MW00790516

Exploring Early
Grand Lodge Freemasonry

EXPLORING EARLY GRAND LODGE FREEMASONRY

Studies in Honor of the Tricentennial of the Establishment of the Grand Lodge of England

CHRISTOPHER B. MURPHY
EDITOR

SHAWN EYER
EXECUTIVE EDITOR

Plumbstone
WASHINGTON, D.C.
2017

Cover art: Detail, illustration from George Bickham's *The Musical Entertainer*, 1735, from the collection of Tyler Vanice, MPS.

The Traditional History from Anderson's *Constitutions* was transcribed by Steven Dieter, MPS.

This book is published in partnership with
The Philalethes Society. *http://www.freemasonry.org*

Publisher's Cataloging-in-Publication data

Murphy, Christopher B., editor.
Eyer, Shawn, editor.
    Exploring early grand lodge Freemasonry : studies in honor of
    the tricentennial of the establishment of the Grand Lodge of
    England / Christopher B. Murphy, editor ; Shawn Eyer,
    executive editor.
    530 p. 25 cm. Includes bibliographical references and index.
    ISBN-13 978-1-60302-062-6 (cloth)
    ISBN-13 978-1-60302-061-9 (pbk.)
    ISBN-13 978-1-60302-063-3 (ebook)
    1. Freemasonry—History—18th century. 2. Freemasonry—Lodges.
    3. Freemasonry—Philosophy. 4. Freemasons. 5. Masonic music.
    I. Title.
    HS416.E97 2017   366'.1—dc23.

Library of Congress Control Number: 2017962404

http://plumbstone.com

Here's a Health to our Society, and to every faithful Brother that keeps his Oath of Secrecy. As we are sworn to love each other. The World no Order knows like this our Noble and Antient Fraternity: Let them wonder at the Mystery.

1724

…Solomon sent and ffet hiram out off tyre he being a widdows son of the tribe of naphtale and his father was a man of tyre a worker in brass filled with wisdom and Cunning to work all works in brass and he came to king sollomon and wrought all his work ffor him—the Exsplanation of these verses is as ffollows—the word Cunning renders ingenuity as ffor wisdom and understanding when they are found in one person he can want nothing: so by this present scripture must be allowed that the widows Son whose name was hiram had a holy inspiration….

1726

The Essential Secrets of masonry indeed are Everlastingly Safe, & never can be Revealed abroad, because they can never be understood by such as are unenlightened.

1734

Our Profession so honourable, that the greatest Monarchs glory in being admitted amongst us; and so ancient is the Lodge, that no Records can fix its Origin. For, how can it be otherwise than permanent, which has its Foundation fix'd on the stable Centre of the Earth, and its Heaven aspiring Superstructure supported by Columns of Divine Attributes.

1735

May the ROYAL ART go on and prosper, and spread itself from *Pole* to *Pole*, from *East* to *West*!

1738

Contents

Foreword   ix

Introduction   1

The Traditional History   7
JAMES ANDERSON

"A Just and Exact Account of Masonry":   53
A Survey of the Constitutions and
Pocket Companions of 1723 to 1756
CHRISTOPHER B. MURPHY

"The Essential Secrets of Masonry":   152
Insight from an American Masonic Oration of 1734
SHAWN EYER

"Spiritual and Heavenly People in Corners":   216
Embracing Masonic Ethos through the Eyes
of James Anderson
DANA SCOFIELD

Freemasonry, the London Irish,   241
and the Antients Grand Lodge
RIC BERMAN

"Genius of Masonry": The Preservation of Masonic   280
Tradition in the Songs of the Freemasons
NATHAN A. ST. PIERRE

The Grand Lodge of All England Held at York: 313
An Independent Grand Lodge in England
in the Eighteenth Century
DAVID HARRISON

John Desaguliers: The Balance of Religion and Science   348
JEDEDIAH FRENCH

Assessing Authentic Lodge Culture: 390
Moving Beyond the Tavern Myth
CHRISTOPHER B. MURPHY

About the Contributors   457
The Philalethes Society   460
Index   464

Foreword

We are informed by the records of the Craft that over three hundred years ago, London Freemasons from four lodges—predominantly or wholly of the non-operative type—gathered at the Apple Tree Tavern at Covent-Garden. At this meeting, they resolved to form a Grand Lodge *pro tempore* and restore what they called the Annual Assembly. Later, on June 24, 1717, which is the Feast Day of Saint John the Baptist, they gathered at the Goose and Gridiron Tavern near St. Paul's and established what is known to scholars as the premier Grand Lodge. It is highly possible that, as evidence suggests, this was the first formal Grand Lodge of Freemasonry, although dozens of lodges also existed that were not part of it.

Because of this event, this year the Fraternity celebrates the tricentennial of the Grand Lodge era. Freemasons from around the world are planning events, great and small, to join in this great milestone.

But what does it mean to celebrate this tricentennial? After all, scholars have shown that some aspects of Freemasonry are at least as old as the 1500s, and of course we realize that the 1717 Grand Lodge was only a byproduct of the fact that during the 1600s, what came to be termed speculative Freemasonry was growing in depth, scope, and popularity. Still, the tercentenary is an opportunity to reflect deeply upon exactly what, culturally speaking, the practice of Freemasonry was like three hundred

years ago. We might ask ourselves: *of what* is this the tricentennial? On reflection, the answer must be more than the organizational genesis of the first Grand Lodge. In this volume of essays,
numerous Masonic scholars have asked such questions as: What
did Masons of the early Grand Lodge era actually do in their
lodges? How did these brethren think of themselves and their
Craft? What were their motivations and ideals? What was their
experience of Freemasonry? By posing such questions, our writers have been able to study not just an institutional beginning,
but the cultural realities of Masonic life in the first decades of
the Grand Lodge's history.

Although modern Masonic research is, on the one hand, well
over a century underway, many of these questions are insufficiently explored. Critical narratives exist that attempt to delineate the origins of Freemasonry or explain the sociological
impact of Freemasonry. Many of these interpretations are very
impressive and a few of them have attained significant academic
currency. Despite the general advancement of the discipline, one
often comes away from much of recent scholarship with only im-
pressionistic ideas about the lived culture of British Freemasons
in the early years of the premier Grand Lodge.

Some well-regarded treatments of Masonic history, in fact,
cite remarkably little in the way of the literature of Freemasonry, which can give the uninformed reader the impression
that only scant traces of such material still survive. Such approaches may rely upon sociopolitical contexts and extremely
detailed prosopographic analysis to reveal very illuminating—
if sometimes highly conjectural—dimensions of the subject.
This manner of approaching Masonic history can only be made
more effective by a thorough reckoning with the literary and
ritualistic remains of the lodge participants of the time. With a
few exceptions—perhaps most notably the superbly perceptive
phenomenological study of Alexander Piatigorsky—the early

Grand Lodge era Freemasons have had too small a voice in the historical interpretations of their endeavors. Their self-perceptions and the descriptions of Masonry as they experienced and regarded it have been neglected. The relative exclusion of such a significant portion of the early literature has contributed to a considerable problem in the field: the fortification of historical theories about early lodge life that are difficult to square with the full body of evidence. At times, our characterizations of the ultimate aims of Freemasonry have inadequately comported with the stated opinions of the Masons of the time period, the content of the rituals that they used to transmit their actual values, and the overall corpus of evidence.

This problem is found equally in the work of academic scholars working outside of Freemasonry as well as participant scholars. The reasons for this defect in so many analyses of Masonry are certainly complex, and may be largely rooted in the methodological approaches of late nineteenth-century researchers. One specific stimulus for the uneven treatment of primary sources is likely to be the disdain that scholars of that era had for the heavily mythological accounts that are so prominent in early Masonic publications and manuscripts. Owing to a tendency to view statements only as either truthful and valuable or false and worthless, many participant scholars came to regard key early Masonic writers in a negative light. A general sense that Masonic history could and should be conducted without a close examination of this "tainted" literature became widely accepted. The most representative example of this rejected literature is Anderson's *Constitutions*, which is largely concerned with mythography. A critical literature with scant patience for mythology has treated this work—and all works similarly mythographic (which is to say nearly all early Masonic writings)—as though it possesses value only for its aspects that can be demonstrated as factual and not mythic.

There are some signs that this approach—which was never truly formalized—is being questioned by a new generation of scholars, possibly in response to the relative ease of access to primary sources that today's researchers possess. Aspects of early Masonry that were once artificially isolated as the caprices of particular authors are now more easily identified as common refrains and themes. Early Masonic writing "defined the parameters of an enduring Masonic discourse," observes Paul Kléber Monod. This discourse "represented the Craft in exalted terms, as the inheritor of fundamental secrets" of a sacred nature.[1]

This discourse interrogated, elaborated, and sought to apply the foundational mythology of the Craft. It is time for both those myths and the Masonic discourse that flourished in their context to be studied in a more comprehensive and integrated manner. Fortunately, researchers have become more sophisticated in terms of how mythology can be critically engaged.

For example, improving upon the dipolar model of the past, recent theorists have developed language appropriate to the negotiation of Masonic legendary histories. Arthur Versluis, for example, refers to Masonic "parahistory."[2] Dan Edelstein describes the category of writing to which the Traditional History belongs as a process of "historical mythologisation."[3] In recent decades, numerous scholars—most notably Joseph Mali—have argued that the term "mythistory" might be employed, not in the derogative sense of "history amalgamated with fable," but in a rehabilitated way that finds value in such narratives that would not otherwise be available in a non-mythologized account. As Mali

1   Paul Kléber Monod, *Solomon's Secret Arts* (New Haven: Yale University Press, 2013), 187.

2   Arthur Versluis, *Magic and Mysticism: An Introduction to Western Esotericism* (Lanham, Md.: Rowman & Littlefield, 2007), 94.

3   Dan Edelstein, "Introduction to the Super-Enlightenment." In *The Super-Enlightenment: Daring to Know Too Much*, edited by Dan Edelstein (Oxford: The Voltaire Foundation, 2010), 11.

states in *Mythistory: The Making of a Modern Historiography*:

> [H]istorical myths are now commonly perceived as "foundational narratives," as stories that purport to explain the present in terms of some momentous event that occurred in the past. Stories like these are in many ways historical—though rarely, if ever, do they refer to an actual past. Rather, they refer to a virtual past, to the fact that historical communities, like religions or nations, consist in the beliefs that their members have about them—more concretely, in the stories they tell about them. As Wendy Doniger O'Flaherty has put it, "a myth is a story that is sacred to and shared by a group of people who find their most important meanings in it; it is a story believed to have been composed in the past about an event in the past, or, more rarely, in the future, an event that continues to have meaning in the present because it is remembered." These stories tend to be events that occurred in what Mircea Eliade calls *illud tempus*, the primordial mythical time that precedes historical time, and therefore they are likely to remain forever beyond historical verification or refutation. Yet, as Eliade points out, stories like that usually relate "a creation," in which "something *new, strong,* and *significant* was manifested," something that is still very actual even if it is not quite factual. Myths are not strictly historical, then, but since they serve to "reveal that the world, man, and life have a supernatural origin and history, and that this history is significant, precious, and exemplary," they impart meaning to history. However legendary a myth may be, it does not signify fabrication or pure fiction because it usually contains or refers to certain crucial issues in the history or territory of the community. These issues require and inspire *historical* myths because they pertain not only to such metaphysical mysteries as

the ultimate origins and destinies of the community, but primarily to those practical verities in which the members of the community all believe and live, even though (or precisely because) they are mythical rather than logical or historical deductions.[4]

Most of the studies in this collection break with the unofficial tradition prevailing among certain researchers whereby they substantially discard the self-definitional statements of the Masons of the early Grand Lodge era. It seems as though scholars have almost systematically set aside the texts that discuss the mythopœic essence of Freemasonry as the early participants saw it, and then set about the task of developing a new, often artificial, narrative of what those participants valued in Freemasonry. Although a critical approach is essential in historiography—including our acknowledgment that the historical importance of a phenomenon may have been unknown or even unknowable in its time, and that the motivations of the individuals involved were perhaps more complex, multilayered, and contradictory than they themselves realized—no responsible historian can discount the artifacts of a culture while proposing to get to the truth about that culture.

Academic characterizations of the activities, aims, and values of the early Grand Lodge Freemasons have been, as it were, all over the map. For some, the premier Grand Lodge's version of Freemasonry was created as a vehicle to proselytize a Hanoverian political agenda, promote Newtonian science, or to spread a new secular awareness. For others, it was simply an innocuous but highly pretentious "club" intended as a form of entertainment, civil conversation, and mutual support. For others still, Freemasonry has been viewed as an evolution of late Renais-

4   Joseph Mali, *Mythistory: The Making of a Modern Historiography* (Chicago: The University of Chicago Press, 2003), 4.

sance philosophy, perhaps including esoteric and mystical ideas, expressed socially through initiatic ritual rather than privately through literature alone. There are reasons for each of these interpretations, and in some cases they are not mutually exclusive.

However, a compelling question upon which to reflect when reading any historian's interpretation of early Grand Lodge Freemasonry is whether, given the model presented, we might accurately predict the spirit and content of the Masonic literature and ritual of the time period. If we had to recreate this literature using a particular narrative as a template, how well would our production match with the material that actually survives? The experience of many of us who have immersed ourselves in the literature is that none of the narratives appear so far to have told the whole story of eighteenth-century Masonic life. We also observe that interpretive models possess the danger of preemptively limiting one's encounter with the field of evidence. This results, too frequently, in tendentious conclusions and general interpretations that do not reconcile naturally with the content of the Fraternity's literary remains. Certain popular narratives verge on the ahistorical: particularly the notion of early Freemasonry as a strictly clubby phenomenon, quite devoid of serious speculation, whose aims were merely amusement, fellowship, and epicurean indulgence. From the beginning, Masonic literature and ritual run strongly counter to the grain of such a characterization. It is virtually impossible to reconcile the surviving evidence with the "merely epicurean" interpretation of Masonry. Certain other narratives fare little better when put to the same test.

This is why the original scholarship of today is so refreshing. A new generation of Masonic historians are fundamentally reconsidering key questions of early lodge life and culture. The studies assembled here have been chosen because of the authors' extensive work in the primary sources and willingness to critically interrogate the interpretations of the past. The result is a xvi

collection that delves deeply into the early evidence—whether familiar, neglected, or obscure—to provide fresh perspectives on many aspects of the Masonic story.

This volume has been made possible by the encouragement of the Philalethes Society, North America's oldest independent Masonic research organization. The Society publishes a quarterly journal, *Philalethes*, of which I have had the pleasure to be Editor since 2009.[5] I would like to thank Ed Halpaus, the 2014–2016 President of the Philalethes Society, for proposing a volume of articles about the tercentenary. Although the original idea that President Halpaus suggested was a collection of papers on the subject of the premier Grand Lodge drawn from the Society's publications dating back to 1931, as an editor it struck me that a volume of original essays reflecting the latest research would be most useful to readers. The Society's executive committee agreed with this concept, and over the last two years, through the efforts of scholars from both the United States and England, *Exploring Early Grand Lodge Freemasonry* took shape.

Special thanks are due also to current President John L. Cooper III for his unflagging support of the project. The contributors to this volume—nearly all of them members of the Society and regular contributors to *Philalethes*—have displayed an impressive amount of erudition and originality, and the articles they have produced are some of the best I have seen. Most of all, I would like to express my deep gratitude toward Christopher Murphy, for his editorial prowess as well as his impressive scholarship. Undeterred by incomplete maps, he explores the territory of Masonic history—via roads both familiar and obscure—in ways that are truly enlightening.

Shawn Eyer
Alexandria, Virginia

5   Learn more about the Philalethes Society in the article on page 460 of this volume, or on the web at *http://www.freemasonry.org*.

Introduction

Christopher B. Murphy

THE SUMMER OF 2017 marked a momentous event in the history of Freemasonry: the three-hundredth anniversary of the founding of the first Grand Lodge, widely among scholars as the Premier Grand Lodge or as the Grand Lodge of London and Westminster.[1] The story is familiar to many Freemasons: acting on plans laid down the year prior, it was in 1717 that the members of four London Lodges assembled in the Goose and Gridiron tavern, and elected Brother Anthony Sayer to be the Grand Master of the newly-formed Grand Lodge. As per the 1738 *Constitutions*, their aim was to "revive" the quarterly assemblies and annual feasts of old.[2]

Of course, Freemasonry existed long before this. Examples of Masonic catechism, for instance, are dated to the late seventeenth century. References to the "Mason's Word" date to the

1   The Grand Lodge was originally formed by lodges meeting in London and Westminster, and apparently its jurisdiction was limited to that area. See James Anderson, *The Constitutions of the Freemasons, Containing the History, Charges, Regulations, &c. of that most Ancient and Right Worshipful Fraternity* (London: William Hunter, 1723), 88 & 103.

2   James Anderson, *The New Book of Constitutions of the Antient and Honourable Fraternity of Free and Accepted Masons, Containing Their History, Charges, Regulations, &c.* (London: Richard Chandler, 1738), 109.

early seventeenth century. The "Old Charges," i.e. the early legends and specific behavioral expectations of the Craft, date to
the late fourteenth century. Moreover, the operative dimensions
of Masonry, such as geometry and architecture, are clearly older
than 1717. The same is true of the various speculative traditions—
such as esoteric Christianity, Kabbalah, and Hermeticism—that
are widely agreed to have also influenced the Craft. In a 1981
work, Alex Horne, FPS, proposed that some elements of Masonic
practice could "have had [their] origin in our general cultural heritage; or in some communal activity; or perhaps in some
item of folk-lore; or perhaps even in some popular superstition,"[3]
thereby having those elements also predate 1717. That men who
were not actual stonemasons were admitted to lodges in the seventeenth century is proof enough that the Craft itself was not
created from whole cloth in 1717. However, the establishment of
the Grand Lodge acting originally in London and Westminster
represented a pivotal stage in the development of how Freemasonry would be practiced and (eventually) administrated, and
with this understanding the year 1717 is regarded by many as the
beginning of Freemasonry as it is known today. The birth of the
Grand Lodge era was a quiet but transformational event that,
within a few decades, resulted in a tremendous growth in the
scope of Masonic activity.

   In the three centuries since these four Lodges cemented
themselves together, the Craft has undergone some modifications. Certain symbols have been incorporated into the larger
scope of Craft iconography, while others have fallen out of use.
Side degrees and appendant bodies have developed out of the
Craft Lodge system. Regional Masonic practice has been influenced by societal trends and the social mores or certain times
and places. Thomas W. Jackson, FPS, has observed that contemporary Freemasonry, when considered from a global perspective,

3   Alex Horne, *Sources of Masonic Symbolism* (Richmond: Macoy
      Publishing, 1981), 15.

has found expression in different "styles": philosophical, social, political, sociological, and charitable.[4] These are just some of the alterations that can be seen when comparing Masonry then to Masonry now.

Undoubtedly, some of these modifications and additions aid in the Freemasons' quest for Light. However, it may also be asserted that each shift away from the early period of Grand Lodge-era Masonic development is a step away from the genuine spirit of Masonry. In other words, regardless of the value that may be evident, such developments necessarily mean that the Craft has been distanced from what Charles Leslie called "its primitive lustre."[5]

Whether one views these accretions as degrading the three Great Pillars of the Lodge, or as essential ornamentation of the Temple, the fact remains that the superstructure of Freemasonry in its current form was erected upon a foundation laid in the early decades of the eighteenth century. Therefore, in order for Masons and non-Masons alike to best understand the three-century-old edifice of the Craft, students of Masonry must become acquainted with what early Grand Lodge era Masonry was, as well as what these Masons did and believed. It is a recognition of this fact that inspired the present volume. The intent of this work is to present a study of this formative period. An invaluable resource in understanding this era of the fraternity is the vast array of surviving Masonic writing, from the 1720s through the next half-century. There is no better means by which to understand the *what* and *why* of early Freemasonry than absorbing the explanations given by the early Masons themselves.

4   For example, Jackson shared these observations in an unpublished speech delivered June 27, 2009, at Glasgow, Montana.
5   Charles Leslie, "A Vindication of Masonry and Its Excellency Demonstrated in a Discourse at the Consecration of the Lodge of Vernon Kilwinning, On May 15, 1741," In Anon., *The Free Masons Pocket-Companion* (Edinburgh: Auld & Smellie, 1765), 161.

The works in this collection seek to answer questions regarding the central belief system of early Lodges. How did Freemasons conceive of their institution? What were their customs, norms, and conduct? Certainly, important dates and persons are considered, but far more consideration is paid to examining that culture of early Freemasonry. Such an approach is particularly important to those Freemasons in the present who have adopted a restorative, or observant, mode of Masonic practice. A volume such as the present collection examines the belief system extant during early Freemasonry—what contributor Dana Scofield, MPS, refers to as the "Masonic ethos" of the time. Only in understanding the predominant practices and self-concepts of the early Grand Lodge era, can Masonic restoration be authentic in its attempts and goals. But it is not only the restorative Mason who will benefit from this work. Contemporary Masons of every stripe, of any of Jackson's styles, can benefit from learning the historic themes of their fraternity. By knowing what came before him, today's Freemason can better understand his role as a steward of the Craft, but also himself as the beneficiary of all his Masonic forebears.

Contributors Jedediah French and Dana Scofield engage in this process by seeking to understand two of the most important figures in early Freemasonry: the third Grand Master of the Premier Grand Lodge, Jean Theophilus Desaguliers, FRS, and Dr. James Anderson, author of the first two editions of the Masonic *Constitutions*, respectively. French examines the religio-philosophic worldview of Desaguliers, and the evidence of such as reflected in early Masonic thought. This study stands in contrast to more recent assertions that Desaguliers was primarily focused on a religious science, and sought to make Freemasonry reflect that orientation. Scofield examines Anderson's two books of *Constitutions* alongside his more obscure work, *News from Elysium*. In this survey, Scofield creates a robust reconstruction of James Anderson's belief regarding Craft provenance, purpose, and import. Because the *Constitutions* were such critical documents in these formative years of Freemasonry, Anderson's understanding of the Craft might be said to be the most influential of all Masonic interpretations.

David Harrison outlines the history of the Grand Lodge at York, the very creation of which was couched in an active engagement with early Masonic legend and myth by those brethren in the north of England. The detailed history that Harrison provides is all reflective of a pedigree York Masons believed dated to the reign of Prince Edwin in 926 A D. Nathan St. Pierre discusses the use of music in Masonic Lodges of the eighteenth century. In so doing, St. Pierre examines how Masonic songs grew from Masonic self-concept, how the music of the Freemasons was an extension of Masonry itself—not music as a reflection of Masonic culture, but music "in-or-as" Masonic culture.

The editor offers two contributions. The first is a survey of nine books of Masonic constitutions published between 1723 and 1756. Particular attention is paid to overarching themes within these books, and what they reveal about the nature of Freemasonry and its practice in the first half of the eighteenth century. The second contribution from the editor offers a counterargument to the reductionist vision of early Freemasonry that holds that the fraternity was a mere social organization devoid of any deeper purpose or intent. A thorough review of primary sources is presented which demonstrates that there was far more to early Grand Lodge era Freemasonry than food, fellowship, and exclusivity. Esoteric and religious elements of foundational Masonic philosophy are discussed and analyzed.

In his essay, Shawn Eyer details the discovery of an obscure Masonic sermon, *A Dissertation upon Masonry*, given in a lodge in the English colonies of North America on June 24, 1734. This document preserves what appears to be the oldest surviving private Masonic oration in the world. His commentary explores the oration's prelapsarian and paradisaical themes as well as its explicit references to the esoteric nature of the "essential secrets" of the Craft. He also offers compelling evidence that the *Dissertation*—although it was never published—was circulated among American Freemasons and influenced at least one Masonic leader very directly.

Ric Berman discusses the issues that spurred the creation of the Grand Lodge of the Antients. Although the stimuli came from different sources, it was an unwavering dedication to Craft antiquity, and an utter fidelity to Masonic tradition that motivated the likes of Grand Secretary Laurence Dermott and his Antient Brethren.

The attentive Craftsman questions the teachings and function of the Masonic institution. He seeks the meaning of Masonry. These answers can be elusive, particularly if he ignores the concepts and context of the foundational Freemasonry of the early 1700s. The same, of course can be said for the non-Masonic student: without knowing the roots of Freemasonry, one can never fully appreciate its flower, particularly if one is not acquainted with the knowledge reserved only for its participants. The contributors of the present volume seek to foster an increase in the appreciation and understanding of the formative years of the Masonic Order, via a thorough examination of the writing of early Freemasons themselves. This volume is collected in celebration of three hundred years of Grand Lodge Masonry. It is our collective wish that an appreciation of early Grand Lodge era culture may embolden Freemasonry to thrive for another three centuries and beyond.

The Traditional History

JAMES ANDERSON

Introductory Note

Masonic symbolism and lore is deeply connected to a special account of human progress known most commonly as the Traditional History. In fact, as many of the most important Masonic rituals are dramatically set in the mythical past, the ceremonies may be considered a performative expression of parts of the Traditional History. This foundational myth appears in many forms within the Old Charges and later printed constitutions and handbooks. In all of them, events and personages from sacred history become interwoven with thinkings and developments within the classical world, and "Masonry" becomes synonymous with the upward progress of humanity as witnessed through architectural sophistication and æsthetics. These accounts have often been discarded by positivist scholars as simply fraudulent history, crafted to impress outsiders and cull new members. However, the Traditional History represents more than such a characterization would indicate. It is more properly considered Freemasonry's "mythistory," a special perspective on the world that frames the role of the Craft as working to preserve valuable ancient mysteries while cultivating the arts and sciences.

As it is impossible to understand early Grand Lodge era Free-masonry without a working knowledge of the counter-mythology conveyed by the Traditional History, the editors determined that it would be appropriate to include a version of the story within this volume. Here we reprint key sections from one redaction of this Masonic *hieros logos*: the version compiled by James Anderson for the 1738 second edition of his *Constitutions*. In its grand sweep, it encompasses the story of humanity from the first people up to the time of the writer. It relates that Adam was created with a special knowledge of geometry implanted within his being, which he was able to discover by study of the paradise-temple of Eden. This information passes into the hearts of his progeny, and across all the centuries of human development, as the Traditional History expounds a generally optimistic story of improvement that culminates in the architectural triumphs of Inigo Jones and Christopher Wren, the growth of Freemasonry in the British Isles, and ultimately the creation of the Grand Lodge of England.

Here, as generally within this volume, the typographical expression and orthography of original sources have been closely imitated. The folios of the original edition are indicated between vertical lines for convenient reference to the source material. Notations within Anderson's version have been transformed into regular, numbered footnotes.—Shawn Eyer

| 1 |

The
CONSTITUTIONS
OF THE
Right Worshipful FRATERNITY
OF THE
Free and *Accepted* MASONS.

Collected from Their old *Records* and faithful *Traditions*.

TO BE READ

At the Admission of a NEW BROTHER, when the *Master*
or *Warden* shall begin, or order some other Brother to
read, as follows.

PART I.

The History of Masonry *from the* Creation *throughout the known*
Earth; *till true old* Architecture *was demolish'd by the* 𝕲𝖔𝖙𝖍𝖘 *and*
at last revived in Italy.

CHAPTER I.

From the Creation *to* 𝕲𝖗𝖆𝖓𝖉 𝕸𝖆𝖘𝖙𝖊𝖗 NIMROD.

THE ALMIGHTY Architect and *Grand-Master* of the Universe having created all Things very Good and according to *Geometry*, last of all formed ADAM after his own Image, ingraving on his heart the said noble science; which *Adam* soon discover'd by surveying his Earthly Paradise and the fabrication of the *Arbour* or Silvan Lodgment that God had prepared | 2 | for him, a well-proportion'd and convenient place of shelter from heat, and of retirement, rest, and repast after his wholesome labour in cultivating his Garden of Delights, and the first *Temple* or place of worship, agreeable to his original, perfect and innocent state.

    A.M. or Year of the World   1 ⎱
    B.C. or before the Christian Era[1]   4003 ⎰

But tho' by Sin *Adam* fell from his original happy State, and was expell'd from his lovely *Arbour* and Earthly *Paradise* into the wide World, he still retain'd great Knowledge, especially in GEOMETRY; and its Principles remaining in the Hearts of his Offspring, have in Process of Time been drawn forth in a convenient Method of Propositions, according to the Laws of Proportion taken from *Mechanism*: and as the *Mechanical* Arts gave occasion to the Learned to reduce the Elements of *Geometry* into Method; so this noble *Science*, thus reduced and methodized, is now the Foundation of all those Arts (especially of *Architecture*) and the Rule by which they are conducted and finish'd.

    ADAM, when expell'd, resided in the most convenient natu-

---

1   The first *Christians* computed their times as the Nations did among whom They lived till *A.D.* 532 when *Dionysious Exiguus*, a Roman *Abbot*, taught them first to compute from the Birth of *Christ*: but He lost 4 Years or began the *Christian* Era 4 Years later than just. Therefore, tho' according to the *Hebrew* Chronology of the old Testament and other good Vouchers, CHRIST was truly born in some Month of the Year of the World or *A.M.* 4000, yet these 4 Years added make   4004 ⎱
Not *before the Birth of Christ*, but *before the Christian Era*, viz. 1737 ⎰
For the true *Anno Domini* or Year after *Christ's* Birth is   1740
But the MASONS being used to compute
by the Vulgar *Anno* Domini or Christian *Era*   1737
And adding to it not 4004 as it ought, but
the strict Years before *Christ's* Birth, *viz.*   4000
                                                                     ———
They usually call this the *Year of* MASONRY   5737
Instead of the accurate Year   5740
and we must keep to the Vulgar Computation.
The *A.M.* or *Anno Mundi* is the same follow'd by *Usher* and *Prideaux*, &c. and so these letters *A.M.* signify *Anno Mundi* or Year of the World: and here *B.C.* is not *Before Christ* but *Before the Christian Era*.

ral Abodes of the Land of *Eden*, where be could be best shelter'd | 3 | from Colds and Heats, from Winds, Rains and Tempests and from Wild Beasts; till his Sons grew up to form a *Lodge*, whom he taught *Geometry* and the great Use of it in *Architecture*, without which the Children of Men must have liv'd like *Brutes*, in Woods, Dens and Caves, &c. or at best in poor Huts of Mud or Arbours, made of Branches of Trees, &c.

Thus, KAIN, when expell'd[2] with his Family and Adherents from *Adam*'s Altars, built forthwith a strong City, and call'd it DEDICATE or CONSECRATE, after the name of his eldest Son *Enoch*; whose Race follow'd the Example, improving the Arts and Sciences of their Patriarch: for TUBAL KAIN wrought in *Metals*, Jubal elevated *Musick*, and Jabal extended his *Tents*.

Nor was his brother SETH less instructed, the Patriarch of the other half of Mankind, who transmitted *Geometry* and *Masonry* to his late Posterity, who were the better skill'd by *Adam*'s living among them till he died. *A.M.* 930.

ADAM was succeeded in the Grand Direction of the Craft by SETH, ENOSH, KAINAN, MAHALALEEL, and JARED, whose Son *Godly* ENOCH died not, but was translated alive, Soul and Body, into Heaven, aged 365 Years, *A.M.* 987. He was expert and bright both in the *Science* and the *Art*, and being a Prophet, He foretold the Destruction of the Earth for Sin, first by *Water*, and afterwards by *Fire*: therefore *Enoch* erected *Two* large PILLARS,[3] the one of *Stone* and the other of *Brick*, whereon he engraved the Abridgement of the Arts and Sciences, particularly *Geometry* and *Masonry*.

JARED liv'd after his Son *Enoch* Years 435 and died aged 962,[4]

2   *A.M.* 130.
3   Some call them SETH's *Pillars*, but the old *Masons* always call'd them ENOCH's *Pillars*, and firmly believ'd this Tradition: nay *Josephus* (Lib. i. cap. 2) affirms the *Stone-Pillar* still remain'd in *Syria* to his Time.
4   *A.M.* 1422.

the oldest Man except his Grandson METHUSELAH the Son of *Enoch*, who succeeded *Jared*; but *Methuselah* ruled not long: for the Immoral Corruption universally prevailing,

METHUSELAH, with his Son LAMECH and Grandson NOAH, | 4 | retired from the corrupt World, and in their own peculiar Family preserved the good old Religion of the promised *Messiah* pure, and also *Royal Art*, till the *Flood*: for LAMECH died only five Years before the *Flood*, and METHUSELAH died a few Days before It, aged 969 years: and so He could well communicate the Traditions of his learned Progenitors to *Noah's* 3 Sons; for JAPHET liv'd with him 100 Years, SHEM 98 and HAM 96.

At last, when the World's Destruction drew nigh, God commanded NOAH to build the *great* Ark or floating Castle, and his 3 Sons assisted like a *Deputy* and two *Wardens*: That Edifice though of Wood only, was fabricated by *Geometry* as nicely as any Stone-Building (like true *Ship-Building* to this Day) a curious and large Piece of *Architecture*, and finish'd when *Noah* enter'd into his 600 Year; aboard which he and his 3 Sons and their 4 Wives passed, and having received the Cargo of Animals by God's Direction, they were saved in the *Ark*, while the rest perished in the Flood for their Immorality and Unbelief.[5]

And so from these MASONS, or four *Grand Officers*, the whole present Race of Mankind are descended.

After the *Flood*, NOAH and his 3 Sons, having preserved the Knowledge of the Arts and Sciences communicated It to their growing Off-spring, who were all of *one Language and Speech*. *And it came to pass*[6] *as they journeyed from the* East (the Plains of Mount *Ararat*, where the *Ark* rested) towards the *West*, they found *a Plain in the Land of* SHINAR, *and dwelt there* together,

5   *B.M.* 1656.⎱
     A.C. 2348.⎰
6   *Gen.* XI. 1, 2.

as NOACHIDÆ,[7] or Sons of *Noah*: and when *Peleg* was born there to *Heber*, after the Flood 101 years, Father *Noah* partition'd the *Earth*, ordering them to disperse and take Possession; but from a fear of the ill Consequences of Separation, they resolved to keep together.

| 5 |

CHAP. II.

From NIMROD *to* 𝕲𝖗𝖆𝖓𝖉-𝕸𝖆𝖘𝖙𝖊𝖗 SOLOMON

Nimrod[8] the Son of *Cush*, the Eldest Son of *Ham*, was at the Head of those that would not disperse; or if they must separate, They resolved to transmit their Memorial illustrations to all future Ages; and so employed themselves under *Grand Master* NIMROD, in the large and fertile Vale of 𝖘𝖍𝖎𝖓𝖆𝖗 along the Banks of the *Tygris*, in building a great and stately *Tower* and *City*, the largest Work that ever the World saw (described by various Authors) and soon fill'd the Vale with splendid Edifices; but They over-built it, and knew not when to desist 'till their Vanity provoked their Maker to confound their *Grand Design*, by confounding their *Lip* or Speech. Hence the city was called 𝕭𝖆𝖇𝖊𝖑 *Confusion*.

Thus they were forced to disperse about 53 Years after they began to build, or after the Flood 154 years,[9] when The General MIGRATION from 𝖘𝖍𝖎𝖓𝖆𝖗 commenced.

They went off at various Times, and travell'd North, South, *East* and *West*, with their mighty Skill, and found the good Use

---

7   The first Name of *Masons*, according to some old Traditions.

8   NIMROD signifies a *Rebel*, the name that the *Isrælites* gave him; but his Friends call'd him 𝕭𝖊𝖑𝖚𝖘 Lord.

9   *A.M.*   1810.⎫
     B.C.   2194.⎭

of it in settling their Colonies.

But NIMROD went forth no farther than into the Land of *Assyria*, and founded the *first* Great *Empire* at his Capital 𝔑𝔦𝔫𝔦𝔳𝔢𝔥, where he long reign'd; and under him flourish'd many learned Mathematicians, whose Successors were, long afterwards, called *Chaldees* and *Magians*: and though many of them turned Image-Worshippers, yet even that Idolatry occasion'd an Improvement in the *Arts* of 𝔇𝔢𝔰𝔦𝔤𝔫𝔦𝔫𝔤:[10] for NINUS King of *Nineveh* or *Assyria*, ordered his best Artists to frame the *Statue* of 𝔅𝔞𝔞𝔩, that was worshipped in a gorgeous *Temple*.

| 6 | From SHINAR, the *Science* and the *Art* were carried to the distant Parts of the Earth, notwithstandng the *Confusion* of *Dialects*: That indeed gave Rise to the *Masons* Faculty and universal Practice of conversing without speaking, and of knowing each other by *Signs* and *Tokens*[11] (which they settled upon the *Dispersion* or Migration, in case any of them should meet in different Parts, who had been before in *Shinar*) but It hinder'd not the Propagation of *Masonry*, which was cultivated by all the first Nations; till the Negligence of their Chiefs, and their horrid Wars, made them turn ignorant, and lose their original Skill in Arts and Sciences.

Thus the *Earth* was again planted and replenish'd with MASONS from the Vale of SHINAR, whose various Improvements we shall trace.

MITZRAIM or *Menes*, the second Son of HAM, led his Colony from *Shinar* to EGYPT (which is *Mitzraim* in *Hebrew*, a dual Word, signifying both *Egypts*, Upper and Lower) after the *Flood* 160 years, and after the *Confusion* six Years, *A.M.* 1816, where they preserved their original Skill, and much cultivated the *Art*: for antient History informs us[12] of the early fine Taste of the

10   viz. *Architecture, Sculpture, Statuary, Plastering and Painting*.
11   This old *Tradition* is believed firmly by the old *Fraternity*.
12   *Diod. Sicul.* lib. I.

Egyptians, their many magnificent Edifices and great Cities, as *Memphis, Heliopolis, Thebes* with 100 Gates, &c. besides their *Palaces* and *Sepulchres*, their *Obelisks* and *Statues*, the Colossal *Statue* of SPHINX, whose Head was 120 Foot round, and their famous 𝔓𝔶𝔯𝔞𝔪𝔦𝔡𝔰, the greatest[13] being reckoned the *first* or earliest of the seven *Wonders* of *Art* after the general *Migration*.

The *Egyptians* excell'd all Nations also in their amasing LABYRINTHS, One of them cover'd the Ground of a whole Province, containing many fine Palaces and | 7 | 100 *Temples*, disposed in its several Quarters and Divisions, adorned with Columns of the best Porphyre, and the accurate *Statues* of their Gods and Princes; which *Labyrinth* the *Greeks*, long afterwards, endeavour'd to imitate, but never arrived at Its *Extension* and *Sublime*.

The Successors of 𝔐𝔦𝔱𝔷𝔯𝔞𝔦𝔪 (who stiled themselves the *Sons of antient Kings*) encouraged the *Royal Art* down to the last of the Race, the learned King AMASIS. See Chap. IV.

But History fails us in the South and West of *Africa*. Nor have we any just Accounts of the fair and gallant Posterity of *Noah*'s eldest Son JAPHET, that first replenish'd vast *old Scythia*, from *Norway* Eastward to *America*; nor of the 𝔍𝔞𝔭𝔥𝔢𝔱𝔦𝔱𝔢𝔰 in *Greece* and *Italy, Germany, Gaul* and *Britain*, &c. 'till their original Skill was lost: But, no doubt, they were good Architects at their first *Migration* from *Shinar*.

SHEM, the second Son of *Noah*, remain'd at UR of the *Chaldees* in *Shinar*, with his Father and great Grandson HEBER, where they liv'd private and died in Peace; but *Shem*'s Offspring travell'd into the South and East of *Great Asia*, *viz*. ELAM,

---

13   Some say it was built of Marble Stones brought from the Quarries of *Arabia*; for there is no Vestige of a Quarry near it. Others call them artificial Stones made on the Spot, most of them 30 Foot long. The *Pile* at Bottom was 700 Foot square, and 481 Foot high; but Others make it much higher: And in rearing it 360,000 *Masons* were employ'd for 20 Years, as if all the People had join'd in the GRAND DESIGN.

ASHUR, ARPHAXAD, LUD and ARAM, with SALA the Father of
Heber; and their Off-spring propagat'd the *Science* and the *Art*
as far as CHINA and 𝕵𝖆𝖕𝖆𝖓: while NOAH, SHEM and HEBER di-
verted themselves at *Ur*, in Mathematical Studies, teaching *Peleg*
the Father of *Rehu*, Father of *Serug*, Father of *Nachor*, Father of
Terah, Father of ABRAM, a learned Race of Mathematicians and
Geometricians.[14]

Thus ABRAM, born two Years after the Death of *Noah*,[15] had
learned well the *Science* and the *Art*, before the GOD of GLORY
call'd him to travel from *Ur* of the *Chaldees*, and to live a Peregrin,
nor in *Stone* and *Brick*, but in 𝕿𝖊𝖓𝖙𝖘 erected also by *Geometry*.
So travelling with his Family and Flocks through *Mesopotamia*,
he pitched | 8 | at *Charran*,[16] where old TERAH in 5 Years died
and then ABRAM aged 75 Years, travell'd into the Land of the
Canaanites:[17] but a Famine soon forced him down to *Egypt*; and
returning next Year, he began to communicate his great Skill to
the Chiefs of the *Canaanites*, for which they honour'd him as a
Prince.

ABRAM transmitted his *Geometry* to all his Off-spring;
Isaac did the same to his two Sons, and JACOB well instructed
his Family; while his Son JOSEPH was 𝕲𝖗𝖆𝖓𝖉-𝕸𝖆𝖘𝖙𝖊𝖗 of the *Egyp-
tian* Masons, and employ'd them in building many Granaries and
Store-Cities throughout the Land of *Egypt* before the *Descent* of
Jacob and his Family.

Indeed this *peculiar Nation* were chiefly conversant in *Tents*
and *Flocks* and military Skill, for about 350 Years after *Abram*
came to *Canaan*, till their Persecution began in *Egypt*, about 80

14   The old *Constitutions* affirm this strongly, and expatiate on
     ABRAM's great Skill in *Geometry*, and of his teaching it to many
     Scholars, tho' all the Sons of the *Freeborn* only.
15   *A.M.* 2008.
16   *A.M.* 2078.
17   *A.M.* 2083.⎱
     B.C. 1921.⎰

Years before the *Exodus* of *Moses*: But then the 𝕰𝖌𝖚𝖕𝖙𝖎𝖆𝖓𝖘 having
spoil'd and enslaved the *Hebrews*, train'd them up in *Masonry*
of 𝕾𝖙𝖔𝖓𝖊 and 𝕭𝖗𝖎𝖈𝖐, and made them build two strong and stately
Cities for the Royal Treasures, *Pithom* and *Raamses*. Thus the divine Wisdom appeared in permitting them to be thus employ'd,
before they possess'd the promis'd Land then abounding with
fine *Architecture*.

At length, after *Abram* left *Charran* 430 years,[18] MOSES
marched out of *Egypt* at the Head of 600,000 *Hebrew* Males,
marshall'd in due Form; for whose sake God divided the *Red
Sea*, to let them pass through, and drowned *Pharaoh* and the
Egyptians that pursu'd them.

While marching through *Arabia* to *Canaan*, 𝕲𝖔𝖉 was pleased
to inspire their 𝕲𝖗𝖆𝖓𝖉 𝕸𝖆𝖘𝖙𝖊𝖗 MOSES, *Joshuah* his Deputy, and
Aholiab and *Bezaleel*, 𝕲𝖗𝖆𝖓𝖉 Wardens, with Wisdom of Heart[19];
and so next year they raised the curious TABERNACLE or *Tent*
(where the divine 𝕾𝖍𝖊𝖈𝖍𝖎𝖓𝖆𝖍 | 9 | resided, and the holy *Ark* or
Chest, the Symbole of God's Presence) which, though not of
Stone or *Brick*, was framed by *Geometry*, a most beautiful Piece
of true symmetrical Architecture, according to the Pattern that
God discover'd to *Moses* on Mount *Sinai*, and it was afterwards
the Model of SOLOMON's 𝕿𝖊𝖒𝖕𝖑𝖊.

MOSES being well skill'd in all the *Egyptian* Learning, and
also divinely inspired, excell'd all *Grand Masters* before him,
and ordered the more skillful to meet him, as in a *Grand Lodge*,
near the Tabernacle in the *Passover*-Week, and gave them wise
Charges, Regulations, &c. though we wish they had been more
distinctly transmitted by Oral Tradition. But of this enough.

When MOSES King of *Jessurun* died A.M. 2553.

JOSHUAH succeeded in the Direction with *Kaleb* as Deputy,

18   *A.M.*   2513. ⎫
     B.C.   1491. ⎭
19   *Exod* XXXII. 6.

and *Eleazar* with his son *Phineas* as *Grand Wardens.* He marshall'd his *Isrælites*, and led them over the *Jordan* (which God made dry for their March) into the promis'd Land: and *Joshuah* soon found the *Canaanites* had so regularly fortified their great Cities and Passes, that without the special intervention of EL SHADDAI, in behalf of his *Peculiar*, They were impregnable and invincible.

JOSHUAH having finish'd his Wars in 6 Years, *A.M.* 2559. fixed the 𝕿𝖆𝖇𝖊𝖗𝖓𝖆𝖈𝖑𝖊 at *Shiloh* in *Ephraim*, ordering the *Chiefs* of *Isræl* not only to serve JEHOVAH their God, and to cultivate the Land, but also to carry on the *Grand Design* of Architecture in the best 𝕸𝖔𝖘𝖆𝖎𝖈 𝕾𝖙𝖎𝖑𝖊.

Indeed the *Isrælites*, refined in Cities and Mansions, having many expert Artists in every *Tribe* that met in *Lodges* or Societies for that Purpose, except for when for their Sins they came under Servitude; but their occasional Princes, call'd *Judges* and *Saviours*, revived the *Mosaic Stile* along with Liberty and the *Mosaic Constitution;* and only came short of the *Phenicians* and *Canaanites* in 𝖘𝖆𝖈𝖗𝖊𝖉 Architectures of *Stone*; for the *Phenicians* had many 𝕿𝖊𝖒𝖕𝖑𝖊𝖘 for their many Gods: and yet the one *Temple* or 𝕿𝖆𝖇𝖊𝖗𝖓𝖆𝖈𝖑𝖊 of the one true God at *Shiloh*, exceeded them all in *Wisdom* and *Beauty*, though not in *Strength* and *Dimensions*.

| 10 | Mean while, in *Lesser Asia*, about 10 years before the *Exodus* of *Moses*, Troy was founded and stood sublime till destory'd by the emulous *Greeks*, about the 12th year of *Tola* Judge of *Isræl. A.M.* 2819.

And soon after the *Exodus*, the famous *Temple* of JUPITER HAMMON in *Libian Africa* was erected, that stood till demolish'd by the first Christians in those Parts.

The SIDONIANS also, expert Artists, first built *Tyre*, and a colony of *Tyrians* first built CARTHAGE; while the *Greeks* were obscure, and the *Romans* existed not yet.

But the *Phenicians* improved in their *sacred* Architecture; for we read of the *Temple* of 𝕯𝖆𝖌𝖔𝖓 in *Gaza*, very magnificent and capacious of 3000 People under its *Roof,* that was artfully supported only by *Two Columns,* not too big to be grasped in the arms of SAMSON, who tugg'd them down; and the large Roof, like a Burst of Thunder, fell upon the Lords and Ladies, the Priests and People of the *Philistins*; nay *Samson* was also intangled in the same death that he drew upon his Enemies for the Loss of Liberty and Eyes. After the *Exodus* of *Moses* 379. Before the *Temple* of *Solomon* 101.[20]

ABIBALUS, King of *Tyre,* beautified that City; and so did his Son King HIRAM who built 3 stately *Temples* to **Jupiter, Hercules,** and **Astarte,** the *Tyrian* Gods, and assisted *David* King of *Isræl* in erecting his *Palace of Cedar.*

Many Monuments of the primitive Architecture are obscured with Fables; for the true old Histories are lost, or worn out by the Teeth of Time, and also the *oral* tradition is darkened by the Blending of the Nations.

| 11 |

CHAP. III.

From SOLOMON *to* **Grand Master** CYRUS

But the most magnificent Structures of *Gaza, Gath* and *Askelon, Jebusi,* and *Hebron, Tyre* and *Sidon, Egypt* and *Assyria, &c.* were not comparable to the *Eternal's* **Temple** at *Jerusalem,* built by that wisest mere Man and most glorious King of *Isræl,* SOLOMON, (the Son of *David,* who was denied the Honour for being a Man of Blood) the Prince of Peace and Architecture, the GRAND MASTER MASON of his Day, who performed all by

20   The *Tradition* of old Masons is, that a learned *Phenician* called SANCONIATHON was the Architect, or *Grand Master,* of this curious *Temple*: And that SAMSON had been too credulous and effeminate in revealing his Secrets to his Wife, who betray'd him into the Hands of the *Philistins*; for which he is not numbered among the antient *Masons.* But no more of this.

divine Direction, and without the Noise of Tools; all the Stones, Timbers and Foundings being brought ready cut, fram'd and polish'd to *Jerusalem*.

It was founded in the 4th year of SOLOMON, on the second Day of the second Month of the Year after the *Exodus* —— 480 and SOLOMON employ'd about it, tho' not all upon *A.M.* 2993⎫ it, the following Number of Operators, *viz.*   *B.C.* 1011⎭

1. 𝕳𝖆𝖗𝖔𝖉𝖎𝖒, Rulers or *Provosts*, call'd also 𝕸𝖊𝖓𝖆𝖙𝖟𝖈𝖍𝖎𝖒, *Overseers*, and Comforters of the people in working, that were expert *Master Masons*, in Number   3600

2. 𝕲𝖍𝖎𝖇𝖑𝖎𝖒, *Stone-Cutters* and *Sculptors*, and 𝕴𝖘𝖍 𝕮𝖍𝖔𝖙𝖟𝖊𝖍, *Men of Hewing*, and 𝕭𝖔𝖓𝖆𝖎, *Setters*, Layers or Builders, or bright *Fellow-Crafts*, in number   80000

3. The levy of Assistants, under the noble ADONIRAM who was the *Junior* 𝕲𝖗𝖆𝖓𝖉 𝖂𝖆𝖗𝖉𝖊𝖓   30000

———————

In all *Free-masons*   113600

Besides the *Labourers* called, 𝕴𝖘𝖍 𝕾𝖆𝖇𝖇𝖆𝖑, or *Men of Burden*, who were of the Remains of the old *Canaanites*, and being *Bondmen*, are not to be reckoned among *Masons*,   70000

———————

In all   183,600

| 12 | SOLOMON had the *Labourers* of his own; but was much obliged to HIRAM King of *Tyre*, for many of the 𝕲𝖍𝖎𝖇𝖑𝖎𝖒 and 𝕭𝖔𝖓𝖆𝖎, who lent him his best Artists, and sent him the Firs and Cedars of *Lebanon*: but above all, he sent his Name sake[21] HI-

21   In 2 *Chron.* II. 13 HIRAM King of *Tyre* (called there HURAM) in his Letter to King SOLOMON, says, *I have sent a Cunning Man* le Huram Abbi; which is not to be translated, like the Vulgate *Greek* and *Latin*, HURAM *my Father*; for his Description verse 14 refutes it; and the Words import only HURAM of *my Father's*, or the Chief *Master Mason* of my Father ABIBALUS. Yet some think that King HIRAM might call the Architect HIRAM his Father, and

RAM ABBIF, the most accomplish'd Designer and Operator upon Earth, who in *Solomon*'s Absence fill'd the Chair as *Deputy* 𝕲𝖗𝖆𝖓𝖉 𝕸𝖆𝖘𝖙𝖊𝖗, and in his Presence was the *Senior* 𝕲𝖗𝖆𝖓𝖉 𝖂𝖆𝖗𝖉𝖊𝖓, or prin-

> learned and wise Men were wont to be call'd by Royal Patrons in old Times: Thus JOSEPH was call'd ABRECH, or the King's Father; and this same HIRAM the Architect is called SOLOMON's Father, 2 *Chron.* iv. 6.

𝕲𝖓𝖆𝖘𝖆𝖍 𝕮𝖍𝖚𝖗𝖆𝖒 𝕬𝖇𝖇𝖎𝖋 𝕷𝖆 𝕸𝖊𝖑𝖊𝖈𝖍 𝕾𝖍𝖊𝖑𝖔𝖒𝖔𝖍

> *Did* HIRAM *his Father make to King* SOLOMON

But the Difficulty is over at once by allowing the Word ABBIF to be the Surname of HIRAM the Artist call'd above *Hiram Abbi*, and here call'd *Huram Abbif,* as in the *Lodge* he is called HIRAM ABBIF, to distinguish himself from KING HIRAM: For this Reading makes the Sense plain and compleat, *viz.* that Hiram King of *Tyre*, sent to King SOLOMON the cunning Workman call'd HIRAM Abbif.

He is described in two Places, 1 *Kings* vii 13, 14, 15 and 2 *Chron* ii. 13, 14. In the first he is call'd *a Widow's Son of the Tribe of* Naphtali, and in the other he is called *the Son of a Woman of the Daughters of* Dan; but in both, that his Father was *a Man of* Tyre: that is, she was of the Daughters of the City *Dan,* in the Tribe of *Naphtali,* and is call'd a *Widow* of Naphtali, as her husband was a *Naphtalite*; for he is not call'd a *Tyrian* by Descent, but a Man of *Tyre* by Habitation, as *Obed Edom* the *Levite* is call'd a *Gittite,* and the Apostle *Paul a man of* Tarsus.

But tho' HIRAM ABIFF had been a *Tyrian* by Blood, that derogates not from his vast Capacity; for the *Tyrians* now ere the best Artificers, by the Encouragement of King HIRAM: and those *Texts* testify that God had endued this HIRAM ABIFF with Wisdom, Understanding and mechanical Cunning to perform every Thing that SOLOMON required, not only in building the TEMPLE with all its costly Magnificence; but also in founding, fashioning and framing all the holy *Utensils* thereof, according to *Geometry,* and *to find every Device that shall be put to him*! And the Scripture assures us that He fully maintain'd his Character in far larger Works than those of *Aholiab* and *Bezaleel,* for which he will be honoured in the *Lodges* till the End of Time.

cipal Surveyor and *Master of Work*.

| 13 | SOLOMON partition'd the *Fellow Crafts* into certain *Lodges*, with a *Master* and *Wardens* in each; that they might receive Commands in a regular manner, might take Care of their Tools and Jewels, might be regularly paid every Week, and be duly fed and clothed, &c. and the *Fellow Crafts* took Care of their Succession by educating 𝕰𝖓𝖙𝖊𝖗'𝖉 𝕻𝖗𝖊𝖓𝖙𝖎𝖈𝖊𝖘.[22]

Thus a solid Foundation was laid of perfect *Harmony* among the Brotherhood, the *Lodge* was strongly cemented with Love and Friendship, every Brother was duly taught Secrecy and Prudence, Morality and good Fellowship, each knew his peculiar Business, and the *Grand Design* was vigorously pursued at a prodigious Expense.

For besides King DAVID's vast Preparations, his richer Son SOLOMON, and all the wealthy *Isrælites*, nay even the Princes of the neighbouring *Gentiles*, largely contributed towards It, in Gold, Silver and rich Jewels, that amounted to a Sum almost incredible: but was all needful;

For the *Wall* round It was in Compass 7700 Foot, the Materials were the best that the Earth produced, and no Structure was ever like it for exactly proportion'd and beautiful Dimensions, from the most magnificent PORTICO on the *East*, to the glorious and reverend 𝕾𝖆𝖓𝖈𝖙𝖚𝖒 𝕾𝖆𝖓𝖈𝖙𝖔𝖗𝖚𝖒 on the *West*, with numerous Apartments, pleasant and convenient Chambers and Lodgings for the Kings and Princes, the *Sanhedrin*, the Priests and Levites | 14 | of *Isræl*, and the outer *Court* of the *Gentiles* too, It being an *House of Prayer for all Nations*, and capable of receiving in all its Courts and Apartments together about 300000 People.

It was adorned with 1453 *Columns* of *Parian Marble* twisted, or sculptured or fluted, with twice as many *Pillasters*, both having exquisite *Capitels* or Chapiters of several different noble *Orders*,

22   According to the *Traditions* of old Masons, who talk much of these Things.

and about 2246 Windows, besides those in the curious Pavement; and it was lined with massy Gold, set with innumerable
Diamonds and other precious Stones, in the most harmonious,
beautiful and costly *Decoration*: tho' much more might be said, if
it had not been so often delineated, particularly by *Villalpandus*.

So that its *Prospect* highly transcended all that we are now
capable to imagine, and has been ever esteemed the finest Piece
of *Masonry* upon Earth, before or since, the 2d and *Chief* of the
7 *Wonders of Art*, since the general *Migration* from *Shinar*.

It was finish'd in the short Space of 7 Years and 6 Months, to
the Amazement of all the World; when the *Cape-Stone* was celebrated by the *Fraternity* with great Joy.[23] But their Joy was soon
interrupted by the sudden Death of their dear Master HIRAM
ABBIF, whom they decently interr'd in the *Lodge* near the *Temple*
according to antient Usage.

After HIRAM ABBIF was mourn'd for, the 𝕿abernacle of MOSES
and its holy Reliques being lodged in the 𝕿emple, SOLOMON in a
General Assembly dedicated or consecrated It by solemn Prayer
and costly Sacrifices past Number, with the finest Music, vocal
and instrumental, praising JEHOVAH, upon fixing the *Holy* ARK
in its proper Place between the *Cherubims*; when JEHOVAH fill'd
his own 𝕿emple with a *Cloud of Glory!*

But leaving what must not, and indeed what cannot be committed to Writing, we may certainly affirm, that however ambitious and emulous the *Gentiles* were in improving the *Royal Art*,
it was never perfected till the building of the 𝖌𝖔𝖗𝖌𝖊𝖔𝖚𝖘 *House* of
GOD fit for the special Refulgence of his Glory upon Earth, where
he | 15 | dwelt between the *Cherubims* on the *Mercy Seat* above
the *Ark*, and from thence gave his People frequent oraculous
Responses This glorious Edifice attracted soon the inquisitive
Connoisseurs of all Nations to travel, and spend some Time in

23   A.M.   3000.⎫
     B.C.   1004.⎭

Jerusalem, to survey its peculiar Excellencies, as much as was allow'd to the *Gentiles*; as they soon discover'd that all the World, with their joint Skill, came far short of the *Israelites* in the *Wisdom*, *Strength* and *Beauty* of Architecture; when the *wise* King SOLOMON was 𝕲𝖗𝖆𝖓𝖉 𝕸𝖆𝖘𝖙𝖊𝖗 of all *Masons* at *Jerusalem* and the *learned* King HIRAM²⁴ was *Grand Master* at *Tyre*, and inspired HIRAM ABBIF, had been *Master* of *Work*; when true compleat *Masonry* was under the immediate Care and Direction of Heaven; when the NOBLE and the *Wise* thought it their Honour to be the Associates of the ingenious Craftsmen in their well form'd *Lodges*; and so the 𝕿𝖊𝖒𝖕𝖑𝖊 of JEHOVAH, the one true God, became the just Wonder of all *Travellers*, by which, as by the most perfect Pattern, they resolved to correct the *Architecture* of their own Countries upon their Return.

SOLOMON next employ'd the *Fraternity* in carrying on his other Works, *viz.* His two PALACES at *Jerusalem* for himself and his Queen. The stately HALL of Judicature with his *Ivory Throne* and *Golden Lyons*. MILLO, or the *Royal Exchange*, made by filling up the Great Gulph, between Mount *Moriah* and Mount *Zion*, with strong Arches, upon which many beautiful *Piazzas* were erected with lofty *Collonading* on each Side, and between the Columns a spacious *Walk* from *Zion Castle* to the *Temple* where Men of Business met. The HOUSE of the *Forrest* of *Lebanon* built upon 4 Rows of *Cedar-Pillars*, his Summer-House to retire from the Heat of the Business, with a *Watch Tower* that looked to the road to *Damascus*. Several *Cities* on the road between *Jerusalem* and *Lebanon*. Many Store-houses *West* of | 16 | the *Jordan* and

24   The *Tradition* is, that King HIRAM had been *Grand Master* of all *Masons*; but when the TEMPLE was finish'd, HIRAM came to survey It before its Consecration, and to commune with SOLOMON about *Wisdom* and *Art*; and finding the Great *Architect* of the Universe, had inspired SOLOMON above all mortal Men, HIRAM very readily yeelded the Pre-eminence to SOLOMON JEDIDIAH, the *Beloved of God*.

several Store Cities *East* of that River well fortitify'd,—and the City 𝕿𝖆𝖉𝖒𝖔𝖗 (call'd afterwards by the *Greeks Palmyra*) with a splendid Palace in it, the glorious Ruins of which are seen by Travellers to this Day.

All these and many more costly Buildings were finish'd in the short Space of 13 Years after the *Temple*, by the care of 550 𝕳𝖆𝖗𝖔𝖉𝖎𝖒 and 𝕸𝖊𝖓𝖆𝖙𝖟𝖈𝖍𝖎𝖒: for *Masonry* was carried on throughout all his Dominions, and many particular *Lodges* were constituted under *Grand Master* SOLOMON, who annually assembled the 𝕲𝖗𝖆𝖓𝖉 𝕷𝖔𝖉𝖌𝖊 at *Jerusalem* for transmitting their Affairs to Posterity: tho' still the Loss of good HIRAM ABBIF was lamented.

Indeed this wise *Grand Master* SOLOMON shew'd the Imperfection of *human* Nature, even at its Hight of Excellency, by loving too much many *strange Women*, who turn'd him from the true Religion: But our Business with him is only as a MASON; for even during his Idolatry he built some curious *Temples* to 𝕮𝖍𝖊𝖒𝖔𝖘𝖍, 𝕸𝖔𝖑𝖊𝖈𝖍 and 𝕬𝖘𝖍𝖙𝖆𝖗𝖔𝖙𝖍, the Gods of his Concubines, till about 3 Years before he died, when he composed his penitential Song, the *Ecclesiastes*; and fixed the true Motto on all earthly Glory, *viz.* VANITY of VANITIES, ALL *is* VANITY *without the* Fear *of* God *and the keeping of his Commands, which is the whole Duty of Man!* And died aged 58 Years.[25]

Many of SOLOMON's *Masons* before he died began to travel, and carry'd with 'em the *High Taste* of Architecture, with the Secrets of the Fraternity, into *Syria, Lesser Asia, Mesopotamia, Scythia, Assyria, Chaldæa, Media, Bactria, India, Persia, Arabia, Egypt,* and other Parts of great ASIA and AFRICA; also into EUROPE, no doubt, tho' we have no History to assure us yet of the Transactions of *Greece* and *Italy*: But the Tradition is that they travell'd to HERCULES PILLARS on the *West*, and to CHINA on the *East*: and the old *Constitutions* affirm, that one call'd NINUS,

25   A.M.   3029. ⎞
       A.C.   975. ⎠

who had been at the building of *Solomon's Temple*, brought the refined Knowledge of the *Science* and the *Art* into *Germany* and *Gaul*.

| 17 | In many Places being highly esteem'd, they obtain'd special Privileges; and because they taught their *liberal Art* only to the *Freeborn*, they were call'd FREE MASONS; constituting *Lodges* in the Places where they built stately Piles, by the Encouragement of the Great and Wealthy, who soon requested to be accepted as Members of the *Lodge* and *Brothers* of the *Craft*; till by Merit those *Free* and *accepted Masons* came to be *Masters* and *Wardens*.

Nay Kings, Princes and Potentates became 𝕲𝖗𝖆𝖓𝖉 𝕸𝖆𝖘𝖙𝖊𝖗𝖘, each in his own Dominion, in Imitation of King *Solomon*, whose Memory, as a *Mason*, has been duly worshipp'd, and will be, till *Architecture* shall be consumed in the general Conflagration; for he never can be rivall'd but by one equally inspired from above.

After SOLOMON's death, the Partition of his Empire into the Kingdoms of *Isræl* and *Judah*, did not demolish the *Lodges*: For in *Isræl*, King JEROBOAM erected the curious *Statues* of the two 𝕲𝖔𝖑𝖉𝖊𝖓 𝕮𝖆𝖑𝖛𝖊𝖘 at *Dan* and *Bethel*, with 𝕿𝖊𝖒𝖕𝖑𝖊𝖘 for their Worship; King *Baasha* built *Tirzah* for his Palace, and King *Omri* built *Samaria* for his Capital; where his son King ACHAB built a large and sumptuous 𝕿𝖊𝖒𝖕𝖑𝖊 for his *Idol* 𝕭𝖆𝖆𝖑 (afterwards destroy'd by King *Jehu*) and a *Palace of Ivory*, besides many Castles and fenced Cities.

But SOLOMON's Royal Race, the Kings of *Judah*, succeeded him also in the GRAND MASTER's *Chair*, or deputed the High Priest to preserve the *Royal Art*. Their Care of the Temple with the many Buildings they raised, with strong Forts, are mention'd in holy Writ down to JOSIAH the last good King of *Judah*.

SOLOMON's 𝕿𝖗𝖆𝖛𝖊𝖑𝖑𝖊𝖗𝖘 improved the *Gentiles* beyond Expression. Thus the *Syrians* adorned their *Damascus* with a lofty *Temple* and a Royal *Palace*. Those of *Lesser Asia* became excellent *Masons*, particularly at *Sardis* in *Lydia*, and along the Sea Coasts in the mercantil Cities, as at 𝕰𝖕𝖍𝖊𝖘𝖚𝖘.

[…]

| 20 | Mean while, *Nebuchadnezzar* was carrying on his Grand Design of inlarging and beautifying BABYLON, and employ'd the more Skillful Artists of *Judah*, and of his other captivated Nations, to join his *Chaldees* in raising the *Walls*, the *Palaces*, the *Hanging Gardens*, the amazing *Bridge*, the *Temples*, the long and broad Streets, the Squares, &c. of that proud *Metropolis*, accounted the 4th of the 7 *Wonders of Art*, described at large in many Books, and therefore needless to be rehearsed particularly here.

| 21 | But for all his unspeakable Advantages of Wealth and Power, and for all his vast Ambition, he could not arrive at the *sublime* of the *Solomonian Stile*. 'Tis true, after his Wars, He was a mighty Encourager of Architecture, a sumptuous 𝕲𝖗𝖆𝖓𝖉 𝕸𝖆𝖘𝖙𝖊𝖗; and his Artists discover'd great Knowledge in raising his *Golden Image* in the Vale of *Dura* 60 Cubits high and 6 broad, and also in all the beautiful Parts of his *Great* BABYLON: Yet It was never fully peopled; for his Pride provoked God to afflict him with Brutal Madness for 7 Years, and when restored, He liv'd about one Year only and died *A.M.* 3442, but 23 Years after, his Grandson *Belshazzar* was slain by CYRUS, who conquer'd that Empire and soon removed the Throne to SUSIANA in *Persia*.

The MEDES and PERSIANS had much improved in the *Royal Art*, and had rivall'd the *Assyrians* and *Chaldeans* in *Masonry* at 𝕰𝖐𝖇𝖆𝖙𝖆𝖓𝖆, 𝖘𝖚𝖘𝖎𝖆𝖓𝖆, 𝕻𝖊𝖗𝖘𝖊𝖕𝖔𝖑𝖎𝖘, and many more fine Cities, before They conquer'd 'em in War; tho' They had nothing so large as 𝕹𝖎𝖓𝖎𝖛𝖊𝖍 and 𝕭𝖆𝖇𝖞𝖑𝖔𝖓, nor so accurate as the 𝕿𝖊𝖒𝖕𝖑𝖊 and the other Structures of *Solomon*.

The *Jewish* Captives, after *Nebuchadnezzar*'s Death, kept themselves at Work in regular *Lodges*, till the set Time of their Deliverance; and were thus the more capable, at the *Reduction*, of Rebuilding the *Holy Temple* and the *City* of *Salem* upon the old Foundations; which was ordered by the *Decree* of CYRUS, according to God's word that had foretold his Exaltation and that Decree, publisht *A.M.* 3468, *B.C.* 536.

[...]

| 25 | At length the ROYAL ART flourish'd in *Greece*. Indeed we read of the old *Dedalus* and his Sons, the Imitators of the *Egyptians* and *Phenicians*, of the little Labyrinth in *Crete*, and the larger at Lemnos, of the Arts and Sciences early at *Athenes* and *Sicyon*, *Candia* and *Sicily* before the *Trojan War*; of the *Temples* of **Jupiter** *Olympius*, **Esculapius**, *&c.* of the *Trojan Horse*, and other Things: But we are all in Darkness, Fable and Uncertainty till the *Olympiads*.

| 26 | Now the 35th year of *Uzziah* King of *Judah* is the first Year of the first OLYMPIAD[26] when some of their bright Men began to travel. So that their most antient famous Buildings, as the Cittadel of *Athenes*, the Court of *Areopagus*, the *Parthenion* or *Temple* of **Minerva**, the *Temples* of *Theseus* and **Apollo**, their *Porticos* and *Forums*, *Theatres* and *Gymnasiums*, stately publick *Halls*, curious *Bridges*, regular *Fortifications*, stout *Ships* of War, and magnificent *Palaces*, with their best *Statues* and *Sculpture*, were All of 'em, either at first erected, or else rebuilt fine, even after the *Temple* of ZERUBBABEL; for

THALES MILESIUS, their first Philosopher, died eleven Years only before the *Decree* of *Cyrus*; and the same Year 3457, PY-THAGORAS, his Scholar, travell'd into *Egypt*; while PISISTRATUS, the Tyrant of *Athenes*, began to collect the *first Library* in *Greece*.

PYTHAGORAS liv'd 22 Years among the *Egyptian* Priests till sent by *Cambyses* to *Babylon* and *Persia*, *A.M.* 3480, where he

26   *A.M.*   3228. }
      B.C.   776. } before the Founding of Rome 28 years

pickt up great Knowledge among the *Chaldæan Magians* and *Babylonish Jews*; and return'd to *Greece* the Year that *Zerubabbel's* 𝔗𝔢𝔪𝔭𝔩𝔢 was finish'd, *A.M.* 3489.

He became, not only the Head of a new Religion of Patch Work, but likewise of an *Academy* or *Lodge* of good *Geometricians*, to whom he communicated a Secret[27] *viz. That amazing Proposition which is the Foundation of all Masonry, of whatever Materials or Dimensions,* call'd by *Masons* his HEUREKA; because They think It was his own Invention.

But after *Pythagoras,* GEOMETRY was the darling Study of the *Greeks*, and their learned Men reduced the noble Science to the Use of the ingenious *Mechanicks* of all Sorts, that perform by *Geometry* as well as the Operators in *Stone* or *Brick.*

| 27 | And as MASONRY kept pace with *Geometry*, so many *Lodges* appear'd, especially in the *Grecian* Republicks, where *Liberty, Trade* and *Learning* flourish'd; as at *Sicyon, Athenes, Corinth* and the Cities of *Ionia*, till They arrived at their beautiful DORIC, IONIC and CORINTHIAN *Orders*: And their Improvements were soon discover'd to the *Persians* with a Vengeance, when They defeated *Xerxes, A.M.* 3525.

GREECE now abounded with the best *Architects, Sculptors, Statuaries, Painters* and other fine *Designers*, most of 'em educated at the Academies of *Athenes* and *Sicyon*, who Instructed many Artists and *Fellow Crafts* to be the best Operators upon Earth: So that the Nations of *Asia* and *Africa*, who had taught the *Greeks*, were now taught by 'em.

The learned *Greeks* rightly judging, that the Rules of the beautiful Proportions in *Architecture* should be taken from the Proportions of the *Human Body*, their fine *Painters* and *Statuaries* were esteem'd *Architects*, and were then actually so (even as afterwards true old *Masonry* was revived in *Italy* by the *Painters*[28])

27 *Euclid. Lib.* I *Prop.* XLVII.
28 See Chap VII. No country but *Greece* could now boast of such

nor could They have been fine *Painters* without being *Architects*.

Therefore several of those in the *Margin below*, excellent *Painters* and *Philosophers*, are in the List of *antient Architects*: Nay They all openly taught *Geometry*, and many of 'em practis'd *Masonry*; and being Gentlemen of good Repute, They were generally at the *Head* of the *Craft*, highly useful to the *Fellow Crafts*, by their Designs and fine Drawings, and bred them up | 28 | clever Artists: Only by a Law in *Greece*, no *Slave* was allowed to learn the 7 liberal Sciences, or those of the *Freeborn*[29]; so that in *Greece* also they were call'd FREE MASONS, and in their many *Lodges*, the Noble and Learned were accepted as Brothers, down to the days of ALEXANDER the *Great*, and afterwards for many Ages.

[…]

| 40 | HEROD became the greatest Builder of his Day, the Patron or *Grand Master* of many *Lodges*, and sent for the most expert *Fellow Crafts* of *Greece* to assist his own *Jews*: For after the Battle of *Actium* B.C. 30, Before *Christ's* Birth 26.

HEROD, being reconciled to *Augustus*, began to shew his

men as *Mycon, Phidias, Demon, Androcides, Meton, Anaxagoras, Dipænus* and *Scyllis, Glycon, Alcamenes, Praxitiles, Polycletus, Lysippus, Peneus, Euphranor, Perseus, Philostratus, Zeuxis, Appolodorus, Parhasius, Timanthes, Eupompus, Pamphilus, Apelles, Artemones, Socrates, Eudoxus, Metrodorus* (who wrote of *Masonry*) and the excellent *Theodorus Cyrenarus*, who amplify'd *Geometry*, and publisht the *Art Analytic*, thn [sic] Master of the divine PLATO from whose School came *Xenocrates* and *Aristotle* the Preceptor of ALEXANDER *the Great*.

Plato died   A.M. 3656. }
           B.C.   348. }

29   According to the old *Constitutions* these are, 1. *Grammar.* 2. *Rhetoric.* 3. *Logic.* 4. *Arithmetic.* 5. GEOMETRY. 6. *Music.* 7. *Astronomy.*

mighty Skill in *Masonry* by erecting a splendid *Grecian* THE-ATRE at *Jerusalem*, and next built the stately City *Sebaste*, (so called from *Sebastos* or *Augustus*), formerly *Samaria*, with a curious little *Temple* in It like That of *Jerusalem*. He made the City *Cæsarea* the best Harbour in *Palestine*, and built a *Temple* of white Marble at *Paneas*—the cities *Antipatris*, *Phasaelis* and *Cypron*, and the *Tower* of *Phasael* at *Jerusalem*, not Inferior to the *Pharo* of *Alexandria*, &c.

But his most amazing Work was his Rebuilding of the 𝕿𝖊𝖒-𝖕𝖑𝖊 of ZERUBBABEL; for having prepared Materials (which with those of the old Temple were enough) and proper Instruments, HEROD employ'd 10000 *Masons* (besides Labourers) and mar-shall'd 'em in *Lodges* under 1000 Priests and Levites that were skilful Architects, as *Masters* and *Wardens* of the *Lodges*, and acted as GRAND MASTER himself with his Wardens HILLEL and SHAMMAI, two learned *Rabbins* of great Reputation.

He began to pull down the *Temple* of *Zerubbabel*, not all at once, but Piece by Piece, and levelled the Foot-stone of this *Temple* of *Jerusalem*, viz.

After the founding of the *Second Temple* 518 years; In the 21st Year of *Herod* and 13 Year of *Augustus* and 29th *Julian* Year. In the 4th Year of *Olympiad* CXC and of *Rome* 732.[30]

Just 46 Years before the second Passover of *Christ*'s Ministry, for the *Jews* said 46 *Years was this Temple in Building*. (John xi.20.)

| 41 | The *Holy Place*, and the *Holy of Holiest* in the West, and the great *Portico* in the East, were finished at a wondrous Cost, and in the short Space of 1 Year and 6 Months and the Rest de-sign'd by *Herod* in 8 Years more.[31]

---

30   A.M.   3987 ⎫
      Before the *Chr. Æra*   17 ⎬
      Before *Christ's Birth* 14
31   9 Y. and 6 M.

When the *Fraternity* celebrated the *Cape Stone* with great
Joy and in due Form, and the King solemniz'd Its *Dedication* by
Prayer and Sacrifice, on his Coronation Day, of the 31st Year of
his reign, And 23ᵈ of *Augustus*.[32]

Josephus describes It,[33] as he view'd It, with the Additions
built after *Herod* died, a number of the most curious and magnificent Marble Edifices that had been rais'd since the Days of
SOLOMON; yet more after the *Grecian Stile*, and much Inferior
to *Solomon's* TEMPLE in Extent and Decoration, tho' larger than
That of *Zerubbabel*, and was by the *Romans* esteemed the same;
for *Tacitus* calls It the same that *Pompey* walk'd thro'.

But It was not fully finish'd, in all Its Appartments, till about
6 Years before It was destroy'd, viz. A.D. 64.

At length

AUGUSTUS having shut up the *Temple* of JANUS; for that all
the World was at Peace, In the 26ᵗʰ Year of his Empire, after the
Conquest of *Egypt*,

The WORD was made FLESH, or the LORD JESUS CHRIST
IMMANUEL was born, the Great Architect or *Grand Master* of
the *Christian* Church.[34]

[…]

| 47 | For when the *Gothic Nations*, and those conquer'd
by them, began to affect stately Structures, They wanted both
Heads and Hands to imitate the Antients, nor could They do it
for many Ages (as in the next Chapter) yet not wanting Wealth

---

32 *A.M.*   3997)
    Before the Christian Era   7)
    Before *Christ's Birth*

33 *Antiq.* lib. xv. cap. xi.

34 After *Solomon's* Death 971)   In the Year of the *Julian Period* 4710
    In the Year of *Rome*   745)   In the Year of *Masonry* or *A.M.*   4000
    In the Year of *Herod*   34)   B.C. or Before the *Christ. Æra*   4

and Ambition, They did their best: and so the more Ingenious gradually coalesced in Societies or *Lodges*, in Imitation of the Antients, according to the remaining Traditions that were not quite obliterated, and hammer'd out a *New Stile* of their own, call'd the GOTHIC.

But tho' This is more expensive than the *old Stile*, and discovers now to us the Ignorance of the *Architect*, and the Improprieties of the *Edifice*; yet the Inventions of the *Artists* to supply the Want of good old Skill, and their costly Decorations, have manifested their great Esteem of the *Royal Art*, and have render'd their *Gothic* Structures *Venerable* and *Magnificent*; tho' not Imitable by Those that have the true *High Taste* of the *Grecian* or AUGUSTAN STILE.

[…]

| 97 |

Part III

The 𝕳istory of MASONRY in *Britain*, from the
Union of the *Crowns* to these Times

Chap I

The AUGUSTAN STILE in *Britain*, from the *Union* of the
CROWNS 1603. till the RESTORATION 1660.

Before this *Period*, some Gentlemen of fine Taste returning from their Travels full of laudable Emulation, resolved, if not to excel the *Italian Revivers*, at least to imitate them in old *Roman* and *Grecian* MASONRY. But no Remains being here, no Vestiges of the good old AUGUSTAN Stile, those ingenious Travellers brought home some Pieces of *old Columns*, some curious Drawings of the *Italian Revivers*, and their Books of *Architecture*; especially

INIGO JONES, born near St. *Paul's London*, A.D. 1572 (Son of Mr. *Ignatius* or *Inigo Jones*, a citizen of *London*) bred up at *Cambridge*, who naturally took to the *Arts* of *Designing*, and was first known by his Skill of *Landskip-Painting*; for which he was patroniz'd by the noble and learned WILLIAM HERBERT (afterwards Earl of *Pembroke*) at whose Expence *Jones* made the Tour of *Italy*, where he was instructed in the *Royal Art* by some of the best Disciples of the famous

ANDREA PALLADIO.

| 98 | INIGO JONES, upon his Return, laid aside his *Pencil*, and took up the *Square*, *Level* and *Plumb*, and became the 𝔙𝔦𝔱𝔯𝔲𝔳𝔦𝔲𝔰 𝔅𝔯𝔦𝔱𝔞𝔫𝔫𝔦𝔠𝔲𝔰, the rival of *Palladio* and of all the *Italian* Revivers; as it soon appear'd after

The UNION of the CROWNS, *A.D.* 1603.
When the ROYAL TEWDORS expired,
and the ROYAL STEWARTS succeeded.

SCOTTISH Kings of All *Britain*.

I. JAMES I. *Stewart*, now the *first* King of *all* Britain, a *Royal* Brother *Mason*, and *Royal Grand Master* by Prerogative, wishing for proper Heads and Hands for establishing the *Augustan Stile* here, was glad to find such a Subject as 𝔍𝔫𝔦𝔤𝔬 𝔍𝔬𝔫𝔢𝔰; whom he appointed his General *Surveyor*, and approv'd of his being chosen *Grand Master* of *England*, to preside over the *Lodges*.

The King order'd him to draw the Plan of a *new* Palace at *Whitehall*, and so when the old *Banquetting-House* was pull'd down, the KING with *Grand Master* 𝔍𝔬𝔫𝔢𝔰 and his *Grand Wardens*, (the foresaid WILLIAM HERBERT Earl of *Pembroke*, and *Nicholas Stone* the Sculptor,) attended by many Brothers in due Form, and many eminent Persons, walk'd to *Whitehall* Gate, and levell'd the *Footstone* of the *New Banquetting-House* with 3 great

Knocks, loud Huzza's, Sound of Trumpets, and a Purse of broad
Pieces of Gold laid upon the Stone for the *Masons* to Drink.

To the King and the Craft!
A.D. 1607

Tho' for want of a Parliamentary Fund, no more was built but
the said glorious Banquetting-House, the finest single Room of
that large Extent since the Days of *Augustus*, and the Glory of
this Reign. Afterwards the lofty Ceiling was adorned by the fine
Pencil of *Peter Paul* RUBENS.

The best *Craftsmen* from all Parts resorted to *Grand Master*
JONES, who always allow'd good Wages and seasonable Times
for Instruction in the Lodges, which he constituted with excellent By-Laws, and made 'em like the *Schools* or *Academies* of
the | 99 | Designers in Italy. He also held the Quarterly *Com-
munication*[35] of the Grand Lodge of *Masters* and *Wardens*, and the
Annual General Assembly and *Feast* on St. *John*'s Day, when he
was annually rechosen, till *A.D.* 1618 when the foresaid WILLIAM
Earl of *Pembroke* was chosen *Grand Master*; and being approved
by the King, he appointed Inigo Jones his *Deputy* Grand Master.

Masonry thus flourishing, many eminent, wealthy and
learned Men, at their own Request, were accepted as *Brothers*, to
the Honour of the *Craft*, till the King died 27 *March* 1625 leaving
two Children, *viz.*

2. CHARLES I. *Stewart*, | *Elizabeth Stewart*, Queen of *Bohemia*.
aged 25 Years succeeded; | Princess *Sophia*, Electress of *Brunswig*.
also a Royal Brother and | *George* I. King of Great *Britain*. Below.
Grand Master by Prerogative: Being well skill'd in the Arts of
Designing, he encouraged the best foreign *Painters*, *Sculptors*,
Statuaries, *Plaisterers*, &c. but wanted no Foreigners for *Archi*-

35   So said Brother Nicholas Stone his Warden, in a Manuscript burnt
      1720.

tecture; because none of 'em equall'd his own *Inigo Jones* and his excellent Disciples. When *Grand Master* PEMBROKE demitted, *A.D.* 1630.

HENRY DANVERS Earl of *Danby* succeeded in *Solomon's Chair* by the King's Approbation; and at his own Cost erected a small but most accurate Piece of the old Architecture, by the Design of his *Deputy* 𝔍𝔬𝔫𝔢𝔰, even the famous beautiful *Gate* of the *Physic* Garden at *Oxford* with this Inscription.

GLORIÆ DEI OPTIMI MAXIMI HONORI CAROLI REGIS,
IN USUM ACADEMIÆ ET REIPUBLICÆ, A.D. 1632
HENRICUS COMES DANBY.

THOMAS HOWARD Earl of *Arundel* (the Progenitor of our late *Grand Master* NORFOLK) then succeeded *Danby* at the Head | 100 | of the Fraternity, a most excellent Connoisseur in all the *Arts* of *Designing*, and the great Reviver of learned Antiquities, who will be ever famous for his *Marmora Arundeliana*! But *Deputy* 𝔍𝔬𝔫𝔢𝔰 was never out of Office; and join'd *Grand Master* ARUNDEL, in persuading 𝔉𝔯𝔞𝔫𝔠𝔦𝔰 ℜ𝔲𝔰𝔰𝔢𝔩 Earl of *Bedford*, to lay out his Grounds of *Covent-Garden* in an Oblong-Square *East* and *West*, where he built the regular Temple of St. *Paul* with its admirable *Portico*, made Parochial *A.D.* 1635. when

Grand Master BEDFORD succeeded, and employ'd his *Deputy* 𝔍𝔬𝔫𝔢𝔰 to build the *North* and *East* Sides of that Square with large and lofty *Arkades* (commonly call'd *Piazzas*) which, with the said Church on the *West* End, make a most beautiful Prospect after the *Italian* or antient manner.

INIGO JONES succeeded *Bedford* in *Solomon's Chair* again; and before the Wars the King employ'd him to build the stately great *Gallery* of Somerset-House fronting the *Thames*: And the King intended to carry on *Whitehall* according to *Jones's* Plan, but was unhappily prevented by the *Civil* Wars: for the *Parlia-*

ment's Army conquer'd the *King* and *Parliament* too, and murder'd him at his own Gate on 30 *January* 164$\frac{8}{9}$.

Yet even during the Wars, the *Masons* met occasionally at several Places: Thus **Elias Ashmole** in his Diary Page 15 says, *I was made a Free Mason* at Warrington, Lancashire, *with Colonel* Henry Manwaring, *by Mr.* Richard Penket *the Warden, and the fellow Crafts* (there mention'd) *on* 16 Oct. 1646.

The *Great* INIGO JONES aged 80 Years died at *London*, and was buried at St. *Bennet's* Church at *Paul's* Wharf on 26 *June* 1652, the **Grand Master** of *Architects*, who brought the *Augustan* Stile into *England*.

He shew'd his great Skill also in designing the magnificent *Rowe* of great *Queen-street,* and the *West* Side of *Lincoln's-Inn-Fields,* with beautiful *Lindsey-House,* the *Chirurgeons Hall* and *Theatre, Shaftsbury-House* in *Aldersgate-Street, Southampton-House Bloomsbury* (now the Duke of *Bedford's*) *Berkeley-House Piccadilly* (now the Duke of *Devonshire's*) lately burnt and rebuilt; accurate *York-Stairs* at the *Thames, &c.* And in the Country, | 101 | *Gunnerysbury-House* near *Brentford, Wilton-House Wiltshire, Castle-Abby Northamptonshire, Stoke-Park, &c.*

Some of his *best Disciples* met privately for their mutual Improvement till the *Restoration,* who preserved his clean Drawings and accurate Designs (still preserved by the skilful Architect, the noble RICHARD BOYLE the present Earl of *Burlington*) and after the Restoration they propagated his *lofty Stile.*

Chap. II.
From the RESTORATION 1660 till the REVOLUTION 1688.

3. CHARLES II. *Stewart*, succeeded his Father, and was magnificently restor'd, aged 30 Years, on his own Birth-Day, 29 *May* 1660. In his travels he had been made a *Free Mason*, and having observed the exact Structures of foreign Countries, he

resolved to encourage the *Augustan* Stile by reviving the *Lodges*, and approved their Choice of

HENRY JERMYN Earl of St. *Albans* as their 𝕲𝖗𝖆𝖓𝖉 𝕸𝖆𝖘𝖙𝖊𝖗, who appointed Sir JOHN DENHAM his *Deputy Grand Master*, Sir **Christopher Wren** ⎰ *Grand* ⎱ According to a Copy of the Mr. **John Web** ⎱ *Wardens.* ⎰ of the *old Constitutions*, this *Grand Master* held a *General* Assembly and *Feast* on St. John's Day 27 *Dec* 1663 when the following *Regulations* were made.

1. *That no person of what Degree soever, be made or accepted a* Free Mason *unless in a regular Lodge, whereof one to be a* Master *or a* Warden *in that Limit or Division where such Lodge is kept, and another to be a* Craftsman *in the trade of* Free Masonry.

2. *That no Person hereafter shall be accepted a* Free Mason, *but such as are of able Body, honest Parentage, good Reputation. And an Observer of the Laws of the Land.*

3. *That no Person hereafter who shall be accepted a* Free Mason *shall be admitted into any* Lodge *or Assembly until he has brought a Certificate of the Time and Place of his Acceptation from the* | 102 | *Lodge that accepted him until the* Master *of that* Limit *or Division where such Lodge is kept: And the said Master shall enrol the same in a Roll of Parchment to be kept for that Purpose, and shall give an Account of all such Acceptations at every General* Assembly.

4. *That every Person who is now a* Free Mason, *shall bring to the Master a Note of the Time of his Acceptation, to the End the same may be enroll'd in such Priority of Place as the Brother deserves; and that the whole* Company *and* Fellows *may the better know each other better.*

5. *That for the Future the said Fraternity of* Free Masons *shall be regulated and govern'd by* ONE GRAND MASTER, *and as many* Wardens *as the said Society shall think fit to appoint at every Annual General* Assembly.

6. *That no Person shall be accepted unless he be* 21 *Years old*

or more.

THOMAS SAVAGE Earl of *Rivers* succeeded St. *Albans* as 𝕲𝖗𝖆𝖓𝖉 𝕸𝖆𝖘𝖙𝖊𝖗, 24 June 1666, ⎧ Mr. *John Web*,   ⎫ Grand
who appointed Sir 𝕮𝖍𝖗𝖎𝖘𝖙𝖔𝖕𝖍𝖊𝖗 ⎩ Mr. *Grinlin Gibbons*,⎭ Wardens.
𝕎𝖗𝖊𝖓 his *Deputy;* but the *Deputy* and *Wardens* manag'd all things.

This Year on 2 *Sept.* the Great Burning of *London* happen'd, and the *Free Masons* became necessary to rebuild it.

Accordingly,

The *King* and *Grand Master* order'd the *Deputy* 𝕎𝖗𝖊𝖓 to draw up a fine Plan of the new City with long, broad and regular Streets; but tho' private Properties hinder'd it's taking Effect, yet that noble City was soon rebuilt in a far better *Stile* than before.

The *King* levell'd the *Footstone* of the *New Royal-Exchange* in solemn Form, on 23 *Oct.* 1667 and it was open'd, the finest in *Europe,* by the Mayor and Aldermen on 28 Sept. *1669.* Upon the Insides of the *Square* above the *Arkades,* and between the Windows, are the *Statues* of the Soveraigns of *England.* Afterwards the *Merchant* Adventurers employ'd *Grand Warden* 𝕲𝖎𝖇𝖇𝖔𝖓𝖘, to erect in the Middle of the Square the KING's *Statue* | 103 | to the Life, in *Cæsarian* Habit, of white Marble, with an elegant Inscription, below.[36]

GILBERT SHELDON Archbishop of *Cantebury,* an excel-

36   CAROLO SECUNDO CÆSARI BRITANNICO
            PATRIÆ PATRI
REGUM OPTIMO CLEMENTISSIMO AUGUSTISSIMO
        GENERIS HUMANI DELICIIS
        UTRIUSQUE FORTUNÆ VICTORI
        MARIUM DOMINO AC VINDICI
    SOCIETAS MERCATORUM ADVENTUR ANGLIÆ
    QUÆ PER CCCC JAM PROPE ANNOS
        REGIA MAJESTATE FLORET
FIDEI INTEMERATÆ ETR GRATITUDINIS ÆTERNÆ
            HOC TESTIMONIUM
        VENERABUNDA POSUIT
    ANNO SALUTIS HUMANÆ MDCLXXXIV

lent Architect, shew'd his great Skill in designing his famous *Theatrum Sheldonianum* at *Oxford*, and at his Cost it was conducted and finish'd by *Deputy* 𝔚𝔯𝔢𝔫 and *Grand Warden* 𝔚𝔢𝔟; and the *Craftsmen* having celebrated the *Cape-Stone*, it was open'd with an elegant Oration by Dr. *South*, on 9 *July* 1669. D.G.M. 𝔚𝔯𝔢𝔫 built also that other *Master Piece*, the pretty *Museum* near the *Theatre*, at the Charge of the *University*. Mean while

LONDON was rebuilding apace; and the Fire having ruin'd St. *Paul's* Cathedral, the KING with *Grand Master* RIVERS, his Architects and Craftsmen, Nobility and Gentry, Lord Mayor and Aldermen, Bishops and Clergy, &c. in due Form levell'd the *Footstone* of New St. *Paul's*, design'd by D.G. *Master* 𝔚𝔯𝔢𝔫 A.D. 1673 and by him conducted as *Master of Work* and Surveyor, with his Wardens Mr. *Edward Strong* Senior and Junior, upon a Parliamentary Fund.

The City rear'd beautiful *Moor-Gate*, and rebuilt *Bedlam-Hospital* in the best *Old Stile*, A.D. 1675 and where the Fire | 104 | began, the City rais'd the famous *Monument* of White Stone, a fine fluted *Column* of the *Doric* Order, 202 Foot high from the Ground, and the *Shaft* is 15 Foot in Diameter, with an easy *Stair* of black Marble within the Shaft leading up to an *Iron Balcony*, guilded at the Top, the highest *Column* upon Earth. It's *Pedestal* is 21 Foot Square and 40 Foot high, with most ingenious *Emblems* in Baffo Relievo, wrought by the foresaid *Gabriel Cibber*, with *Latin Inscriptions*. It was finish'd A.D. 1677.

So where the Fire stopt at Temple-Bar, the City built a fine *Roman* Gate, with the Statues of Queen ELIZABETH and King JAMES I on the *East* Side, and those of King CHARLES I and CHARLES II on the *West* Side.

The 𝔓𝔥𝔶𝔰𝔦𝔠𝔦𝔞𝔫𝔰 discover'd also their fine Taste by their accurate *College*, a *Master-Piece*; and the 𝔏𝔞𝔴𝔶𝔢𝔯𝔰 by the Front of *Middle Temple-Lane*.

And after the Fire, the *Parish* Churches were many of 'em elegantly rebuilt, especially St. *Mary-le-Bow* with it's Steeple of several orders, and St. *Mary Wool-Church* with it's admiral *Cupola, &c.*

The KING also founded *Chelsea-Hospital* for old Soldiers, and a most curious New *Palace* at *Greenwich* from a Design of *Inigo Jones*, conducted by *Grand Warden* 𝔚𝔢𝔟 as *Master* of Work; and another *Palace* at *Winchester*, designed by *Grand Master* WREN, an excellent Pile of the richest *Corinthian* Order, cover'd in before the King's Death, but never finish'd, and now in Ruins.

The King order'd Sir WILLIAM BRUCE, *Baronet, Grand Master* of *Scotland*, to rebuild his Palace of *Holyrood-House* at *Edinburg* in the best *Augustan* Stile, and the *Scottish* Secretary-Office at *Whitehall*. G. *Master* Bruce built also his own pretty Seat at *Kinross*.

| 105 | So that the *Fellow Crafts* were never more employ'd than in this Reign, nor in a more lofty Stile[37]; and many *Lodges* were constituted throughout the Islands by Leave of the several noble G. Masters: for after G. *Master Rivers* demitted, A.D. 1674.

GEORGE VILLARS Duke of *Bucks*, an old *Mason*, succeeded as G. *Master* of *England*; but being indolent, he left all Business to his *Deputy* 𝔚𝔯𝔢𝔫 and his *Wardens*; and when he demitted A.D. 1679.

HENRY BENNET Earl of *Arlington* succeeded, who was too deeply engag'd in Affairs of *State* to mind the *Lodges*: Yet in his *Mastership* the Fraternity was considerable still, and many Gentlemen requested to be admitted. Thus the foresaid Brother *Ashmole* (in his *Diary* Page 66) says,

On the 10 *March* 1682, *I received a Summons to appear next Day at a Lodge in* Masons-Hall London, *when we admitted into*

---

37   For besides many other find *Structures* in and about *London*, many
      noble *Mansions* in the Counrty were built or founded; as *Wing-House Bedfordshire; Chevening* in *Kent; Ambrosebury* in *Wiltshire; Hotham-House* and *Stainsborough Yorkshire;* Palace of *Hamilton* in *Clydesdale; Sterling-House* near the Castle; *Drumlanrig* in *Nidsdale;* and many more.

the Fellowship of Free Masons Sir William Wilson, *Capt.* Richard Borthwick, *and four more. I was the Senior Fellow, it being* 35 *Years since I was admitted; and with me were Mr.* Thomas Wise (*Master of the* London Company *of Masons*) *and eight more old Free Masons. We all dined at the* Half-Moon *Tavern in* Cheapside, *a noble dinner, prepared at the Charge of the new accepted Masons.*

But many of the Fraternity's *Records* of this and former Reigns were lost in the next and at the Revolution; and many of 'em were too hastily burnt in our Time from a Fear of making Discoveries: So that we have not so ample an Account as could be wish'd of the *Grand Lodge, &c.*

King *Charles* II dying on 6 *February* 168⅘. his Brother succeeded, *viz.*

4. JAMES II *Stewart*, aged 51 Years. A most excellent *Statue* of him still stands in *Whitehall*. But not being a *Brother Mason*, the *Art* was much neglected, and People of all sorts were | 106 | otherwise engag'd in this Reign: Only upon the Death of Grand Master *Arlington* 1685 the *Lodges* met and elected

Sir CHRISTOPHER WREN 𝕲𝖗𝖆𝖓𝖉 𝕸𝖆𝖘𝖙𝖊𝖗, who appointed Mr. *Gabriel Cibber,* ⎫ *Grand Wardens,* ⎧ and while carrying on Mr. *Edward Strong* ⎭   ⎩ St. *Paul's*, he annually met those Brethren that could attend him, to keep up good old Usages, till the Revolution, then

𝖂𝖎𝖑𝖑𝖎𝖆𝖒 of *Nassau* Prince of *Orange*, landed on 5 *Nov.* 1688 and King JAMES sail'd to *France* on 23 *Dec.* following, and died there on 6 *Sept.* 1701.

Chap. III
From the REVOLUTION to *Grand Master* MONTAGU, 1721.

U PON King *James*'s going off, the *Convention* of *States* entail'd the Crown of *England* upon King *James*'s two Daughters and their Issue, *viz.* MARY Princess of *Orange*, and ANN Princess of *Denmark*: And failing them on WILLIAM Prince of *Orange*; for his Mother *Mary Stewart* was King *James*'s eldest Sister: But ORANGE was to reign during Life. Accordingly on 13 *Feb.* 168$\frac{8}{9}$.

5. King WILLIAM III. aged 38 Years, and his Wife

6. Queen MARY II *Stewart*, aged 26 Years,

She died at *Kensington* without Issue on 28 *Dec.* 1694.

} were proclaim'd *King* and *Queen*, Joint *Soveraigns* of *England*; and *Scotland* soon proclaim'd them.

Particular *Lodges* were not so frequent and mostly *occasional* in the *South*, except in or near the Places where great Works were carried on. Thus Sir Robert Clayton got an *Occasional* Lodge of his Brother *Masters* to meet at St. *Thomas*'s *Hospital Southwark*, A.D. 1693 and to advise the Governours about the best Design of rebuilding that Hospital as it now stands | 107 | most beautiful; near which a *stated* Lodge continued long afterwards.

Besides that and the *old* Lodge of St. *Paul*'s, there was another in *Piccadilly* over against St. *James*'s Church, one near *Westminster* Abby, another near *Covent-Garden*, one in *Holborn*, one on *Tower-Hill*, and some more than assembled statedly.

The *King* was privately made a *Free Mason*, approved of their Choice of G. *Master* WREN, and encourag'd him in rearing St. *Paul*'s *Cathedral*, and the great *New* Part of 𝕳𝖆𝖒𝖕𝖙𝖔𝖓 𝕮𝖔𝖚𝖗𝖙 in the *Augustan Stile*, by far the finest *Royal* House in *England*, after an old Design of *Inigo Jones*, where a bright *Lodge* was held during the Building. The King also built his *little* palace of *Kensington*, and finish'd *Chelsea Hospital*; but appointed the fine *new*

Palace of *Greenwich* (begun by King *Charles* II) to be an *Hospital* for old *Seamen*, A.D. 1695 and order'd it to be finish'd as begun after *Jones's* old *Design*.

This Year our most noble Brother CHARLES LENNOS Duke of *Richmond* and *Lennox* (Father of the present Duke) *Master* of a Lodge at *Chicester*, coming to the annual Assembly and Feast at *London*, was chosen *Grand Master* and approv'd by the King. Sir **Christopher Wren** was his D.G. *Master*, who acted as {Edward Strong, sen.} {Grand Wardens.} {Edward Strong, jun.} before at the Head of the *Craft*, and was again chosen *Grand Master*, A.D. 1698.

In this Reign *Naval* Architecture was wonderfully improv'd, and the *King* discover'd his High Taste in building his elegant Palace at *Loo* in *Holland*, till he died at *Kensington* 8 *March* 170$\frac{1}{2}$ when

7. Ann *Stewart*, the other Daughter of King *James* II, aged 38 Years, succeeded as Queen *Soveraign*. Wife of GEORGE Prince of *Denmark*: he was the Patron of *Astronomers* and *Navigators*, and died at *Kensington* 28 *Oct.* 1708.

Queen Ann enlarg'd St. *James's* Palace, and after the famous Battle of *Blenheim*, A.D. 1704 demolish'd the *old* Royal Castle of *Woodstock* in *Oxfordshire*, and built in its stead the Castle of *Blenheim* for her General *John Churchill* Duke of *Marleborough*.

| 108 | The Queen, in her 5th Year, united the *two* Kingdoms of *England* and *Scotland* into the *one* Kingdom of *Great-Britain*, which commenced on 1 *May* 1707.

After the *Union* of the *Crowns* 104 Years.

The *Queen* and *Parliament* enacted the building of 50 new *Churches* in the Suburbs of *London*; and the Surveyors shew'd their Skill in *Buckingham* House and *Marleborough* House in St. *James's* Park, *Powis* House in *Ormond-Street*, the *Opera* House in *Haymarket*, and many more about Town: As in the Country the Duke of *Devonshire's* fine *Chatsworth* in *Derbyshire*, *Stourton*

Wiltshire, the Earl of *Carlisle*'s Castle *Howard* near *York*, *Helmsley* House or *Duncomb-Park*, *Mereworth* House in *Kent*, *Wilbury* House in *Wiltshire*, &c. Nay after the Peace of *Utrecht* many rich old Officers in the Army, returning home good Connoisseurs in Architecture, delighted in raising stately Mansions.

But the *Augustan Stile* was mostly richly display'd at *Oxford* in the *New* Chapel of *Trinity* College by Dr. 𝕭at𝕳urst, in *Peek-Water-Square* of *Christ's-Church* College by Dr. 𝕬l𝕯rige, in *Queen's-College* by Dr. 𝕷ancaster elegantly rebuilt, in *Allhallow*'s Church, the new *Printing* House, &c.

Yet still in the *South* the Lodges were more and more disused, partly by the Neglect of the *Masters* and *Wardens*, and partly by not having a *Noble Grand Master* at *London*, and the annual Assembly was not duly attended.

G.M. WREN, who had design'd St. *Paul*'s *London*, A.D. 1673 and as *Master of Work* had conducted it from the *Footstone*, had the Honour to finish that noble Cathedral, the finest and largest *Temple* of the *Augustan* Stile except St. Peter's at *Rome*; and celebrated the *Capestone* when he erected the Cross on the Top of the Cupola, in *July* A.D. 1708.

Some few Years after this, Sir *Christopher Wren* neglected the Office of *Grand Master*; yet the *Old Lodge* near St. *Paul*'s and few more continued their stated Meetings til

Queen *Ann* died at *Kensington* without Issue on 1 *Aug.* 1714. She was the last of the Race of King *Charles* I upon the Throne of *Britain*; for the Others, being *Romans*, are excluded by the | 109 | Act of Parliament for settling the *Crown* upon the *Protestant* Heirs of his sister ELIZABETH *Stewart* Queen of *Bohemia* above, *viz.* on her Daughter the Princess SOPHIA Electress Dowager of *Brunswig-Luneburg*; and she dying a little before Queen ANN, her Son the *Elector* succeeded on the said 1 *Aug.* 1714.

𝔖𝔞𝔵𝔬𝔫 *Kings of Great-Britain*

1. King GEORGE I enter'd *London* most magnificently on 20 *Sept.* 1714 and after the Rebellion was over *A.D.* 1716 the few *Lodges* at *London* finding themselves neglected by Sir *Christopher Wren*, thought fit to cement under a *Grand Master* as the Center of Union and Harmony, *viz.* the *Lodges* that met,

1. At the *Goose* and *Gridiron* Ale-house in St. *Paul's Church-Yard.*

2. At the *Crown* Ale-house in *Parker's-Lane* near *Drury-Lane.*

3. At the *Apple-Tree* Tavern in *Charles-Street, Covent-Garden.*

4. At the *Rummer* and *Grapes* Tavern in *Channel-Row, Westminster.*

They and some old Brothers met at the said *Apple-Tree*, and having put into the Chair the *oldest Master* Mason (now the *Master* of a *Lodge*) they constituted themselves a GRAND LODGE pro Tempore in *Due Form*, and forthwith revived the Quarterly *Communication* of the *Officers* of Lodges (call'd the 𝔊𝔯𝔞𝔫𝔡 𝔏𝔬𝔡𝔤𝔢) resolv'd to hold the *Annual* ASSEMBLY and *Feast*, and then to chuse a GRAND MASTER from among themselves, till they should have the Honour of a *Noble Brother* at their Head.

Accordingly

On St. *John Baptist's* Day, in the 3ᵈ Year of King GEORGE I *A.D.* 1717 the ASSEMBLY and *Feast* of the *Free and accepted Masons* was held at the foresaid *Goose and Gridiron* Ale-house.

Before Dinner, the *oldest Master* Mason (now the *Master* of a *Lodge*) in the Chair, proposed a List of proper Candidates; and the Brethren by a Majority of Hands elected

| 110 | Mr. ANTONY SAYER Gentleman, *Grand Master* of *Masons*, who { Capt. *Joseph Elliot*,   ⎱ Grand
being forthwith { Mr. *Jacob Lamball*, Carpenter, ⎰ *Wardens.*
invested with the Badges of Office and Power by the said *Oldest Master*, and install'd, was duly congratulated by the Assembly

who pay'd him the *Homage.*

Sayer *Grand Master* commanded the *Masters* and *Wardens* of Lodges to meet the *Grand* Officers every *Quarter* in *Communication*,[38] at the Place that he should appoint in his Summons sent by the *Tyler.*

ASSEMBLY and *Feast* at the said Place 24 *June* 1718.

Brother *Sayer* having gather'd the Votes, after Dinner proclaim'd aloud our Brother

GEORGE PAYNE Esq; *Grand Master* of *Masons*, who being duly invested, { Mr. *John Cordwell*, City Carpenter, } *Grand* install'd, con- { Mr. *Thomas Morrice*, Stone Cutter, } *Wardens.* gratulated and homaged, recommended the strict Observance of the Quarterly Communication; and desired any Brethren to bring to the Grand Lodge and old *Writings* and *Records* concerning *Masons* and *Masonry* in order to shew the Usages of antient Times: And this Year several old Copies of the *Gothic Constitutions* were produced and collated.

ASSEMBLY and *Feast* at the said Place, 24 *June* 1719.

Brother *Payne* having gather'd the Votes, after Dinner proclaim'd aloud our Reverend Brother

JOHN THEOPHILUS DESAGULIERS, L.L.D. and F.R.S. *Grand Master* of *Masons,* { Mr. *Antony Sayer*, foresaid, } *Grand* and being duly { Mr. *Tho. Morrice*, foresaid, } *Wardens.* invested, install'd, congratulated and homaged, forthwith reviv'd the old regular and peculiar Toasts or Healths of the *Free Masons.*

Now several *old* Brothers, that had neglected the *Craft*, visited the *Lodges*; some *Noblemen* were also made Brothers, and more *new* Lodges were constituted.

| 111 | ASSEMBLY and *Feast* at the foresaid Place 24 *June* 1720.

38 It is call'd the *Quarterly Communication*, because it should meet *Quarterly* according to antient Usage. And When the *Grand Master* is present it is a Lodge in *Ample Form*; otherwise, only in *Due Form*, yet having the same Authority with *Ample Form.*

Brother *Desaguliers* having gather'd the Votes, after Dinner proclaim'd aloud

GEORGE PAYNE Esq; again *Grand Master* of *Masons;* who being duly ⎰Mr. *Thomas Hobby*, Stone-Cutter, ⎱ *Grand* invested, ⎱Mr. *Rich. Ware*, Mathematician, ⎰ *Wardens.* install'd, congratulated and homag'd, began the usual Demonstrations of Joy, Love and Harmony.

This Year, at some *private* Lodges, several very valuable *Manuscripts* (for they had nothing yet in Print) concerning the Fraternity, their Lodges, Regulations, Charges, Secrets, and Usages (particularly one writ by Mr. *Nicholas Stone* the Warden of *Inigo Jones*) were too hastily burnt by some scrupulous Brothers; that those papers might not fall into strange Hands.

At the *Quarterly* Communication or *Grand Lodge*, in *ample* Form, on St. *John Evangelist's* Day 1720 at the said Place

It was agreed, in order to avoid Disputes on the *Annual* Feast-Day, that the *new Grand Master* for the future shall be named and proposed to the *Grand Lodge* some time before the Feast, by the present or *old Grand Master*; and if approv'd, that the Brother proposed, if present, shall be kindly saluted; or even if absent, his Health shall be toasted as *Grand Master Elect.*

Also agreed, that for the future the *New Grand Master*, as soon as he is install'd, shall have the sole Power of appointing both his *Grand Wardens* and a *Deputy* Grand Master (now found as necessary as formerly) according to antient Custom, when *Noble* Brothers were *Grand* Masters.

Accordingly,

At the 𝕲𝖗𝖆𝖓𝖉 𝕷𝖔𝖉𝖌𝖊 in *ample* Form on *Lady-Day* 1721, at the said Place *Grand Master* PAYNE proposed for his Successor our most Noble Brother

JOHN Duke of MONTAGU, *Master* of a Lodge; who being present, was forthwith saluted *Grand Master Elect*, and his Health drank in *due* Form; when they all express'd great Joy at the happy

Prospect of being again patronized by *noble Grand Masters*, as in the prosperous Times of *Free Masonry*.

| 112 | PAYNE *Grand Master* observing the *Number* of Lodges to encrease, and that the General *Assembly* requir'd more Room, proposed the next *Assembly* and *Feast* to be held at *Stationers-Hall Ludgate-Street*; which was agreed to.

Then the *Grand Wardens* were order'd, as usual, to prepare the Feast, and to take some *Stewards* to their Assistance, Brothers of Ability and Capacity, and to appoint some Brethren to attend the Tables; for that no Strangers must be there. But the *Grand Officers* not finding a proper Number of *Stewards*, our Brother Mr. 𝕵𝖔𝖘𝖎𝖆𝖍 𝖁𝖎𝖑𝖑𝖊𝖓𝖊𝖆𝖚, Upholder in the B*urrough Southwark*, generously undertook the whole himself, attended by some Waiters, *Thomas Morrice, Francis Bailey, &c.*

Chap. IV.
From *Grand Master* the Duke of MONTAGU to *Grand Master* RICHMOND

ASSEMBLY and *Feast* at *Stationers-Hall*, 24 June 1721. In the 7th Year of King GEORGE I.

PAYNE *Grand Master* with his Wardens, the former *Grand Officers*, and the *Masters* and *Wardens* of 12 Lodges, met the *Grand Master Elect* in a *Grand Lodge* at the *King's-Arms* Tavern St. *Paul's Church-yard*, in the Morning; and having forthwith recognized their Choice of Brother MONTAGU, they made some new Brothers, particularly the noble PHILIP Lord *Stanhope*, now Earl of *Chesterfield*: And from thence they marched on Foot to the *Hall* in proper Clothing and due Form; where they were joyfully receiv'd by about 150 *true* and *faithful*, all clothed.

After Grace said, they sat down in the antient Manner of *Masons* to a very elegant Feast, and dined with Joy and Gladness. After Dinner and Grace said, | 113 | Brother PAYNE the old

Grand Master made the *first Procession*[39] round the *Hall,* and when return'd, he proclaim'd aloud the most noble Prince and our Brother JOHN MONTAGU Duke of 𝔐𝔬𝔫𝔱𝔞𝔤𝔲 GRAND MAS-TER of *Masons!* and Brother *Payne* having invested his *Grace's* WORSHIP with the Ensigns and Badges of his Office and Author-ity, install'd him in *Solomon's* Chair and sat down on his Right Hand; while the Assembly own'd the Duke's Authority with due Homage and joyful Congratulations, upon this Revival of the *Prosperity* of *Masonry.*

MONTAGU *G. Master,* immediately call'd forth (without nam-ing him before) as it were carelesly, 𝔍𝔬𝔥𝔫 𝔅𝔢𝔞𝔩, M.D. as his *Deputy Grand Master,* whom Brother *Payne* invested, and install'd him in *Hiram Abbiff's* chair on the *Grand Master's Left Hand.*

In like Manner his *Worship* ⎰ Mr. *Josiah Villeneau* ⎱ *Grand* call'd forth and appointed,   ⎱ Mr. *Thomas Morrice* ⎰ *Wardens.* who were invested and install'd by the last *Grand* Wardens.

Upon which the *Deputy* and *Wardens* were saluted and con-gratulated as usual.

Then MONTAGU *G. Master,* with his *Officers* and the *old Of-ficers,* having made the 2d *Procession* round the *Hall,* Brother 𝔇𝔢𝔰𝔞𝔤𝔲𝔩𝔦𝔢𝔯𝔰 made an eloquent Oration about *Masons* and *Mason-ry:* And after Great Harmony, the Effect of brotherly Love, the *Grand Master* thank'd Brother *Villeneau* for his Care of the *Feast,* and order'd him as *Warden* to close the *Lodge* in good Time.

—The 𝔊𝔯𝔞𝔫𝔡 𝔏𝔬𝔡𝔤𝔢 in *ample* Form on 29 *Sept.* 1721 at *King's-Arms* foresaid, with the former *Grand* Officers and those of 16 *Lodges.*

His Grace's *Worship* and the *Lodge* finding fault with all the Copies of the *old Gothic Constitutions,* order'd Brother *James Anderson,* A.M. to digest the same in a new and better Method.

---

39   See the Form of it at *Richmond.* Page 117. [This original note refers to a section of the 1738 *Constitutions* that not included in this transcription.—Ed.]

—The 𝕲𝖗𝖆𝖓𝖉 𝕷𝖔𝖉𝖌𝖊 in *ample* Form on St. JOHN's Day 27 *Dec.* 1721 at the said *King's-Arms*, with former *Grand* Officers and those of 20 *Lodges*.

| 114 | MONTAGU *Grand Master*, at the Desire of the *Lodge*, appointed 14 learned Brothers to examine Brother *Anderson*'s Manuscript, and to make Report. This *Communication* was made very entertaining by the Lectures of some *old Masons*.

—𝕲𝖗𝖆𝖓𝖉 𝕷𝖔𝖉𝖌𝖊 at the *FountainStrand*, in *ample* Form 25 *March* 1722 with former *Grand* Officers and those of 24 *Lodges*.

The said *Committee* of 14 reported that they had perused Brother *Anderson*'s Manuscript, *viz.* the *History, Charges, Regulations and Master's Song*, and after some Amendments had approv'd of it: Upon which the *Lodge* desir'd the *Grand Master* to order it to be printed. Mean while

Ingenious Men of all Faculties and Stations being convinced that the *Cement* of the *Lodge* was Love and Friendship, earnestly requested to be made *Masons*, affecting this amicable Fraternity more than other Societies then often disturbed by warm Disputes.

Grand Master MONTAGU's good Government inclin'd the better Sort to continue him in the Chair another Year; and therefore they delay'd the prepare the *Feast*.

But *Philip* Duke of *Wharton* lately made a Brother, tho' not the *Master* of a *Lodge*, being ambitious of the Chair, got a Number of Others to meet him at *Stationers-Hall* 24 *June* 1722 and having no *Grand* Officers, they put in the Chair the *oldest Master Mason* (who was not the *present* Master of a *Lodge*, also irregular) and without the usual decent Ceremonials, the said *old Mason* proclaim'd aloud

Philip Wharton Duke of *Wharton* Grand Master of *Masons*, and

{ Mr. *Joshua Timson*, Blacksmith }	*Grand*	but his Grace
{ Mr. *William Hawkins*, Mason, }	*Wardens.*	appointed no

Deputy, nor was the *Lodge* opened and closed in due Form.

Therefore the *noble* Brothers and all those that would not

countenance irregularities, disown'd *Wharton's* authority, till worthy Brother MONTAGU heal'd the Breach of Harmony by summoning

—The 𝕲rand 𝕷odge to meet 17 *January* 172⅔ at the *King's-Arms* foresaid, where the Duke of *Wharton* promising to be *True* and *Faithful, Deputy Grand* Master *Beal* proclaim'd aloud the most noble Prince and our Brother.

| 115 | PHILIP WHARTON Duke of *Wharton* GRAND MASTER of *Masons*, who appointed Dr. 𝕯esaguliers the *Deputy Grand* Master,

⎰ *Joshua Timson,* foresaid,⎱ ⎰for *Hawkins* demitted
⎱ *James Anderson*, A.M.   ⎰ *Grand Wardens.* ⎱as always out of Town.

When former *Grand* Officers, with those of 25 Lodges paid their homage.

G. Warden *Anderson* produced the *new* Book of *Constitutions* now in Print, which was again approv'd, with the Addition of the *antient Manner of Constituting a Lodge.*

Now *Masonry* flourish'd in Harmony, Reputation and Numbers; many Noblemen and Gentlemen of the first Rank desir'd to be admitted into the *Fraternity*, besides other Learned Men, Merchants, Clergymen and Tradesmen, who found a *Lodge* to be a safe and pleasant Relaxation from Intense Study or the Hurry of Business, without Politicks or Party. Therefore the *Grand Master* was obliged to constitute more *new Lodges*, and was very assiduous in *visiting* the *Lodges* every Week with his *Deputy* and *Wardens*; and his *Worship* was well pleas'd with their kind and respectful Manner of receiving him, as they were with his affable and clever Conversation.

"A Just and Exact Account of Masonry"

A Survey of the Constitutions and Pocket Companions of 1723 to 1756

CHRISTOPHER B. MURPHY

NOTWITHSTANDING THE VARIOUS cathedrals and other surviving feats of architecture, the oldest arte-facts of the Fraternity are its written documents. The earliest of these is known as the Regius Poem as recorded in the Halliwell MS, which is dated to approximately 1425. This work is a long-form poem of 724 lines, that describes the moral and behavioral expectations of "thys onest craft of good masonry"[1] in fifteen "articles" and fifteen "points." Also briefly mentioned is a legend pertaining to the passage of the arts and sciences, specifically referencing the Great Flood and the Tower of Babel.

The next oldest Masonic document dates to c. 1450, and is known as the Cooke MS. The manuscript itself was written "principally to treat of the first foundation of the worthy science of

---

1   Regius Poem, line 20.

Geometry."[2] The text does so by tracing geometry's emergence out of the arts and sciences developed by the children of the Biblical Lamech, of the line of Cain, seven generations removed from Adam. The lore of Cooke continues with these children preserving their arts and sciences upon two pillars—the Primordial Pillars—through which the knowledge was passed down to Pythagoras, Hermes, Euclid, and beyond. Also included are rules of conducts for Masons, as was seen in the Regius Poem.

The two primary attributes of these works are the rules of conduct—what became known as "charges"—and the legendary path of Geometry/Architecture/Masonry through the ages— which became known as the "traditional history." The subsequent Masonic writing over the next three centuries adopted and adapted these. This body of work, dating from c. 1425 to the opening years of the eighteenth century are known, collectively, as the "Old Charges" or "Gothic Constitutions." Masonic scholars have spent years identifying, analyzing, interpreting, and categorizing these works, creating taxonomies and tracing lines of influence between the various "families" of these Old Charges.

The year 1717 brought the genesis of the Grand Lodge system. With this shift soon came the impetus for a new generation of digested (and now printed and published) books of charges and Constitutions for the use of the new, and increasingly non-operative, brethren. These books largely followed the examples of these Gothic Constitutions, in that they both reiterated the mythic pedigree of the Royal Art of Freemasonry, and clearly outlined the moral and behavioral expectations of Craftsmen.

The following piece is a survey of these publications, from James Anderson's first edition of the *Constitutions* in 1723, through the first edition of the *Ahiman Rezon* of the Antients'

---

2   Cooke MS, lines 77–80; The original reads, "Owr entent is príncipally to trete of first fundacíon of þ worthe scyés of Gemetry."

Grand Lodge in 1756, *viz*:

- Anderson's *Constitutions*, 1723
- Pennell's *Constitutions*, 1730
- Cole's *Constitutions*, second edition, 1731
- Franklin's *Constitutions*, 1734
- Smith's *Pocket Companion*, 1735
- Anderson's *Constitutions*, second edition, 1738
- Spratt's *Constitutions*, 1751
- Scott's *Pocket Companion*, 1754
- Dermott's *Ahiman Rezon*, 1756

There are two books of Constitutions that fall within this time period, but which are not analyzed within this survey. These are *The Old Constitutions Belonging to the Ancient and Honourable Society of Free and Accepted Masons* (1722), commonly known for its author as "Roberts' *Constitutions*," and *A Book of the Antient Constitutions of the Free & Accepted Masons* (1728), commonly referred to as "Cole's *Constitutions*" for their engraver, Benjamin Cole. The information in these two books are drawn from the Gothic Constitutions, and therefore represent the Fraternity when it was primarily comprised of operative stonemasons. The myths are those beginning with the children of Lamech, such as is found in the Cooke MS (summarized above) and the charges are of a decidedly operative slant. They are excluded from this survey because they do not capture the shift in mythos, nor the decidedly speculative nature of the other early Grand Lodge-era texts. With that said, Cole's second edition from 1731 is included; that work still maintains the flavor of the Gothic Constitutions, but contains several additional elements that are germane to the subject at hand.

This paper will outline some of the features of these works, as they relate to the Masonic self-concept and praxis of the time.

While some notation may be given on the authors, or their Masonic careers, this is largely an examination of the texts themselves; that is to say, the focus is on the content of these books, and what they demonstrate about the practice of Freemasonry at the time of their publication. By understanding what was within these publications, a clearer understanding of Freemasonry of the time—its beliefs and practices—may be reached. These works represent a view into the authentic Masonry of the first decades of the eighteenth century, and therefore represent the very foundation of Freemasonry today.

Anderson's Constitutions, 1723

THE

CONSTITUTIONS

OF THE

FREE-MASONS.

CONTAINING THE

History, Charges, Regulations, &c.

of that most Ancient and Right

Worshipful *FRATERNITY*

For the Use of the LODGES

LONDON:

Printed by WILLIAM HUNTER, for JOHN SENEX at the Globe,
And JOHN HOOKE at the *Flower-de-luce* over-against *St. Dunstan's*
Church, in Fleet-street.

In the Year of Masonry   5723

Anno Domini   1723

This book is, arguably, the most important Masonic work ever published. While some corners of Masonic research have claimed that Anderson was acting without sanction, and simply seeking to profit from the fraternity, there is ample evidence to support the position that Anderson's work was, indeed, approved and adopted by the Grand Lodge, *viz*:

- The book opens with a four-page dedication to the incoming Grand Master, the Duke of Montagu, by John Theophilus Desaguliers, the Deputy Grand Master under Grand Master Phillip Duke of Wharton; this carried the tacit approval of the outgoing Grand Master.
- Desaguliers states that the work of the "learned AUTHOR" had met with Grand Master Montagu's "Perusal and Approbation."[3]
- As per the Approbation, Anderson was ordered by the Duke of Montagu to "peruse, correct, and digest, into a new and better Method, the *History*, *Charges*, and *Regulations*, of the *ancient* FRATERNITY."[4]
- The work itself was subsequently vetted by "the *late* and *present* DEPUTY *Grand-Masters*," "other learned *Brethren*," and the "*Masters* and *Wardens* of particular *Lodges*."[5]

The book begins with a now-iconic frontispiece engraved by Freemason John Pine. The scene includes two bands of Brethren, each represented by a Grand Master. Grand Master Wharton is passing the *Constitutions* and compasses to Grand Master Montagu. The exchange is occurring in a low dale, under a well built arch, along an arcade lined with columns of the five Orders of

3   James Anderson, *Constitutions of the Free-Masons*, (London: William Hunter, 1723), [iv], [v].
4   Anderson, *Constitutions* (1723), 73.
5   Ibid.

Architecture. While not checkered, *per se*, the pavement is drawn into individual squares. Superimposed between the Grand Masters is a rendering of the 47th Proposition of Euclid; below, the word *eureka* is inscribed in Greek. Above, the god Apollo rides the chariot of the sun through the clouds. The figure of Apollo may be read as an allusion to the religious pluralism built into Grand Lodge Freemasonry; more on this concept below.

There are references in the text that convey that Anderson compiled and curated several older Masonic traditions. In other words, what follows in Anderson's work is not cut from whole cloth, but rather is the result of his own research. For instance, in the Dedication, Desaguliers notes that Anderson's work was "compil[ed] and digest[ed]… from the old *Records*" and accurately reflects the "*History* and *Chronology*" of the Craft.[6] Anderson himself stated that his work was "COLLECTED From [Freemasons'] general RECORDS, and their faithful TRADITIONS of many Ages."[7] On page 34, an extensive footnote appears that Anderson advises is "collected from the *Records* of ancient Times."[8] The quote itself is taken from lines 901–960 of the Cooke MS, thereby demonstrating that Anderson was in possession of at least some of the old records avowed by Dr. Desaguliers.

The first forty-eight pages of the work contains the Traditional History, the mythic origin story of the nature and propagation of the Craft. As has already been demonstrated, such a legendary view of the roots of the Order was not an invention of Anderson. The Craft had long been associated with the children of Lamech, Primordial Pillars, Nimrod, etc. These ideas are contained within the earliest Masonic documents, but they did not originate there. The Regius Poem implies an inspirational older text in its line,

6   Ibid., [iv].
7   Ibid., 1.
8   Ibid., 34.

"By olde tyme wryten y fynde."[9] The Cooke MS names its sources, referencing the Bible and such medieval writers as Higden,
Bede, and St. Isadore.[10] This demonstrates an established practice
of seeking Masonic truths in older texts. Anderson continues
in this quest, when he breaks from the story of the children of
Lamech, and instead cites a source far older that the medieval
influences referenced in Cooke. Although he does not identify
his source until the second edition of his *Constitutions*, fifteen
years later, Anderson draws his inspiration from the works of
first-century scholar Flavius Josephus when he delivers his "new"
version of the Traditional History.

A superficial reading of the Traditional History may leave
one to view it simply as a fanciful tale for the amusement of the
brethren. Such a reading may be tied to the misperception of
early eighteenth-century Lodges being convened merely as social
institutions. Two facts contradict such an assertion: First, as noted immediately above, such myths harken back to a time when
Masonic Lodges most certainly had no non-operative members;
the purpose for their gathering, therefore, was centered on the
builder's craft and not for amusement. Secondly, this legend was
deemed so important as to necessitate its being read whenever a
new Mason was initiated.[11] Added to these arguments is the additional point that the Grand Lodge approved a book that began
with the Traditional History; it is the first section following the
Dedication. If the Traditional History was just for amusement,
then it would arguably not be given a place of prominence within
the text, but more likely be placed after the Charges and Regulations. Another root of the perception that the lore should not
be taken seriously is the argument that, as a "history," elements
found within it are objectively false.

9   Regius Poem, line 143.
10   Cooke MS, lines 140–145.
11   Anderson, *Constitutions* (1723), 1.

J.M. Hamill, when he addressed the members of Quatuor Coronati Lodge № 2076 on the occasion of his installation as Master, spoke of some of the reasons for this characterization of the Traditional History. He stated, "Too often past Masonic historians have been damned and the whole of their work rejected out of hand because their, or their period's, view of what constituted good history does not coincide with our own."[12] He continued:

> Are we right to criticize Anderson? As historians I think that the answer must be yes, *provided* that it is criticism with an understanding of what the contemporary conception of history was in his time. Scientific research was in its infancy and its scrupulous discipline was not applied to other subjects. To Anderson and his contemporaries history was an amalgam of folk memory, legend, established fact and recent events...they had few means of checking the accuracy of any folk lore more than a generation old and saw nothing wrong in manufacturing information to fill a gap.[13]

Hamill is acknowledging the cultural context of 1723. He observes that it is unfair to levy the academic standards of one time onto another time. He states that a reader ought not to dismiss this Masonic legend because of perceived flaws in the methodology of the writer. This is an important defence of the Traditional History. There are, however, two important points missing in Hamill's address. First is to recognize a point made above, that Anderson did, indeed, labor to "fill gaps" through research. Secondly, Hamill does not take into account the philosophical and spiritual intent of the legend. This will be addressed in detail below.

12   Hamill, "Masonic History and Historians," 1.
13   Ibid., 2.

To be sure, the Traditional History reflected and reinforced Masonic self-concept, as a divinely-inspired manifestation of perennialist philosophy. Masons of the time would not have identified it in those terms, but Masonic literature of the early eighteenth-century is rife with reflections of the idea that the Craft was given by God, and has survived as part of a hidden stream of teachings that has passed through many lands and many hands throughout all human history. This is what is conveyed in the legendary origin story of the Craft. In order to begin to appreciate how these ideas informed Masonry in the beginning of the Grand Lodge era, one must examine the Traditional History itself, and consider it with the sincerity with which it was most certainly written. To aid in this, a summary of the myth is in order.

The legend begins:

> A DA M, our first Parent, created after the Image of God, *the great Architect of the Universe*, must have had the Liberal Sciences, particularly *Geometry*, written on his Heart.[14]

Whereas the Lamechian legend rooted the Craft in the most distant antiquity, as the invention of some of Man's earliest ancestors, Anderson's legend frames it as a God-given institution. Moreover, according to Anderson, while the Craft is descended through Cain's line (and eventually through to Lamech's children), it is more successfully propagated by the line of Seth, Adam's third son. Geometry is also explicitly paired with Masonry, being named as the "Foundation" of the art.[15]

The sacred knowledge is passed through the generations of Seth, unto godly Enoch, six generations from Adam. Just as the children of Lamech are aware of the approaching punishment of

14   Anderson, *Constitutions* (1723), 1.
15   Ibid., 2.

God, as relayed in the Old Charges, so here can Enoch foretell of the wrath. As such, he is the one who inscribes the Arts and Sciences onto two pillars, one made to withstand flame, the other to withstand flood; the knowledge is therefore preserved through God's purification of the Earth. Noah and his sons, Ham, Shem, and Japheth, are then named as the holders of the knowledge, as those who carry the "Traditions and Arts of the *Ante-delu-vians*" into the cleansed world.[16] For the next century, the sons of Noah repopulated the world, until the successive generations found themselves assembled in the plains of Shinar, under the direction of King Nimrod at the building of the Tower of Babel. Concurrent to this, Geometry was also supported by the "learned *Priests* and *Mathematicians*, known by the Names of CHALDEES and MAGI...."[17]

Whereas the Tower of Babel has been generally cast as a cautionary tale, the Masonic story of the Tower of Babel carries a different message and thus represents an example of counter-mythology. The narrative speaks of the multitude of workmen employed in this plan to reach Heaven. God confounds the plan, and confuses the tongues, thereby ceasing the building and dispersing the workmen. And yet, such a dispersion "hinder'd not the Improvement of *Masonry*"—in fact, it gave rise "to the Masons Faculty and ancient universal Practice of conversing without speaking, and of knowing each other at a Distance."[18]

Therefore, not only was the Institution of Masonry unimpeded by the confusion of tongues, but God's intervention actually created the Masonic landmark of modes of recognition (which is to say nothing of the possibility of more esoteric elements of the Mason's Word[19]). As such, the Traditional History reframes

16   Ibid., 3.
17   Ibid., 4–5.
18   Ibid., 5.
19   For examples, see Stevenson, chapter 6.

two Divine interventions—the great flood and the confusion of tongues—as serving the purpose of purifying the Craft. Noah and his sons, the keepers of the art, were cleansed of any foul influences, and the true Craftsmen at Shinar were left unimpeded after the cowans were dispersed.

The generations from Noah moved forth from Shinar and continued to populate the Earth, while the true Masons continued to spread their divine learning. Some of these would later reassemble in the ruins of the Tower, and perfect Seth's art of Astronomy.[20] Abraham was instructed, and he passed the secrets unto his sons, Isaac and Ishmael, and they to the twelve patriarchs.[21] The Jews subsequently added the knowledge of "good" Masonry to their use of "*Military Architecture*."[22]

The Great Architect also touched Bezaleel and Aholiab with divine inspiration for the design of the Tabernacle. Although this structure was a tent, it was still crafted by the rules of Geometry, and therefore was deemed "a most beautiful Piece of Architecture" into which the Shekinah—the immediate and palpable Presence of God—manifested.[23] The design of the Tabernacle thus served as the model for the Temple of Solomon, as revealed to "GRAND MASTER MOSES."[24] It was in the wilderness following the exodus, that Grand Master Moses gave the Jews the first Charges of Masonry, following which they improved in the Art "by the special Direction of Heaven."[25]

The description of the building of King Solomon's Temple begins on page 9, and extends until page 15—nearly half of the book until this point. This fact alone speaks to the importance of

20   Anderson, *Constitutions* (1723), 17.
21   Ibid., 7.
22   Ibid.
23   Ibid., 8.
24   Ibid.
25   Ibid., 9.

the events of the building of this Temple, even though it would be another seven years before similar importance was found in Ritual exposures. It should also be noted that while Anderson provides copious footnotes throughout the work, the footnotes offered in his discussion of the Temple stand out as being particularly detailed. For instance, ample space within the footnotes is devoted to seeking greater meaning from the original Hebrew terms related to King Solomon and his Temple.

One of these footnotes speaks of the workforce at the Temple. It attempts to reconcile the discrepancy between the numbers of overseers of the works, the *Harodim* or *Menatzchim*, as mentioned in both 1 Kings and 2 Chronicles. The text above the footnote specifically names this class as being Master Masons. Also within the workforce are 80,000 stone cutters, known as *Ish Chotzeb, Ghiblim*, or *Bonai*, but who Anderson calls the "Fellow Craftsmen." Finally, there is another class of workmen, the *Ish Sabbal*, who are the bearers of burden, but who Anderson specifically notes are not Masons.[26]

A second footnote, the lengthiest of the entire work, is devoted to an examination of the name and parentage of Hiram Abif. Anderson proposes that "Abif" is simply the surname of the Master Craftsman, and is not indicative of a filial relationship between Hiram Abif and Hiram King of Tyre. The connection between the two is that the Artificer is named in honor of the Monarch. Further, Hiram Abif's parentage is determined, reconciling the two seemingly opposing descriptions of him being "a Widow's Son of the Tribe of *Naphthali*"[27] and "Son of a Woman of the Daughters of *Dan*,"[28] all while simultaneously having his father be named as Tyrian. Anderson writes:

26 Ibid., 10.
27 1 Kings 7:14; Anderson, *Constitutions* (1723), 11.
28 2 Chronicles 2:14; Anderson, *Constitutions* (1723), 11.

which Difficulty is remov'd, by supposing his Mother was ei-
ther of the Tribe of Dan, or of the Daughters of the City called
Dan *in the Tribe of* Naphthali, *and his deceased Father had*
been a Naphthalite, *whence his Mother was call'd a* Widow
of Naphthali; for his Father is not call'd a Tyrian *by Descent,*
but a Man of Tyre *by Habitation....*[29]

The finished Temple was 30,000 square cubits in floor space. It contained 1,453 columns and 2,906 pilasters representing the orders of architecture, and 2,246 windows and "was justly esteem'd by far the finest Piece of *Masonry* upon Earth before or since."[30] Anderson continues by saying that the Royal Art was "never perfected" until God allowed this Temple to be built.[31] So perfect was this construction, crafted "under the immediate Care and Direction of Heaven" that it allowed for Divine manifestation upon the Mercy Seat within the *Sanctum Sanctorum.*[32] Also by its construction, King Solomon and King Hiram were named Grand Masters of their jurisdictions, and Hiram Abif as Master of Works. Following the completion of the Temple, the Craftsmen, now schooled in the perfect Art, dispersed around the world to propagate Masonry.

In Greece, only those works which post-date the Temple at Jerusalem provide any demonstration of perfection in Architecture. Similarly, there are no proofs of earlier advancement in Geometry. It is only with the "Greater PYTHAGORAS" that a Grecian mastery of the science emerges, as he was "prov'd the Author of the 47th *Proposition of Euclid*"[33] which is the "Foundation of all

29   Anderson, *Constitutions* (1723), 11–12n.
30   Ibid., 13.
31   Ibid.
32   Ibid., 14.
33   Ibid., 20.

Masonry, sacred, civil, and military."[34] It is specifically noted that
Pythagoras was instructed by the "Chaldean MAGI" who, as was
noted above, were learned in the arts and traditions of Noah.[35]

Pythagorean teachings became a staple of Grecian learning,
and were embraced in successive generations by "*the divine* PLA-
TO" and by Euclid.[36] Euclid himself shared the teachings with
his patron, the King of Egypt, Ptolomeus Philadelphus, who also
became a Master Mason. Following the example set by King Ptolomeus, all of Africa was soon enriched by the Art of Masonry.

The "prodigious Geometrician" Archimedes is next named
as proliferating Masonry among the Romans.[37] Rome thereafter
became a "*Center* of *Learning*," and a cradle for the improvement
of the Arts and Sciences under the peaceful rule of Grand Master Augustus Caesar.[38] It was in this environment that Vitruvius
was nurtured to become the "Father of all true Architects to
this Day" and the Augustan Style of Architecture was brought
to perfection.[39] Likewise, the traditions and Masonic knowledge
of the Britons was cultivated, and under the aegis of French King
Charles Martell, architects were sent into Briton and encouraged
Gothic architecture to flourish in those lands.

In all times of war, the Royal Art is suppressed, and this was
the case at the time of the Danish invasion. Once those troubles
ceased, however, vitality returned to Masonry, particularly under the nurturance and support of King Athelstane and his son,
Prince Edwin. So great was Edwin's love for the Craft that he
sought initiation into the Fraternity, eventually becoming the
Grand Master and presiding over the annual Communication of

34   Ibid., 21.
35   Ibid.
36   Ibid., 22.
37   Ibid., 24.
38   Ibid., 25.
39   Ibid.

the guilds at York. Grand Master Edwin declared that the Constitutions and Charges should be read to every newly-made Mason.

One purpose of the annual assemblies at York was for the congregated Masons to determine the wages that they, as a single band of Brethren, would demand for their labor. Seemingly in answer to this early example of collective bargaining, King Henry VI outlawed these meetings: "*our said* Sovereign Lord *the* King… *hath ordained and established, that such Chapters and Congregations shall not be hereafter holden*," the punishment for which will be adjudication as felons, imprisonment, and "*Fine and Ransome at the King's Will.*"[40]

As evidenced by the continuation of an organized labor force, as well as the existence of a Speculative Craft today, it is clear that this statute was not widely recognized by Masons. Anderson states this, when he declared, "Masons never neglected their *Lodges*" as a result of the law.[41] Anderson offers a fascinating footnote explanation reconciling the apparent lawlessness with which Masons ignored King Henry's Act:

> That Act was made in ignorant Times, when true Learning was a Crime, and Geometry condemned for *Conjuration*; but it cannot derogate from the Honour of the ancient *Fraternity*, who to be sure, would never encourage any such Confederacy of their working Brethren. But by *Tradition* it is believ'd, that the *Parliament-Men* were then too much influence'd by the illiterate *Clergy*, who were not accepted Masons, nor understood Architecture (as the *Clergy* of some former Ages) and generally thought unworthy of this Brotherhood; yet thinking they had an indefeasible Right to know all Secrets, by vertue of auricular *Confession*, and the Masons never confessing any thing thereof, the

40   Ibid., 35.
41   Ibid., 36.

said *Clergy* were highly offended, and it first suspecting them of Wickedness represented them as dangerous to the State during that Minority, and soon influenc'd the *Parliament-Men* to lay hold of such supposed Agreements of the working Masons, for making an Act that might seem to reflect Dishonour upon even the whole worshipful *Fraternity*, in whose Favour several Acts had been both before and after that Period made.[42]

On the face of it, this clarification may appear simply as a tale of politicking, and men seeking power in society. There are, perhaps, more subtle elements to this, that speak to the mythic stream that flows throughout the Traditional History. The notion of anti-Masonic acts being established in times of ignorance offers a potent counterpoint to the Wisdom found in the Masonry of Solomon, and, indeed, from the fact that the Art was bestowed by God. It speaks to the possibility of perversion of religion: Geometry—a knowledge implanted in the core of our First Father by our Heavenly Father—is deemed a dark sort of magic, as "conjuration." The fact that Masons would not confess their secrets (as if there was some sin inherent in the Craft that *required* confession) despite protestations from the clergy themselves speaks to the degree to which Masons held their mysteries dear.

Continuing with the narrative, the Scots are also named as promoters of the Art, with "the Kings being often the *Grand Masters*," and eventually having Grand Masters and Grand Wardens hired and paid by the Crown to oversee and regulate the Craft.[43] As is so often seen, however, warfare disrupted the practice of the Science, and the Civil Wars ended this Scottish custom and halted Masonry throughout the land.

42   Ibid., 36.
43   Ibid., 37.

Queen Elizabeth, not being privy to the secrets of the Craft, initially stood to again outlaw annual assemblies. She was won over, however, and Masons were allowed to continue with their custom. James VI, Elizabeth's successor, ranks as yet another "*Mason* King,"[44] but also as the restorer of Roman architecture to the world, "from the Ruins of *Gothick* Ignorance."[45] As ignorance was dispelled across Europe "*Geometry* recover'd its Ground" and the Augustan Style was revived by a host of famous Architects who assumed the labors of enriching the world.[46] Chief among these was the "*Great* PALLADIO," with the "*great Master-Mason* INIGO JONES" nearly his equal in the Art.[47]

The Traditional History continues to unfurl by naming the successive monarchs of the European realms, as well as some of the celebrated Architects of the time, as promoters of the Craft. Included among the other protectors of the Royal Art are "several *Noblemen* and *Gentlemen* of the best Rank, with *Clergymen* and learned *Scholars* of most Professions and Denominations."[48] There is perhaps another reference to the "Masons Faculty" when Anderson speaks of Accepted Masons' ability to "know and love one another, even without the Help of Speech, or when of different Languages."[49]

Anderson's telling concludes by savoring the peace that has been enjoyed in "BRITISH NATIONS" and the subsequent enjoyment of "the good Fruits of Peace and Liberty."[50] Foremost among these fruits is the revival of the "*drooping Lodges of London*," the establishment of several other Lodges, and the rein-

44   Ibid., 38.
45   Ibid., 38–39.
46   Ibid., 39.
47   Ibid.
48   Ibid., 48.
49   Ibid., 47.
50   Ibid.

statement of the quarterly Grand Lodge Communication.[51] After having been secured and preserved by so many since the Biblical creation of man, the stewardship of the Craft has come to rest in the hands of the various Grand Masters, and finally with the "present worthy *Grand-Master, the most noble* PRINCE *John Duke of* MONTAGUE."[52]

This is really the critical point: Masonry was coeval with the creation of mankind, and has survived throughout the age into the revived Grand Lodge era. Within this Western conception of the creation of humankind, is nested the mythic Masonic concept of a spiritual lineage linking Adam with the Duke of Montague. The link is the secret, sacred knowledge of Masonry. Anderson sums up the narrative by stating that Accepted Masons

> in all Ages, and in every Nation, have maintain'd and propagated their Concernments in a way peculiar to themselves, which the most *Cunning* and the most *Learned* cannot penetrate into, though it has been often attempted ....[53]

To be clear, he is speaking of the Speculative Art. Certainly the operative architects and geometers know the Art, but so do the Ark-builders and tent-makers of the Hebrew Bible; so do the painters and statuaries;[54] so do the "several *Noblemen* and *Gentlemen* of the best Rank, with *Clergymen* and learned *Scholars* of most Professions and Denominations."[55] This is the Speculative Craft with which Adam was created and which all Freemasons may claim as their own.

Following the Traditional History are listed the several

51   Ibid.
52   Ibid., 48.
53   Ibid., 47.
54   Ibid., 26.
55   Ibid., 48.

"Charges of a Free-Mason," which are also to be read at the making of a Mason.[56] In fine, these Charges can be divided into those rules that clearly reflect a Speculative Craft, and those that are derived from rules for an operative craft but into which some speculative instruction may be read. Recall that, according to Masonic legend, Charges have been delivered to Masons since the time of Moses.[57] As such, the repetition of Charges is just as much part of Masonic tradition as is the study of Geometry.

Perhaps the most significant of these Charges is the first: "*Concerning* GOD *and* RELIGION."[58] The universality of the Craft is contained within this Charge, as it opens Freemasonry to all men of faith without concern for specifics of that faith. The Charge "obliges" Masons only to "that Religion in which all Men agree." It continues that to be "*good Men and true*, or Men of Honour and Honesty" are the proper hallmarks of faith, and that "particular Opinions" as well as the "Denominations and Persuasions [by which] they may be distinguish'd" are to be kept private. By doing such:

> Masonry becomes the *Center* of *Union*, and the Means of conciliating true friendship among Persons that must have remain'd at a perpetual Distance.[59]

This was—and in many respects, remains—a revolutionary concept: that good men could be joined by faith alone, regardless of what that faith was. Fifteen years later, Anderson would compile his second edition of the *Constitutions*. In it, this first Charge is expanded in significant ways, as will be seen below.

Some may read this Charge in isolation, and assert that it is a

56 Ibid., 49.
57 Ibid., 8.
58 Ibid., 50.
59 Ibid.

call for Deism. But this Charge was never intended to be taken in
isolation. If Deism is marked by a noninterventionist God, then
Deism is dismissed in the Traditional History. The legend has
God intervening with the Great Flood, at the Tower of Babel, in
Bezaleel and Aholiab's Tabernacle, and at Solomon's Temple. The
Great Architect of the Traditional History is, indeed, involved
with the lives of Masons, and therefore is conceptually incompatible with Deism. Of course, this is not to say that individual
Masons could not, or cannot, be Deists. By keeping his "particular Opinion" to himself, a Mason can conceive of God according
to the views of any system of faith, and still abide by this Charge.
Moreover, because the Traditional History is a mythic story—as
opposed to literal one—it should not be assumed that Masons
are confined within the Judeo-Christian context in which the
Traditional History was conceived. The myth provides a framework for understanding Freemasonry as an extension of religion,
but one that holds truths that may be unavailable within religions
themselves.

This concept of a new religious pluralism may prompt a re-
consideration of the frontispiece, more especially the appearance
of Apollo. Certainly, the sun god riding his chariot across the sky
is symbolic of rebirth and new beginnings, such as those which
come with the installation of a new Grand Master. But also, consider the operative legend of the four crowned martyrs. Briefly,
the legend states that Roman emperor Diocletian called forth
four expert stonemasons—Castorius, Claudius, Nichostratus,
and Symphorianus—to erect a temple to Apollo. Unbeknownst
to Diocletian, these four master masons had secretly converted
to Christianity; because of their new faith, the four refused to
build the temple. At this refusal, Diocletian ordered their execution.[60] One moral to take from this legend may be that reli-

60   For further information on the four crowned martyrs, see Mackey,
       Encyclopædia, 272–75; see also Acaster, "The Special Significance

gious fidelity is to be held above all, even above one's own life. A counter lesson, however, may be that a refusal of allowing differences in matters of faith, when taken to its extreme, is the basis for horrors: men losing their lives, killings perpetrated by the state, and the world losing its skilled artisans. The application of such a lesson may be seen in Pine's frontispiece: in a time when Freemasonry had begun embracing religious pluralism, the god Apollo can peacefully coexist with the Christian rulers of the Craft. In an institution where men are to keep their particular opinions to themselves, there is no need for any man to be executed because of his religion.

The second Charge speaks to the Mason's interaction with civil government. It calls for a Mason to be a "peaceable Subject to the Civil Powers," and reiterates a concept frequently seen in the Traditional History: that Masonry flourishes in times of peace. However, the language of the Charge also makes it clear that mere rebellion against civil authority is not, in and of itself, grounds for expulsion.[61]

"*Of* Lodges" is the subject of the third Charge. A Lodge is herein defined as a "Place where *Masons* assemble and work."[62] In order to ensure regularity, all Masons must belong to a Lodge. Also in this section, the prerequisites for membership are explained:

> The Persons … must be good and true Men, free-born, and of mature and discreet Age, no Bondmen, no Women, no immoral or scandalous Men, but of good Report.[63]

The next Charge regards the qualifications for Masonic of-

of the Quatuor Coronati in Relation to Modern Freemasonry."
61   Anderson, *Constitutions* (1723), 50.
62   Ibid., 51.
63   Ibid.

ficers. The first admonition is that "Preferment" is based upon a Brother's Merit, and not on seniority.[64] Also outlined are the prior accomplishments which must accompany advancement in Stations. All Wardens must have at least attained the Degree of Fellow Craft. The Grand Master must also have attained at least Fellow Craft status, so long as he "also to be nobly born."[65] All Grand Wardens must be Past Masters, as must all Deputy Grand Masters. All officers must serve the Brotherhood "with all Humility, Reverence, Love, and Alacrity."[66]

The fifth Charge, "*Of the Management of the* CRAFT *in working*" reads much like the Charges found in the Gothic Constitutions. While speculative meaning may be read into the fifth Charge, it appears to be firmly rooted in an operative culture, and reflective of the regulations of the working stonemasons.[67]

The sixth Charge speaks to proper Masonic behavior in various settings. When in Lodge, brethren are to act with due decorum, and pay reverence to the Master, Wardens, and Fellows. Violations of this expectation will result in the consequence as set forth by the Brethren. A Mason is also admonished not to "go to the Law about what concerneth *Masonry*, without an absolute Necessity apparent to the *Lodge*."[68]

A certain level of restraint is expected after the Lodge was closed. The mood is more relaxed, and Brethren can engage in "innocent Mirth," but are never to indulge to excess, nor induce

64   Ibid.
65   Ibid., 52.
66   Ibid.
67   Ibid., 52–53. One example of operative language that is actually Speculative thought in the fifth charge may be the statement that "All the Tools used in working shall be approved by the Grand Lodge." (53) There is no reason to believe that tools of stonemasons were submitted to a central authority for approval.
68   Ibid., 54.

another to do so.[69] Nothing that may "forbid an *easy* and *free* Conversation"[70] should occur, just as nothing should be said "ludicrously or jestingly while the *Lodge* is engaged in what is serious and solemn."[71] Specifically noted is a prohibition of religious or political "*Quarrels*" when assembled together after Lodge.[72]

When meeting outside of a Lodge, Brethren are to greet each other in a spirit of equality, while also showing appropriate deference for public distinctions. When meeting outside of Lodge with non-Masons, Masons are admonished to be prudent in their speech so that no Masonic secrets are revealed to the uninitiated. In the community, a Mason is required to be a good family man, neighbor, and citizen. Accordingly, he is to avoid "Gluttony or Drunkenness."[73] If a Mason encounters an unknown Brother, he is to respectfully and prudently examine him, and treat him appropriately given the results of the examination.

These Charges culminate with a statement of the essential quality of Brotherly Love within Freemasonry. Such is "the Foundation and Cape-stone, the *Cement* and *Glory* of this ancient *Fraternity*."[74] Brotherly Love ought to permeate a Mason's every action, and both motivate and emanate from his every decision.

Following the Charges a legal opinion is featured, regarding the statute of Henry VI, noted above. This postscript is drawn from the *Institutes of the Lawes of England*, published by Sir Edward Coke between 1628 and 1644. Briefly stated, the opinion calls the King's statute illegal and unenforceable. Anderson notes that Coke's opinion likely indicates that Coke himself was count-

69   Ibid.
70   Ibid.
71   Ibid., 53.
72   Ibid., 54.
73   Ibid., 55.
74   Ibid., 56.

ed among the Accepted Masons of the seventeenth-century.[75]

The next section of *Constitutions* relates the "General Regulations" compiled by Grand Master George Payne in 1720. At
the direction of Grand Master Montagu, Anderson "digested
them into this new Method."[76] The following regulations can
be generally grouped into four categories, 1) regarding Lodges,
2) regarding Grand Lodge, 3) regarding Quarterly Communications, and 4) regarding selection of Grand Officers. These are
here presented in brief:

1. The Grand Master has the right to attend and preside over
any Lodge, and appoint his Wardens to act as such in a Lodge
on a *pro tempore* basis.

2. The Grand Master can hold a Communication at his dis-
cretion. If the Worshipful Master is absent, the most recent Past
Master sits in the East. Barring a Past Master being present, the
Senior Warden presides.

3. The regulation calls for a Secretary, without specifically
naming him as such. It is his duty to keep the by-laws, rolls, and
minutes.

4. No more than five Masons may be made at a time. Also, a
Candidate must be at least twenty-five years old.

5. One month must pass between acceptance of a petition
and initiation, to allow the brethren to inquire into the character
of the candidate. Please note that there is no specific call for an
Investigation Committee, as is the contemporary practice.[77]

6. Unanimous consent is required to accept a Candidate. This
regulation specifies that this requirement cannot be overturned
even by dispensation from the Grand Master.

7. Candidates shall clothe the Lodge, and make a donation to

75   Ibid., 57.

76   Ibid., 58.

77   For what may be the earliest reference to an investigation
      committee, see D'Assigny, *A Serious and Impartial Enquiry.*

the charity coffers.

8. Brethren required permission from the Grand Master to demit from a Lodge. If the request was granted, such brethren were required to join with another Lodge, thereby avoiding the presence of unaffiliated Masons.

9. A Brother has three opportunities to rectify improper in-Lodge behavior before he is subject to discipline as determined by his Brethren.

10. Masters and Wardens are to represent the wishes and interests of their Brethren when assembled for the Quarterly and Annual Communications.

11. Masons are to observe regularity in their labors, and to frequently visit other Lodges to ensure adherence to the same usages.

12. Grand Lodge is defined as a body consisting of the Masters and Wardens of Lodges, governed by a Grand Master, his Deputy, and Wardens. Grand Lodges assemble quarterly.

13. The business of the Quarterly Communications is to be transacted "quietly, sedately, and maturely." It is here that Apprentices may be "admitted *Masters* and *Fellow-Crafts*." Note the use of the titles of the three grades, yet the apparent synonymy of the titles "Master" and "Fellow-Craft"; for example, it speaks of Apprentices being advanced, but not of Fellow-Crafts being advanced. This charge outlines how the records and monies of the Grand Lodge are to be managed.

14. The oldest, present Lodge Master shall preside over Grand Lodge in the absence of the Grand Master and Deputy Grand Master.

15. Only Lodge Wardens may act as *pro tempore* Grand Wardens.

16. The Deputy Grand Master is the only proper conduit to the Grand Master, and all business and concerns are to be voiced to him and through him.

17. A Grand Lodge officer cannot simultaneously serve as a Lodge officer.

18. If a Grand Master is dissatisfied with his Grand Officers, the issues must first be addressed at a Grand Lodge Communication. If these attempts do not rectify the issue, then the Grand Master can appoint new officers.

19. This regulation calls for a new regulation to be written that addresses what to do if a Grand Master acts in an un-Masonic manner. At the time of the writing, there was no extant regulation to address this, because the situation never previously arose.

20. Grand Masters, with his Deputy and Wardens, shall visit each lodge at least once.

21. This regulation specifies a line of succession in the event of the death or incapacitation of the Grand Master.

22. The Annual Communication of Grand Lodge will be held on St. John the Baptists Day. Ideally, a feast will accompany the assembly, but it is not required.

23. The Grand Wardens are responsible for planning the feasts. The Grand Master or Deputy Grand Master may appoint Stewards to aid in the planning and execution of the feasts.

24. The Grand Wardens and Stewards are also responsible for budgeting the feast, and do so at the direction of the Grand Master, or, barring that, at the direction of the assembled Lodge Master and Wardens.

25. Masters of Lodges are required to dispatch one Fellow-Craft to the Grand Lodge Communications, and these assembled Fellow-Crafts were responsible for testing all men who attended to ensure that they were Masons.

26. Two "Porters, or Door-keepers" were also appointed to assist the Fellow-Crafts.[78]

27. The Grand Wardens will appoint table servers for the feasts.

78   Anderson, *Constitutions* (1723), 67.

28. The Grand Lodge is to attend to any business "long before Dinner."[79] This business includes the specific duty to ensure due decorum and conduct by the Masons assembled.

29. The Lodge Masters and Wardens gather to decide to retain the current Grand Master, or to elect a new Brother for the Chair.

30. After the business of electing is done, the brethren are at ease.

31. After dinner, the Grand Lodge is called to order. Brethren are not to speak unless first addressed.

32. A grand officer other than the Grand Master shall announce that the Grand Master has agreed to serve in that capacity.

33. This regulation allows for the exiting Grand Master to nominate his replacement, if the Masters and Wardens of the constituent Lodges have not made a nomination.

34. If there is not agreement in nominations for the Grand Master, then a balloted vote is held.

35. The Grand Master, whether he is newly elected or serving again, shall then nominate his Deputy and Wardens.

36. If a Brother is nominated to serve in a grand office, but he is not present at the Annual Communication, then he may not be elected unless someone may vouch that the nominated Brother will accept the office.

37. Brethren may then offer Motions for the good of the Order.

38. The Grand Master or Deputy then addresses the Brethren. The Annual Communication is closed after "some other Transactions, that cannot be written in any Language."[80]

39. New regulations can be proposed and adopted at the Annual Communications, "Provided always that *the old* LAND-MARKS *be carefully preserv'd.*"[81]

---

79   Ibid.
80   Ibid., 70.
81   Ibid.

The penultimate Regulation represented a hallmark of Anderson's work: his frequent allusion to the deeper secrets of Freemasonry. He rarely identifies them by that term, but the 1723 *Constitutions* has repeated references to the fact that certain things pertaining to the Craft should not—and perhaps *cannot*—be written. Regulation № 38 is one, but certainly not the only, example. For instance, when speaking of the Chaldees and Magi supporting Geometry, Anderson interrupts himself, declaring, "it is not expedient to speak more plain of the Premises, except in a *formed Lodge*."[82] In describing early Masons' tendency to withhold information even from clergymen, Anderson acknowledges the existence of "what must not, and indeed cannot, be communicated in writing...."[83] In discussing certain modes of teaching the Arts and Sciences, Anderson advises, "But neither what was convey'd, nor the Manner how, can be communicated by writing; as no Man indeed can understand it without the Key of a *Fellow Craft*."[84] Yet another example is the assertion that "It is impossible to describe" the proper qualifications of Lodge officers "in writing."[85]

The last section of the 1723 *Constitutions* is a collection of four Masonic songs. Two of these were by Anderson himself, a third by Freemason Charles Delafaye, and the fourth by Freemason Matthew Birkhead. The first, "The Master's Song," is a twenty-eight-verse retelling of the Traditional History. Moreover, the chorus of the song reiterates the idea that there are Masonic secrets that can never be shared in writing, or with a non-Mason:

> *Who can unfold the* Royal Art?
> *Or sing its* Secrets *in a* Song?

82   Ibid.,5.
83   Ibid., 13.
84   Ibid., 29.
85   Ibid., 51.

They're safely kept in Mason's HEART,
And to the ancient Lodge *belong.*[86]

Next is "The Warden's Song, or Another History of Masonry." As the title promises, a second musical version of the Traditional History is offered within these thirteen verses. The chorus, as in "The Master's Song," reflects the Masonic understanding that certain truths cannot be revealed to the uninitiated:

Their *Secrets*, ne'er to *Strangers* yet expos'd,
Preserv'd shall be
By *Masons Free*,
And only to the *ancient Lodge* disclo'd;
Because they're kept in *Masons* HEART
By Brethren of the ROYAL ART.[87]

"The Fellow-Crafts Song" rendered by Charles Delafaye, consists of nine verses, and is said to be "Sung and Play'd at the Grand-Feast."[88] The song begins by establishing the divine provenance of the song; "HAIL MASONRY! thou *Craft* divine! Glory of Earth, from Heav'n reveal'd." The verses continue by asserting that Masonry contributes to the refinement of man. For instance, one verse is sung, "As Men from Brutes distinguished are, A *Mason* other Men excels." Another states that Masonic "Fellowship" is "from Envy free." The song ends with a reference to the builder's art extending from the Gothic Constitutions to the present day:

Then in our Songs be Justice done
To those who have enrich'd the *Art*,

86   Ibid., 75.
87   Ibid., 82.
88   Ibid., 83.

From Jabal down to BURLINGTON,
And let each Brother bear a Part.[89]

Jabal is one of the children of Lamech, who according to the pre-Andersonian version of the Traditional History, was the creator of the science of measuring land.[90] "Burlington" refers to Richard Boyle, Earl of Burlington, who Anderson called the "best Architect of Britain."[91] Thus, in much the same way as Anderson uses Freemasonry to link Adam and the Grand Master, so too is Delafaye linking Jabal and the Earl of Burlington through architecture.

The final song of the collection is the "Enter'd 'PRENTICES SONG," versions of which had been printed at least from 1709. The author of the song, Matthew Birkhead is listed as being Master of Lodge № 5 ("v"), under the aegis of Grand Master Wharton.[92] Arguably, this is the most well-known of all the fraternity's songs, and addresses the general greatness with which Freemasons considered their Craft: "What Mortal can boast SO NOBLE A TOAST, As a Free and an Accepted MASON?"[93]

---

89   Ibid., 83.
90   Cooke MS, lines 203–213.
91   Anderson, *Constitutions* (1723), 48.
92   Ibid., 74.
93   Ibid., 84.

Pennell's Constitutions, 1730

THE

CONSTITUTIONS

OF THE

FREE MASONS.

CONTAINING

The History, Charges, Regulations,

&c. of that Most Ancient and Right

Worshipful FRATERNITY.

For the Use of the LODGES.

Fraternitatem Diligite.

DUBLIN:

Printed by *J. Watts*, at the Lord *Carteret's*

Head in *Dames-Street*, for *J. Pennell*, at the

three *Blue Bonnets* in St. *Patrick's-Street.*

In the Year of Masonry	5730.
Anno Domini	1730.

Known for John Pennell, the Grand Secretary of the Grand
Lodge of Ireland, this 1730 book of *Constitutions* is, in many
ways, a restatement of Anderson's work. What this demonstrates,
therefore, is a substantial parity in early Masonic practice span-
ning England and Ireland: all of the themes and clues as to
self-concept that could be read in Anderson regarding English
Freemasonry are equally applicable to Irish Freemasonry.

The Latin script found on the title page of Pennell's *Constitutions* can translate as a commandment for Brotherly Love, and is
drawn from the Latin Vulgate translation of 1 Peter 2:17. In full,

the verse reads *omnes honorate fraternitatem diligite Deum timete regem honorificate.* That Pennell drew from the Latin Vulgate, the Bible officially adopted by the Roman Catholic church, may give an indication as to his own religious affiliation. The same verse is rendered in the King James version as "Honour all men. Love the brotherhood. Fear God. Honour the king." The Geneva Bible translates the verse as, "Honor all men: love brotherly fellowship: fear God: honor the King." Either translation is certainly applicable to a book dedicated to Freemasonry.

Pennell's telling of the Traditional History is an almost verbatim recapitulation of Anderson. Pennell lacks the extensive footnotes found in Anderson, but more often than not incorporates the same information into the narrative itself. This being the *Constitutions* of the Grand Lodge of Ireland, it is not surprising that Pennell adds a description of the history of Freemasonry in "the famous Kingdom of *Ireland*."[94] The Kingdom was "inhabited before the Flood,"[95] but it was the line of Japheth which colonized the island after the dispersion at Shinar.[96] Just as Anderson had done for England, Pennell identifies several magnificent works of architecture as a testament to the Craft in Ireland, ultimately boasting:

> Let the curious but examine the Histories and Antiquities of *Ireland*, and they will find it able to vie with most Kingdoms, in ancient Abbeys and venerable *Gothick* Buildings" [as well as those in the *Augustan* Stile].[97]

In charting the development of the Craft in Ireland, Pennell cites the works of Bede, among others. This is important to note,

---

94 Pennell, *The Constitutions of the Free Masons,* 38–45.
95 Ibid., 38.
96 Ibid., 39.
97 Ibid., 41–42.

given that Bede was one of the writers specifically cited in the Cooke MS. It seems then, in a manner of speaking, that Bede is a traditional source for Masonic tradition.

Pennell's presentation of the Charges is likewise sourced from Anderson's, albeit with variations and paraphrases in some instances. Of note, Charge IV, "*Of* Masters, Wardens, Fellows, *and* Apprentices," includes a reference to Deacons, which is not present in Anderson.[98] Also, when discussing decorum "In the LODGE while *constituted*," the charge is the same as that in Anderson, but the phrase "set them to worship" is omitted.[99] Most notably, the first Charge "*Concerning* GOD *and* Religion" omits Anderson's lines referring to the fluidity of the Mason's religion in ancient times, as well as to the adherence to "that Religion in which all Men agree" and the admonition to keep private one's religious identity.[100] The rest of the Charge reads the same as Anderson, and includes the acceptance of good men regardless of "Denominations or Persuasions."[101]

This omission may be related to what is arguably the most important part of the 1730 *Constitutions*, the "Prayer to be said at the opening of a *Lodge*, or making of a *Brother*:"

> MOST *Holy and Glorious* LORD GOD, *thou Great Architect of Heaven and Earth, who art the Giver of all good Gifts and Graces and hast promis'd that where two or three are gathered together in thy Name, thou wilt be in the Midst of them; in thy Name we assemble and meet together, most humbly beseeching thee to bless us in all our Undertakings, to give us thy Holy Spirit, to enlighten our Minds with Wisdom and Understanding, that we may know, and serve thee*

98   Ibid., 50–51.
99   Ibid., 55.
100 Ibid., 50.
101 Ibid., 48.

aright, that all our Doings may tend to thy Glory, and the
Salvation of our Souls.

And we beseech thee, O LORD GOD, to bless this our
present Undertaking, and grant that this, our new Brother,
may dedicate his Life to thy Service, and be a true and faith-
ful Brother *among us, endue him with Divine Wisdom, that*
he may, with the Secrets of Masonry, *be able to unfold the*
Mysteries of Godliness and Christianity.

This we humbly beg in the Name and for the Sake of
JESUS CHRIST our LORD and SAVIOUR.
AMEN.[102]

There are two points of note with this prayer. First is that Pennell captured language that remains present in common modes of Masonic working even today. In many Grand Jurisdictions of North America, for example, similar language is used in the prayer at the Opening of a Lodge, invoking the presence of the Divine. Additionally, in many English-speaking systems, the prayer offered just prior to initiation contains similar pleas for understanding and wisdom. As such, with the possible exception of some early Masonic catechisms, the 1730 *Constitutions* is among the earliest sources for some of the oldest surviving language in Masonic ritual. Second, is the specific message being conveyed in the second paragraph of the prayer. The Brotherhood is entreating God for "Divine Wisdom" in the form of the "Secrets of *Masonry*." But this is not simply a request for wisdom in the cause of acting with prudence and justice, but instead as a specific means by which to reach a knowledge of God. In other words, this prayer reveals an early Masonic belief that Freemasonry offers some sort of special understanding of spiritual knowledge. This is different than Freemasonry being a handmaiden to religion; Freemasonry, instead, was characterized as

102 Ibid., 59.

a gateway to a more robust understanding of the very source of religion. Such a concept of the Craft was repeated throughout the century, in Ireland, England, Scotland, and the American colonies, and echoed by such Masonic luminaries as Wellins Calcott, Isaac Head, and William Preston.[103]

As noted above, the abridged Charge regarding God and religion may be tied to this prayer, particularly to the specific pairing of Godliness with Christianity. Perhaps naming Christianity indicates a less tolerant stance on religious pluralism within the Grand Lodge of Ireland than within the Premier Grand Lodge. Perhaps, it is just reflective of the overwhelming religious majority of the island, and not so much a dilution of the concept of Masonic universality. It is important to note that one of the accusations leveled by some scholars against the Antients Grand Lodge, established in 1751, was one of religious intolerance; specifically, some allege that the Antient Grand Lodge attempted to promote Freemasonry as a distinctly Christian institution while the Moderns had no such commitments.[104] While this particular argument tends to be unconvincing (for reasons to be given below), these sections from Pennell's *Constitutions* demonstrate the presence of explicit Christian mysticism within the Irish lodges of the late 1720s and 1730s.

103   For example, see See Calcott, *Candid Disquisition*, 198–99; Head, *Confutation*, 102; and Preston, *Illustrations*, 210. For a near-contemporary example from the American colonies, see Shawn Eyer's essay in this volume, "'The Essential Secrets of Masonry': Insight from an American Masonic Oration of 1734," p. 151ff.

104   For a typical example of this narrative, see Daniel Ligou, *Le Dictionnaire de la Franc-maçonnerie* (Paris: Quadrige, 2006), 518. For the view that the religious nature of the rituals and legends was merely an affectation of the Moderns perhaps designed to assuage authorities, see C. Révauger, "Freemasonry and Religion in Eighteenth-Century Britain," in Trevor Stewart, Ed., *The Canonbury Papers, Volume Three: Freemasonry and Religion* (London: Canonbury Masonic Research Centre, 2006), 93–104.

Cole's Constitutions, 1731

THE ANTIENT

CONSTITUTIONS

OF THE

Free and Accepted MASONS,

Neatly ENGRAV'D on

COPPER PLATES.

WITH A

SPEECH deliver'd at the Grand Lodge at *York*.

ALSO

A SPEECH of EDWARD OAKLEY, Architect, M.M.

late Senior Grand Warden in *Carmarthen, South Wales*.

LIKEWISE

A PROLOGUE spoken by MR. MILES, and an EPILOGUE spoken by a MA-
SON's Wife, at the Theater-Royal in *Drury-Lane*, on *Friday* the 27th Day
of *December*, 1728, when was acted the Second Part of King *Henry* IV.

To which is added,

A Curious COLLECTION of the most Celebrated Songs in Honour of
MASONRY, as they are Sung at All the Regular Lodges of the Antient and
Honourable Fraternity of Free and Accepted MASONS in
Great Britain and Principality of *Wales*, &c.

____ *Ingenuas didicisse fideliter artes,*
Emollit mores, nec sinit esse feros. OVID.

The SECOND EDITION

LONDON:

Printed for B. CREAKE, at the *Red Bible* in *Ave-Mary-*
Lane, Ludgate-Street, near *St. Paul's*; and B. COLE
Engraver, the Corner of *King's Head-Court*, near
Fetter-Lane, Holbourn. M.DCC.XXXI.

This second edition of Cole's *Constitutions* reprints the engraved copper plates of the Traditional History and Masonic Charges as found in the 1728 edition. As noted above, because of its close affinity with the Old Charges, Cole's 1728 *Constitutions* were excluded from this survey. The 1731 edition, however, is not merely a reprint, but is instead greatly expanded; these expansions chart important elements of early-eighteenth-century Freemasonry thus requiring their examination herein. The quotation from Ovid on the title page pairs nicely with the introduction to the seven liberal arts and sciences found in the opening pages of Cole: "A faithful study of the liberal arts humanizes character and permits it not to be cruel."[105]

The work features a frontispiece engraved by Cole. In the foreground are three men, one of whom is wearing an apron and holds an opened pair of compasses in his right hand. He is flanked by two men, one of whom holds a square in his right hand. Behind the gentlemen are three pillars, one each of the Corinthian, Doric, and Ionic orders, from left to right. In the background are several workmen, distributed about some scaffolding, above a well built arch. In the sky, we have the sun and moon, concurrently, with the emblem of seven stars between them. This may be the earliest surviving example of this particular Masonic symbol.

As the lengthy title page indicates, there are several additions to this volume. The most important of these is the song book. This song book, it should be noted, was printed with its own cover page, naming the section *A Curious Collection of the Most Celebrated Songs in Honour of Masonry*, and has its own pagination. One year earlier, in 1730, a book entitled *A New Model for the Rebuilding of Masonry on a Stronger Basis Than the Former* was printed, and this book contained a collection of songs, on par with the scope of the *Curious Collection*. As such, while

105   Ovid, *Epistulæ ex Ponto* 2.9.47.

Cole's second edition does not hold the distinction of being the first Masonic song book, it does mark a new practice: including a wide variety of Masonic songs within books of *Constitutions*. As noted above, the 1723 *Constitutions* contained four Masonic songs, but the sheer size of the collection found in Cole's 1731 edition marked a shift in practice that stretched into the late nineteenth century.

The *Curious Collection* is broken up into two sections. The first section is comprised of five songs, and is likely their earliest date of publication of each. A brief synopsis of each of the songs:

- "THE NEW FAIRIES: OR, THE Fellow-Craft's SONG. As Sung in the Lodge in *Carmarthen South-Wales*."[106] This 24-stanza song is an allegorical tale featuring Elves who sneak into a tyled Lodge room. The song itself is deeply annotated, offering explanations of the allegorical and symbolic meanings behind the pervasive mystical themes and imagery.
- "THE Candidate's SONG, FROM *Horace's Blandusia*, Lib. iii. Ode 13. As Sung at the LODGE in *Carmarthen, South-Wales*."[107] Like "The New Fairies," this song is both heady and contains thorough annotations.
- An untitled song "Sung by Brother WILLIAMS."[108] This song is of the self-congratulatory variety, as the author notes the "stupidity" of "those that rail against the Art."[109] The song also makes reference to an allegation of "Disobedience to a Queen."[110] This is likely a reference to the suspicion Queen Elizabeth once held for the Craft, as noted in Anderson's

---

106 Anon., *Curious Collection*, 1–11.
107 Ibid., 12–14.
108 Ibid., 14–15.
109 Ibid., 15.
110 Ibid.

Traditional History.[111]

- "Masons SONG, Sung by Brother OATS."[112] By using the elements of the Traditional History specific to the development of architecture, "The Masons SONG" credits the beautifying of the world to the Craft, and celebrates the eternal spirit of the fraternity.
- "SONG in the *Generous Free Mason*. Sung by Brother OATS."[113] Both the Universality of the Craft, as well as the "Godlike Actions"[114] of its votaries are the themes of this song.

The second section reprints both of Anderson's Traditional History songs, Delafaye's song, and Birkhead's song. Additionally, twelve other songs are printed, some likely for the first time. They are, in brief:

- "The Fairies, with the Mason's Chorus." This is an earlier version of the "NEW FAIRIES" from the first section of the collection. Here can be read traces of the mystic themes of the newer version.[115] Additionally, the song contains a chorus similar to those seen in the "NEW FAIRIES," and which is found under the title "The Fairy Elves Song" in Cole's 1728 *Constitutions*. This song had earlier appeared the 1730 work, *A New Model for the Rebuilding of Masonry*, by a Peter Farmer.[116]
- An untitled song. This song celebrates the feats and beauties of Masonry, evoking King Solomon. The chorus rings out, "Sing then my Muse to Masons Glory! Your Names are so

---

111 Anderson, *Constitutions* (1723), 38.
112 *Curious Collection*, 16–17.
113 Ibid., 17.
114 Ibid.
115 Ibid., 26–28.
116 Farmer, *New Model*, 19–21.

rever'd in Story, That all th' admiring World do now adore ye."[117]

- Untitled song "Composed by a Member of the One Tun Lodge in Noble-Street." Beginning with the lines "As I at Wheeler's Lodge one Night / Kept Bacchus company," this brief contribution is of the toasting variety.[118] While not mentioned in Cole's Traditional History, it is noteworthy that other books of *Constitutions* in this survey equate Bacchus with Grand Master Nimrod.[119] This song had also appeared in Farmer's *A New Model*, and is credited to Mr. Moses Harris.[120]

- Untitled song. Another song extolling the virtues of Masonry, here can be found a reference to alleged Masonic exposures printed in the *Post-Boy* and *Flying Post* newspapers, disclosed by "some false-hearted Brother."[121]

- Untitled song.[122] This song begins with a reflection of a self-concept of Masonry being God-given: "Guardian Genius of our Art Divine." The first stanza continues with the instruction not to "pine" over "Ruins of the East," but rather to look to the beauties yet to unfold: "Behold what strength our rising DOMES appears."[123] The beauties are not "confin'd" to architecture, but rather found along all "Paths of Virtue."

- Untitled song. This song borders on the bawdy. It speaks of "A Mason's Daughter" who maintains her "Virgin Zone" bound in chastity; only a Freemason is worthy to share with

---

117 *Curious Collection*, 28–30.
118 Ibid., 30.
119 For example, see Anderson, *Constitutions* (1723), 4 (footnote).
120 Farmer, *New Model*, 18. See Crawley, "Wheeler's Lodge"; see also Hextall, "Wheeler's Lodge."
121 *Curious Collection*, 32–32.
122 Ibid., 32–33.
123 Ibid., 33.

her the "Conubial Joys of their Days."[124]
- Untitled song. Beginning with the line, "We have no idle Prating," the theme of this song is that Masons do not delve into matters of church or state. The song further states that Masonic labors are serious, and their refreshment is merry.[125] This song also appeared in Farmer's *A New Model*.[126]
- Untitled song. This song opens with an admonishment not to spar with the enemies of Freemasonry: "Let malicious People censure; They're not worth a Mason's Answer." Instead, let Brethren rejoice in their time together, knowing that "Masons Foes" will be stymied by their jealousy.[127] This was also featured in *A New Model*.[128]
- Untitled song. The two stanzas of this song recall the wisdom that has passed through the ages, and manifested at the building of King Solomon's Temple, and which is embodied by the virtuous Freemason. It begins with the line, "Sing to the honor of those…."[129]
- Untitled song. Here, Freemasonry is identified as a heavenly blessing, and the Lodge room compared to Eden. "Grant me kind Heav'n what I request! In *Masonry* let me be blest."[130]
- Untitled song. This is another celebratory song of the "Glorious *Craft*." It harkens to Masonry's reformation of "*Adam's Race*" through the temples, columns, and domes that now "adorn this happy Land."[131]
- Untitled song. Another song in honor of women, this is per-

124 Ibid., 33–34.
125 Ibid., 35–36.
126 Farmer, *New Model*, 23–25.
127 *Curious Collection*, 37.
128 Farmer, *New Model*, 22.
129 *Curious Collection*, 38–39.
130 Ibid., 39–40.
131 Ibid., 40–41.

haps less bawdy than the last, thanking "our *Sisters*" for the "chiefest Delight."[132]

Two epilogues follow the song book. The first speaks to the refinement of a Mason, from a woman's perspective. The second speaks to the Mason's masculinity and prowess as a provider, husband, and father.

Cole's 1731 *Constitutions* concludes with reprints of two Masonic orations which became quite famous, and often republished, in the eighteenth-century. The first presented is by Francis Drake from his address before Grand Master Bathhurst of the Grand Lodge of York in 1726; the second is a speech delivered by Edward Oakley in 1728. Space precludes a full examination of these, suffice it to say that both examples are classics of early Masonic oratory, and are worthy of further study.[133]

132 Ibid., 43.
133 For a systematic treatment of Drake, see Eyer, "Drake's Oration," 14–25.

Franklin's Constitutions, 1734

THE

CONSTITUTIONS

OF THE

FREE-MASONS.

CONTAINING THE

History, Charges, Regulations, &c.

of that most Ancient and Right

Worshipful FRATERNITY.

For the Use of the LODGES.

LONDON Printed; *Anno* 5723.

Re-printed in *Philadelphia* by special Order, for the Use

of the Brethren in NORTH-AMERICA.

In the Year of Masonry 5734, *Anno Domini* 1734.

In 1734, in Philadelphia, Benjamin Franklin reprinted James Anderson's 1723 *Constitutions*, for the "Use of the Brethren in NORTH-AMERICA."[134] This work constitutes the first Masonic book to be printed in on the American continent. The fact that it is a near-verbatim duplication of Anderson's work means that the same themes and instructions that informed Masonic practice in England and Ireland carried over into the English colonies.

Some variations between the 1723 edition and Franklin's version bear highlighting. Franklin's edition lacks an engraved frontispiece. The lack of Hebrew text in the notes about Hiram Abiff and the Solomonic stonemasons, likely because Franklin lacked access to a Hebrew typeface. The sheet music that was found in Anderson is absent in the Franklin reprint. Additionally, in

134 James Anderson, *Constitutions of the Freemasons* (Philadelphia: Benjamin Franklin, 1734), title page.

the instructions for the singing of "The Master's Song," Franklin added a parenthetical clause to Anderson's original instruction:

> To be sung with a *Chorus,* when the MASTER shall give Leave (*no Brother being present to whom Singing is disagreeable*) either one Part only, or all together, as he pleases.[135]

When these are taken together, a suggestion may be inferred that singing was less important in colonial Masonic practice than it was in the British Isles. Indeed, it may have been. Just as noteworthy, however, is that to the four songs originally featured in Anderson, Franklin added a fifth. This uncredited song, aptly titled "A New SONG," is of the self-congratulatory variety: It speaks to the refinement and loyalty demonstrated by Freemasons and the self-improvement inherent within the Craft, as well as to the "Stupidity" of "those that do despise the Art."[136] A version of this song had appeared three years earlier in Cole and Creake's 1731 collection of Masonic songs.[137] A shorter version appeared in 1730, in Farmer's *A New Model for the Rebuilding of Masonry.*[138] There are several variations in the lyrics between these three versions, and this may either be due to the regional differences and alterations that inadvertently slip into a song largely propagated mouth-to-ear, or due to attempts to improve the song by Franklin or one of his contemporaries. This expansion in the number of songs recommended for use in the lodges would tend to disqualify any theory suggesting that songs were less a part of Masonic practice among the Brethren of North America.

135 Ibid., 81. Emphasis in the original.
136 Ibid., 91.
137 *Curious Collection,* 14. Royster is therefore incorrect both in stating that the song first appeared in print here and suggesting the possibility that Franklin wrote the song. See Royster, "Editorial Note," 94.
138 Farmer, *New Model,* 28–29.

Smith's Pocket Companion, 1735

A

POCKET COMPANION

FOR

FREE-MASONS.

Deus nobis Sol & Scutum

Dedicated to the SOCIETY.

LONDON:

Printed and Sold by E. RIDER in Blackmore-
street, near Clare-market.

MDCCXXXV.

Along with books of *Constitutions*, Masonic *Pocket Companions* were also important in early Masonic literature. This entry by William Smith follows the same pattern as, and borrows much of the phrasing from, Anderson, just as Pennell and Franklin had done before him. The title page of the Irish edition, which also appeared in 1735, touts that it is "*Approved of, and Recommended by the* Grand-Lodge."[139] Further, in 1740, this book was adopted by the Grand Lodge of Scotland as its *de facto* Book of Constitutions.[140] Both of these facts further support Smith's inclusion here. The impetus behind this work was, in Smith's words, an oft repeated request for "*a small Volume easily portable, which will render what was before difficult to come at, and troublesome to carry about, of more extensive Use.*"[141] The Latin motto inscribed

139   Smith, *Pocket Companion*, Dublin edition, title page. In Williams & Cerza, *D'Assigny*, 123.
140   Crawley, "Old Charges," 48.
141   Smith, *Pocket Companion* (London: 1735), [v].

onto the title page translates to "God is our sun and shield," and
refers to Psalm 82:11:

> For the LORD God is a sun and shield: the LORD will give
> grace and glory: no good thing will he withhold from them
> that walk uprightly.[142]

The reference to walking uprightly has two Masonic connotations. First is to a common explanation of the symbolic lesson
of the working tool of the plumb. The other refers to Noah, who
not only was viewed as one of the chief patriarchs of the Craft
in its Traditional History, but who was described as being upright.[143] Because Noah walked uprightly, he was spared from the
Deluge and allowed to propagate the Craft—each being a very
"good thing."

The Dublin edition, also published in 1735, was likewise printed by E. Rider, but also by T. Jones and J. Pennell. The contents
of the two books are nearly identical. One difference is that the
London edition cites the manner of constituting a new Lodge "As
practis'd by the Right Honourable the Earl of CRAWFURD," John
Lindsay, the Grand Master of the Premier Grand Lodge;[144] the
Dublin edition carries the same instruction *vis-à-vis* new Lodges, but does not name a Grand Master in the same context. Another difference is that the Dublin edition carries an approbation
by the Irish Grand Master, Henry Barnewall, the 4th Viscount of
Kingsland,[145] while the London edition has no approbation. In
both editions, the work is dedicated to the "Brethren and Fellows
of the Most Antient...Society of Free and Accepted Masons." In

---

142 Authorized Version.

143 Genesis 6:9.

144 Smith, *Pocket Companion* (London: 1735), 40.

145 Smith, *Pocket Companion* (Dublin: 1735). In Williams & Cerza,
     D'Assigny, 159.

an interesting point of variation in nomenclature, the Irish society is deemed "Right Worshipful"[146] whereas the English society is referred to as "Honourable."[147] Unless otherwise specified, the citations from Smith are taken from the London edition; with that said, the differences between the two editions are negligible, and are mainly confined to differences in punctuation and emphasis.

The book features a handsome frontispiece by T. Worlidge and J. Clark. The scene features two craftsmen prominent in the foreground, with one taking measurements from a tracing board. In the distance can be found several workmen erecting an edifice. The sun and moon are each present in the sky. The engraving also features several working tools, an archway, and a broken pillar.[148]

Smith subtly uses his Dedication and Preface to caution the growing Brotherhood to guard the secrets of the Craft. The Dedication opens by happily celebrating "THE great Increase of our SOCIETY of late," with the hope that society will be rewarded with a revival of the "AUGUSTAN AGE."[149] In this Preface that follows, he explains more of his reasoning in issuing the work:

> For it has been often remarked that great Numbers, especially of the younger Masons, (who have been desirous of knowing every thing relating to the Craft) have been a long time frustrated in their Pursuits for want of something of this Kind, which they might have records to at any time. I need not say more in relation to the Book itself, but must here beg leave to

---

146 Smith, *Pocket Companion* (Dublin: 1735), title page [i]. In Williams & Cerza, *D'Assigny*, 123.

147 Smith, *Pocket Companion* (London: 1735), [iii].

148 For a treatment of this frontispiece, see Murphy, "The Broken Pillar," 55–56.

149 Smith, *Pocket Companion* (London: 1735), [iii].

exhort the Brotherhood, *that avoiding all Innovations they adhere strictly to the antient Practices of the* ORDER *when all the social Virtues shone conspicuously amongst us, and the World admir'd us rather for our Veracity, Brotherly Love, and Relief of one another, than for those invaluable Secrets which have ever kept....*[150]

Smith is speaking of the delineation between the exoteric elements of the Craft ("Veracity, Brotherly Love, and Relief") and the esoteric ("invaluable Secrets"). It is important to note that Francis Drake, the Grand Junior Warden of the Grand Lodge of York, made this same distinction at a speech initially given at a St. John the Baptist feast in 1726. Drake's speech was published and reprinted several times, and it is impossible to say how often it was recited in Masonic lodges. Whether Smith heard a recitation of Drake's speech, or whether Drake and Smith captured what was a common Masonic understanding of the time, or if Drake informed the Craft's self-awareness of what could be termed exoteric and esoteric material, cannot be known for sure. It will suffice to note that the words of Drake and Smith both reflect the existence of a Masonic concept of esotericism within the York, Irish, and Scottish Grand Lodges.

Following the dedication and preface, Smith provides a fresh telling of the Traditional History. All of the Old Testament elements of the Andersonian myth are present, but phrased in Smith's own words. He provides a full account of Adam, Seth, Enoch and the Primordial Pillars, Noah and his sons, Nimrod and the builders at Babel, and the construction of King Solomon's Temple. A telling of the history, greatly abridged from Anderson's version, follows, with Pythagoras and Euclid mentioned briefly, as well as a variety of architectural feats. The only element of the Traditional History that Smith quotes directly from

150   Smith, *Pocket Companion* (London: 1735), [v].

Anderson is the legend of King Athelstan and Prince Edwin.[151] Smith also added four paragraphs in honor of Irish Masonry, a subject absent from Anderson but represented in Pennell.

In his Traditional History, Smith refers to two Masonic concepts that are familiar to contemporary Craftsmen, but that had only appeared in print a few years prior to the publication of the *Pocket Companion*. In the infamous Masonic exposure, *Masonry Dissected* (1730), a catechism was printed, purporting to reflect secret Masonic ritual. In this, the following exchange is seen:

> Q.   What do you come here to do?
> A.   Not to do my own proper Will,
>   But to subdue my Passion still....[152]

Whether he was inspired by Pritchard, or was merely reflecting the workings he had used in Lodge, Smith alludes to a failure of this chief duty as the explanation behind Adam's expulsion from Eden:

> *Our first Father Adam was left without excuse when he transgress'd the Divine Command*, as having this unerring Rule to direct him, without any Seeds of Corruption in his Body or jarring the Principles in his Mind; *but after his Default the Passions usurp'd the Throne of Reason*, lately their Master, and thro' his unhappy Race have but too much born the sway.[153]

Pritchard's exposure is also the earliest written record of the triple pillars of Wisdom, Strength, and Beauty serving as the sup-

---

151   Ibid., 7–9; cf. Anderson, *Constitutions* (1723), 31–41.
152   Pritchard, *Masonry Dissected*, 9.
153   Smith, *Pocket Companion* (London: 1735), 1. Emphasis added.

ports of a Lodge.[154] Smith also evokes these, when he described Geometry as the means by which to "trace out the Wisdom, Strength and Beauty display'd in all the wondrous Works of the great Architect of Nature, and thence with adoration reflect them to their all-wise, all-potent and most amiable Origin."[155] Such imagery not only frames the Lodge as the microcosm of God's created universe, but it also proposes that Geometry, "which is the Basis of MASONRY," is the means by which to understand the Divine.[156] As such, Smith provides us with a narrative complement to the same belief revealed in Pennell's prayer referenced above: Freemasonry is a means to divine knowledge.

The Charges and Regulations found in Smith are duplicates of those found in Anderson. Smith includes a Charge to be delivered to a new Brother. In this Charge can be traced language that is still present in many forms of English-language workings.[157]

To the London edition, Smith attached a songbook, which also included prologues and epilogues "SPOKEN At the THE-ATRES in *London*, for the Entertainment of FREE-MASONS."[158] Included are the four songs printed in Anderson, along with "several other songs in Praise of Masonry."[159] Each of these additional songs was earlier printed in Creake and Cole's 1731 *A Curious Collection of the Most Celebrated Songs in Honour of Masonry*. Of the other material:

1. "A PROLOGUE": this was earlier printed in 1734, appended

---

154 Pritchard, *Masonry Dissected*, 13.

155 Smith, *Pocket Companion* (London: 1735), 1.

156 Ibid.

157 See Smith, *Pocket Companion*, 43–45. For derivative Charges in British and American Freemasonry, see Preston, *Illustrations* (1772), 191–99; Jones, *Masonic Miscellanies*, 292–93; Cross, *True Masonic Chart*, 20–21; Claret, *The Whole of Craft-Freemasonry*, 67–72.

158 Smith, *Pocket Companion* (London: 1735), 48.

159 Ibid., 71.

to an edition of Drake's famous oration of 1726.

2. "An EPILOGUE *Spoken by Mrs.* Thurmond, *a* Mason's *Wife*": this was earlier printed in the same 1734 printing of Drake's speech.

3. "An EPILOGUE By MR. RAULINS. *Spoken by Mrs.* Horton": This had been earlier published in Creake and Cole's 1731 collection noted above.

With the exception of some advertisements on the last four printed pages of the book, the remainder of Smith catalogues the "Regular LODGES according to their Seniority and Constitution."[160]

160 Ibid., 95–115.

Anderson's Constitutions, 1738

THE

NEW BOOK

OF

CONSTITUTIONS

OF THE

Antient and *Honourable* FRATERNITY

OF

FREE and ACCEPTED MASONS.

CONTAINING

Their *History, Charges, Regulations,* &c.

COLLECTED and DIGESTED

By Order of the GRAND LODGE from their old *Records,*
faithful *Traditions* and *Lodge-Books,*

For the Use of the LODGES.

By JAMES ANDERSON D.D.

LONDON:

Printed for Brothers CÆSAR WARD and RICHARD CHANDLER,
Booksellers, at the *Ship* without *Temple-Bar;* and sold at their
Shops in *Coney-Street,* YORK, and at SCARBOROUGH-SPAW.

M DCC XXXVIII

In the *Vulgar* Year of Masonry 5738.

Fifteen years after the publication of the first book on Freemasonry, the author, James Anderson saw his second edition of the
same published under the aegis of the Grand Lodge. As in the
1723 edition, this volume begins with a dedication, this time by
Anderson himself. He states that the outgoing Grand Master,
the Marquis of Caernarvon, ordered Anderson to dedicate this
edition to Prince Friderick Lewis, while specifically noting that
Freemasons meddle not in affairs of state.

In his forward, addressed to the reader, Anderson outlines the
ways in which this second edition is expanded from the first. In
the closing of this forward, Anderson speaks of the Craft's elevat-
ing nature, and the essential secrets of the Fraternity. He writes:

> Most regular Societies have had, and will ever have, their
> own *Secrets*; and, to be sure, the *Free-Masons* always had
> theirs, which they never divulged in *Manuscript*; and there-
> fore cannot be expected in *Print*: Only, an expert Brother,
> by the true Light, can readily find many useful Hints in
> almost every Page of this Book, which *Cowans*, and Others
> not Initiated, cannot discern.[161]
>
> [...]
>
> It is good to know WHAT NOT TO SAY![162]

Although indirectly, Anderson is contesting the common
accusation that Masonic secrets are simply the modes of recognition. Such grips and passwords could certainly be conveyed
in writing, and would not require either an "expert Brother"
nor "true Light" to learn them. Anderson also repeats a concept he presented in his first edition, that there are some things

161 Anderson, *The New Book of Constitutions* (1738), ix.
162 Anderson, *Constitutions* (1738), x.

that simply cannot be shared in a form potentially accessible to non-Masons. Another example of this is found when describing the Holy of Holies and "leaving what must not, and indeed cannot be committed to Writing."[163] Anderson echoes this warning again as it relates to forming a new Lodge.[164] Yet another is found at the conclusion of the Charges, when he writes:

> All these *Charges* you are to observe, and also Those that shall be communicated unto you in a Way that cannot be written.[165]

It may well have been this very understanding—that there are Masonic secrets that may never be committed to writing—that induced some Brethren of the late-seventeenth-century to "too hastily" destroy some Lodge records "from a Fear of making Discoveries."[166] This purge of the written word occurred again in 1720, with the burning of various manuscripts "by some scrupulous Brothers, that those Papers might not fall into strange Hands."[167]

The book also contains a sanction from the Grand Lodge, attesting that Anderson's version is the only permissible printed *Constitutions* for use in Lodges. Other versions "have been condemn'd as pyratical and stupid."[168] Later in the text, Anderson notes that the "*Free Mason's Vade Mecum* was condemn'd by the G. Lodge as a pyratical and silly thing."[169] In 1736, a song book was published under that name, but it seems curious that

163   Ibid., 14.
164   Ibid., 151.
165   Ibid., 149.
166   Ibid., 105.
167   Ibid., 111.
168   Ibid., xi.
169   Ibid., 133.

a song collection would warrant such a response from the Grand Lodge. Even if the *Vade Mecum* was a collection of anti-Masonic songs, such a condemnation is odd given that none of the other anti-Masonic works of the era were similarly defamed. Perhaps, then, Anderson's reference is to a different text. The term *vade mecum* generally denotes a handbook. Perhaps this is a reference to William Smith's *Pocket Companion for Free Masons.* Certainly, a book that gives a Traditional History and a list of Charges could more easily be described as "pyratical" of Anderson's work than a song book could, and given the similarity in structure between Anderson's and Smith's works, one can more easily see why Smith would be cast aside as unsanctioned.

In addition to a reprinting of the frontispiece featured in the 1723 edition, this volume includes two more engravings by John Pine. The first is a mark of heraldry with the working tools of a Mason scattered about; this is paired with the dedication to Prince Lewis. The second piece, based upon a design by Freemason James Thornhill (1675–1734), features Hiram Abif, square in hand, explaining his trestleboard to King Solomon. Behind Solomon are featured two guards with their rods; behind Hiram Abif, a figure who perhaps represents an apprentice helps hold his designs.

The Traditional History is vastly expanded in this second edition.[170] As in the first edition, the directive specifies that this history is "TO BE READ at the Admission of a NEW BROTHER."[171] Some of the expansion is due to the inclusion of figures being newly counted as Brethren, and feats of architecture being newly counted as representative of the Royal Art. An example of this is when Anderson offers the possibility that "STONEHENG [was] rais'd...by the Art of *Marvellous* MERLIN"; Anderson couches

170 A considerable portion of the 1738 edition of the Traditional History is reproduced in this volume; see page 7ff.
171 Ibid., 1.

this suggestion, however, by acknowledging the conclusions of Inigo Jones and John Web that Stonehenge was a Roman Temple.[172] The majority of the increase, however, is due to an expansion of the descriptions, histories, and contributions of Brethren previously named in earlier tellings of the Traditional History.

Before reintroducing the reader to Adam, Anderson makes a point of declaring that all of the Great Architect's creation was rendered "according to *Geometry*."[173] This may have naturally occurred to him as part of the general growth of the myth, but it bears noting that Smith made a similar statement.[174] Adam is again proposed as having been created with Geometry at his heart. Additionally, Adam was said to have formed his sons into a Lodge, wherein he taught them the noble science. As the myth continues to describe Enoch's Primordial Pillars, Anderson offers a note:

> Some call them SETH's *Pillars*, but the old *Masons* always call'd them ENOCH's *Pillars*, and firmly believ'd this Tradition: nay *Josephus* (Lib. i. cap. 2.) affirms the *Stone-Pillar*

172 Ibid., 60. John Webb (1611–1672) is also among those who Anderson names as a Freemason. Specifically, Anderson names John Webb and Christopher Wren as Grand Wardens under Grand Master Jermyn, the Earl of St. Albans [p. 101]. In 1669, Webb authored *An Historical Essay Endeavoring a Probability That the Language of the Empire of China is the Primitive Language*. In this work, Webb proffers a history, partially drawn from Josephus, wherein Adam is forewarned of a cataclysm, Seth or Enoch engraves knowledge onto two pillars made to withstand torch and tempest, Noah and his sons become the sole keepers of a certain knowledge, and after the confusion of tongues at the building of the Tower of Babel, Noah and his sons retain the knowledge unadulterated. The similarities between Webb's history and Anderson's history are clear, and are being developed by this author for future publication.
173 Ibid., 1.
174 Smith, *Pocket Companion* (London: 1735), 1.

still remain'd in *Syria* to his Time.[175]

There are two important elements to this statement. First is a recognition that parallel traditions exist which may stray from the Masonic myth, but a belief that the mythology as propagated by Freemasons is correct. Second, is that here Anderson demonstrates that he is drawing from ancient sources to inform his Traditional History. He had used the writings of Josephus in his first edition, but it is here that he cites the source. This indicates that Anderson himself was doing research into the origins of Freemasonry, seeking evidence of the Craft in antiquity.

As the rains cleansed the Earth, Noah and his sons were aboard they Ark, and they, too, formed a Lodge: "his 3 Sons assisted like a *Deputy* and two *Wardens*."[176] This particular expansion is highly important, as it is in this edition that Noah is to take on an even more prominent role than he had in previous versions of the myth. The story continues:

> After the *Flood*, NOAH and his 3 Sons, having preserved the Knowledge of the Arts and Sciences, communicated It to their growing Off-spring, who were all *of one Language and Speech*. [...T]hey found a Plain in the Land of SHINAR, and dwelt there together, as NOACHIDÆ, or Sons of *Noah*.[177]

A side note identifies "Noachidæ" as "The first Name of *Masons*, according to some old Traditions."[178] This is the first of several important references to this concept within this edition of the *Constitutions*, as is detailed below.

175 Anderson, *Constitutions* (1738), 3.
176 Ibid., 4.
177 Ibid.
178 Ibid.

In describing the building of the Tower of Babel, a familiar Masonic term is defined for the first time. The builders at Babel sought to attain a knowledge of God by constructing a Tower to the heavens. This aim is here defined as the Masons' "*Grand Design*."[179] While the term was used as early as 1723 (in "The Warden's Song," for instance) here it is explained: the Grand Design is an attempt to lift humanity closer to God, specifically illustrated in this instance by a mythic feat of architecture.

After Zerubbabel finished his Temple, another Mason is newly introduced: Zoroastres. Naming him the Grand Master of Magians, and crediting him and his disciples for having been "Improvers of Geometry in the liberal Arts."[180] Anderson goes on to say:

> Yet a Remnant of 'em are scatter'd in those Parts to this Day, who retain many of the old Usages of the *Free Masons*, for which they are here mention'd, and not for their Religious Rites that are not the Subject of this Book: For we leave every Brother to Liberty of Conscience; but strictly charge him carefully to maintain the *Cement of the Lodge*, and the 3 Articles of NOAH.[181]

Noteworthy in this selection is the idea that a lost society assembled under the aegis of Zoroaster could display workings that are recognizable as Freemasonry. What is more striking, however, is that this part of the myth seems to have been understood as an actual opportunity within the Grand Lodge. In 1735, three years before this edition was published, Grand Secretary John Revis sent a letter from Grand Master Lord Weymouth to the Provisional Grand Master of Calcutta, advising:

179   Ibid., 5.
180   Ibid., 23.
181   Ibid.

> Providence has fixed your Lodge near those learn'd Indi-
> ans that affect to be called Noachidæ, the strict observance
> of his Precepts taught in those Parts by the Disciples of
> the great Zoroastres, the learned Archmagus of Bactria,
> a Grand Master of the Magians, whose Religion is much
> preserved in India (which we have no concern about), and
> also many of the Rituals of the Ancient Fraternity used
> in his time, perhaps more than they are themselves. Now
> if it was consistent with your other Business, to discover
> in those parts the Remains of Old Masonry and transmit
> them to us, we would all be thankful....[182]

The remainder of the Traditional History follows much the
same path as Anderson's 1723 telling. Additionally, because a
decade and a half's worth of Grand Lodge activity had passed
between editions, Anderson undertook to capture some details of the fifteen-year span, as well as provide some details of
the founding of the Grand Lodge. Many detractors have found
fault with elements of this part of Anderson's history, and used
such fault as reasons to cast aside almost the entirety of his con-
tributuion to Masonic thought. Because the current work is a
survey of Masonic self-concept and practice, it will not delve
into measuring the accuracies of Anderson's history. It must be
remembered, however, that much of what he captured in the
Traditional History was of a mythic nature. Anderson was faced
with the challenge of integrating a legendary view of the Craft
with verifiable historical facts. If he claimed the Masonic membership of historical figures for whom no Masonic evidence is
available, these should be viewed through the lens of legend, and
not as statements of deliberate falsehood. If there are aspects of
Anderson's telling that contradict the traceable history of the
revival of Grand Lodge, such errors prove neither Anderson's

182 Crawley, "Masonic MSS," 35–36.

intent to deceive, nor do they invalidate the whole of Anderson's contributions to Freemasonry. In considering this, one should recall the words of J. M. Hamill, as noted earlier in the discussion.

Moving to the Charges, the second edition offers some addenda and revisions, but the content in none of these is substantially changed from the first to second editions. The Charge that was most revised is the first, "*Concerning* GOD *and Religion*":

> A MASON is obliged by his Tenure to observe the Moral Law, as a true *Noachida*; and if he rightly understands the *Craft*, he will never be a stupid Atheist, nor an Irreligious Libertine, nor act against Conscience. In antient Times the *Christian Masons* were charged to comply with the *Christian* Usages of each Country where they travell'd or work'd: But *Masonry* being found in all Nations, even of divers Religions, they are now only charged to adhere to that Religion in which all Men agree (leaving each Brother to his own particular Opinions) that is, to be Good Men and True, Men of Honour and Honesty, by whatever Names, Religions or Persuasions they may be distinguish'd: For they all agree in the 3 great *Articles* of NOAH, enough to preserve the Cement of the Lodge. Thus *Masonry* is the Center of their Union, and the happy Means of conciliating Persons that otherwise must have remain'd at a perpetual Distance.[183]

In this new Charge, Anderson has of course maintained the religious pluralism and universality of the Craft, but has defined it in terms relative to the story of Noah. In obeying the moral law, a Freemason embodies the Sons of Noah, the *Noachidæ*. Recall that Anderson advised that such was the oldest name given to Masons, and calls those assembled for the building of

183   Anderson, *New Book* (1738), 143–44.

the Tower of Babel by the same term. Similarly, the "Cement of the Lodge"—that is, the common religious values that bond the Brotherhood together—are a shared belief in the "3 great *Articles* of NOAH."

The term *Noachide* certainly has a literal connotation—to Ham, Shem, and Japheth, the actual sons of Noah[184]—however, "Noachide laws" have historically been used to prescribe "the path of the righteous gentile."[185] Traditionally observant Jews are beholden to the 613 commandments found in the Torah, and many of these commandments are also available to the Gentile to observe. But to be righteous, that is, to remain in good moral standing with God, Rabbinical tradition holds that, minimally, the Gentile must observe the Noachide laws. These are the laws of the rainbow covenant made with Noah and his family after the Flood, and therefore are the only commandments that apply to the entire human race. It is likely that in referring to the articles of Noah, Anderson is invoking this concept.[186]

As such, Anderson is making a profound statement about the Craft, one that speaks to every man "by whatever Names, Religions, or Persuasions they may be distinguish'd." To call Free-masons "Noachidæ" is a potent equalizer, in that it recognizes all non-Jewish religions ("Gentile" refers to any non-Jew), and simultaneously honors Judaism by using terms derived from that tradition. If the *Constitutions* meant to exclude any one religion, or to promote one over others, it would have done so explicitly. Instead, a concept was employed denoting true universality. It is quite brilliant, as it captures the cultural reality of Anderson's

184 See Genesis 6:10.

185 See Clorfene & Rogalsky, *Path of the Righteous Gentile*. This 1987 work is an excellent primer on the discipline, citing specific Talmudic references to explain the requirements of the righteous gentile.

186 See Eyer, "The Anchor and the Ark," and Murphy, "'Our Old Noachian Ark': Craft Masonry and the Traditions of Noah."

time and place—early eighteenty-century England as an over-whelmingly Christian land[187]— and encompasses a Masonic religiosity to the exclusion of none.

But when examining this Charge, it is critical to consider the 1735 letter from the Grand Secretary to the Provisional Grand Master in Calcutta. Therein is a description of a religious community, considered by the Grand Lodge as *Noachidæ*, following the teachings of Zoroastres, and practicing something recognizable in some way to English Brethren as Freemasonry. This knowledge must have been viewed as evidence of the belief, propagated by means of the Traditional History, that Freemasonry represents the manifestation of a hidden stream of secret teaching that has survived throughout the ages. But the Noachide belief espoused in the 1738 Charge may not exclusively be the product of what was revealed in the Grand Secretary's letter.

When the Chevalier Ramsay addressed the Craft in 1737, he gave a discourse on the nature and origin of the Fraternity. Throughout his speech, Ramsay compared Freemasonry to institutions of antiquity; in this context he avowed:

> Yes, sirs, the famous festivals of Ceres at Eleusis, of Isis in Egypt, or Minerva at Athens, or Urania amongst the Phoenicians, of Diana in Scythia were connected with ours. In those places mysteries were celebrated which concealed many vestiges of the ancient religion of Noah and the Patriarchs.[188]

This reference to the Masonic Institution having traces of the "ancient religion of Noah" clearly parallels the view of the Grand Lodge that a Zoroastrian community in Calcutta might—as Noachidæ—possess traits of "old Masonry." These ancient

187   See Shaftesley, "Jews in English Freemasonry," 25–63.
188   Ramsay, "Oration." In Gould, *History of Freemasonry*, 2:11.

fragments of an original, more pure form of human sacred knowledge could have been perceived as pointing to a common root for what Anderson deemed the "Religion in which all Men agree." It was this same sense that had informed the 1723 Charge, and was seen as reflected in the *ur*-Masonic, Noachide practices of India's Zoroastrians, and which is evident in the stream of perennialist teachings of the Craft.

The sixth Charge, second paragraph, relating to the "Behavior after the Lodge is closed and the Brethren not gone" still maintains the call for "innocent Mirth" and the prohibition of pushing a man "beyond his own Inclination" as in the 1723 edition.[189] To this, Anderson adds a Biblical justification, citing King Ahasuerus. According to the Book of Esther, chapter 1, King Ahasuerus held a great feast, with copious amounts of wine available for his royal guests. Esther 1:8 states, "And the drinking was according to the law; none did compel...." This Chapter and verse are cited in the genealogies presented in the Traditional History section, under the entry for Artaxerxes.[190]

Because fifteen years of Grand Lodge activity had passed between editions of his *Constitutions*, Anderson was obliged to update the several Regulations to reflect modifications made to them. Many of these are to further clarify the responsibilities of Grand Officers, in providing for quarterly assemblies and annual feasts, and naming which officers can fill vacancies pro tempore. There are Regulations that mandate the use of various colors in Lodge regalia: Grand Lodge officers are to wear gold jewels hung by blue ribbons, and have their aprons lined with blue silk; Masters and Wardens of Lodges are to use white ribbons by which to hang their jewels, and wear aprons of white silk; and Stewards have silver jewels hung from red ribbon, white rods,

189 Anderson, *New Book of Constitutions* (1738), 147.
190 Ibid., 23–24.

and aprons lined with red silk.[191] Regulation XIII notes that the jewel of the Grand Secretary is to be "two Golden Pens across on his Left Breast."[192]

Some modification was also made to Regulation VI, which had previously demanded unanimous ballots for initiation. In the new version of the same Regulation, a provision is added which allows a waiving of unanimity and the admission of a candidate if no more than three nay votes are cast, "although some Lodges desire no such Allowance."[193]

Clarity is also given with regard to clandestine lodges. If a Brother was found to have made Masons clandestinely, Regulation VIII disqualified him from visiting any lodge until he made amends. If a brother is made clandestinely, or is making Masons clandestinely, then he shall never be permitted to hold a Grand Office, nor to receive relief.[194]

An entirely new Regulation, XL, is added, which speaks to the "Decency of Assemblies and Communications."[195] Quiet and stillness is required, and anyone violating this expectation is "publickly reprimanded," with a third offence bringing dismissal from the Lodge for the evening.[196] Additionally, section 10 of this Regulation calls for quiet in times of voting, and defines what is commonly known today as the "voting sign of a Mason:" votes were "to be signified by each [Brother] holding up one of his Hands."[197]

The history of the Grand Lodge Committee on Charity follows. Of note, Charity is herein defined as being "for the Relief

191   Ibid., 153 & 167.
192   Ibid., 161.
193   Ibid., 155.
194   Ibid., 156–57.
195   Ibid., 176.
196   Ibid., 146–47.
197   Ibid., 178.

of distressed Brethren," as opposed to, for instance, charitable donations to non-Masons or to other relief organizations.[198] A list of Lodges "in and about London and Westminister," one hundred-six in all, is then provided, followed by a list of Deputations. Then follows an Approbation by Grand Master Darnley, and signed by other Grand Officers.

Featured next is a collection of songs. Many of these songs had been earlier printed in either the 1723 *Constitutions*, or the 1731 *Curious Collection* of songs attached to Cole's second edition (see above). Of note:

- The title "The Deputy Grand Master's Song" is given to the first of two songs credited to "Brother OATS" noted above in the 1731 collection.[199] Added to this is a new stanza by "Brother Goston" celebrating the expected child of Prince Friedrick Lewis, to whom the book is dedicated, and who was made a Mason the year prior. This new stanza wishes, "May a LEWIS be born, whom the World shall admire."[200] This is a clever bit of word play, as the son of the Prince would be named Lewis, matching the name of a stone worker's device used to lift ashlars. The term "Lewis" has come to be used to denote a brother who is also the son of a Mason. As such, Brother Goston may be credited with coining a Speculative meaning for this Operative tool.
- The title "The Grand Warden's Song" is given to an untitled, anonymous song from the 1731 *Curious Collection*.[201]
- The title "The Treasurer's Song" is given to an untitled, anonymous song from the 1731 collection.[202]

198 Ibid.
199 Ibid., 206.
200 Ibid., 207.
201 Ibid., 207–208. Compare *Curious Collection*, 28–30.
202 Ibid., 209. Compare *Curious Collection*, 39–40.

- A new song, entitled, "The Secretary's Song" is included.[203] Of this four-stanza song, the first and fourth celebrate the Craft and the Grand Master, while the middle two are in answer to an anti-Masonic essay by Nicholas Amhurst (writing under the pseudonym of Caleb D'Anvers).[204]
- The title "The Swordbearer's Song" is given to an untitled, anonymous song from the 1731 collection.[205]
- The title "An Ode to the Free Masons" is given to the "SONG in the *Generous Free Mason*" by Brother Oats.[206]
- Also included is "An Ode to Masonry" by J. Bancks. This Ode had been published the year before, in a proposal for subscriptions.[207] The 1737 version contained several footnotes, one including a definition of Freemasonry as "A famous Art, Science, or Mystery." Another offers a statement as to the esoteric intent of the work: "As our Author is a Brother of the Craft, and as such will be understood by every True Adept; so he desires every one who is not so, to look upon his Poem as they would upon the Rhapsodies of an ancient Priest, when treating of his Oracles, or the Secrets of his Religion. Every Word is to be accounted a Mystery in itself...."[208]

Also added to this edition is a reprint of the 1730 *Defence of Masonry*, and the pseudonymous 1738 "Brother EUCLID's *Letter to the Author* Against unjust Cavils."[209] Briefly, the 1730 *Defence* was written in response to *Masonry Dissected*, and includes a

203 Ibid., 210.
204 Crawley, "Contemporary Comments," 201–10.
205 Anderson, *New Book of Constitutions* (1738), 211–12. Compare *Curious Collection*, 31–32.
206 Ibid., 212. Compare *Curious Collection*, 17.
207 See Bancks, *Proposals*, 33–39.
208 Bancks, *Proposals*, 34.
209 Anderson, *New Book of Constitutions* (1738), 226–28.

point-by-point rebuttal to Pritchard's accusations regarding secrets and oaths. The *Defence* continues by tracing various Masonic elements found in the world's mystery traditions, such as
the Pythagoreans, Essenes, Cabalists, and Druids.

Brother Euclid's letter quickly dismisses accusations of devil
worship, misogyny, and jealously. It further helps to frame the
self-concept of Masonry at the time. The author names Freemasons as Noachidæ, speaks out against false brethren, and
dismisses accusations of drunkenness. The letter advises that
lodges treat in "the great Lessons of their old Religion, Morality,
Humanity and Friendship" and teach brethren "to abhor Persecution."[210]

The allonymous letter continues in stressing the importance
of gentlemanly conversation on important topics, which was a
common theme of Masonic literature of the period, and supported by many lodge minute books:

> Indeed, the *antient Lodges* were so many Schools or *Acad-
> emies* for teaching and improving the *Arts* of *Designing*,
> especially *Architecture*; and the present *Lodges* are often
> employ'd that Way in *Lodge-Hours*, or else in other agree-
> able Conversation, tho' without Politicks or Party Causes;
> and none of them are ill employ'd, have no Transactions
> unworthy of an honest Man or a Gentleman, no personal
> Picques, no Quarrels, no Cursing or Swearing, no cruel
> Mockings, no obscene Talk, nor ill Manners: For the *noble*
> and eminent *Brethren* are affable to the *Meanest*; and These
> are duly respectful to their Betters in *Harmony* and *Propor-
> tion*; and tho' on the *Level*, yet always within *Compass*, and
> according to the *Square* and *Plumb*.[211]

210 Ibid., 227.
211 Ibid., 228.

The letter is signed "Your true and faithful Brother Euclid," under which is a diagram of the 47th Proposition.[212]

This edition ends with a list of acknowledgements by the author, and list of Lodges. The 1738 *Constitutions* were reprinted in 1746, under the title *The History and Constitutions of the Most Ancient and Honourable Fraternity of Free and Accepted Masons.*[213]

212 Ibid.
213 Anderson, *History and Constitutions.*

Spratt's Constitutions, 1751

THE

NEW BOOK

OF

CONSTITUTIONS

OF THE

Most Antient and Honourable FRATERNITY of

FREE and ACCEPTED MASONS.

CONTAINING

Their History, Charges, Regulations, &c.

ALSO

Some RULES necessary to be observed

By the Committee of Charity, not Published before,

TOGETHER

with a Choice Collection of MASON's Songs, Poems, Prologues, and Epi-

logues, published by the Order, and with the Sanction of the

GRAND-LODGE.

COLLECTED

(From the Book of Constitutions Published in England

in the Year 1738, by our worthy Brother JAMES ANDERSON, D.D.)

For the Use of the LODGES in IRELAND.

By EDWARD SPRATT, Sec.

And the Light shineth in Darkness,

and the Darkness comprehended it not.

St. JOHN cap. 1 ver. 5.

DUBLIN:

Printed by EDWARD BATE in George's Lane, for the

EDITOR, and sold at his House, at the Sun in Nicholas-street, 1751.

Edward Spratt, the Grand Secretary of the Grand Lodge of Ireland, published a book of constitutions in 1751. This was largely a reproduction of Anderson's second edition. Just as Pennell two decades earlier had indicated parity in Irish and English Masonic practice by borrowing so liberally from the 1723 *Constitutions*, so too is Spratt reflecting the same parity, in the same manner.

In addition to notes drawn from Anderson, Spratt's *Constitutions* include other content, such as Pennell's prayer noted above. Spratt also included a song book with its own title page and own pagination. The collection included many songs already referenced herein, as well as two songs, and two epilogues;[214] these had been previously printed in a 1734 work entitled, *A Prologue, and an Epilogue. And Songs, Spoken and Sung To the Antient and Rt. Worshipful Society of Free-Masons, at the Theatre-Royal, on Thursday November the 29th, 1733, being Mr. GRIFFITH's Benefit.* Thomas Griffith, the beneficiary of that production, was an actor and poet who also worked as the first Grand Secretary of Ireland, serving from 1725 to 1732.[215]

Spratt's work features, perhaps for the first time, certain toasts affixed to familiar songs; for instance, following the "Enter'd Prentice's Song," the Brethren are instructed to toast "To all the worthy Fraternity round the Globe."[216]

There are also several seemingly new song editions, identified here by their first lines:

- XIX Song: "HAIL, sacred Art! by Heaven design'd."[217]
- XX Song: "COME as you prepar'd"; this is arranged in the

---

214 Spratt, *New Book*, 12, 13, 36 & 37.

215 J.M.K. MacAlpine, "The Entered Apprentice's Song and The Fellowcraft's Song." *Ars Quatuor Coronatorum* 109(1996): 244–45.

216 Spratt, "A Collection of Songs." In Spratt, *New Book*, 5.

217 Ibid., 19–20.

cadence of "The Enter'd Prentice's Song."[218]
- XXI Song: "The Curious vulgar could never devise."[219]
- XXII Song: "We brethren, Free-Masons, let's mark the great name."[220]
- XXVI Song: "Come, come my Brothers dear."[221]
- XXVII Song: "Come follow, follow me."[222]
- XXVII Song: "With plumb, level, and square, to work let's prepare."[223]
- XXIX: "King Solomon, that wise projecter."[224]
- XXXI: "To the science that virtue, and art do maintain."[225]
- XXXII, by Brother J—— C——: "When earth's foundation first was laid."[226]
- XXXIII Song: "Come, boys, let us more liquor get."[227]

218 Ibid., 20–21.
219 Ibid., 21–22.
220 Ibid., 22–23.
221 Ibid., 26–27.
222 Ibid., 27–28.
223 Ibid., 28–29.
224 Ibid., 29–30.
225 Ibid., 32–33.
226 Ibid., 34.
227 Ibid., 35.

Scott's Pocket Companion, 1754

THE

POCKET COMPANION

AND

HISTORY

OF

FREE-MASONS,

CONTAINING THEIR

Origine, Progress, and present State:

AN

ABSTRACT

OF

Their LAWS, CONSTITUTIONS, CUSTOMS,

CHARGES, ORDERS and REGULATIONS,

FOR THE

Instruction and Conduct of the Brethren:

A

CONFUTATION

OF Dr. Plot's False INSINUATIONS;

AN APOLOGY,

Occasioned by their PERSECUTION in the Canton

Of Berne, and in the POPE's Dominions:

And a select NUMBER of SONGS and other

PARTICULARS, for the USE of the SOCIETY

Per bonam famam et infamiam

LONDON:

Printed for J. SCOTT, at the Black-Swan, in Duck Lane, near
West-Smithfield, and Sold by R. BALDWIN, at the Rose in
Pater-Noster-Row M.DCC.LIV.

Scott's 1754 *Pocket Companion* carries all of the hallmarks of the other books covered by this survey: traditional history, charges, regulations, and songs.

The frontispiece for the volume was engraved by Louis-Philippe Boitard. The scene includes King Solomon, and to his right, Tyrian King Hiram. The attention of the kings is being directed by Hiram Abif to placards displayed by two craftsmen. One craftsman's plate reads, "The Constitutions of Masonry Universal," while the other man's plate outlines the number of workmen required to construct the Temple. Behind the scene, sits a Lodge room. The checkered pavement is illuminated by three burning tapers, as well as by the sun and moon perched upon pillars, and by a blazing star in the sky. In the center of the blazing star is the Hebrew letter ע, *ayin*. *Ayin* also translates to "eye," meaning that Boitard may have meant this as a representation of the All-Seeing Eye of Providence.[228]

Scott's telling of the Traditional History traces the same path as the Andersonian myth. In describing the Noachian covenant with the Great Architect, Scott includes a degree of specificity that may offer some clarity to what Anderson called the "3 great Articles of Noah." Scott writes:

> The first Thing [Noah] did upon his landing, was to build an Altar, and offer a burnt Sacrifice of every clean Beast and Fowl. God having accepted the Sacrifice, blessed Noah, and gave him Power over all living Creatures, with a Permission to eat them as freely as of the Produce of the Ground: However, he forbid him to eat the Blood of Animals, or to shed that of Man; ordering him to punish Manslaughter with Death, and to people the World as fast as he could.[229]

228 Eyer, "Exploration of Themes."
229 Scott, *Pocket Companion*, 9.

As mentioned above, traditionally, there are seven Noachide Laws. Of the four Divine commands mentioned by Scott, three have correspondence with the Noachide Laws, viz: do not consume blood, do not commit murder, and impose justice on those who commit murder, i.e. establish a system of justice; the fourth commandment to procreate does not have a match in any of the seven Noachide Laws. Even though Scott's *Pocket Companion* does not include the Noachide language in its Charge regarding God and religion, it does provide an interpretation of what Anderson—and all those who subsequently used his language—may have meant when referencing the three points of moral agreement among all Freemasons.

Interestingly, Scott is more reserved in referring to characters of the Traditional History as "Brother" than previous writers had been. With that said, he claimed a Masonic *bona fides* for some characters who had been overlooked by previous writers—Charlemagne and the architect and philosopher Leon Battista Alberti, being two examples. Additionally, Scott uses Masonic nomenclature to describe non-Masonic circumstances. For instance, he refers to Zoroastres as "Grand-Master of the Magians,"[230] he states that Pythagoras held a "Lodge of good Geometricians,"[231] and calls Caesar the "GRAND-MASTER of the Roman Republic."[232] This may have been Scott's way to indicate the polymorphic character of Freemasonry as viewed through a perennialist lens: namely, that even though the Craft did not always exist under that name, the teaching and practices of which it is comprised had always existed in a some approximate form.

Scott's Traditional History ends with a brief synopsis of the events under each of the Grand Masters from the Duke of Montagu to John Proby, Lord Carysfort. From there is given the history

230 Ibid., 36.
231 Ibid., 40.
232 Ibid., 50.

and laws of the Committee for Charity, the Charges, the Regulations with amendments listed by Grand Master, and list of "The GENTLEMEN, who have served the Office of STEWARDS to the SOCIETY of FREE and ACCEPTED MASONS, from 1728 to 1753."[233]

Next, Scott reprints Dr. Robert Plot's *An Account of the Free-Masons*, which had originally run in Plot's 1686 work, *The Natural History of Stafford-Shire*. This work has been extensively examined in the Masonic literature of the nineteenth and twentieth-centuries, and so an analysis is not required here. Suffice to say that Plot outlined some of the customs of the fraternity, and spoke of "a large Parchment Volume... Containing, the History and Rules of the Craft of Masonry"[234]—this was a copy of the Old Charges. Plot also levels accusatory and insulting language at the Craft, calling its Traditional History "false or incoherent"[235] to the highest degree and that assemblies of Masons cause "much Mischief."[236]

In response, Scott adds *A Detection of Dr. Plot's Account of the FREE-MASONS*. The text challenges Plot's

> rude and insipid Conjectures and Misrepresentations of the Free-Masons, to whose Foundation and History he was an absolute Stranger, are not more false and groundless, than his Conduct in that Affair was base, insidious and unworthy of any Writer who had the last Regard for the Truth....[237]

The *Detection* cites Elias Ashmole's membership in the fraternity as proof of its virtue, and calls Plot ungrateful for deriding

233 Ibid., 186.
234 Ibid., 193.
235 Ibid., 194.
236 Ibid., 196.
237 Ibid., 197.

Freemasonry while eating Ashmole's bread. With regard to establishing pedigree, the writer staunchly defends the St. Alban legend, citing the sixth-century works of Gildas the Wise, and the eighth-century works of Venerable Bede (just as Pennell did in 1730, and the Cooke MS had three centuries earlier). The text then turns to a defense of the Athelstane-Edwin legend, citing a variety of historical sources as evidence. To underscore these points, the Detector includes the Leland-Locke Pseudepigraphon; this document claimed to date to the time of Henry VI, but was ultimately determined to be a product of Masonic speculation dating not much earlier than 1753.[238] Ultimately, the *Detection* concludes, "…it is most certain, a Man of less Judgment, and more Credulity never lived than Dr. Plot."[239]

Next is reprinted *An Apology for the Free and Accepted Masons, Occassioned by their Persecution in the Canton of Berne, with the Present State of Masonry in Germany, Italy, France, Flanders and Holland*. The reproduced cover page states that the pamphlet was "translated from the FRENCH, by a Brother," and printed at Frankfort in 1748.[240] The pamphlet recounts the various governmental and religious edicts, assaults, and accusations leveled at the fraternity. What begins with a sense of annoyance and hurt, turns impassioned, as the writer cries out against the Inquisition:

> Dare they in a christian Country attack the Innocent in such a Manner as Barbarians would look upon with Horror! False Devotees accustom themselves to infuse into the

238 See Shawn Eyer's article in this volume for a discussion of this document relative to an American Masonic oration of 1734.
239 Scott, *Pocket Companion*, 236.
240 Ibid., 237. See Oliver, *Masonic Persecution*, 52. Oliver states that this pamphlet was printed earlier, in 1739 in Dublin, written by "J.G.D.M.F.M." The version reprinted in Scott is a revised version of the original, as it contains referenced to events which occur later than 1739.

> Minds of the credulous Multitude a baseful Poison against every Thing that they imagine may affect their Reveries, and particularly against the moral Virtues, which they only know by Theory....[241]

In answer, the author extolls the virtues of Freemasonry, "the Daughter of Heaven," counting the ways in which it appeals to men of honor and intellect, and stating unequivocally that its enemies are beneath the Craft.[242] Yet ultimately, the writer ends with a prayer, asking God to "pardon and forgive our Enemies... and take from them those fatal Prejudices with which they bar their Breasts against the Force of Truth, and fortify themselves in Darkness, Ignorance and Falsehood...."[243]

Next are two well-known Masonic orations: Martin Clare's address from December 11, 1735, and Charles Brockwell's sermon in Boston from the Feast of St. John the Evangelist, 1749. Both of these works have been reproduced multiple times, making a review of them in this present work unnecessary. Briefly, however, each speaks to a level of refinement and expectation of excellence inherent in the Craft, and shared by Freemasons. Each is an excellent example of Masonic oratory, and worthy of attention.[244] Echoing the same lessons is a Charge delivered by Isaac Head on April 21, 1752, which follows Brockwell's sermon. Head's Charge calls for virtuous and generous conduct, and admonishments against swearing and drunkenness. He also calls for divine inspiration through "our holy Brother the Apostle

241 Ibid., 278.
242 Ibid., 272.
243 Ibid., 281.
244 For more on Clare's oration, see Eyer, "Inward Civility," 58–63; see also Eyer, "Discourse on Good Behavior," 64–67.

Paul"[245] and that "Piece of Divine Furniture," the Holy Bible.[246] In addition to Head's Charge, Scott also includes the "Short Charge" for the newly initiated, from Smith's 1735 *Pocket Companion.*

Next, three prayers are featured. One of these mirrors the prayer featured in Pennell's *Constitutions* (1730), and another is billed as "A PRAYER to be used of Christian Masons at the empointing of a Brother: Used in the Reign of Edward IV."[247] If this point of reference is accurate, then the prayer would date to the late 1400s. While some manuscripts have similarly-phrased opening prayers, one of the closest matches is found in the Dowlands MS of 1600:

> Scott, 1754
> THE mighty God and Father of Heaven, with the Wisdom of his glorious Son, through the Goodness of the Holy Ghost, that hath been three Persons in one Godhead, be with us at our Beginning, give us Grace to govern in our living here, that we may come to his Bliss that shall never have an End.[248]

> Dowlands MS, c. 1600
> THE might of the Father of Kings, with the wisdome of his glorious Son, through the grace of the goodness of the Holy Ghost, there bene three persons in one Godheade, be with us at our beginning, and give us grace so to governe us here in this mortall life liveinge, that wee may come to his kingdome that never shall have endinge. Amen.[249]

245 Ibid., 301.
246 Ibid., 306.
247 Ibid., 309.
248 Ibid.
249 Hughan, *Old Charges*, 25.

Lastly, thirteen songs are offered. Of the collection, only three have not been otherwise been covered in this survey:

- Song x is credited to Brother Oates, and begins, "TIS Masonry unites Mankind, To generous Actions form the Soul."[250]
- Song xi begins, "When a Lodge of Free-Masons, are cloath'd in their Aprons", and is written to match the cadence of the Enter'd Prentices Song.[251]
- "An ODE on MASONRY" is credited to Brothers Jackson and Gilding, and begins, "Wake the Lute and quiv'ring Strings, Mystic Truths Urania brings."[252]

250 Scott, *Pocket Companion*, 323–24.
251 Ibid., 324–26.
252 Ibid., 326–27.

Dermott's Ahiman Rezon, 1756

AHIMAN REZON:

OR,

A Help to a Brother;

Shewing the

EXCELLENCY of SECRECY,

And the first Cause, or Motive, of the Institution of

FREE-MASONRY;

THE PRINCIPLES of the CRAFT,

And the Benefits arising from a strict Observance thereof;

What Sort of MEN ought to be initiated into the MYSTERY,

And what Sort of MASONS are fit to govern LODGES,

With their Behavior in and out of the Lodge.

Likewise the Prayers used in the *Jewish* and *Christian* Lodges,

The Ancient Manner of

Constituting new Lodges, with all the Charges, &c.

Also the

OLD and NEW REGULATIONS,

The Manner of Chusing and Installing *Grand-Master* and *Officers*,

and other useful Particulars too numerous here to mention.

To which is added

The greatest Collection of MASONS SONGS ever presented to

public View, with any entertaining PROLOGUES and EPILOGUES;

Together with

SOLOMON'S TEMPLE an ORATORIO,

As it was performed for the Benefit of

FREE-MASONS.

By Brother LAURENCE DERMOTT, Sec.

LONDON:

Printed for the EDITOR, and sold by Brother *James Bedford,* at the

Crown in St. *Paul's* Church-Yard.

MDCCLVI

Much has been written about the development of the Grand
Lodge of the Antients. Whether it was a result of Irish brethren
being excluded from English Lodges when traveling, the Premier
Grand Lodge reversing vital elements of the first and second
degrees, disagreement over the role of the Royal Arch degree, or
some combination of these factors and others, in 1751 a Grand
Lodge was formed, that would stand as a bitter rival to the Premier "Moderns" Grand Lodge for the next six decades.

Arguably the most vocal and influential member of the Antients' Grand Lodge was Secretary Laurence Dermott (1720–1791).
In 1756, five years after the formal creation of the Antients' Grand
Lodge, Dermott published his Grand Lodge's first book of constitutions, *Ahiman Rezon*.[253] The purpose of this book was for the
edification of the Brethren about the quality of the Craft, and of the
men seeking admission therein. The title page makes this clear, as
does the statement in the first sentence of the Dedication: "wherein I have endeavored to let the young Brethren know how they
ought to conduct their Actions, with Uprightness, Integrity, Morality, and Brotherly Love, still keeping the ancient Land-Marks
in View."[254]

The message from Dermott to the Reader contains, on the
face of it, the story of Dermott's doomed attempt to write a
Traditional History.[255] He meets his goals despite, superficially,
missing the mark. In fact, Dermott is masking his true message
within a meta-context. First, he excuses his academic shortcom-
ings by explaining that he is of low birth, and wishes he could
aspire to the heights reached by greater men of similar origin.
In offering some thirty-two specific examples of learned men

253 The title of the book, *Ahiman Rezon*, combines two Hebrew names
     from the Bible: אחימן from 1 Chronicles 9:17 and רזון from 1 Kings
     11:23. Dermott features Ahiman as a character in his fascinating
     "The Editor to the Reader" (v–xvii).
254 Dermott, *Ahiman Rezon* (1756), [i].
255 Ibid., v–xvii.

from low birth, from throughout time and area of distinction, Dermott actually demonstrates his own academic acumen. Of course, this is done purposefully. This same method is used in delivering his Traditional History.

Dermott states that in order to be best inspired, and best informed, he surrounds himself with the works of numerous Masons, identifying the books by each author's name. He references Anderson, Spratt, Smith, Pennell, and Scott, all of whom authored works covered in this survey. He names Desaguliers, the Past Grand Master. He references Dr. Fifield D'Assigny, the Irish Mason who wrote at least three Masonic treatises, *An Answer to the Pope's Bull; With the Character of a Free Mason* (1738), *An Impartial Answer to the Enemies of Free-Masonry* (1741), and *A Serious and Impartial Enquiry in to the Cause of the present Decay of Free-Masonry in the Kingdom of Ireland* (1744). Dermott also makes reference to having two sets of the Old Charges, and a "Pamphlet printed at Frankfort"[256] which is the *Apology for the Free and Accepted Masons* printed in Scott's *Pocket Companion*. Dermott wrapped all of these materials "in the *Public Advertiser* of Friday, October 19, 1753, and threw them under the Table"[257]—the particular newspaper to which he refers included a printing of the Leland-Locke Pseudepigraphon (inaccurately cited by some scholars as the Leland MS), which features an alleged Masonic catechism dating to the time of King Henry VI. This text had also appeared in Scott.

Among the various Masonic authors Dermott looked to for inspiration is a name that does not align with any known Masonic text of the time: "Lyon." There is, for instance, no mention of a "Lyon" in *The Rare Books of Freemasonry* (1923), by Lionel Vibert, FPS. Also, in Vibert's entry on *Ahiman Rezon*, he cites Dermott's "references to the current histories of the Craft with allusions

256 Ibid., vii.
257 Dermott, *Ahiman Rezon* (1756), vii.

to other works, not all of which can now be traced;"[258] Vibert must be speaking of "Lyon." William John Chetwode Crawley proposed that "Lyon" was an anglicized version of "Leon," as in Rabbi Jacob Jehuda Leon.[259] Crawley rightly identified that the work of Rabbi Leon, particularly his analysis of King Solomon's Temple had a great impact on Dermott. In his comments on Crawley's paper on Leon, William James Hughan concurs that Lyon and Leon are one and the same, noting at least one publication, a 1778 reprint of Leon's work on the Temple, was credited to "Jacob Luda Lyon."[260]

Dermott reports having written a more detailed history of Masonry than had ever before been committed to paper. Not only did his history include Adam and his progeny, but looked to earlier times, speaking of Milton's *Paradise Lost* as a tale of the first Grand Lodge formed in heaven, and the expulsion of "unruly Members."[261] Exhausted from his labor, Dermott falls asleep, and awakes to find that a dog has eaten his manuscript. What Dermott offers, instead, are the details of his dream, wherein he was visited by four strangers. Despite speaking in a different language than he, Dermott "immediately answered them after the Pantomime Fashion,"[262] thereby alluding to the Freemason's faculty.[263] One of the figures, Ahiman, identifies the quartet as head porters at King Solomon's Temple, and can therefore give Dermott an account of the building of that magnificent edifice. Ahiman also informs Dermott that his history has only superficially captured the depth of the Craft. A fifth figure, clad in the jeweled breast plate of a High Priest of the Israelites, approach-

258   Vibert, *Rare Books*, 17.
259   Crawley, "Rabbi Jacob Jehudah Leon," 150–163.
260   Crawley, "Rabbi Jacob Jehudah Leon," 159.
261   Dermott, *Ahiman Rezon* (1756), vii.
262   Ibid., x–xi.
263   See Anderson, *Constitutions* (1723), 5.

es Dermott, and—after reading Dermott's draft history of the
Craft—intones, "Thou hast div'd deep in the Water, and hast
brought up a Potsherd."[264] The Priest continues, identifying some
Old Testament characters as Masons, while stating that most
figures who had been given that title in earlier writing were, in
actuality, "Strangers to the secret Mystery of Masonry."[265] The
Priest leaves Dermott with the following words:

> If thou be made the Master, lift not thyself up, but be among
> them as one of the rest: Take diligent Care for them, and so
> sit down. And when thou hast done all thy Duty, sit down,
> that thou mayst be merry with them; and receive a Crown
> for thy good Behavior. Speak thou that art the elder, for
> it becometh thee; but with sound Judgment: And hinder
> not Music. And at all Times let thy Garments be White.[266]

And so, by not giving a standard telling of the Traditional
History, Dermott is able to tell a richer version of the same. Freemasonry retains its polymorphic and perennialist foundation—
the Priest says, "Certain it is … that Free-Masonry has been from
the Creation (though not under that Name)"[267]—while making
the Craft more rarefied by eschewing the over-embellishment of
other versions of the myth.

The first chapter is entitled, "The Excellency of Secrecy," and
Dermott reinforces the absolute necessity of this virtue. He does
so by offering various examples of how secrecy has been employed among the ancients. He shares the story of Papirius, son
of a Roman Senator, who withstood threats and violence from
his mother after she learned that he was privy to the secrets of

264 Dermott, *Ahiman Rezon* (1756), xiii–xiv.
265 Ibid., xv.
266 Ibid. Citing Wisdom of Sirach 32:1–3 and Ecclesiastes 9:8.
267 Ibid., xiv.

the Senate. Dermott relates the tale of Anaxarchus, who bit out his own tongue and spat it at his enemies rather than disclose his secret knowledge. The Roman goddess Angerona, and her Greek god counterpart Harpocrates, deities of secrecy and silence, are invoked in the text. The Pythagorean practice of obliging Initiates to seven years of silence, as well as King Solomon's admonition to avoid wine, as "Drunkenness is the enemy of Secrecy,"[268] are also referenced by Dermott. All of this is to underscore the concept present in the Antients' Grand Lodge that the mysteries of Masonry were safely lodged in the faithful breast.

Ahiman Rezon abounds with praises of Freemasonry, all reflecting Masonic self-concept. Dermott asserts that "the Welfare and Good of mankind was the Cause or Motive of so grand an Institution as Free-Masonry," and cites "true Religion, Morality, and Virtue" as "Precepts of the Royal Art."[269] He promises "our Privileges and Instructions, when rightly made Use of, are not only productive of our Welfare in this Side of the Grave, but even our eternal Happiness hereafter."[270] Along this same theme, Dermott calls Masonry "the most sovereign Medicine to purge" out sin and vice, and that "regular Lodges" are "the only Seminaries where Men...may hear, understand, and learn their Duty to God; and also to their Neighbors."[271]

Much of what remains of Dermott's first chapter is a recapitulation of the Charges found in Anderson. Primary among these are an assertion of religious pluralism, admonishments to be peaceable citizens, selecting officers based on merit, and stating expectations of behavior both in and out of Lodge. This then leads into a reprinting of the same charges as were found in Anderson's

268 Ibid., 8. Referencing Proverbs 31:4–5.

269 Ibid., 10.

270 Dermott, *Ahiman Rezon* (1756), 17; this phrase is borrowed from D'Assigny, *Impartial Enquiry*. In Williams *&* Cerza, *D'Assigny*, 40.

271 Ibid., 23.

1738 *Constitutions.* Next is a reprinting of the "Short Charge" featured in Smith's 1735 *Pocket Companion.* To the admonition not to neglect one's "necessary Avocations for the Sake of Masonry," Dermott notes that a Mason should "not belong to a Number of Lodges at one Time, nor run from Lodge to Lodge."[272] A description of the "Antient Manner of Constituting a Lodge" follows the other examples noted in previous books of constitutions.

Dermott next includes three prayers that may be said in Lodge, as well as a fourth that is meant to be recited at a Royal Arch Lodge. The first prayer is to be "used by Jewish Free-Masons:"

> O Lord, excellent art thou in thy Truth, and there is nothing great in Comparison to thee; for thine is the Praise, from all the Works of thy Hands, for evermore.
>
> ENLIGHTEN us, we beseech thee, in the true Knowledge of Masonry: By the Sorrows of Adam, thy first made Man; by the Blood of Abel, thy holy one; by the Righteousness of Seth, in whom thou art well pleased; and by thy Covenant with Noah, in whose Architecture thou was't pleased to save the Seed of thy beloved; number us not among those that know not thy Statutes, nor the divine Mysteries of the secret Cabbala.
>
> But grant, we beseech thee, that the Ruler of this Lodge may be endued with Knowledge and Wisdom, to instruct us and explain his secret Mysteries, as our holy Brother Moses did (in his Lodge) to Aaron, to Eleazar and Ithamar, (the Sons of Aaron, and the seventy Elders of Israel.
>
> And grant that we may understand, learn, and keep all the Statutes and Commandments of the Lord, and his holy Mystery, pure and undefiled unto our Lives End. Amen, Lord.[273]

272 Ibid., 37.
273 Ibid., 43.

Obviously, this prayer evokes the characters of the Hebrew Bible feature in the Traditional History. But this prayer was not the invention of Dermott, at least not entirely. Compare it with this prayer found in a mid-fourth-century manuscript known as the *Arabick Catena* (or "Arabic Extracts"):

> O Lord, excellent art thou in thy truth, and there is nothing great in comparison of thee. Look upon us with the eie of Mercy and compassion, Deliver us from this deluge of waters, and set our feet in a larger Room. By the sorrows of Adam thy first made Man, By the blood of Abel thy holy one, By the Righteousness of Seth in whom thou art well pleased, Number us not among those who have transgressed thy Statutes, but take us into thy mercifull care: for thou art our Deliverer, and thine is the praise from all the works of thy hands for evermore.[274]

According to the manuscript, this prayer was said aboard the Ark by Noah and his sons, as they daily prayed before their cargo, the sarcophagus of their Patriarch Adam. By utilizing such a prayer, Freemasons are invoking the spirit of the Noachidæ, and claiming that spirit as their own, thereby connecting themselves in a practical way with their own mythic history.

The next prayer offered by Dermott was to be "used amongst the primitive Christian Masons," and is clearly modeled on the opening invocation found in many of the Old Charges. In noting the similarity between this prayer and one from Calcott (1769), Wallace McLeod, FPS, notes that both prayers are likely derived from a document dating to c. 1680, known as the Embleton MS, which is part of the Sloan family of Old Charges.[275]

The last prayer comes from a tradition noted in the Hebrew

274 See Gregory, *Notes and Observations*, 120.
275 McLeod, *Candid Disquistion*, 23.

Mishna, and was reported to have been said "in the Royal Arch Lodge at Jerusalem;"[276] it is titled the *Ahabath Olam*. This prayer is taken from the Jewish evening prayer service, the *Maariv*. From here, Dermott makes a plain statement about the Royal Arch Degree, which he calls "the Root, Heart, and Marrow of Free-Masonry:"[277] No Brother can become a true Royal Arch Mason without first serving as the Master of his Lodge. Any brothers initiating men into the Royal Arch in any other manner are likened to a "Heap of Miscarriages."[278] He then goes on to cite D'Assigny as the authority behind the true prerequisites for candidates to this degree. Embedded within Dermott's statements relative to the Royal Arch is a lesson about how Brethren ought to treat each other. Dermott makes these statements in response to one particular Mason's practice of exalting unqualified men to the degree of the Holy Royal Arch. Despite how incensed Dermott is at this practice, he does not identify the offending brother. In choosing not to name names, Dermott demonstrates that he is both subduing his passions, and expressing brotherly love for this wayward brother.

Dermott then prints the Regulations, new and old, and the Regulations for Charity "As practiced in Ireland and by York-Masons in England."[279] Next is a collection of sixty songs, with more than a third of those perhaps never having been printed before. Space constraints preclude even a brief summary or analysis of each; however, these songs cover the wide variety already seen in this survey, from self-celebratory songs to songs dismissive of anti-Masonic sentiment, from mystic, heady songs to rollicking drinking anthems. The songs not already discussed herein are noted by first line, with title and/or author when noted:

276 Dermott, *Ahiman Rezon* (1756), 46.
277 Ibid., 47.
278 Ibid., 48.
279 Ibid., 89.

- xxii, "What tho' they call us Masons fools."[280]
- xxxv, Progress of Masonry, "Pray lend me your Ears my dear Brethren awhile."[281]
- xxxvi, by Laurence Dermott, "As Masons once on Shinar's Plain."[282]
- xxxvii, Dermott, "With Harmony and flowing Wine." [283]
- xxxviii, Dermott, "Ye ancient sons of Tyre."[284]
- xxxix, "From the Depths let us raise."[285]
- xl, "Tis Masonry that unites Mankind."[286]
- xli, by Alexander Kennedy, schoolmaster, "Once I was blind and I cou'd not see."[287]
- xlii, Kennedy, "Attend loving Brethren and to me give Ear."[288]
- xliii, by John Jackson, "See in the East the Master plac'd."[289]
- xliv, by John Cartwright, "Attend, attend the Strains."[290]
- xlv, Cartwright, "To Masonry your voices raise."[291]
- xlvi, Cartwright, "Bless'd be the Day that gave to me."[292]

280 Ibid., 124–25.
281 Ibid., 144–48.
282 Ibid., 148–50.
283 Ibid., 151–52.
284 Ibid., 152–53.
285 Ibid., 153–56.
286 Ibid., 157–58.
287 Ibid., 158–60.
288 Ibid., 160–62.
289 Ibid., 162–63.
290 Ibid., 163–64.
291 Ibid., 164–66.
292 Ibid., 166 67.

- XLVII, by Alexander Dixon, "How bless'd are we from Igno-rance free'd."[293]
- XLVIII, by E.P., "Come fill up a Bumper, and let it go round."[294]
- XLIX, "Urania sing the Art divine, Beauty, Strength, and Wis-dom grace each line." Note that this song quotes the *Arabick Catena* MS cited above.[295]
- LVII, "Hail! MASONRY divine."[296]
- LIII, "Let Masons be merry each Night when they meet."[297]
- LIV, "If Unity be good in every Degree."[298]
- LV, "How happy a Mason whose Bosom still flows."[299]
- LVI, "When Masonry by Heaven's Design."[300]
- LVII, "Let worthy Brethren all combine."[301]
- LIX, "With cordial Hearts lets drink a Health."[302]
- LIX, "Whoever wants Wisdom, must with some Delight."[303]

One theory as to the impetus for the formation of the Antients' Grand Lodge was the religious universality that marked the Pre-mier Grand Lodge. The argument follows that the Antients, as part of their adherence to older Masonic practice, objected to a supposed process of the de-Christianization of Freemasonry, and the admission of men regardless of "whatever Denomina-

---

293 Ibid., 167–70.
294 Ibid., 170–71.
295 Ibid., 171–74.
296 Ibid., 177–78.
297 Ibid., 178–79.
298 Ibid., 179.
299 Ibid., 180.
300 Ibid., 180–81.
301 Ibid., 181–82.
302 Ibid., 183–84.
303 Ibid., 185.

tions or Persuasions they may be distiguish'd."[304] However, if a rejection of religious universality contributed to the formation of the Antients Grand Lodge, supporting evidence seems quite absent from *Ahiman Rezon*. In fact, there is ample evidence within Dermott's book to suggest that the Antients agreed with and accommodated religious diversity.

The most striking piece of evidence is the fact that Dermott used Anderson's own wording for the charge regarding God and Religion.[305] If Anderson's words in this Charge were seen as embracing religious pluralism, then their appearance in *Ahiman Rezon* would carry the same connotation. In other words, the Premier Grand Lodge and the Antient Grand Lodge had the same regulation as to religious universality. Elsewhere, Dermott borrows, almost exactly, the language of Fifield D'Assingy's 1744 *Serious and Imparial Enquiry*:

> A Mason is obliged by his tenure, to believe firmly in the true worship of the Eternal God, as well as in all those sacred Records which the Dignitaries and Fathers of the Church have compiled and published for the Use of all good Men: So that no one who rightly understands the Art, can possibly tread in the irreligious Paths of the unhappy Libertine, or be induced to follow the arrogant Professors of Atheism or Deism....[306]

If one were tempted to see Christian bias in Dermott here, note that the only place in which Dermott has altered D'Assingy's text is where the earlier writer describes the "sacred records

---

304 Anderson, *Constitutions* (1723), 50.

305 Compare Dermott, *Ahiman Rezon* (1756), 25–26 to Anderson, *New Book of Constitutions* (1738), 144–44. Stylistic differences are present, but they in no way affect the meaning of the charge.

306 Dermott, *Ahiman Rezon* (1756), 14; cf. D'Assingy, *A Serious and Imparial Enquiry* (1744), 14.

which the dignitaries, fathers, *and apostles* of the church have compiled and published for the use *of christians*."[307] Dermott has shortened this statement to recommend "sacred Records which the Dignitaries and Fathers of the Church have compiled and published for the Use of *all good Men*."[308] This revision would not have been made were Dermott attempting to promote the exclusion of non-Christian Masons.

There are other statements that support this observation. For instance, Dermott acknowledges that Masons "are not all of the same Opinion in Matters of Faith, yet they are ever in one Mind in Matters of Masonry."[309] Additionally, *Ahiman Rezon* features the 1735 Charge featured in Smith, stating, "religious disputes are never mentioned within the Lodge, for as Masons we only pursue the universal Religion, or the Religion of Nature; this is the Cement which unites the most different Principles in one sacred Band."[310] Moreover, that Dermott included a prayer for a Jewish Lodge should dismiss any idea that the Antients thought Masonry was meant for Christians only, and this is only underscored by the use of an additional Jewish prayer, the *Ahabath Olam*, for what was, in Dermott's view, the pinnacle of Freemasonry.

Conclusions

The nine works addressed in this survey span the first four decades of the Grand Lodge era. As these works were official Grand Lodge publications, written for Grand Lodges, or were adopted by the early Grand Lodges, they represent the Masonic mainstream of the time. It follows, therefore, that these books also lay

307 D'Assingy, *Enquiry* (1744), 14; emphasis added.
308 Dermott, *Ahiman Rezon* (1756), 14; emphasis added.
309 Dermott, *Ahiman Rezon* (1756), 17.
310 Ibid., 36.

the foundation for the Craft in contemporary times.

As noted above, the myth of the "Old Charges" credited the creation of Masonry to the children of Lamech. When James Anderson undertook to compile a "Book from the old Records,"[311] he looked to sources that predated the extrabiblical stories that inspired the medieval Traditional History. By researching such works as those of the first-century writer Flavius Josephus, Anderson found the seeds of an older myth, one that anchored the Craft in the lore of far more distant antiquity.

This Andersonian version of the Traditional History, tells of the Almighty creating the first man with Geometry on his heart, and is the tale that was carried forth throughout the first century of the Grand Lodge era. This mythic origin shaped Masonic self-concept in the decades and centuries that followed, and established the fraternity's view of the Craft as a divinely-sourced manifestation of perennialism—a stream of secret, sacred teachings that was coeval with creation itself. This myth was given to each new brother, thereby underscoring the importance and sincerity with which these early Masons regarded their own mythos. Contemporary students of the fraternity seeking to understand Freemasonry would be well advised, therefore, to consider the Traditional History with the same sincerity.

If the Traditional History captures the self-concept of the fraternity, then the Charges reflect their philosophical orientation. The religious and political universality, combined with the egalitarian attitudes toward socioeconomic class, are all represented within these Charges. Also addressed are the basic expectations for behavior. But even the behavioral expectations illustrate the sincere approach of early Masons; serious intent requires serious conduct, and virtuous aims require virtuous attempts.

Also germane are the administrative Regulations listed within these works. These outlined how things were done within

311   Anderson, *Constitutions* (1723), [iv].

Masonic governance. Researchers and participant-scholars alike can find the early traces of Masonic practices that are ubiquitous today. For instance, today's "voting sign of a Mason" and the jewel distinguishing the office of Secretary each trace to the regulations first printed in 1738. Because of this fact, the Regulations have great historical value, as they allow researchers to identify when practices entered into Masonic usage. These encapsulate the praxis of the Craft, which is just as important as the belief and self-concept of the Craft.

In *Ahiman Rezon*, Dermott wrote of his vision, saying that he was instructed to "Hinder not music."[312] This seems to not have been an issue, judging by the proliferation of Masonic music in the four decades covered in this survey. Beginning with the four songs featured in the 1723 *Constitutions*, and growing to the sixty songs of the 1756 *Ahiman Rezon*, the Brethren of the first half of the eighteenth-century found music, the sixth of the Liberal Arts and Sciences, to be a natural outlet for the inspiration engendered by the fraternity. Some of these songs reiterated the fraternity's mythic context; some celebrated the virtues of the Craft; some were odes to Deity; some were boisterous anthems; and some decried the enemies of the fraternity. The number and varieties of these songs reflect how widely spread the practice of singing was amongst Masons and their Lodges.

The works of Anderson, Pennell, Cole, Smith, Spratt, Scott, and Dermott all capture the practice and beliefs of early Freemasons. Indeed, along with ritual and the Masonic speeches and sermons of the time, there is no better source for understanding the authentic ideology of the early Grand Lodge era. Given this, we may reflect on the words of Freemason H.L. Haywood, FPS. In a 1921 work, Haywood remarked that "there is no authorized interpretation of Freemasonry" and that one must "think Masonry out for himself."

312   Dermott, *Ahiman Rezon* (1754), xv.

Haywood continued:

> But to think Masonry out for one's self is no easy task. It requires that one can see it in its own large perspectives; that one knows the main outlines of its history; that one knows it as it actually is, and what it is doing; and that one knows it as it has been understood by its own authentic interpreters and prophets.[313]

By examining the books of constitutions and pocket companions covered within this survey, the student of Freemasonry can begin identifying the essential themes of the Fraternity in the early eighteenth-century. Through the works of the "authentic interpreters and prophets," Masonry's "own large perspectives" are revealed. By this process, a deeper understanding of the intent, self-concept, and practice of Freemasonry is achieved, whereby one is able to "think Masonry out for himself."

Bibliography

Acaster, E. John T. "The Special Significance of the Quatuor Coronati in Relation to Modern Freemasonry." *Ars Quatuor Coronatorum* 127(2014): 1–24.

Anderson, James. *The Constitutions of the Freemasons, Containing the History, Charges, Regulations, &c. of that most Ancient and Right Worshipful Fraternity.* London: William Hunter, 1723.

———. *The Constitutions of the Freemasons. Containing the History, Charges, Regulations, &c. of that most Ancient and Right Worshipful Fraternity.* Philadelphia: Benjamin Franklin, 1734.

———. *The History and Constitutions of the Most Ancient and Honourable Fraternity of Free and Accepted Masons.* London: J. Rob-

313 Haywood, *Great Teachings*, 14.

inson, 1746.

———. *The New Book of Constitutions of the Antient and Honourable Fraternity of Free and Accepted Masons, Containing Their History, Charges, Regulations, &c.* London: Richard Chandler, 1738.

Anonymous. *A Curious Collection of the Most Celebrated Songs in Honour of Masonry.* London: B. Creake, 1731.

———. *A Prologue, and an Epilogue, and Songs, Spoken and Sung to the Antient and Rt. Worshipful Society of Free-Masons, at the Theatre-Royal, on Thursday November the 29th, 1733, being Mr. GRIFFITH's Benefit.* Dublin: Geo. Faulkner, 1734.

Bancks, Jonathan. *Proposals for Printing by Subscription, Miscellaneous Works, in Verse and Prose, of Mr. John Bancks.* London: Mr. Ares's Printing House, 1737.

Calcott, Wellins. *A Candid Disquisition of the Principles and Practices of the Most Ancient and Honourable Society of Free and Accepted Masons.* London: Brother James Dixwell, 1769.

Cherry, Martin. "Illustrations of Masonry: The Frontispieces of the Book of Constitutions, 1723–1819." In John Wade, Ed., *Reflections on 300 Years of Freemasonry.* London: Lewis Masonic, 2017.

Claret, George. *The Whole of Craft-Freemasonry.* London: G. Claret, 1860.

Clorfene, Chaim & Rogalsky, Yakov. *Path of the Righteous Gentile.* Southfield, Michigan: Targum Press, 1987.

Cole, Benjamin. *The Antient Constitutions of the Free and Accepted Masons, Neatly Engrav'd On Copper Plates.* London: B. Creake, 1731.

Crawley, W. J. Chetwode. "Contemporary Comments on the Freemasonry of the Eighteenth Century." *Ars Quatuor Coronatorum* 18 (1905): 201–216.

———. "The Masonic MSS in the Bodleian Library." *Ars Quatuor Coronatorum* 11 (1898): 4–44.

———. "The Old Charges and the Papal Bulls." *Ars Quatuor Coronatorum* 14 (1911): 47–64.

———. "Rabbi Jacob Jehudah Leon." *Ars Quatuor Coronatorum* 12

(1899): 150–63.

————. "Wheeler's Lodge." *Ars Quatuor Coronatorum* 14 (1901): 205–10.

Cross, Jeremy Ladd. *The True Masonic Chart: Or Hieroglyphic Monitor.* New Haven, Conn.: T.G. Woodward & Co., 1826.

D'Assigny, Fifield. *A Serious and Impartial Enquiry into the Cause of the Present Decay of Free-Masonry in the Kingdom of Ireland.* Dublin: Edward Bate, 1744.

Dermott, Laurence. *Ahiman Rezon: Or, A Help to a Brother.* London: James Bedford, 1756.

[Drake, Francis]. *A Speech Deliver'd to the Worshipful and Ancient Society of Free and Accepted Masons.* London: B. Creake, 1734.

Eyer, Shawn. "An Exploration of Themes Expressed in the Frontispieces of Early Masonic Literature, 1723 to 1775." Unpublished paper.

————. "A Discourse on Good Behaviour for the Guidance of the Members of the Craft." *Philalethes: The Journal of Masonic Research and Letters* 69 (2016): 64–67.

————. "Drake's Oration of 1726." *Philalethes: The Journal of Masonic Research and Letters* 67 (2014): 14–25.

————. "The Anchor and the Ark: Symbols of Faith, Hope and the Persistence of Tradition." *Philalethes: The Journal of Masonic Research and Letters* 64 (2011): 35–38.

————. "The Inward Civility of the Mind: The 1735 Grand Oration of Martin Clare, F.R.S." *Philalethes: The Journal of Masonic Research and Letters* 69 (2016): 58–63.

Farmer, Peter. *A New Model for the Rebuilding of Masonry on a Stronger Basis Than the Former.* London: J. Wilford, 1730.

Gregory, John. *Notes and Observations Upon Some Passages of Scripture.* 2nd ed. London: R.C., 1650.

Gould, Robert. *Gould's History of Freemasonry Throughout the World.* New York: Charles Scribner's Sons, 1936.

————. *The History of Freemasonry.* New York: Yorston & Co., 1885.

Hamill, J. M. "Masonic History and Historians." *Ars Quatuor Corona-*

torum 100 (1986): 1–8.

Haywood, H.L. *The Great Teachings of Masonry*. Enlarged Edition. Richmond, Virginia: Macoy, 1986.

Head, Isaac. *A Confutation of the Observations on Free Masonry By an Anonymous Author of a Pamphlet, Entitled Masonry the Way to Hell.* Exeter: A Brice and B. Thorn, 1769.

Hextall, William. "Wheeler's Lodge." *Ars Quatuor Coronatorum* 22 (1909): 219-220.

Hughan, William James. *The Old Charges of British Freemasons*. London: Simpkin, Marshall & Co., 1872.

Hunt, Charles Clyde. *Masonic Concordance*. Cleveland: World Publishing Company, 1948.

Jones, Stephen. *Masonic Miscellanies, In Poetry and Prose*. London: Vernor & Hood, 1797.

Knoop, Douglas, G.P. Jones & G. Hamer, Eds. *Early Masonic Pamphlets*. London: Quatuor Coronati, 1978.

———. *The Two Earliest Masonic MSS*. Manchester: Manchester University Press, 1938.

MacAlpine, J.M.K. "The Entered Apprentice's Song and The Fellowcraft's Song." *Ars Quatuor Coronatorum* 109 (1996): 244–46.

Mackey, Albert G. *An Encyclopædia of Freemasonry and its Kindred Sciences*. Philadelphia: Moss & Co., 1874.

McLeod, Wallace (Ed.). *A Candid Disquisition of the Principles and Practices of the Most Antient and Honourable Society of Free and Accepted Masons*. Bloomington, Ill.: The Masonic Book Club, 1989.

Moore, Charles Whitlock. *The New Masonic Trestle-board*. Boston: C.W. Moore, 1856

Murphy, Christopher. "The Broken Pillar." *Philalethes: The Journal of Masonic Research and Letters* 69 (2016): 50–57.

———. "'Our Old Noachian Ark': Craft Masonry and the Traditions of Noah." *Philalethes* 66 (2013): 107–12, 128–29.

Oliver, George. *History of Masonic Persecution in Different Quarters of the Globe*. London: Richard Spencer, 1867.

Pennell, John. *The Constitutions of the Free Masons. Containing the History, Charges, Regulations, &c. of that most Ancient and Right Worshipful Fraternity.* Dublin: J. Watts, 1730.

Preston, William. *Illustrations of Masonry.* London: J. Williams, 1772.

Pritchard, Samuel. *Masonry Dissected.* London: J. Wilford, 1730.

Ramsay, Michael. *Oration.* In Gould, *Gould's History of Freemasonry Throughout the World.* New York: Scribner's Sons, 1936: 3:10–15.

Royster, Paul. "Editorial Note." In Anderson, James, & Benjamin Franklin, "The Constitutions of the Free-Masons (1734). An Online Electronic Edition." Paul Royster, Ed. Faculty Publications, University of Nebraska at Lincoln Libraries. Paper 25.

Scott, J. *The Pocket Companion and History of Free-Masons.* London: J. Scott, 1754.

Shaftesley, John. "Jews in English Freemasonry in the Eighteenth and Nineteeth-centuries." *Ars Quatuor Coronatorum* 92 (1979): 25–63.

Smith, William. *A Pocket Companion for Free-Masons.* Dublin: E. Rider, 1735.

———. *A Pocket Companion for Free-Masons.* London: E. Rider, 1735.

Spratt, Edward. *The New Book of Constitutions of the Most Ancient and Honourable Fraternity of Free and Accepted Masons.* Dublin: Edward Bate, 1751.

———. "A Collection of Songs." In Spratt, *The New Book of Constitutions of the Most Ancient and Honourable Fraternity of Free and Accepted Masons.* Dublin: Edward Bate, 1751.

Stevenson, David. *The Origins of Freemasonry.* Cambridge: Cambridge University Press, 1988.

Vibert, Lionel. *The Rare Books of Freemasonry.* London: The Bookman's Journal, 1923.

Williams, Louis & Alphonse Cerza, Eds. *D'Assigny.* Bloomington, Ill.: The Masonic Book Club, 1974.

"The Essential Secrets of Masonry"

Insight from an American Masonic Oration of 1734[1]

SHAWN EYER

FREEMASONRY IS DRIVEN by heritage. Our Craft looks to various pasts to determine its identity in the present: to sacred history through the Volume of Sacred Law, to the mythopoetic past of the so-called Traditional History, and to our organizational history as traced through regular Masonic institutions and their leaders. Added to all this is the special attention that modern Masonic historians direct toward authentic fragments of the fraternity's history, for such evidence often sheds much-needed light upon the actions and motivations of early participants. However, there are times when, despite all of these deep concerns with the past, some key evidence is simply overlooked.

This article is the story of one such treasure: a short speech

---

1   An abbreviated version of this paper appeared in *The Plumbline: The Quarterly Journal of the Scottish Rite Research Society*, Vol. 23, No. 2 (Winter 2016): 1–7.

preserved only in a single manuscript, titled *A Dissertation Upon Masonry, Deliver'd to a Lodge in America*. A fresh transcription of the text was recently published, with critical annotations by the present writer, in the journal of the Philalethes Society.[2] The *Dissertation* is an approximately eighteen-minute lodge oration or sermon, and is one of dozens of Masonic orations that survive from the eighteenth century. However, what makes this one so special is its early date. It was, according to the manuscript, given on June 24 (the Feast of Saint John the Baptist), 1734. This makes it the third oldest surviving Masonic speech, the earlier two being the oration of Francis Drake at the York Grand Lodge on December 27, 1726,[3] and the talk delivered by Edward Oakley in London at the Lodge at the Carpenters' Arms tavern on December 31, 1728.[4] Although the early orations of Drake and Oakley and later ones by Martin Clare (1735) and Chevalier Ramsay (1737) have received moderate to extensive degrees of recognition and anal-

2   Shawn Eyer, "A *Dissertation Upon Masonry*, 1734, with Commentary and Notes," in *Philalethes: The Journal of Masonic Research and Letters* 68(2015): 62–75. The author gratefully acknowledges the assistance of Walter H. Hunt, MPS, Librarian of the Samuel Crocker Lawrence Library at the Grand Lodge of Massachusetts; Georgia Hershfeld, Library Cataloguer, Livingston Masonic Library; Bill Kreuger, Assistant Librarian at the Iowa Masonic Library; Larissa Watkins, Assistant Librarian at the House of the Temple in Washington, D.C.; Christopher B. Murphy, MPS; Arturo de Hoyos, FPS, Grand Archivist and Grand Historian at the Supreme Council, 33°, AASR, S.J.; and S. Brent Morris, FPS, Managing Editor of *The Scottish Rite Journal*.

3   Reprinted with a critical introduction in Douglas Knoop, G.P. Jones, & Douglas Hamer, *Early Masonic Pamphlets* (Manchester, UK: Manchester University Press, 1945), 196–207. Retranscribed with full textual commentary in Shawn Eyer, "Drake's Oration of 1726, with Commentary and Notes," *Philalethes: The Journal of Masonic Research and Letters* 67(2014): 14–25.

4   Reprinted in Knoop, Jones & Hamer, *Early Masonic Pamphlets*, 210–14.

ysis within Masonic scholarship, the *Dissertation Upon Masonry* is comparatively unknown, and thus, unexamined.

1849: A Discovery in the Library

A Dissertation Upon Masonry was discovered in manuscript form in 1849 within the archives of the Grand Lodge of Massachusetts by Charles Whitlock Moore (1801–1873). Moore was a native Bostonian who apprenticed in newspaper publishing, and later established himself as a leading Masonic journalist of his era.[5] For purposes of scholarly reference, the manuscript is properly named the C.W. Moore MS, after its discoverer. According to Moore, the manuscript contained two documents: the previously-unknown 1734 *Dissertation* followed by a transcript of the so-called Leland MS.

Moore transcribed the *Dissertation* and published it in the August 1, 1849, edition of his *Freemasons' Monthly Magazine* under the headline, "The First Masonic Discourse Delivered in America."[6] Introducing the item, he offered a number of questionable opinions:

> The following is probably the first address ever delivered before a Masonic Lodge in America. The first Lodge chartered in this country was in July, 1733. This address was delivered in Boston, the 24th of June, 1734. Earlier addresses may have been delivered on some particular occasions; but if so, we have no record of them. Nor is such a supposition hardly probable, in view of the condition of the Fraternity

---

5   William W. Wheildon, "Charles W. Moore." *The New England Historical and Genealogical Register* 30 (1876): 399–405.

6   Charles Whitlock Moore, "The First Masonic Discourse Delivered in America." *The Freemasons' Monthly Magazine* 8 (1849): 289–93.

prior to 1733. We think, therefore, that it is safe to assume, that this is the first public Masonic discourse ever delivered in America. We discovered it in the archives of the Grand Lodge of Massachusetts. The name of the author is not attached to it. We give the spelling, punctuation, and capital letters, as they appear in the original. The Bodlean [sic] Manuscript, with Mr. Locke's notes, appended to the address by the author, we omit. The address has never before been published; and we give it to the readers of this Magazine, as one of the most interesting papers with which we have recently been enabled to enrich our pages.[7]

This preface makes some presumptions about which we ought to be cautious. Moore matter-of-factly states that the *Dissertation* was given in the Lodge at Boston, although there is no indication of that in the manuscript itself. He also opines that "in view of the condition of the Fraternity prior to 1733," it seemed unlikely to him that there could have been any earlier oration given either in the lodge at Boston or any other lodge, and that therefore the *Dissertation* was "the first public Masonic discourse ever delivered in America." These interpretations are overeager—but not by much.

Moore's idea that the oration must have been given in Boston is likely based upon the fact that the manuscript was found in the library of the Grand Lodge of Massachusetts, and reinforced by the fact that there were few lodges operating in America on the Feast of Saint John the Baptist, 1734. But, while it is true that there were few documented lodges operating in America at the time, even the fact that there *were* several means that we cannot automatically assume the oration was given in the Lodge at the Bunch of Grapes Tavern in Boston.[8] It is highly possible that the

7   Moore, "The First Masonic Discourse," 289.
8   For convenience, this lodge is often referred to as The First Lodge

oration is from that lodge, but it cannot be known for certain at this time.

More unlikely is Moore's finding that the oration is "the first public Masonic discourse ever delivered in America." First, a careful review of the language of the oration shows that it was not addressed to the public in any way, but to Freemasons alone. The title of the *Dissertation* says that it was "Deliver'd to a *Lodge* in America," and the text frequently relies upon internal Masonic rhetoric. It is possible that by "public," Moore simply intended to imply that the address was spoken to the assembled brethren. Even so, it is doubtful that it was the first Masonic oration ever given on the American continent. Orations were a typical feature of many lodges, and lodges that did not have speeches by the brethren elucidating Masonic topics were seen as lacking an important aspect of Freemasonry.[9]

That said, the status of the *Dissertation* is impressive, despite the document's obscurity. It is surely one of the earliest American Masonic orations. It is the third oldest Masonic oration that survives in the world. It is the oldest American Masonic speech that is preserved. We must not overlook the fact that we have the orations of Drake and Oakley in published form alone, both of which, while originally given in private lodge settings, were also intended for, and possibly redacted for, public distribution. The 1734 *Dissertation* was never intended to be published, and its content makes it clear it could only have been delivered within a lodge of Master Masons, which makes it *the oldest surviving*

in subsequent Massachusetts Masonic history. In 1736, it was known as Lodge Nº 126 on the register of the Grand Lodge of England (later characterized as the Moderns).

9   See the earlier orations of Francis Drake (1726) and Edward Oakley (1728) in which it is clear that discussions on topics relevant to Masonry were recommended. Drake openly criticizes the York lodge for neglecting such lectures, but emphasizes that the London lodges were regularly engaging in them.

example of private Masonic instruction in the world.[10]

Thus, Moore's enthusiasm for the document he discovered is fully justified. Unfortunately, his publication of the oration did not have the impact that he had hoped. Not only has the *Dissertation* escaped the thorough scholarly analysis that it deserves, but it has even failed to accrue a general awareness of its existence within the corpus of early Masonic literature.

The Masonic and Academic Reception

An extensive literature review reveals that as few as four Masonic writers (excluding the present author) ever wrote anything about the *Dissertation* after Moore's initial publication: Rob Morris, Albert G. Mackey, Lawrence Greenleaf, and Henry W. Coil.

Rob Morris mentioned the *Dissertation* in two of his works, but offered no interpretations of it in either.[11]

In 1865, Albert G. Mackey wrote a short article, "The Eloquence of Masonry," in which he accepted Moore's assignment for the *Dissertation* to Boston, and offered a short assessment: "This address is well written, and of a symbolic character, as the author represents the Lodge as a type of heaven."[12] This article became the basis for Mackey's entry, "Addresses, Masonic," in his classic *Encyclopædia of Freemasonry and Its Kindred Sciences.*[13]

In 1896, Lawrence N. Greenleaf cited the *Dissertation* as evidence of the antiquity of Freemasonry in general and of the

10   This statement applies to the Grand Lodge era.

11   Rob Morris, *The History of Freemasonry in Kentucky*, 5; Rob Morris, *William Morgan*, 49.

12   Albert G. Mackey, "The Eloquence of Masonry," 147. For a discussion on the special meaning of "type" here, see the section of this paper on the subject of typological interpretation, below.

13   Albert G. Mackey, *Encyclopædia of Freemasonry and Its Kindred Sciences*, 14–15.

trigradal system in particular.[14]

Henry W. Coil is apparently the only twentieth century Masonic author to refer to the *Dissertation*, although his reference is derivative of Mackey's.[15] In his 1961 *Encyclopedia*, Coil acknowledged the oration, but was careful not to adopt the assumptions made by prior authors, stating: "On June 24, 1734, an unknown speaker delivered to an unknown American lodge 'A *Dissertation Upon Masonry*,' which was reprinted in *Moore's Masonic Magazine* [sic], Vol. 8, p. 289 (1849)."[16]

A review of the cumulative indices of *Ars Quatuor Coronatorum* from 1886 to 2014 reveals no reference to the 1734 oration.[17] It appears that the only Freemasons ever to write about the *Dissertation* between Moore's discovery in 1849 and the 2015 critical edition in *Philalethes* are the four mentioned above.

Luckily, the *Dissertation Upon Masonry* was not quite as neglected within the academic world. The first academic study performed was within a 1968 M.A. thesis by Ross Frank Cooke.[18] Cooke's thesis attempted to analyze the structure of the address, but was limited by a rather superficial knowledge of Freemasonry.

Steven C. Bullock's *Revolutionary Brotherhood* cited the *Dis-*

14   *Grand Lodge of Colorado Proceedings* (1896), 294–95.

15   A comparison of the entries on "Addresses, Masonic" in the encyclopedias of each author demonstrates the relationship.

16   Henry W. Coil, *Coil's Masonic Encyclopedia* (New York: Macoy, 1961), 6.

17   This index is not exhaustive, so it may be that the *Dissertation* has been mentioned in AQC without being featured in the index— although if so, it is likely that such references would be slight.

18   Ross Frank Cooke, "An Analysis of Four Speeches Delivered by Masons in Colonial America" (M.A. thesis, Brigham Young University, 1968). Images of the C.W. Moore MS are available currently only because photographic reproductions of the original manuscript were included by Cooke in his thesis. The original MS is not catalogued, and it is not currently available for inspection.

sertation repeatedly as evidence of the ideals of Colonial Freemasonry, and illustrations of the social challenges and trans-
formations of which the Fraternity was a part. Bullock found
that lodge sermons "often provide the most accessible means of
understanding Masonic self-perceptions."[19]

David G. Hackett's survey of early American Freemasonry
from a religious perspective, *That Religion in Which All Men
Agree*, noted the *Dissertation* as evidence of a degree of heterodoxy within Colonial Freemasonry: "Most Saint John's sermons
stressed polite Christianity, yet [the 1734] oration suggests a divergence between it and Freemasonry."[20]

These examples apparently describe the entire response to the
discovery of this important early Masonic speech.

The Critical Summer of 1734

The date of the address confirms that it was an oration for the
Feast of Saint John the Baptist, perhaps the most essential holi-
day of the Masonic Order. The title indicates that the oration was
given to "a Lodge in America." There is no information available
to identify the specific lodge.[21]

19   Steven C. Bullock, *Revolutionary Brotherhood: Freemasonry and
the Transformation of the American Social Order, 1730–1840*, 321.
Bullock's discussion of the 1734 *Dissertation* is found on pp. 63,
65, 66, 73, & 80.
20   David G. Hackett, *That Religion in Which All Men Agree:
Freemasonry in American Culture*, 51.
21   Several commentators have assumed that the location of the
address was Boston (Moore, Morris, Mackey, Cooke, Bullock,
and Hackett). Although the *Dissertation* could have been
delivered in any of the American lodges—the locations of most
of which in 1734 are unknown—it seems likely that it originated
either in Boston or Philadelphia. However, when the content of
the *Dissertation* is taken into account, it is possible to develop

The summer of 1734 was a pivotal period for American Freemasonry. Two June 24 lodge meetings are documented. *The Pennsylvania Gazette* of June 27 recorded that:

> Monday last, a Grand Lodge of the Ancient Honourable Society of Free and Accepted Masons in this Province, was held at the Tun Tavern in Water-Street, when BENJAMIN FRANKLIN being elected Grand-Master for the Year ensuing.... After which a very elegant entertainment was provided, and the Proprietor, the Governor, and several other persons of distinction, honored the Society with their presence.[22]

The same day's events in Boston are recorded as follows:

> 5734 June 24. Being the anniversary of Sᵗ John the Baptist the Brethren Celebrated the Feast in due manner and Form, and chose Our Rᵗ Worshˡ Bro: Mʳ Frederick Hamilton Master of the Lodge.[23]

Both of these are potential locations of the *Dissertation*'s original delivery—the question will be taken up in more detail below.

That summer, Franklin released his edition of Anderson's *Constitutions*, which was first advertised on May 16. Franklin shipped 70 copies to Boston in August.[24] A few months later,

a theory that Boston was the most likely provenance (see the section "The Question of Authorship," below.)

22 Reprinted in *Proceedings of the Right Worshipful Grand Lodge of the Most Ancient and Honorable Fraternity of Free and Accepted Masons of Pennsylvania, and Masonic Jurisdiction Thereunto Belonging* (1906), 82.

23 *Proceedings in Masonry, St. John's Grand Lodge, 1733–1792, Massachusetts Grand Lodge, 1769–1792* (1895), 4.

24 Paul Royster (Ed.), *The Constitutions of the Free-Masons (1734). An*

Franklin applied for a charter from Henry Price in Boston, ultimately bringing the Pennsylvania Masons under the Grand Lodge of England. Thus, this particular Feast of Saint John the Baptist took place during an important time of growth.

A *Dissertation Upon Masonry*, composed and delivered at the center of all this activity, provides valuable insight into the internal activities and self-conceptualizations of the Masons of that crucial period.

The Question of Authorship

The C.W. Moore MS betrays no overt indication as to the author of the 1734 *Dissertation*. David G. Hackett suggested that the *Dissertation* was given by Rev. Charles Brockwell (d. 1755).[25] However, there are indications that Brockwell could not have been the author. He did deliver a Masonic sermon that has come down to us, but that was in 1749 (fifteen and a half years after the *Dissertation* was given).[26] While Brockwell might at first seem to be a possible author of the *Dissertation*, a comparison of the 1734 document to Brockwell's 1749 sermon reveals no significant stylistic or thematic similarities. Furthermore, Brockwell was English by birth, and was apparently studying at Cambridge at the time the *Dissertation* was given. Church histories show that Brockwell was not in America in 1734, but crossed the Atlantic in May of 1737 to lead a church at Scituate, Massachusetts. Brockwell went to Salem in 1738, serving there until he was moved to

Online Electronic Edition (Lincoln, Nebr.: University of Nebraska, 2006), 94.

25   Hackett, *That Religion*, 51.
26   Charles Brockwell, *Brotherly Love Recommended: In a Sermon Preached...in Christ-Church, Boston, on Wednesday the 27th of December, 1749*.

King's Chapel, Boston, in 1746. He died in Boston in 1755.[27]

An unpublished theory by John M. Sherman, a former Librarian of the Samuel Crocker Lawrence Library at the Grand Lodge of Massachusetts, holds merit. A photocopy of Moore's original publication of the *Dissertation* located in the Livingston Masonic Library of the Grand Lodge of New York exists with a typewritten note attached, inscribed that it is from the "Boston Mass Masonic Library Sept. 11, 1971." The note reads:

> We have an original ms. of this with our rare books but it is not in the handwriting of the speaker, in my opinion. I think it was copied, maybe by the Lodge Secretary. I think it may have been delivered by Thomas Harward, Who was King's Lecturer (asst. minister) at King's Chapel, 1731–1736, when he died. Whoever it was, he must have been a Mason. But I have no record of Harward as a Mason. Probably was made in England before he came over.   jms
>
> It may not be possible to prove who did write it.[28]

An examination of published sermons by Thomas Harward reveals good reason for Sherman's suggestion. A particularly strong structural, stylistic, and thematic resemblance to the *Dissertation* may be found in Harward's 1732 sermon, *The Fulness*

---

27 For these and other details of Brockwell's life, see "History of St. Peter's Church, Salem, Mass." *The Gospel Advocate*, 2 (1822): 341–52; also W.M. Willis, *Journals of the Rev. Thomas Smith, and the Rev. Samuel Deane, Pastors of the First Church in Portland* (Portland: Joseph S. Bailey, 1849), 155.

28 Private correspondence with Georgia Hershfeld, Library Cataloguer, Livingston Masonic Library. This note from John M. Sherman provides important documentation for the fact that the C.W. Moore ms was extant in the Samuel Crocker Lawrence library as late as 1971—three years after Cooke's M.A. thesis included photographic reproductions of it.

of Joy in the Presence of God.[29] As such, while objective proof of authorship will remain elusive, Sherman's suggestion that the orator was Thomas Harward should be given due consideration. Moreover, if Harward is the likely author of the 1734 Masonic address, then it follows that the Lodge at the Bunch of Grapes in Boston appears the most likely setting for its original delivery.

A Summary of the 1734 Dissertation

SAINT PAUL'S INITIATIC VISION

The *Dissertation* begins by invoking aspects of the Traditional History of Freemasonry, including the legend that a "Vast number of Emperors & Princes, Inventors of usefull arts, Divines and Philosophers...have in all ages voluntarily taken upon themselfs, the Badge of our profession."[30] The speaker then singles out Saint Paul, who he calls "the powerfull propagator of the Gospel, the profound Scholar, the skilfull architect, the Irresistable orator,"[31] as a notable example as such great men who were legendarily part of the Craft. While it seems novel to think of Saint Paul as a Masonic brother, it was in fact a fairly common theme in eighteenth century Masonic literature and sermons, and is obliquely referenced in Anderson's *Constitutions.*[32]

29   See Thomas Harward, *The Fulness of Joy in the Presence of God, Being the Substance of a Discourse Preach'd Lately in the Royal Chappel at Boston in New-England. By the Reverend Mr. Harward, Lecturer at the Royal Chappel.* Boston: B. Green, 1732.

30   C.W. Moore MS, lines 6–8.

31   Ibid., lines 13–15.

32   The identification of Saint Paul as an initiate of the Craft is a primitive feature not unique to the *Dissertation.* Robert Samber (1682–1745), writing under the pseudonym Eugenius Philalethes,

While Paul was in darkness prior to his initiation, "he was an Enemy to the Lodge, like some of us before admission, he despis'd the Sacred Institution, and Ridicul'd it with all his witt and Elo-

Jr., wrote a dedication to the Grand Master, Wardens, and Brethren of England and Ireland dated March 1, 1721, in which he refers to "Brother St. *Paul*" (*The Long Livers*, xii & xlvi) and "holy Brother Saint *Paul*" (xlviii & liii). He emphasized the early Masonic theme of false brethren: "Our holy Brother St. *Paul*, though he suffered infinite Perils, as he recounts himself, yet the Perils among False Brethren were what seemed most to touch his righteous Soul; for most dangerous are a Man's Enemies, when they are of his own House." (xlviii)

The Bodleian Library contains a manuscript in Samber's hand, likely from the same time period, which carries another reference in similar terms: "Hear what is promised to the Brotherhood from the words of our Holy Brother St. Paul: *Brethren, says he, be of good Comfort, live in peace, and the God of love and peace shall be with you.*" (Mss Rawlinson Poetry 11, folio 74 verso; see Edward Armitage, "Robert Samber," 108) This is echoed in the 1728 Masonic oration of Edward Oakley: "Finally, Brethren, (I speak now to you in holy Brother St. *Paul's* Words,) 'Farewel: Be perfect, be of good Comfort, be of one Mind, live in Peace, and the God of Love and Peace shall be with you.'" (Oakley, *A Speech Deliver'd to the Worshipful Society of Free and Accepted Masons*, 34.)

Other references to Paul as a Freemason occur in a 1737 sermon of John Henley (1692–1756), the Chaplain of the Grand Lodge of England for many years. (*On Scripture Masonry*, 4, 8, 15) References to Paul adhering to this formula are found in some later Masonic rhetoric as well. Isaac Head, who was the first Provincial Grand Master of the Scilly Isles, invokes "our holy Brother the Apostle Paul" in a charge given in Cornwall on April 21, 1752. (Scott, *Pocket Companion*, 301) In another charge, given January 21, 1766, Head lauds Paul as "our excellent Brother, and great Orator, the holy and great Apostle Paul," and encourages the assembled brethren to seek to "be made Partakers of the Beatifick Vision" that Paul experienced. (*A Confutation of the Observations on Free Masonry*, 88 & 90) This is far from an exhaustive inventory for such references. For a short survey of Masonic traditions about St. Paul, see Carl Hermann Tendler, "The Apostle St. Paul, a Mason," *Ars Quatuor Coronatorum* 1(1886–1888):74–75.

quence, but he afterward became its Glory & Support."[33] The *Dissertation* considers Paul's statement in 1 Corinthians 13:11: "When I was a child, says he, I understood as a Child...but when I became a man (an Expression Emphatically Significant among us) when I became a man then...I put away Childish things."[34] The speaker finds a special inference in this transformation from a childish to a manly mental state, connecting it to Masonic initiation.

This pattern continues as he considers another text, paraphrased from 2 Corinthians 12:2–5. Before going into it in detail, the *Dissertation* makes an assertion that might be startling to a modern reader, but was probably not that unusual within the early Masonic context. The 1734 speaker holds that Freemasons have the advantage of a special insight by means of sharing in an ancient fraternal bond:

> ...the whole passage is well worth Repeating & I propose therefrom to Continue my present Discourse; only observing by the way, that the learned annotators & Interpreters of Scriptures, however penetrating & clear they have been in other dark places, yet none of them been of ye lodge, they Could not possibly Conceive the apostle's true meaning in this mysterious part of his Epistle & I have therefore given the World an uninteligible Explication.[35]

The *Dissertation* then continues into the hidden interpretation of 2 Corinthians 12:2–5, which is the central theme for the remainder of the oration.

> I knew a man, Say's he, meaning himself, above 14 years ago whither in the body, or out of the Body I cannot tell,

33   C.W. Moore MS, lines 17–20.
34   Ibid., lines 22–26.
35   Ibid., lines 32–39.

but I knew such a one taken up into the third heaven into paradice where he heard unspeakable words which it is not lawful for any Man to utter, of such a one will I Glory. Freemasons know very well why the apostle calls himself a Man, they know why he could not tell whether, when he was made a mason he was in the Body or out of the Body, and what is meant by the body,[36] they know also that by the third heaven or paradice is figur'd out the third & Chief degree of Masonry, & they are very well acquainted with those unspeakable words, which is not lawful for a man to utter, as a particular Explication of these things to the well Instructed Mason would be needless, so to the World it is needless and Improper.[37]

A HEAVENLY STANDARD OF BEHAVIOR

Now, the *Dissertation* turns to elucidating the comparison of the tiled Masonic lodge to Paul's vision of paradise or heaven. Many reasons are given for this celestial identification:

1) The lodge is like heaven in that "it is an absolute Monarchy, in which the Will of the Sovereign is a law, but so wisely

36   It is intriguing to note that the subtle inference drawn here by the author of the *Dissertation* is understandable by Freemasons today because of the preservation of the same phraseology of being within or without "the body"—that is, the assembled lodge. In his article, "The Sociology of the Construct of Tradition and Import of Legitimacy in Freemasonry," scholar Henrik Bogdan notes that "Freemasonry, in its various forms, is a highly conservative form of organization in the sense that it has changed very little from the eighteenth century to the twenty-first century. The basic organizational structure, the initiatory system, central symbols and even the language (choice of words, phraseology, etc.) have remained more or less intact." (236)

37   C.W. Moore MS, lines 40–53.

Contrived & Established, that the Sovereign can never will nor
Command any thing which is not exactly agreable to the nature
& reason of things, & by the Subjects Received and Submitted
to with Pleasure; the pecul[i]ar light of Masonry Enabling to
discern what is best with Regard to the Lodge...."[38]

2) The lodge is like heaven "on account of the universal understanding which subsistes therein betwixt brethren of vastly
different Languages and Countrys...."[39]

3) The lodge is like heaven "on account of that human[,] Kind
& fraternal treatment of each other which is therein used among
the Brethren." "In Heaven and in the lodge only are to be Seen
humility without contempt, and dignity without Envy."[40]

4) The lodge is like heaven because "it is been Composed of
good people of all Religions, Sects[,] perswasions & Denominations, of all nations and countrys, & I might add of all Generations of men in all ages since the Beginning of mankind."[41]

38 Ibid., lines 59–65.
39 Ibid., lines 83–85. The ability of Freemasons to communicate
    ideas despite language barriers was a common theme of early
    Masonic literature, tied to the story of the Masons who labored
    on the Tower of Babel. See the discussion of The Masons' Faculty
    elsewhere in this paper.
40 Ibid., lines 105–101 & 113–115.
41 Ibid., lines 118–121. Masonic scholars have often interpreted
    Masonic texts that mention Biblical themes (other than the
    Temple of Solomon, King Solomon, Hiram of Tyre, the Holy
    Saints John, and the various Biblical passages found in the
    degree work) as an indication of the exclusion of non-Christians.
    The Dissertation's language here may provide some corrective
    insight. If the oration did not contain this line about accepting
    "all Religions, Sects[,] perswasions & Denominations," many
    would have tended to interpret the document as exclusively
    Christian. The specific language used here makes it clear that
    "all Religions" means far more than all Christian denominations,
    because it extends to the religions of "all nations and countrys,"
    and "all Generations of men in all ages since the Beginning of

The 1734 speaker then shifts his discourse to the "Instruction to younger Bretheren,"[42] and delineates some ways in which Masons ought to strive to make their lodge resemble paradise:

1) The lodge ought to be like paradise because "you that are members thereof should[,] like the Inhabitants of that happy place, as far as possible, Endevour to preserve a pure and unblemish'd life and Conversation...."[43]

2) The lodge "ought to resemble Heaven in the most Cheerfull good humour, and the most perfect love and Charity among the Brethren: let there be no heart burning among us, let evry brother who happens to think himself disobliged by another, open his Soul to the lodge & he shall be made Easy...."[44]

3) The lodge ought to be like heaven "in absolutely refusing admission to improper persons: people of selfish ungenerous illnatur'd dispositions are utterly unfit to be made Masons, tis the Human Benevolent mind only, that deserves & is Capable of this Felicity: Such will naturally desire to join with us, as being pleased with evry thing, that tend to make mankind more happy; and such will apply with a suitable earnestness, of their own Freewill & voluntary motion[,] for by no means should we Invite or Endevour to entice any-man...."[45]

4) The lodge "ought to Resemble Heaven in the most perfect secrecy of all their Transactions."[46]

As the speaker articulates this last point, he distinguishes between two kinds of Masonic secrecy. His advice for the "younger" brethren is not to share the lodge's business with friends and

mankind." Thus, while thoroughly Christian in character, the 1734 *Dissertation* is almost certainly expressing that men of all religions were properly welcome in the Masonic lodge.

42   Ibid., lines 138–139.
43   Ibid., lines 142–145.
44   Ibid., lines 167–172.
45   Ibid., lines 189–198.
46   Ibid., lines 204–205.

family, echoing Anderson's *Constitutions* and many other early sources. But his reference to another class of Masonic secrecy is one of the *Dissertation*'s most salient statements. He says that "The Essential Secrets of masonry indeed are Everlastingly Safe, & never can be Revealed abroad, because they can never be understood by such as are unenlightened."[47]

The *Dissertation* culminates in some beautiful language based upon the Wisdom of Solomon 11:20:

> Reverenc'd be the memory of the Widow's Son, and Blessed be the name of the all Mighty architecte, son of the virgin: Infinitly honnour'd be the name of the great Geometrican, who made all things, by weight and measure, and let love, peace, and unanimity Continue forever among Masons. Be it So.[48]

Some Notable Features

The 1734 *Dissertation* displays several features that inform our knowledge of American Freemasonry in the Colonial period, particularly in terms of its intellectual culture.

ESOTERIC WISDOM

One of the most striking traits of the *Dissertation* is its emphasis on esoteric concepts. Secret transactions, secret interpretations, and secret wisdom are expressed at different points within the oration. On one level, this is not surprising, as Freemasonry has stressed secrecy in one form or another since well before the

47   Ibid., lines 210–212.
48   Ibid., lines 238–244.

founding of the first Grand Lodge. Moreover, the 1734 *Dissertation* comes at a moment in which exposures of the Masonic catechisms and modes of recognition were becoming more widely distributed, more accurate, and more complete.[49] Despite this, Freemasons did not back away from the position that the Craft represented a mystery that outsiders could not penetrate: in addition to the esoteric working of the rituals, which might easily be published and spread verbally outside of bounds, Masons referred to another level of secrecy—an interpretive layer that represented special knowledge.

In order to avoid the vagueries that can result from the unqualified use of the term esotericism to refer to these different kinds of secret knowledge, the author has proposed a practical classification of the forms of esotericism in Freemasonry.[50] Each of these taxons is defined by its function. The first order is the *social-exclusionary* function—referring both to a binary concept of access (i.e., whether the subject is an initiate and thus entitled to a group's esoteric culture, or is not initiated and blocked from any lawful exposure to the esoteric culture of the group), as well as to a scalar concept of progressive access (i.e., through a series

49   These exposures largely emanated from London, which experienced rapid growth in the number of lodges during the decade following 1717. Scholars consider that Samuel Prichard's 1730 pamphlet, *Masonry Dissected*, which was the first exposure to reveal catechetical details of the three degrees, was especially concerning to the Grand Lodge due to its accuracy. The appearance and popularity of *Masonry Dissected* (apparently among opponents and initiates alike) generated Masonic responses such as the erudite essay, *A Defence of Masonry*. It is highly possible, even probable, that American Masons were aware of catechism exposures. It is notable that no contemporary Masonic testimony regarded the Craft's secrets as actually having been revealed by these documents.

50   Eyer, "Esoteric and Mystical Themes." For a popular article about this taxonomy, see Eyer, "Defining Esotericism from a Masonic Perspective."

of degrees). This first taxon is proximal and status-based. The second order is the *textual-interpretive* taxon—referring both to the belief that a "text" (broadly defined) has an esoteric layer of meaning, and to the intellectual endeavor of attempting to elucidate and understand that latent meaning. This is distinct from the first taxon in that merely social entitlement by virtue of belonging to a group, or of initiation to a certain degree, is independent of both the perception that there is esoteric meaning in the private culture of the group, as well as distinct from the pursuit of intellectual activity directed toward the understanding of that meaning. The perception of the presence of such meanings is indicated in a wide range of eighteenth-century Masonic literature, from private sources such as the 1734 *Dissertation* to the classical expressions of Masonic thought in the 1770s, such as William Preston's *Illustrations*, which encouraged the "investigation" of Masonry's "latent doctrines."[51]

The third taxon is *systematic*, referring to esoteri*cism* as a system, discussible in the abstract rather than in terms of a particular unit of content or a particular esoteric insight. This wider taxon could denote the macroscopic perspective of Freemasonry in which it is taken as an intentional philosophical program in which the sum of social-exclusionary knowledge and textual-interpretive arcana are understood as a deliberate system of esoteric meaning—as Preston put it in the 1770s, "a regular system of morality conceived in a strain of interesting allegory, which readily unfolds its beauties to the candid and industrious enquirer."[52] The third taxon is also applicable to the phenomenon of so-called Western Esotericism, an "artificial category"[53] of thought that includes a range of ideas, such as Hermeticism, kabbalism,

---

51   William Preston, *Illustrations of Masonry* (1775), 75; Colin Dyer,
       William Preston and His Work, 212.
52   Dyer, *William Preston*, 207.
53   Hanegraaff, *Western Esotericism*, 3.

neoplatonism, etc., which has been delineated extensively in academic literature.[54]

54   The most influential academic definition of Western Esotericism
     is that given by Antoine Faivre; see his *Western Esotericism: A
     Concise History*, 1–7. Similar definitions, with salient nuances
     and distinctions, are offered by Nicholas Goodrick-Clarke (*The
     Western Esoteric Traditions*, 3–14), Wouter J. Hanegraaff (*Western
     Esotericism*, 1–11), and Arthur Versluis (*Magic and Mysticism*,
     1–2). Kocku von Stuckrad argues for a discursive approach in
     contrast to an essentialist definition (*Western Esotericism*, 5–11).
         In *Esotericism and the Academy*, Wouter Hanegraaff
     critiques various approaches to conceptualizing esotericism
     as a phenomenon (352–67). Arguing against an intellectual
     "eclecticism" which encourages researchers to filter and exclude
     historical information and phenomena according to their post-
     Enlightenment biases, Hanegraaff states that "The point is...to
     provide an antidote against the view that historians should
     select their materials on the basis of normative, doctrinal, or
     philosophical judgments. More specifically, the point is to be aware
     of how the hegemonic discourses of modernity are themselves
     built upon earlier mnemohistorical narratives...rather than on
     critical and evenhanded attention to all the available evidence."
     (378) This point is highly applicable in the field of Masonic studies
     as well, in which the studies of myth, symbolism, and esotericism
     have been regarded as nearly immaterial to the formal study
     of the subject, despite the central role they occupy in Masonic
     culture. Arguably, such "eclectic" filtering is one reason why the
     contents of much of the early Masonic literature—such as the 1734
     Dissertation and other items from the 1720s and 1730s—have left
     so little trace in the academic scholarship of early Freemasonry.
     This largely subconscious process may also account for the
     perception, recently expressed by academic historian Róbert
     Péter, that certain texts "seem to have been deliberately ignored
     by masonic historians." (See Péter, "General Introduction," xii.)
     Perhaps it is not that the texts are ignored deliberately; rather,
     they may be automatically regarded as irrelevant because they
     express ideas that are understood as incompatible with normative
     post-Enlightenment scholarly narratives. This topic is deserving
     of further exploration as historiographical approaches to Masonic
     studies continue to develop.

It is possible for a particular object of study characterized as "esoteric" to refer to any combination of these three distinct categories. This taxonomy is introduced here because it allows for a more precise discussion of the esoteric content of the 1734 *Dissertation*. The *Dissertation* strongly communicates both *social-exclusionary* (first taxon) and *textual-interpretive* (second taxon) concepts of esotericism. These two types of esoteric content are expressed concisely in one section of the sermon:

> Fourthly and lastly, the Lodge ought to Resemble Heaven in the most perfect secrecy of all their Transactions.

> All that we know of those Above,
> Is that they Sing, and that they Love:,... says the Poet.

> In like manner, all that is known of the Lodge should be that in our meetings we are Good natur'd and Chearfull, & love one another. The Essential Secrets of masonry indeed are Everlastingly Safe, & never can be Revealed abroad, because they can never be understood by such as are unenlightened[.] They are not what I am Speaking of, but I mean the Common private transactions of the Lodge, as if a Brother in necessity ask Relief, if an Erring Brother be Reprouv'd & Censur'd, if possibly little differences and animositys should happen to arise, such things as theys should never be heard of abroad. Learn to be Silent: a Babler is an abomination. Remember the fate of that unhappy man Strong indeed in body, but weak in mind; he discover'd his Secret to his Wife & thus his Ennemys came to the Knowledge of them, this prouv'd his destruction & eternal dishonnour, for he is now as a Brother never named among Masons.[55]

---

55   C.W. Moore MS, lines 204–223. The cited poet is Edmund Waller.

This is a lengthy statement of esotericism of the first type, with second-taxon esotericism noted along the way. The first-taxon *social-exclusionary* function is demonstrated by the *Dissertation* author's view that the basic transactions of a lodge be kept secret from outsiders. His reference here is not to the ritual or secret lore of the Craft, but to the necessity of its social privacy in the maintenance of dignity and propriety. If a Mason were to be sanctioned for misbehavior, or a member were in need of charitable aid, this information was to be kept within the confines of the lodge. And, invoking the Biblical example of Samson, the orator makes clear that violation of the *social-exclusionary* boundary will result in a loss of insider status—that is, the social exclusion of the violator.[56]

Sandwiched within this exhortation to maintain first-taxon privacy is an impressive statement of second-taxon esotericism:

56   The symbolic use of Samson as a disgraced member of the Freemasons is not unique to the *Dissertation*, but is found in numerous contemporary Masonic writings. Samson is mentioned in two songs in Anderson's *Constitutions* of 1723. The second has: "But Samson's Blot / Is ne'er forgot / He blabb'd his Secrets to his Wife / that sold Her Husband / who at last pull'd down / The House on all in Gaza Town." (91) A footnote in the 1738 second edition of Anderson's *Constitutions* also expresses the blotting out of Samson's name: "The *Tradition* of old Masons is, that a learned *Phenician* called SANCONIATHON was the Architect, or *Grand Master*, of this curious *Temple*: And that SAMSON had been too credulous and effeminate in revealing his Secrets to his Wife, who betray'd him into the Hands of the *Philistins*; for which he is not numbered among the antient *Masons*. But no more of this." (*New Book*, 10) Samson also figures in Masonic lore apart from his later exclusion for violating his oath of secrecy. In 1754, Alexander Slade recorded what purports to be a primitive Masonic practice of using a sign derived from the Biblical story of Samson drinking from a miraculous spring in Judges 15:19. Because this legend took place before Samson became disgraced by revealing secrets, it was still celebrated by Masons. (*The Free Mason Examin'd*, 21)

> The Essential Secrets of masonry indeed are Everlasting-
> ly Safe, & never can be Revealed abroad [i.e., outside the
> Lodge—Ed.], because they can never be understood by
> such as are unenlightened.[57]

It is also extremely interesting to note that the author of the *Dissertation* is fully aware of the distinction, because he immediately follows this by a statement that "They [the Essential Secrets] are not what I am Speaking of,"[58] contrasting them against the transactions of the lodge.

Although it is commonly suggested by modern interpreters that in early Freemasonry the only secrets were the modes of recognition, this statement shows that the "Essential Secrets" were conceived of as something only attainable by initiates through special understanding—a *textual-interpretive* layer of meaning. This higher order of Masonic secret was considered secure from exposure in a way that the password, grips, rituals, and catechisms were not. Relative to this more rarefied level of Masonic secrecy, scholar Henrik Bogdan remarks that "The construct of tradition in masonic societies thus centres on the transmission of something that in part is not communicable...."[59] While verbally non-communicable, this insight is passed through the experience of initiation and subsequent reflection thereon.

> The experience of going through the various degrees
> can...be interpreted as an internalisation of the esoteric
> form of thought in the sense that the degrees ritually cor-
> respond to the stages of a transmutative process leading to
> the realisation of *gnosis*—the non-communicable experi-

---

57   C.W. Moore MS, lines 210–212.
58   Ibid., lines 212–213.
59   Bogdan, "The Sociology of the Construct of Tradition and Import of Legitimacy in Freemasonry," 220.

ence of the self and its relation with the godhead.[60]

In Bogdan's perspective, the external rituals of initiation correspond with a transpersonal process of a "realisation" that is essentially non-communicable and perhaps mystical.

However, as much as these secrets that "can never be understood by such as are unenlightened" might be conceived as a form of personal enlightenment, they could also be approached a second way within the dimensions of the *textual-interpretive* taxon. A large portion of the text is concerned with the location of esoteric Masonic meaning within the Bible, such as the claim that:

> …the learned annotators & Interpreters of Scriptures, however penetrating & clear they have been in other dark places, yet none of them been of ye lodge, they Could not possibly Conceive the apostle's true meaning in this mysterious part of his Epistle & I have therefore given the World an [otherwise] uninteligible Explication.[61]

Allusions to the belief that Freemasons could obtain special insight that allowed them to understand esoteric meanings in Biblical passages can be found in other early Masonic literature: the *Dissertation* is not the only example of this concept. The location of esoteric lessons in the Bible is a significant feature in the literature of early Grand Lodge era Freemasonry, although this aspect of Masonic culture has not been adequately developed in prior scholarship. While the authors of the Old Charges of prior centuries freely interwove Masonic legends and Biblical stories, by the end of the seventeenth century, there were signs of the existence of esoteric readings of the Bible itself. In 1689 and 1691, Robert Kirk recorded that the Mason Word was like a "Rabbin-

60   Bogdan, "The Sociology of the Construct of Tradition," 221.
61   C.W. Moore MS, lines 34–39.

ical mystery" or "Rabbinical Tradition, in way of comment on Jachin and Boaz, the two Pillars erected in Solomon's Temple."[62]

Many examples illustrate how early eighteenth-century Masons probed the Holy Bible in search of Masonic insight. Anderson's *Constitutions* features numerous instances of this, including the examination of the Hebrew text of several passages in order to shed light on Masonic ideas.[63] The earliest published grand lodge era initiation prayer, found in Pennell's *Constitutions* of 1730, entreats the divine Architect to "*endue him* [the initiate] *with Divine Wisdom, that he may, with the Secrets of* Masonry, *be able to unfold the Mysteries of Godliness and Christianity.*"[64] The discovery or unfolding of latent Masonic teachings is alluded to in the chorus of "The Master's Song" by Anderson.[65]

In 1737, the first Chaplain of the Grand Lodge of England, Rev. John "Orator" Henley, taught that "The Book of God, his Will, and his Works, are Patterns of sacred Masonry: They are full of sublime Mysteries, not imparted to all."[66] In a striking parallel to the theme of the 1734 American *Dissertation*, Henley also connected this esoteric approach to certain language used by Paul: "St. *Paul* distinguishes between Milk and strong Meat, in his Instructions; and between Principles and Perfection . . . ."[67]

---

62   Knoop & Jones, *Genesis of Freemasonry*, 88. If accurate, this account could   refer to Masonic adoption of typological interpretations similar to popular works like Samuel Lee's *Orbis Miraculum* (1659) and John Bunyan's *Solomon's Temple Spiritualiz'd* (1688). Typological or symbolic interpretations of the Bible reached their apogee in the seventeenth and eighteenth centuries.

63   Anderson, *Constitutions* (1723), 10, 11–12.

64   Pennell, *The Constitutions of the Free Masons*, 59. See the discussion of this prayer in Christopher B. Murphy's article, "Assessing Authentic Lodge Culture," in this volume.

65   Anderson, *Constitutions* (1723), 105.

66   Henley, *Select Orations on Various Subjects*, 3.

67   Ibid., 8.

Examples like these demonstrate the interest that early Grand
Lodge era Freemasons had in specifically *textual-interpretive* approaches. Through symbolism and the experience of initiation,
they often appear to have believed that it was possible to gain
special insight into sacred matters.

THE MASONS' FACULTY

The "original language" which "none but masons are capable of
learning" is an important theme within early grand lodge era
Freemasonry, and surely antedates it. Although, superficially, it
is easy to understand in simple terms as referring to the modes
of recognition and the signs of distress, a close examination of
the early Masonic writings reveals a more extensive concept:
the notion of a sophisticated primordial language of symbol.
The 1721 dedication to *Long Livers* is written in a heavily symbolic style that Samber calls "the true Language of the Brotherhood," a special form of communication that is found in both
"the holy Scriptures" and "an uninterrupted Tradition."[68] The
Biblical reference is to the story of the Tower of Babel (Genesis
11:1–9), wherein God disrupts the construction by confusing the
language of the builders. In internal versions of this story, Freemasons connected their special language to the original language
or suggested a vestigial connection to it. In other words, the
Masons taught that they had special access to some form of this
earlier, purer language. This may be viewed as a transgressive
theme because the legendary stonemasons sought to mitigate the
divine intervention of the confusion of languages by preserving
their former means of communication—and the knowledge that
would otherwise be lost—through either the preservation of a
special "faculty" or the creation of a new means to facilitate that

68   [Samber], *Long Livers*, iii.

communication. This is reinforced in Anderson's *Constitutions* of 1723, where the Traditional History states that "the *Science* and *Art* were both transmitted to latter Ages and distant Climes, notwithstanding the Confusion of Languages or Dialects," which helped "give Rise to the Masons Faculty and ancient universal Practice of conversing without speaking."[69] In the 1738 second edition, Anderson added a note: "This old *Tradition* is believed firmly by the old *Fraternity*."[70] A lecture delivered most likely by Provincial Grand Master Joseph Laycock on March 8, 1735/6, at the constitution of a new lodge in Gateshead in the north of England, features additional details that are impressively vivid:

> Their Design and End in building this prodigious Tower (as we suppose) was not only for establishing a Name, but also to fix a Centre of Unity and Correspondence, to which they might, upon any Occasion, repair, least for Want of some such Remarkable, they might become dispersed over the Face of the Earth, and by that means loose that Intercourse with one another which they wanted to preserve. But their Designs running counter to the Purpose of the Allmighty, what they endeavoured to avoid, he miraculously brought about by the Confusion of Tongues, which gave Origin to the MASONS antient Practice of conversing without speaking, by means of proper *Signals* expressive of their Ideas. And the Professors of the *Royal* Art, knowing the Necessity they were under of dispersing, in order to populate the Earth, established several mysterious Ceremonials among themselves, to serve as Principles of Unity, and to distinguish one anothers by in Parts remote.[71]

69   Anderson, *Constitutions* (1723), 5.
70   Anderson, *New Book of Constitutions* (1738), 6.
71   Smith, *The Book M*, 1:19.

A 1754 exposure further expounds on the idea, saying that after the confusion of tongues, Belus [Nimrod] "assembled another Grand Lodge, and instructed his Men how to converse by Signs, &c. whereby they were capable of executing his future Designs."[72] A note on this passage reads: "This was what gave Rise to what is called Free-Masonry, being fifty-three Years after the first Assembly, or Lodge held. This Tradition is firmly believed."[73] A footnote later in the same source relates that this skill degenerated over time, from a technique that could convey ideas down to simple communication modes such as a distress sign:

> The Masons Faculty, and ancient, universal Practice of conversing, and knowing each other at a Distance, by Signs, &c is supposed to be greatly lost, by Reason there is so very little remaining, but however trifling the Remains, a Mason is oblig'd to answer all lawful Signs, therefore, if he be at work on the Top of a Building, he is obliged to come down, and answer, if such a Sign be given.[74]

In the Leland-Locke Pseudepigraphon—first published in 1753, and commonly referred to as the Leland MS, although scholars believe that no such manuscript ever existed—it is also clear that this language has extended capability and esoteric connotations.[75] In the "ancient" part of the text, the Masons are described as concealing many things, including "the Wey

72   Slade, *The Free Mason Examin'd*, 10.
73   Ibid.
74   Ibid., 20.
75   Although the Leland MS was a pseudepigraphon, it was accepted throughout in the eighteenth century as authentic, and Freemasons took no issue with its description of their Craft. A copy of it, in fact, follows the *Dissertation Upon Masonry* in the C.W. Moore MS. Sadly, this portion of the manuscript does not appear to have been photographed.

of Wynnynge the Facultye of Abrac, the Skylle of becommynge gude and parfyghte wythouten the Holpynges of Fere, and Hope; and the Universelle Longage of Maconnes."[76] The notes written in the name of John Locke explain this as follows:

> An universal language has been much desired by the learned of many ages. 'Tis a thing rather to be wished than hop'd for. But it seems the MASONS pretend to have such a thing among them. If it be true, I guess it must be something like the language of the PANTOMIMES among the ancient Romans, who are said to be able, by signs only, to express and deliver any oration intelligibly to men of all nations, and languages. A man who has all these arts and advantages, is certainly in a condition to be envied: but we are told, that this is not the case with all MASONS; for tho' these arts are among them, and all have a right and an opportunity to know them, yet some want capacity, and others industry to acquire them.[77]

Clearly, more than modes of recognition are intended here, since 1) this language is supposed to express ideas, and 2) it is said that some Masons lack the sophistication and dedication to learn the language, which is hardly an issue with the modes of recognition and signs of distress. The idea of a secret, information-bearing language understandable only by some Freemasons is difficult to classify, because it is apparent that it existed mostly in fiction. It is, of course, *exclusionary* per the first taxon, but the implication of these accounts is that prior to the degenerated versions (one-dimensional signs of recognition and distress) it was possible to convey complex information through the Masons' Faculty. Since there is no need to conceal information that is commonplace or

76   Anon., "An Antient MS on Free Masonry," 420.
77   Ibid.

unprivileged, the implication is that the content of such messages was esoteric itself and would therefore belong to the *interpretive* function, or the second taxon of Masonic esotericism.

THE TRIGRADAL SYSTEM

The orator's identification of Paul's vision of "the third heaven or paradice" with "the third *&* Chief degree of Masonry" is note-worthy, as it demonstrates that the so-called trigradal system of initiation—which, according to some, originated in the 1720s in London—was apparently well-established in this American lodge, and potentially others like it, by 1734. Although many scholars would suggest that the trigradal division was less than a decade old in 1734, the *Dissertation* gives no indication of the division into three degrees being new. First, of course, the speak-er offers his ideas "by way of Instruction to younger Bretheren" (sic), which indicates that the lodge had members who were not recent initiates. This impression is reinforced by the docu-ment's position that "a particular Explication of these things to the well Instructed Mason would be needless." Thus, there are two classes of hearers: the younger and less instructed, and the older and well-instructed. It is reasonable to proposed that there may be a number of years involved in the distinction between these two categories within the lodge. If it is true that a segment of the original hearers of the sermon had been Masons for sev-eral years—long enough to remember the transition from two degrees into three—then the narrative's central conceit of Saint Paul experiencing the third degree many centuries prior would have met only with amusement. Instead, the lodge of which the *Dissertation* orator is a part seems to believe the trigradal divi-sion to be ancient.

This is a very notable feature, and one which poses some

challenge to the consensus position that the trigradal division originated in London around 1725 and spread from there. The mechanism of its propagation into the lodges remains a problem for scholars, as the premier Grand Lodge's authority was still in its nascent stages, and it does not seem to have had the prerogative to directly command lodges in (and beyond) England to so fundamentally revamp the structure of their degrees. In light of these circumstances, the propagation—and, if we are impartial, perhaps even the origination—of the trigradal system remain an intriguing problem. The *Dissertation* provides an important point of reference for the question.

MASONIC INSTRUCTION

The *Dissertation* reveals that Masonic instruction was offered in this Colonial lodge. As mentioned above, the "well instructed" members of the lodge are explicitly identified as a privileged group who have special understanding. The implication is clear both here and elsewhere in the *Dissertation* that there are both beginning and advanced Freemasons, and this distinction was defined not just by seniority but by the amount of instruction received. The orator says that it would be "needless" to provide an explanation "to the well instructed Mason." This indicates that, at least in the American lodge which received this address, Masonic instruction was taking place. This seems to contradict the popular view that there was no instruction in the lodges at this time beyond the ceremonies themselves. The implication of the orator's statement here is not necessarily that the brethren would already have understood the specific points being made in his speech, but the wording here and the overall nature of the *Dissertation* suggests that Freemasons in this lodge had received sufficient instruction to hear and contemplate his address.

This strongly suggests that a rather complex interpretive function was part of lodge culture within American Freemasonry in the 1730s. This should not surprise us, as it is well-documented that English lodges very often featured educational content. In addition to lectures offered on various outside subjects, orations were delivered by willing brothers explaining the meanings—as they perceived them—of Masonic symbolism, lore, and ritual.[78] Within this wider context, *A Dissertation upon Masonry* contributes to our overall understanding of intellectual activity within the lodges of English and American Masonry of the early Grand Lodge era.

THE LODGE AS A FORM OF PARADISE

Architectural historian James Curl describes how, when Masons gathered in spaces such private halls and taverns, they were actually striving to meet in an imaginary, symbolic space:

> ...Freemasons had to set up their emblems and images in rooms acquired for meetings and so the décor was of a temporary nature, indicating perhaps a Lodge of the imagination, with objects and signs placed in certain positions as to aid in remembering ritual, secrets, and the Mason Word. [...]
>
> It is also clear from Masonic rituals and catechisms that there was an Ideal Lodge, a symbolic building, that Freemasons shared in imagination.[79]

78   See Trevor Stewart's Prestonian Lecture, "English Speculative Freemasonry: Some Possible Origins, Themes and Developments." Stewart often refers to this intellectual activity as "Masonic cerebration," and credits to it the expanding number of degrees.

79   James Stevens Curl, *The Art and Architecture of Freemasonry*, 53.

The imaginal space of the Ideal Lodge often seems to have possessed an aspect of transcending time and referring, paradoxically, to various interconnected sacred contexts: Eden, the Temple of Solomon, and the celestial lodge. The assertion that a Masonic Lodge was a sacred space that may be viewed by initiates as a "type"[80] or representation of Eden was a key idea of eighteenth-century Masonic philosophy, in a manner parallel to the conception of the Lodge as a representation of Solomon's Temple.

Typological interpretation of scripture has existed since ancient times and is found in Biblical literature itself. It is defined as "the interpretation of persons, events, and institutions in light of their resemblance or correspondence to other persons, events, and institutions, within a common framework of sacred history."[81] Allegorical interpretations of this kind were a primary feature of kabbalistic literature in Jewish thought. In Christianity, this method of interpretation flourished after the Reformation.

Poetic interpretations of this kind may be understood as "merely" figurative or as revealing esoteric meanings intentionally concealed within an ancient text. In the *Dissertation*, both the identification of Paul's ascent to the third heaven with the third degree of Masonic initiation and the identification of the Lodge with paradise are examples of typology. The identification of the Lodge as a *typos* of paradise or heaven is, of course, still visible in Freemasonry today in the idea that the tiled Lodge represents or "reflects" the heavenly "celestial lodge."[82]

Typological interpretation fell out of favor after Enlightenment rationalism became the dominant mode of Western thought, perhaps because the connections that most typological

---

80   In the sense of "An imperfect symbol or anticipation of something." (OED).

81   Soulen & Soulen, *Handbook of Biblical Criticism*, 203.

82   See Eyer, "The Lodge Primordial and Eternal," forthcoming.

readings make are considered historically impossible.

The typological readings of the *Dissertation*, however, pre-date that sense of disconnection, and the comparisons that it draws take place within an internally consistent world view: namely, that of the Traditional History of the Order. Freemasonry's Traditional History provides that "common framework of sacred history" needed to infer the kinds of connections that the *Dissertation* draws.

The Masonic literature, lectures, sermons, and songs of the early Grand Lodge era frequently hint at the mythical identification of the Lodge with paradise. This is rooted in the traditional concept of the secrets of Masonry being communicated to Adam and passed down through his sons.[83]

Although they were usually private rooms above taverns in reality, the environs used for Masonic ritual were ritualistically transformed into surrogates for sacred spaces. This sacred space has been viewed as representing Eden, the Jerusalem Temple, and Heaven—not necessarily from a mutually exclusive perspective, but in a simultaneous and multivalent way. It is reasonable to consider that the purpose behind such an identification was not so much that the brethren would "believe" those connections intellectually, but that the activity of the ceremony within the symbolic locus of a timeless and sacred space was intended to have a positive influence upon the affect of the candidate.

Scholar Olaf Kuhlke treats this subject in his 2008 study, *Geographies of Freemasonry: Ritual, Lodge, and City in Spatial Context*: "By symbolically transporting the candidate and the participating lodge members back to a time when a sacred place was built...the lodge temporarily becomes a sacred place and time where the presence of God can be felt."[84] Considered from

---

83   Anderson, *Constitutions* (1723), 1–2, 75, 80; *New Book* (1738), 1–3.
84   Kuhlke, *Geographies of Freemasonry*, 64. Speaking of the experience of the third degree specifically, Kuhlke argues that it

this perspective, the *Dissertation's* language seems less fanciful and more natural. The performative experience of the Master Mason degree becomes mythopoetically charged with meanings that temporarily conflate the individual candidate and his circumstances with the character of Hiram and the circumstances surrounding his fate and the so-called lost word.[85] Consequent to this experience, it would be fitting for the newly "raised" Master Mason to view his participation in the Lodge as an anticipatory *typos* of heavenly perfection.

An early Masonic lecture featured in *The Book M, or Masonry Triumphant* (1736) explicitly connects Masonic enlightenment with celestial life, and includes poetic descriptions of the experience of the heavenly brethren, whose bliss is "continually enlarged" within the celestial lodge:

> IN all our Pursuits of Knowledge we make Truth in the Particular the Summit of our Aim; for when we have attain'd

"should impress upon the candidate the notion that the Masonic Temple is a sacred place, and the times when meetings are held, are to be regarded as sacred time." That the main activity of both the second and third degrees of Freemasonry are dramatically set in the Solomonic era is explicit.

85 Jan Snoek, an academic scholar who has greatly advanced the study of the evolution of Masonic ritual, holds that in the early Grand Lodge era, the candidate's experience of the Hiramic drama was intended to communicate a mystical or symbolic identification of Hiram with the Supreme Architect. Snoek argues that "the candidate is identified with a hero, who turns out to be (a) deity. In that way, the ritual *Unio Mystica* between the candidate and the divinity is expressed and realized." See "The Evolution of the Hiramic Legend," pages 34 & 42. Snoek's understanding of the early version of the Craft working is not inconsistent with the thrust of the 1734 *Dissertation*. The *Dissertation's* comparison of the third degree to Paul's heavenly vision, though dissonant through a later, more rationalist, understanding of Masonry, accords well with the implications that Snoek's research presents.

to that we can go no further: Towards this glorious Height
our Natures, if not depress'd, are continually soaring. Then
open wide your mental Eyes, ye generous Fellows, let
Truth's bright Radiations enter. He is most knowing that
knows most of Truth, and he is wise, who acts according to
it. Was it not Truth that form'd the wide Expanse of Nature,
and rang'd it in such Beauty and Harmony? In fine, it was
Truth that gave every Being to be what it is.

Great is the God of Truth, the only Fountain of true living Pleasures, unfading Joys, and never ending Bliss, such
only worth the Quest, of all that know and love themselves,
such only do as set a true Value on their own immortal
Souls, and are not content to lye grovelling in the present transitory Pleasures, which the corporeal Life affords,
but look farther, even into Eternity, and by that Means in
some Measure prelibate those Soul enchanting Joys that
surround the ineffable Throne of Heaven.

The Universe is that great Volume to which we alone
Confine our Studies, in which, each Line, each Letter,
speaks the Almighty Architect, and in sweet Melody declare his Excellence. These are the Studies in which those
immortal Youths that compose the Celestial Hierarchy,
those Divine Philosophers that tread the Azure Empirean
Plains of Heaven, and stand in Presence of their great Original, continually are exercised: By them the infinite Perfections of the Deity are continually traced thro' all the Footsteps of his Handy work, both in the upper and inferiour
Natures; thus do they happy live in an eternal Increase of
Knowledge; the more they know of him the greater is their
Love, the more they love the greater their Fruition: Thus are
their Minds and Bliss continually enlarged, and each new
Entity by them discovered, or a new Scene of Nature open
laid, proves a sweet Instrument for their skilful Touches

to sound melodiously their Author's Praise. *These glorious Patterns let us Masters strive to imitate, that even, while confined to this narrow and gloomy Prison of our Bodies, we may open to ourselves a Kind of Heaven here below, till that dear Time, when (having finished well our Parts in this Lodge militant) we are called to that triumphant one above.*[86]

It is valuable to note that the celestial lodge is here characterized as the "Lodge triumphant" in contrast to the "Lodge militant" on earth. This direct parallel to ecclesiastical language is employed in order to illustrate the idea of a vital connection between the earthly brethren and those "those Divine Philosophers that tread the Azure Empirean Plains of Heaven, and stand in Presence of their great Original." This connection is dynamic enough, when Freemasonry is properly practiced, to allow earthly Masons to "imitate" the heavenly lodge "even while confined" to physical bodies, so that they might "open to [themselves] a Kind of Heaven here below." This Masonic version of the *communio sanctorum* is conceptually consonant with the main thrust of the 1734 *Dissertation* as given in the American Colonies. It also makes a subtle appearance in a speech given by Martin Clare before the premier Grand Lodge of England on December 11, 1735:[87]

---

86   Smith, *The Book M*, 1:11–12, emphasis added.

87   The speech had originally been given some months earlier at the lodge later known as the Grand Stewards' Lodge. As recently demonstrated, over 87 percent of the speech is actually paraphrased from an essay by John Locke. The sections discussed in this paper are original to Clare. For complete details about the intertextuality of Clare's speech and Locke's *Some Thoughts Concerning Education*, see Shawn Eyer, "The Inward Civility of the Mind: The 1735 Grand Oration of Martin Clare, F.R.S." and Martin Clare, "A Discourse on Good Behaviour for the Guidance of the Members of the Craft," Shawn Eyer, Ed. *Philalethes: The Journal of Masonic Research and Letters* 69 (2016): 64–67.

SHALL it then ever be said, that those, who by Choice are distinguished from the Gross of Mankind, and who voluntarily have enrolled their Names in this most Ancient and Honourable Society, are so far wanting to themselves and the Order they profess, as to neglect its Rules? Shall those who are banded and cemented together by the strictest Ties of Amity, omit the Practice of Forbearance and Brotherly Love? Or shall the Passions of those Persons ever become ungovernable, who assemble purposely to subdue them?

WE are, let it be considered, the Successors of those who reared a Structure to the Honour of Almighty God, the Grand Architect of the World, which for Wisdom, Strength and Beauty, hath never yet had any Parallel. We are intimately related to those great and worthy Spirits, who have ever made it their Business and their Aim to improve themselves, and to inform Mankind. Let us then copy their Example, that we may also hope to obtain a Share in their Praise.[88]

Clare's perspective is that Freemasons are "distinguished from the Gross of Mankind" by their voluntary participation in an Order in which they become "the Successors of those who reared a Structure to the Honour of Almighty God," whereby they become "intimately related to those great and worthy Spirits, who have ever made it their Business and their Aim to improve themselves, and to inform Mankind."

By referring to the legendary Masonic builders of Solomon's Temple as "Spirits" who continue to grow and develop as well as act to benefit humanity, Clare's speech of 1735 parallels the

---

88   The first surviving printing of Clare's speech is from J. Scott, *The Pocket Companion and History of Free-Masons* (1754), 281–91. The section cited is from pages 289–90. For an accessible transcript, see Martin Clare, "A Discourse on Good Behaviour for the Guidance of the Members of the Craft," 67.

speech found in *The Book M* (which likely originated around the
same time) that states that the heavenly Freemasons "live in an
eternal Increase of Knowledge" and that "their Minds and Bliss
[are] continually enlarged."

Alexander Piatigorsky observed that other material found in
early Masonic literature and rhetoric "highlights the elite *religious status* of Masons, describing them as if they not only represented the supreme force among all the world's religions but
also enjoyed a special and highly privileged relationship with
God."[89] Rather than attributing soteriological significance to this
"special" status, it was instead was tied to a privileged kind of
knowledge or wisdom about certain "mysteries." This is illustrated by the prayer at initiation, of which the earliest printed form,
which appeared in 1730, reads:

> And we beseech thee, O LORD GOD, to bless this our pres-
> ent Undertaking, and grant that this, our new Brother, may
> dedicate his Life to thy Service, and be a true and faithful
> Brother among us, *endue him with Divine Wisdom, that
> he may, with the Secrets of* Masonry, *be able to unfold the
> Mysteries of Godliness and Christianity.*[90]

Taken in wider context, the 1734 *Dissertation* seems less and
less anomalous. While many of its themes are obscure and spiritual, they were not at all out of place in the Masonic literature
of the time period.

Moreover, although the idea of transforming a part of one's

89   Alexander Piatigorsky, *Who's Afraid of Freemasons?*, 114.
     Piatigorsky's immediate reference was to the 1728 oration of
     Edward Oakley, using language cited from the March 1, 1721
     Masonic essay of Eugenius Philalethes, Jr. (that is, Robert Samber).

90   John Pennell, *Constitutions*, 59. For a more detailed discussion of
     this passage, see Christopher B. Murphy's "Assessing Authentic
     Lodge Culture" in this collection.

community temporarily into paradise may strike the modern reader as nonsensical, it was a concept that enjoyed significant currency in the American Colonies, even outside of Freemasonry. The setting of the New World inspired ideas of a radical break from history and a new beginning for humanity. The aim of restoring paradise was a notable aspect of religious thought in New England, including Puritan beliefs. As Zachary Hutchins points out, among American Masons this took two forms: the symbolic identification of the Lodge with Eden, and the "hopes that Freemasons could collectively transform the American continent into a prelapsarian paradise."[91]

A clear expression of this is found in the language of a charge given by John Eliot at Boston on June 24, 1783, for the installation of John Warren as Grand Master. Eliot went beyond the idea of the Lodge as Paradise and poetically expressed the concept that Masonic virtues, practiced universally, could *return the world to an prelapsarian state*:

> If men practiced the divine social virtues—The curse would no longer devour the earth—Eden would yield forth her blooms and spices.—[Th]ere would be no prickling briar around the lilies and roses of this beautiful garden.—The sons and daughters of men might repose under the bowers of paradise, and angels of light and love would look down not with pity, but with joy upon us.[92]

And, as late as 1795, a Masonic sermon by a highly influential American Masonic cleric and educator emphatically describes, "without a metaphor, in what respects a Lodge on earth, duly regulated according to its professed principles, grounded in scripture,

---

91 See Hutchins, *Inventing Eden*, 238.
92 C. Gore, *An Oration: Delivered at the Chapel, in Boston* (Boston: William Green, 1783), 17.

may be compared to Heaven, or the Lodge of Paradise above."[93] In fact, as shown below, this sermon demonstrates literary dependence upon the 1734 *Dissertation*.

Evidence of Circulation and Literary Influence

Since *A Dissertation upon Masonry* was not published until its discovery by Charles Whitlock Moore in 1849, it might be supposed that it had no influence on Masonic thought in the eighteenth century beyond its 1734 context. However, the internal evidence of the C.W. Moore MS itself indicates that the *Dissertation* was in at least limited circulation decades after its original delivery. This is clear, because the MS also contains a transcription of the Leland-Locke Pseudepigraphon (or Leland MS), which first appeared in 1753.[94] Discounting the unlikely possibility that the C.W. Moore MS is somehow the earliest specimen of the Leland-Locke item, one concludes that the C.W. Moore MS was copied after 1753. This means that the *Dissertation*, though unpublished, was being actively preserved two decades after it was composed. Although this may indicate only an autograph (now lost) and the C.W. Moore MS copy, there is reason to believe that further pen-and-paper distribution of the *Dissertation* took place.

This is proven by a close review of the text of a sermon given in 1795 at St. Peter's Church, Philadelphia, by Rev. Dr. William

93   William Smith, *The Works of William Smith, D.D.*, 2:82.

94   C.W. Moore recorded that the manuscript he discovered contained the text of the Leland MS "appended" to the *Dissertation*; see Moore, "The First Masonic Discourse," 289. The manuscript is not currently available for inspection. Photographic images of the manuscript strongly support the accuracy of Moore's statement, as the final four lines of page 12 contain material that pertains to the Leland-Locke and has no bearing on the *Dissertation*.

Smith.[95] Smith (1727–1803) was an extremely prominent thought leader in the early Republic. In addition to his clerical duties as an Anglican priest, he was a visionary thinker in the world of higher education. He served as the first Provost of the College of Philadelphia (now the University of Pennsylvania), and founded two important liberal arts colleges in Maryland: Washington College in Chestertown, and St. John's College in Annapolis.[96]

He was also a devoted Freemason, and served as the Grand Chaplain of the Grand Lodge of Pennsylvania (Moderns) in 1755, and then as the Grand Secretary of the Grand Lodge of Pennsylvania (Antients) from 1778 to 1782. Additionally, he was directly involved in the establishment of the Grand Lodge of Maryland.

Smith was sixty-nine years old when he gave his last Masonic sermon at the June 24, 1795, communication of the Grand Lodge of Pennsylvania. He took as his text Ecclesiastes 2:21, understood as the words of King Solomon: "There is a MAN, whose Labour is in Wisdom, and in Knowledge, and in Equity." Near the beginning, the founding father expresses his reluctance to deliver yet another Masonic address:

> The emphatical meaning of the word Man, as used by our master, Solomon, in the Philosophical and Masonic sense of this text, I need not explain in this splendid assembly of Masons. It is understood within the walls of the congregated Lodge, and carried abroad into the world by every true Brother, in the Grand Lodge of the heart.
>
> As such a Man, I would strive to acquit myself on this occasion. Forty years will this day have finished the long period, since I first addressed, from this pulpit, a Grand

95   Smith, *The Works of William Smith*, 2:73–88.

96   An excellent account of Smith's influence in American higher education may be found in Charlotte Fletcher's *Cato's Mirania: A Life of Provost Smith*.

Communication of Brethren, with our great fellow-labour-er, the venerable Franklin, at their head; and frequent have been the calls upon me for similar addresses, during the important æra that hath since succeeded.

It was with reluctance, therefore, that I engaged in this day's duty, knowing that I had little new to offer; and that little must be offered, with a great decay of former vigour, both of body and mind.

But the unanimous request of the Brotherhood oper-ates as a command on me, once more to undertake what I trust they will accept as a final labour among them; squared by the Rules of Wisdom and Equity, and mensurated by the best Compass of my Knowledge; taking as a model not only the labours of Solomon, but of one greater than Solomon, so far as they can be imitated, namely, the Great Architect of the world; all whose labours are in the Infinite Perfection of Wisdom and Knowledge and Equity.[97]

Smith immediately directs the hearer's attention to the word "Man," which he interprets in a technical Masonic sense—a meaning he regards as esoteric (in the *social-exclusionary* mode). This directly parallels the rhetoric of the 1734 *Dissertation*:

When I was a child, says he, I understood as a Child...but when I became *a man (an Expression Emphatically Signif-icant among us)* when I became a man then...I put away Childish things.[98]

I knew a man, Say's he, meaning himself, above 14 years ago whither in the body, or out of the Body I cannot tell, but I knew such a one taken up into the third heaven into paradice

97   Smith, *The Works of William Smith*, 2:73–74. Emphasis added.
98   C.W. Moore ms, lines 22–26. Emphasis added.

where he heard unspeakable words which it is not lawful for
any Man to utter, of such a one will I Glory. *Freemasons know
very well why the apostle calls himself a Man....*[99]

Both of these eighteenth-century Masonic texts use the word
man in a special, technical sense that has to do with the Masonic status of an individual rather than his biological status as a
human being. In 1734, the term is described as "Emphatically
Significant among us." In 1795, it has an "emphatical meaning,"
in the context of a "Philosophical and Masonic sense" which "is
understood within the walls of the congregated Lodge."
    Smith then specifies that he (like, of course, his listeners) is
"such a Man." Then, he connects the concept to St. Paul in terms
nearly identical to those found in the C.W. Moore MS.:

> I knew a Man, says he (still using the word Man in the same
> emphatical sense, well understood by Masons, as it was
> used by Solomon in the text)—"I knew a man in Christ,
> above fourteen years ago—(whether in the body I cannot
> tell, or whether out of the body I cannot tell, God knoweth),
> but I knew such a man caught up to the third Heaven, into
> Paradise, where he heard unspeakable words, which it is
> not lawful for a Man to utter—Of such an one will I glory."
> St. Paul speaks here of his own Trance and Vision, when
> converted and rapt up into the third Heavens ....[100]

The earlier 1734 version of this, already cited, follows:

> I knew a man, Say's he, meaning himself, above 14 years
> ago whither in the body, or out of the Body I cannot tell,
> but I knew such a one taken up into the third heaven into

99   Ibid., lines 40–45. Emphasis added.
100   Smith, *The Works of William Smith*, 2:81. Emphasis added.

paradice where he heard unspeakable words which it is
not lawful for any Man to utter, of such a one will I Glory.
Freemasons know very well why the apostle calls himself
a Man, they know why he could not tell whether, when he
was made a mason he was in the Body or out of the Body,
and what is meant by the body, they know also that by the
third heaven or paradice is figur'd out the third & Chief
degree of Masonry, & they are very well acquainted with
those unspeakable words, which is not lawful for a man to
utter, as a particular Explication of these things to the well
Instructed Mason would be needless, so to the World it is
needless and Improper.[101]

The intertextuality between the 1734 and 1795 sermons is
demonstrated further by the language used in equating the Masonic lodge to heaven. William Smith's version continues:

Returning, therefore, to the words of St. Paul—"I knew a
Man, whether in the body or out of the body, I cannot
tell!" and comparing earthly things with heavenly—The
Brethren here assembled, well understand what is meant
by the emphatical words—"Man and Body;" and not being
able to tell, in certain situations of the Initiated, whether
they "were in the Body or out of the Body;" and also what
is meant by their being taken up to the third Heaven, or
Paradise of their Art and Craft; and hearing the words,
which it is not lawful to utter, but to the true Brethren; to
those who have the Signs and Tokens of fellowship, and the
language of Brotherly-love!
    But passing over all those mysterious expressions (both
in the scripture original, and in the copy brought down to
the practice of the Lodge); I shall consider, in language

101   C.W. Moore MS, lines 40–53.

familiar to all, and without a metaphor, in what respects a Lodge on earth, duly regulated according to its professed principles, grounded in scripture, may be compared to Heaven, or the Lodge of Paradise above.[102]

As seen above, Smith's sermon parallels the 1734 *Dissertation* once more by asserting a technical, "emphatical," meaning to the word "Body." Furthermore, the third degree of Masonry is compared to Paul's ascent to the third heaven. And, finally, Smith echoes the idea that Freemasons might possess traditions that parallel—but are not mere duplications of—the "mysterious expressions" of Biblical texts. As noted earlier, the 1734 sermon claims that only Freemasons can understand such passages fully:

> ...the learned annotators & Interpreters of Scriptures, however penetrating & clear they have been in other dark places, yet none of them been of ye lodge, they Could not possibly Conceive the apostle's true meaning in this mysterious part of his Epistle....[103]

In Smith's language, the "mysterious expressions" exist "both in the scripture original, and in the copy brought down to the practice of the Lodge." Smith's concept appears to be that the practices enacted "within the walls of the congregated Lodge" represent a "copy" that corresponds to a Biblical "original" that has been transmitted or "brought down" through the traditions of the Craft. As notable as Smith's presentation of this idea is, perhaps the fact that he regarded his listeners—the officers and brethren of the Grand Lodge—as familiar with this rhetoric is just as, or even more, remarkable. Smith is not speaking here as one introducing a new idea to his audience, but as one employing the internal parlance of an institution.

102   Smith, *The Works of William Smith*, 2:82.
103   C.W. Moore MS, lines 34–38.

Rev. Smith's sermon continues to delineate three ways in which the Lodge resembles "Heaven, or the Lodge of Paradise above." The first reason pertains to the perfection of the Order's design:

> And first the Lodge below may resemble the Lodge above, by the excellency of its Constitution and Government, which are so devised, that although the Will of the Master, like the Will of God, is a Law to the whole Family; yet He can neither Will nor Do any thing but what is according to Wisdom, and Knowledge, and Justice, and Right Reason; and therefore the obedience of his Lodge is cheerful and unrestrained. For the peculiar light of his profession assists him in discerning what is best for his Houshold or Lodge; and that Love, which is the lasting cement of his Family, disposes all the Brethren to act with One Mind and Heart. But not so hath it been among mankind in general. For although they have busied themselves in all ages, in the framing civil Constitutions, and plans of Government; in forming, and reforming them, in pulling down and building up—yet still their labours have been too much in vain— because they have daubed with untempered mortar, and their corner-stones, have not been laid (as in the Lodge, and according to our text,) in Wisdom and in Knowledge and in Equity of Rights![104]

This tracks closely with the first reason given in the 1734 *Dissertation*:

> 1$^{s[t]}$ In the first place, the Lodge may be likened to heaven on account of the Excellency *&* perfection of its Constitution and Government: it is an absolute Monarchy, in which the Will of the Sovereign is a law, but so wisely Contrived *&* Es-

---

104 Smith, *The Works of William Smith,* 2:82–83.

tablished, that the Sovereign can never will nor Command any thing which is not exactly agreable to the nature & reason of things, & by the Subjects Received and Submitted to with Pleasure; the pecul[i]ar light of Masonry Enabling to discern what is best with Regard to the Lodge, & that love which is the lasting cement of our Society, disposes all the Brethren to agree to it with an unanimity not elsewhere to be practised. Men have in all ages busied themselfs in forming and Reforming Commonwealths, Monarchies, Aristocrasies & many other Species of Governments; but the Experience of all ages has shewn that all their forms were Imperfect, either unable to Support themselfs against outward violence, or dying of their inward deceases, hence we see no State or Constitutions have subsisted many Centuries without Violent convulsions[,] Revolutions & Changes: this has been the Fate of the Syrians, Persian & Grecian Monarchies, the Commonwealths of Sparta, Rome & Athens: but the Constitution of the Kingdom of Masons hapily Tempered, preserves to this day, its ancient and original vigour, and will doubtless last till time itself shall be Swallowed up in the boundless ocean of Eternity.[105]

In the first part of the second reason Smith offers in order to compare the Lodge to Heaven is the uniform prevalence of brotherly love that characterizes both sacred spaces, while a common set of signs unites people of many languages:

Secondly, the Lodge may be said to resemble Heaven, on account of the universal Good Will which reigns therein, among the Brethren, although of different languages and countries. It is not necessary to have the labour of learning various tongues in the earthly, more than in the

105   C. W. Moore MS, lines 57–81.

heavenly Lodge. And although, at the building of Babel, the universal language of the workmen was confounded and divided, because they were divided in their hearts and workmanship; yet among the true Master-builders who have since remained at unity among themselves, there is but one language and the same tokens, which are known and understood by all in every country and clime; namely, the language of Love, and the tokens of Good Will![106]

The 1734 *Dissertation* stresses the same rationale:

2^d I[n] the Second place the apostel might Justly liken the Lodge to a Heaven, on account of the universal understand-ing which subsistes therein betwixt brethren of vastly dif-ferent Languages and Countrys. as in that place of Bliss we are not to suppose that none can converse or be understood but such as are able to speak English, Hebrew or any other particular national languages, so in the universal lodge the Beauty and benefit of masonry would be Extremely faint and narrow if Brethren of all nations, could not with plea-sure know[,] converse with and understand each others Tongues. When God Confounded the Common language of mankind, at the Building of Babel, the language of Masons Remain'd unaffected and Intire; it is true the Building ceas'd because the labourers who were the Bulk of the people could neither understand the master nor one another, therefore the Brethren separated and dispersed with the Rest; but in whatever country they settled and propagated the Royal art, they carefully preserved the original language, which continues among their successors to this day: a language which none but masons are capable of learning, a happiness

---

106   Smith, *The Works of William Smith*, 2:83.

which none but Brethren are capable of enjoying.[107]

Smith's second reason continues, highlighting the classless nature of the Lodge and Heaven, wherein all distinctions of wealth are disregarded:

> In the Lodge, as in Heaven, there are no distinctions of Rich and Poor, but all meet on the Level, and act on the Square; distinguished only by their different Skill in their Craft; and a zealous desire, both in the Lodge and out of the same, to promote all that is praise-worthy among the Brethren, and tending to enlighten and bless mankind, by an amiable conde-scension, and a benevolent freedom, which pervades and ac-tuates every member, and reigns undisturbed in the Lodge.[108]

This closely mirrors the 1734 *Dissertation's* third comparison of the Masonic Lodge and the heavenly realms:

> 3^{ly} In the third place, the apostle might liken the lodge to a heaven on account of that human[,] Kind & fraternal treatment of each other which is therein used among the Brethren. The great, the Riche, or noble of the world, ap-pear in the lodge without pride or Haughtines, an amiable Condescention, a Charming Benevolent freedom brightens their evry actions, those of the lower Rank of life, however they may behave abroad are in the lodge, found modest & peaceable[,] free from petulance or Sauciness to Supe-riours, gentle and loving to each other: In Heaven and in the lodge only are to be Seen humility without contempt, and dignity without Envy.[109]

107 C. W. Moore MS, lines 82–103.
108 Smith, *The Works of William Smith*, 2:83–84.
109 C. W. Moore MS, lines 104–115.

Smith's third reason to correlate the Lodge with Heaven is that both welcome men of all nationalities, creeds, and vocations:

> In the third place, the Lodge may be said to resemble Heaven, because in Heaven, without respect of persons, they who fear God and work righteousness are received into happiness; so likewise the Lodge opens its bosom to receive good men (who come with the proper signs and tokens) of all Nations, Sects and Professions; and entertains them with sincere Love and Friendship—even as the quiet harbour of some hospitable port, opens its arms to the tempest-driven voyager, and offers him that security and rest, which, on the common ocean, he sought to enjoy in vain![110]

This strongly reflects the 1734 *Disseration's* fourth reason:

> 4[thly] In the fourth place I would observe that the apostle might Justly Enough liken the lodge to a Heaven on this account, that it is been Composed of good people of all Religions, Sects[,] perswasions & Denominations, of all nations and countrys, & I might add of all Generations of men in all ages since the Beginning of mankind. the Scriptures says, that with Regard to heaven, Verily God is no Respecter of persons but in ev'ry nation those who fear him and work Rightiousness shall be Saved, in like manner in the Lodge no narrow distinctions are made or Ragarded, but good & worthy men who are so in practise & the general conduct of their lives, of whatsoever Speculatife believe or opinion have a Right to desire & if they apply in a proper manner & from true & laudable motives, will doubtless obtain admission: the lodge stands Reddy with an open

110   Smith, *The Works of William Smith*, 2:84.

Bosom to Receave them all with sincere love & affectionate friendship: thus the Calm & quiet heaven of some hospitable port Extends its open arms to the wandring Tempest driven Voyager, affording him a Security & Repose which in a Restless ocean, (common life) is not to be met with.[111]

In his 1795 sermon, Smith continues to treat the theme of the "Paradisaical Lodge," guarded by the "*celestial Tyler*," using rhetoric that is profoundly beautiful:

> Thus instructed, and thus professing the principles and doctrines of the true Lodge, remember the fate of that first of Masons and of Men, our great progenitor Adam, who being found unworthy of the bliss which he enjoyed in his Paradisaical Lodge, was driven from thence by order of the omnipotent GRAND-MASTER; and a *celestial Tyler*, a mighty Cherubim, with a Sword of fire (mark the emblem)[112] was placed to guard the door, and forbid his future entrance.
>
> Since that time, the Lodges of his posterity have fallen from primitive order and perfection. Yet still they will be a resemblance of the Paradisaical lodge, and even of Heaven itself, so far as you labour earnestly in the exercise of Love, that great badge of your profession.[113]

Taken as a whole, these parallels reveal that, beyond question, William Smith's 1795 sermon demonstrates a direct literary dependency upon the 1734 *Dissertation*. Much of the structure and phraseology is so close that it seems that a copy of the 1734 ser-

111   C.W. Moore MS, lines 116–135.
112   This is a reference of the *flamberge* or wavy sword traditionally carried by the Tyler (or Tiler), an officer whose duty was to delineate the design of the lodge upon the floor of the meeting space and then to guard the lodge from outside during its meeting.
113   Smith, *The Works of William Smith*, 2:86–87.

mon must have been in William Smith's possession in the 1790s. Smith alludes to his borrowing elsewhere in the same sermon in a footnote: "The Masonic reader will readily allow, that in different Masonic Sermons, even by different Authors, repetitions and copying from each other, so far as concerns the mysteries of the Craft, Metaphors, Allusions, &c. are unavoidable."[114]

There is some evidence that Smith had a copy of the *Dissertation* as early as seventeen years prior, because he appears to quote from it directly in the sermon he gave at Christ Church in Philadelphia on December 28, 1778 (with, incidentally, George Washington in attendance):

> Learn when to be silent, and when to speak; for "a Babbler is an Abomination, because of the *unspeakable Words*, which a *Man* may not utter," but in a proper Place.[115]

The 1734 *Dissertation* has parallel language:

> Learn to be Silent: a Babler is an abomination.[116]

> …unspeakable words which it is not lawfull for any Man to utter….[117]

In 1791, Smith was selected to lead a committee to develop an address to congratulate George Washington on his election to the presidency on behalf of the Grand Lodge of Pennsylvania. The January 2, 1792, letter, which is reported to have been delivered personally by Rev. Smith, includes the Masonic concept of the "terrestrial Lodge" as an earthly counterpart of the "Celestial

114 Smith, *The Works of William Smith,* 2:75n.
115 Smith, *Ahiman Rezon,* 154.
116 C.W. Moore MS, line 218, paraphrasing 2 Corinthians 12:4.
117 Ibid., lines 50–51.

Lodge…where Cherubim and Seraphim, wafting our Congratulations from Earth to Heaven, shall hail you Brother."[118]

Interestingly, the 1734 *Dissertation* may be the first literary example of the theme that the harmony of the tiled Lodge reflects the harmony of the heavenly Temple. William Smith was influenced by this idea, and as early as December 28, 1778, expressed it in his prayer given before the sermon at Christ Church in Philadelphia:

> In thy Name we assemble, and in thy Name we desire to proceed in all our doings. Let the wisdom of thy blessed Son, through the grace and goodness of the Holy Ghost, so subdue every discordant passion within us, so harmonize and enrich our hearts with a portion of thine own love and goodness, that the Lodge, at this time, may be a sincere, though humble, copy of that Order and Beauty and Unity, which reign forever before thy Heavenly Throne.[119]

Adapted into a non-sectarian form, this verbiage was recommended as the opening prayer for American lodges in the Baltimore Convention's proposed national system of work and lectures.[120] It was later adopted as an official opening prayer within many American jurisdictions. It is not the contention of this paper that the 1734 *Dissertation upon Masonry* represents the original creation of any of its themes. However, its apparent influence upon William Smith, who in turn influenced American Masonic ritual practice, is of tremendous interest.

118   See Horace Wemyss Smith, *Life and Correspondence of the Rev. William Smith,* 2:347–48.
119   Smith, *The Works of William Smith,* 2:48. This was also printed in Smith's 1783 *Ahiman Rezon,* 165.
120   Charles Whitlock Moore & S.W.B. Carnegy, *The Masonic Trestle-Board,* 13.

Conclusion

The 1734 *Dissertation Upon Masonry* is an exceptionally rare and important document whose obscurity until now is deeply regrettable. The *Dissertation* is, as noted earlier, the oldest extant American lodge oration, and the third oldest surviving Masonic oration in the world. Moreover, unlike the earlier two orations of Drake and Oakley, which have come down to us only in published forms which suggest the possibility or probability of an editorial stage between their initial oral delivery and their incarnations as printed artifacts, the transcript of the 1734 American oration was never intended to be published. It is clearly a lecture that could only be given in a tiled lodge, transcribed unedited. That means that it is *the oldest surviving unmediated record of the private educational speech of speculative Freemasonry anywhere.*

As such, its contents are of profound interest to any student of early Grand Lodge era Masonic thought. A systematic analysis of the *Dissertation* demonstrates that all of its features are consistent with other very early Masonic literature.[121] The special value of the 1734 sermon is that it unites these themes into a narrative that provides a more vital perspective on how early Freemasons may have received and understood various threads of tradition.

The mystical nature of the oration is scarcely deniable, and what it has to say about the role of instruction within the lodges during this period of Masonic history is worth emphasizing. The fact that the *Dissertation* is essentially focused on the Master Mason's degree is relevant to all scholars who investigate the origins and progress of the so-called trigradal system of Masonic degrees. The 1734 sermon's overt claims of esoteric tradition illuminate contemporary Masonic writings, and demonstrate that second-taxon esotericism was acknowledged within the early

---

121   See the author's "A *Dissertation* Upon Masonry, 1734, with Commentary and Notes."

Grand Lodge era—negating the more common finding that the secrets of Masonry were only the various modes of recognition during that phase of development.

The religious character of the *Dissertation* is deeply informative. First, its content—like most Masonic ritual and literature—is diametrically opposite what would be expected if the narrative that Freemasonry was a school of Deism were generally accurate. David Hackett's observation that "Most Saint John's sermons stressed polite Christianity, yet [the 1734] oration suggests a divergence between it and Freemasonry"[122] is worthy of comment. To be certain, there is nothing either impolite or impious in the *Dissertation*. It recommends a moral standard for Masonic society which would be the paragon of any community of faith: it stresses honesty, forgiveness, tolerance, inclusion, and charity. Furthermore, it is a deeply reverential sermon, arcing at times into the mystical and concluding with a stirring and sincere benediction. Its only conceivable point of divergence from what Hackett terms "polite" religion is its teaching—far from unique in early Masonic literature—that Masonic initiates have some special insight into "dark" passages of scripture that others are unable to understand. Hackett found that in this text, "not only did Freemasonry predate Christianity but the Christian story veiled Freemasonry's deeper meaning"—specifically, that "Paul spoke to his fellow Masons in code through the Christian story."[123] He characterizes this and other early religious traits of Freemasonry as heterodoxical.[124]

This aspect of the *Dissertation* clearly displays the deep concern that many Freemasons of the early Grand Lodge era had with locating concealed truth within sacred traditions such as Biblical texts. Although such an approach may strike a rationalist

122   Hackett, *That Religion in Which All Men Agree*, 51.
123   Ibid.
124   Ibid., 52.

reader in modern times as anachronistic and inherently invalid, this mode of interpretation has a long pedigree in mystical literature. It bears a strong resemblance to traditional kabbalistic hermeneutics, and appears to be very consonant with Christian typological interpretation.[125] These techniques allow readers to discern (or develop) esoteric knowledge "concealed" within a text—and there is a long, perfectly orthodox, tradition of engaging in such forms of exegesis.

Despite its obvious historical value, *A Dissertation upon Masonry* has been almost completely ignored since its discovery in 1849, which points to methodological blind spots that can be deleterious to our ultimate task of understanding early Freemasonry. Although academic historians Steven Bullock and David Hackett realized the *Dissertation's* critical value, the contents of the oration have been all but disregarded by Masonic historians. It has therefore failed to leave a trace in historical narratives about the Freemasonry of the 1730s. Few were aware of it, and of those who did mention it, its existence was merely noted: what it had to say was not of interest, despite it being the only surviving example of American Masonic interpretation from the 1730s, the very decade that saw the Craft officially established in the Colonies.

Now that the importance of this document is becoming acknowledged, we may begin to better understand the American Freemasonry that thrived in the days of Henry Price and Benjamin Franklin. The 1734 *Dissertation* offers thought-provoking insight into the culture of early American Freemasonry, and cannot be legitimately excluded from any future historical analysis of the Craft in the American Colonies during the early Grand Lodge era.

125   For a summary of the kabbalistic "four-fold" method of interpretation (which allows for allegorical and "secret" readings), see Idel, *Absorbing Perfections*, 429–37. For background on Christian typological interpretation, see the section labeled "The Lodge as a Form of Paradise" in this paper.

Bibliography

Anderson, James. *The Constitutions of the Freemasons, Containing the History, Charges, Regulations, &c. of that most Ancient and Right Worshipful Fraternity.* London: William Hunter, 1723.

————. *The Constitutions of the Freemasons. Containing the History, Charges, Regulations, &c. of that Most Ancient and Right Worshipful Fraternity.* Philadelphia: Benjamin Franklin, 1734.

————. *The New Book of Constitutions of the Antient and Honourable Fraternity of Free and Accepted Masons, Containing Their History, Charges, Regulations, &c.* London: Richard Chandler, 1738.

Anonymous. "An Antient MS on Free Masonry." *The Gentleman's Magazine,* Vol. 23, No. 9 (September, 1753), p. 417–21.

Armitage, Edward. "Robert Samber." *Ars Quatuor Coronatorum* 11(1898): 103–117.

Bogdan, Henrik. "The Sociology of the Construct of Tradition and Import of Legitimacy in Freemasonry." In *Constructing Tradition: Means and Myths of Transmission in Western Esotericism,* edited by Andreas B. Kilcher, 217–38. Leiden: Brill, 2011.

Brockwell, Charles. *Brotherly Love Recommended: In a Sermon Preached Before the Ancient and Honourable Society of Free and Accepted Masons, in Christ-Church, Boston, on Wednesday the 27th of December, 1749. By Charles Brockwell, A.M. His Majesty's Chaplain in Boston. Published at the Request of the Society.* Boston: John Draper, in Newbury-Street, 1750.

Bullock, Steven C. *Revolutionary Brotherhood: Freemasonry and the Transformation of the American Social Order, 1730–1840.* Chapel Hill, N.C.: University of North Carolina Press, 1996.

Bunyan, John. *Solomon's Temple Spiritualiz'd, or, Gospel Light Fetched Out of the Temple at Jerusalem, To Let Us More Easily into the Glory of New Testament Truths.* London: Printed for, and sold by George Larkin, at the Two Swans without Bishopsgate, 1688.

Clare, Martin. "A Discourse on Good Behaviour for the Guidance of the Members of the Craft." Shawn Eyer, Ed. *Philalethes: The Journal of Masonic Research and Letters* 69(2016): 64–67.

Coil, Henry W. *Coil's Masonic Encyclopedia.* New York: Macoy, 1961.

Cole, Benjamin. *The Antient Constitutions of the Free and Accepted Masons, Neatly Engrav'd On Copper Plates.* London: B. Creake, 1731.

Cooke, Ross Frank. "An Analysis of Four Speeches Delivered by Masons in Colonial America." M.A. thesis, Brigham Young University, 1968.

Curl, James Stevens. *The Art and Architecture of Freemasonry: An Introductory Study.* London: B.T. Batsford, Ltd., 1991.

———. *Freemasonry and the Enlightenment: Architecture, Symbols, and Influences.* London: Historical Publications, 2011.

Dyer, Colin F.W. *William Preston and His Work.* Shepperton, UK: Lewis Masonic, 1987.

Eyer, Shawn. "Defining Esotericism from a Masonic Perspective." *The Journal of the Masonic Society* No. 2 (Autumn 2008): 16–21.

———. "*A Dissertation Upon Masonry*, 1734, with Commentary and Notes." *Philalethes: The Journal of Masonic Research and Letters* 68(2015): 62–75.

———. "Drake's Oration of 1726, with Commentary and Notes." *Philalethes: The Journal of Masonic Research and Letters* 67(2014): 14–25.

———. "Esoteric and Mystical Themes in the Literature of Early Grand Lodge Era Freemasonry." Paper presented at the fourth international conference of the Association for the Study of Esotericism, University of California, Davis, July 21, 2012.

———. "The Inward Civility of the Mind: The 1735 Grand Oration of Martin Clare, F.R.S." *Philalethes: The Journal of Masonic Research and Letters* 69(2016): 58–63.

Faivre, Antoine. *Western Esotericism: A Concise History.* Albany: State University of New York Press, 2010.

Fletcher, Charlotte Goldsborough. *Cato's Mirania: A Life of Provost Smith.* Lanham, Md.: University Press of America, 2002.

Goodrick-Clarke, Nicholas. *The Western Esoteric Traditions: A Historical Introduction.* Oxford: Oxford University Press, 2008.

Gore, C. *An Oration: Delivered at the Chapel, in Boston.* Boston: William Green, 1783.

[Grand Lodge of Massachusetts]. *Proceedings in Masonry, St. John's Grand Lodge, 1733–1792, Massachusetts Grand Lodge, 1769–1792.* Boston: Grand Lodge of Massachusetts, 1895.

[Grand Lodge of Pennsylvania]. *Proceedings of the Right Worshipful Grand Lodge of the Most Ancient and Honorable Fraternity of Free and Accepted Masons of Pennsylvania, and Masonic Jurisdiction Thereunto Belonging.* Philadelphia, Grand Lodge of Pennsylvania, 1906.

Hackett, David G. *That Religion in Which All Men Agree: Freemasonry in American Culture.* Berkeley, Cal.: University of California Press, 2014.

Hanegraaff, Wouter J. *Esotericism and the Academy: Rejected Knowledge in Western Culture.* Cambridge: Cambridge University Press, 2012.

———. *Western Esotericism: A Guide for the Perplexed.* London: Bloomsbury, 2013.

Harward, Thomas. *A Visitation Sermon, in Defence of the Christian Faith, Against the Modern Socinians and Deists. By Thomas Harward, Master of Arts, and Curate of Madington.* London: Printed by R. Janeway, for R. Whitledge, at the Bible and Ball in Ave-Mary-Lane, 1709.

———. *The Fulness of Joy in the Presence of God, Being the Substance of a Discourse Preach'd Lately in the Royal Chappel at Boston in New-England. By the Reverend Mr. Harward, Lecturer at the Royal Chappel.* Boston: Printed by B. Green, sold by Gillam Phillips, over against the south side of the Town-House, 1732.

Head, Isaac. *A Confutation of the Observations on Free Masonry By an Anonymous Author of a Pamphlet, Entitled Masonry the Way to Hell.* Exeter: A Brice & B. Thorn, 1769.

[Henley, John]. *Select Orations on Various Subjects.* London: John Tillotson, 1737.

Hutchins, Zachary McLeod. *Inventing Eden: Primitivism, Millennialism, and the Making of New England.* Oxford: Oxford University Press, 2014.

Idel, Moshe. *Absorbing Perfections: Kabbalah and Interpretation.* New Haven, Conn.: Yale University Press, 2002.

Knoop, Douglas, & G.P. Jones. *The Genesis of Freemasonry: An Account of the Rise and Development of Freemasonry in its Operative, Accepted, and Early Speculative Phases.* Manchester: Manchester University Press, 1947.

Knoop, Douglas, G.P. Jones, & Douglas Hamer, *Early Masonic Pamphlets.* Manchester, UK: Manchester University Press, 1945.

Kuhlke, Olaf. *Geographies of Freemasonry: Ritual, Lodge, and City in Spatial Context.* Lewiston, N.Y.: Edwin Mellen, 2008.

Lee, Samuel. *Orbis Miraculum, or, The Temple of Solomon Pourtrayed by Scripture-Light.* London: Printed by John Streater for Thomas Basset, 1659.

Mackey, Albert G. "The Eloquence of Masonry." *The Masonic Trowel* Vol. 4, No. 10 (October 15, 1865): 147–48.

———. *Encyclopædia of Freemasonry and Its Kindred Sciences.* Philadelphia: Moss & Co., 1879.

Moore, Charles Whitlock. "The First Masonic Discourse Delivered in America." *The Freemasons' Monthly Magazine* 8(1849): 289–93.

Moore, Charles Whitlock & S.W.B. Carnegy, *The Masonic Trestle-Board, Adapted to the National System of Work and Lectures: As Rev. and Perfected by the United States Masonic Convention, at Baltimore, Maryland, A.L. 5843.* Boston: C.W. Moore, 1843.

Morris, Rob. *The History of Freemasonry in Kentucky.* Louisville, Ky.: Rob Morris, 1859.

———. *William Morgan, Or, Political Anti-Masonry: Its Rise, Growth and Decadence.* New York: Macoy, 1884.

Oakley, Edward. *A Speech Deliver'd to the Worshipful Society of Free and Accepted Masons, at a Lodge, held at the Carpenters Arms in Silver-Street, Golden-Square, the 31ˢᵗ of December, 1728.* In [Francis Drake], *A Speech Deliver'd to the Worshipful and Ancient Society of Free and Accepted Masons, at a Grand Lodge, held at Merchant's-Hall, in the City of York, on St. John's Day, December 27, 1726.* 2nd ed. London: B. Creake, 1734.

Pennell, John. *The Constitutions of the Free Masons. Containing the History, Charges, Regulations, &c. of that most Ancient and Right Worshipful Fraternity.* Dublin: J. Watts, 1730.

Péter, Róbert. "General Introduction." In *British Freemasonry, 1717–1813*, edited by R. Péter & C. Révauger. New York: Routledge, 2016.

Piatigorsky, Alexander. *Who's Afraid of Freemasons?: The Phenomenon of Freemasonry.* London: Harvill, 1997.

Preston, William. *Illustrations of Masonry.* 2nd ed. London: J. Wilkie, 1775.

Proceedings of the Right Worshipful Grand Lodge of the Most Ancient and Honorable Fraternity of Free and Accepted Masons of Pennsylvania, and Masonic Jurisdiction Thereunto Belonging (Philadelphia, Grand Lodge of Pennsylvania, 1906), 82.

Proceedings in Masonry, St. John's Grand Lodge, 1733–1792, Massachusetts Grand Lodge, 1769–1792 (Boston: Grand Lodge of Massachusetts, 1895), 4.

Royster, Paul, ed. *The Constitutions of the Free-Masons (1734). An Online Electronic Edition.* Lincoln, Nebr.: University of Nebraska, 2006, 94.

[Samber, Robert, writing as Eugenius Philalethes, Jr.]. *Long Livers: A Curious History of Such Persons of Both Sexes Who Have Liv'd Several Ages, and Grown Young Again.* London: J. Holland, 1722.

Scott, J. *The Pocket Companion and History of Free-Masons.* London: J. Scott, 1754.

Slade, Alexander. *The Free Mason Examin'd, or, The World Brought out of Darkness into Light.* London: R. Griffiths, 1754.

Smith, Horace Wemyss. *Life and Correspondence of the Rev. William Smith, D.D., First Provost of the College and Academy of Philadelphia. First President of Washington College, Maryland. With Copi-*

ous Extracts from his Writings. Philadelphia: S.A. George & Co., 1879–1880.

Smith, William (of Gateshead, County Durham). *The Book M: Or, Masonry Triumphant*. Newcastle upon Tyne: Leonard Umfreville & Co., 1736.

Smith, William (1727–1803). *Ahiman Rezon Abridged and Digested: As a Help to All That Are, or Would Be Free and Accepted Masons. To which is added, a sermon, preached in Christ-Church, Philadelphia, at a general communication, celebrated, agreeable to the constitutions, on Monday, December 28, 1778, as the anniversary of St. John the Evangelist*. Philadelphia: Printed by Hall & Sellers, 1783.

———. *The Works of William Smith, D.D., Late Provost of the College and Academy of Philadelphia*. Philadelphia: Hugh Maxwell & William Fry, 1803.

Snoek, Jan A.M. "The Evolution of the Hiramic Legend in England and France." *Heredom: The Transactions of the Scottish Rite Research Society* 11(2003): 11–53.

———. "The Rituals of the Union." Paper presented at the fourth International Conference on the History of Freemasonry, Edinburgh, Scotland, May 25, 2013.

Soulen, Richard N. & R. Kendall Soulen. *Handbook of Biblical Criticism*. 3rd ed. Louisville, Ky.: Westminster John Knox Press, 2002.

Stewart, Trevor. "English Speculative Freemasonry: Some Possible Origins, Themes and Developments." *Ars Quatuor Coronatorum* 117(2004): 116–82.

Tendler, Carl Hermann. "The Apostle St. Paul, a Mason." *Ars Quatuor Coronatorum* 1(1886–1888):74–75.

von Stuckrad, Kocku. *Western Esotericism: A Brief History of Secret Knowledge*. London: Equinox, 2005.

Versluis, Arthur. *Magic and Mysticism: An Introduction to Western Esotericism*. Lanham, Md.: Rowman & Littlefield, 2007.

Wheildon, William W. "Charles W. Moore." *The New England Historical and Genealogical Register* 30 (1876): 399–405.

"Spiritual and Heavenly People in Corners"

Embracing Masonic Ethos through the Eyes of James Anderson

DANA SCOFIELD

FOR A ROBUST UNDERSTANDING of the elements, ideals, and philosophies of early Masonic practice and culture, one must attempt to understand what and how the early Masons thought, and more importantly, *felt* about Freemasonry. It has been common in Masonic scholarship to suggest that early members presented their beliefs about the Craft in a purely propagandistic way. Accoding to this perspective, early Freemasons lauded the virtues of Masonry largely because those virtues were not really present. When describing the antiquity of the Order and its mythical connection to some of humanity's great leaders in religion, philosophy, architecture, and state, they were desperatly attempting to lay claim to a venerable status on a fraudulent basis. Most of the substantial ideas that early members presented are essentially disregarded by those adherent to this school of thought, who consider that the Freemasons of the early Grand Lodge era cannot be trusted to give an accurate account of how they perceived the Fraternity, nor of their own reasons for participating in it.[1] This attempt to critically engage the primary sources leads some researchers to disregard much of what the early participants said of their own motivations and values. In short, as a result of the fact that early Freemasonry wove legend into its history, the *emic* perspectives of the early Freemasons have been largely ignored—even to the extent that many scholars are unfamiliar with the existence of some of the relevant texts. Yet, the Masonic literature of this era contains some of the most expressive and personal specimens of Masonic writing that are known. The emotional and spiritual impact that Freemasonry had on the men who were responsible for its development is evident throughout the period's texts.

There are many examples of this. Some of the most beautiful are found in poetry, such as John Bancks' "Of Masonry: An Ode" (1737),[2] and Charles Leslie's *Masonry: A Poem* (1739).[3] Inspiration is also found in the orations of the period, such as those reprinted in William Smith's *Book M* (1736).[4] But moving literary testaments to the Craft can also be found within more seemingly administrative documents such as the foundational *Constitutions*. Further, as is posited below, beauty can also be found in the non-Masonic writings of Masons.

Many prominent Masons were often as active in political, religious and civic affairs as they were within the Fraternity. These men authored a variety of works, Masonic and otherwise. Although it could be argued that there is not much of Masonic interest to be found within these ostensibly non-Masonic writings, there is much value in examining such writings in search of Masonic allusions. Another position advanced in the present work is the idea that the eloquence and grandeur with which

1   For an example, see Edwards, "Anderson's Book."
2   Bancks, *Proposals*, 33–39.
3   Leslie, *Masonry: A Poem*.
4   Smith, *The Book M: Or, Masonry Triumphant*.

early Masons described their Craft should not necessarily be interpreted as mere propaganda; while maintaining a critical awareness, scholars should reflect on the possibility that these men may have meant what they said and sincerely expressed what they were experiencing and constructing in Freemasonry.

Modern students of Freemasonry have a plethora of eighteenth-century Masonic documents at their fingertips that can provide a vast amount of insight into early Masonic culture. These writings offer not only a glimpse into *what* was being practiced among these early Masons within their lodges, but *how* they thought about the Craft and its importance in their lives. There is no greater source for understanding Masonic ethos than the writings of those who strongly influenced Masonic culture in the first decades of the Grand Lodge era. Although they are not necessarily the founders of Freemasonry itself, their work was foundational and even defining.

Many early Masons could be noted as key framers and influencers of this type. However, it is without doubt that one of the most influential men in preserving—if not to some extent establishing—what would become the primary Masonic ethos for the first half of the eighteenth-century is Rev. James Anderson. Anderson was best known in Freemasonry for his compilation of the *Constitutions* of the premier Grand Lodge, both the first edition of 1723, as well as the second and greatly expanded edition of 1738. It is through Anderson that the Traditional History of Freemasonry was delivered: a mythological chronology of the Craft from the time of Adam, covering a vast range of early Masonic legend. These works also contain the charges and regulations of the first Grand Lodge. By exploring these writings together with some of Anderson's work not obviously concerning Freemasonry, one can develop a more accurate view of how he may have thought about Freemasonry, and felt about its place in society.

The purpose of this work is not to scrutinize the historical basis of James Anderson's version of the Traditional History; nor, for that matter, any of his writing.⁵ Although historical inaccuracies are found in the Traditional History and elsewhere in his writing, such errors should not lead to a summary disregard for his work, particularly when attempting to assess Anderson's own Masonic views. Additionally, it is invalid to assess Anderson's work as though it had been produced according to the strictures of (or even in alignment with the purposes of) modern academic historiography. There is nothing critical or scholarly about such an anachronistic approach to the study of literature three centuries old. Describing the difficulty that many participant scholars experienced in dealing with Anderson's work, professor David Stevenson wrote:

> There was resentment and embarrassment at the idea that Anderson had tricked Freemasons for generations with false history. There was a judging of him on the basis of late-nineteenth-century and twentieth-century English assumptions, especially about Freemasonry, with little attempt to understand his own age—and indeed what the *Constitutions* were intended to do. There was also, it may be suspected, a determination to prove how 'scientific' the standards of Masonic history had become, after past laxity, with harshness of judgment taken to be a measure of good scholarship.⁶

This "harshness" that Stevenson saw as directed toward Anderson is of the same variety that has been more widely applied to the Craft in general. The fact that this severity comes from so many Freemasons—and not just from the non-Masonic world—

---

5   Anderson was not the first to pen such a history. The so-called "Old Charges," predating the founding of the 1717 Grand Lodge also contain a mythic origin of the Craft. Although the Regius Poem, c. 1425, is the oldest of these, the first fully developed legend is found in the Cooke MS, c. 1450.

6   Stevenson, "James Anderson," 94.

is, perhaps, almost more alarming. Many contemporary Freemasons seem focused on finding and exploiting inconsistencies or errors in early Masonic writing. Many seem set on invalidating any spiritual or philosophical meaning which may be gleaned from Freemasonry. Many flatly deny the true Masonic ethos of the Freemasonry of Anderson's time, thereby insisting that the Craft is ineffectual to meet the needs of modern day Brethren, or potential Brethren.

It is not the intention of the author to fall in to the trappings of unfettered "determination" to disprove such an important figure as James Anderson. Rather, the intent is to place a light on Anderson's love of the Craft and how he may have passed that zeal on to future generations of Freemasons.

Antiquarian Inquiry in the 1723 and 1738 Books of Constitutions

The Constitutions of the Free-Masons is very likely James Anderson's greatest contribution the Fraternity. Throughout the *Constitutions* is found abundant evidence pointing to the importance that was placed on establishing Grand Lodge Masonry as an ancient and honorable fraternal order. The desire to do this was held not only by the Grand Lodge itself, but arguably by Anderson as an individual as well. It is understood that histories of the time were legendary and often embellished; Anderson asserted no claim to do otherwise in his Traditional History of the Craft.

Although Anderson had motives driven by the Grand Lodge, he was writing the *Constitutions* based largely upon traditions established long before his time. Anderson was to take this collection of old documents and collect them into a manageable system to be used by the Institution, his work being vetted by the Grand Lodge itself.

It is critical to acknowledge the substantial amount of study

Anderson undertook to find traces of the Craft throughout history. This should not be understood as Anderson expressing the Traditional History as a literal history, but as a testament to Anderson's belief that a deeper understanding of Freemasonry could be developed by seeking the traces of Masonic traditions in antiquity.

In both the 1723 and 1738 *Constitutions*, Anderson leaves evidence of his own study and process of explaining the traditions that he collected. Beginning with John Theophilus Desaguliers, Deputy Grand Master of the Premier Grand Lodge, and his dedication in the 1723 edition, one can see that Anderson's work in exploring the old documents was recognized by the Grand Lodge:

> I need not tell your GRACE what Pains our learned AUTHOR has taken in compiling and digesting this Book from the old *Records*, and how accurately he has compar'd and made every thing agreeable to *History* and *Chronology*, so as to render these NEW CONSTITUTIONS a just and exact Account of *Masonry* from the Beginning of the World to your *Grace's* MASTERSHIP, still preserving all that was truly ancient and authentick in the old ones....[7]

Desaguliers recognized the extensive work that Anderson put into preparing the *Constitutions*, adding legitimacy and validation of the seriousness of his efforts. Also, in the 1738 edition, Anderson himself explains that he was charged by the Grand Master to peruse the old records:

> But they had no *Book* of Constitutions in Print, till his *Grace* the present Duke of MONTAGUE, when *Grand Master*, order'd me to peruse the old *Manuscripts*, and digest the Constitutions with a just *Chronology*.[8]

7   Anderson, *Constitutions* (1723), [iv–v].
8   Anderson, *New Book of Constitutions* (1738), vii.

Other traces of Anderson's study are scattered throughout the Traditional History of both editions of the *Constitutions*. In a footnote in the 1723 edition, for example, Anderson states:

> *For by some Vestiges of Antiquity we find one of 'em, godly* ENOCH, *(who dy'd not, but was translated alive to Heaven) prophecying of the* final Conflagration *at the Day of Judgement* (as St. Jude tells us) *and likewise of the* GENERAL DELUGE *for the Punishment of the World: Upon which he erected his two large Pillars, (tho' some ascribe them to Seth) the one of* Stone, *and the other of* Brick, *whereon were engraven the Liberal Sciences, &c. And that the Stone* Pillar *remained in* Syria *until the Days of* Vespasian *the Emperor.*[9]

In Josephus' *Antiquities of the Jews*, we find the same story concerning the construction of the Pillars. Anderson cites Josephus in the 1738 edition as a source of this information:

> Some call them Seth's Pillars, but the old Masons always call'd them ENOCHs Pillars, and firmly believ'd this Tradition: nay Josephus (Lib. i. cap. 2.) affirms the Stone-Pillar still remain'd in Syria to his Time.[10]

Other footnotes used by Anderson in the 1723 Traditional History further illustrate the extensive amounts of time he spent reading and delving into source material to explain the traditions. In his telling of the employment of Craftsmen at work on the Temple, he explains in a footnote that "though there were employ'd about it no less than 3600 Princes," offering his own attempt to gain a deeper understanding of 1 Kings and 2 Chronicles by studying the original Hebrew:

9   Anderson, *Constitutions* (1723), 3.
10   Anderson, *New Book of Constitutions* (1738), 3.

> *In* 1 Kings v. 16. *they are call'd* הרדים Harodim, *Rulers or Pro-*
> *vosts assisting King* Solomon, *who were set over the Work,*
> *and their Number there is only 3,300: But* 2 Chron. ii. 18. *they*
> *are called* מנצחים Menatzchim, *Overseers and Comforters of*
> *the People in Working, and in Number 3,600; because either*
> *300 might be more curious Artists, and the* Overseers *of the*
> *said 3,300; or rather, not so excellent, and only* Deputy-Mas-
> ters, *to supply their Places in case of Death or Absence, that*
> *so there might be always 3,300 acting* Masters *compleat; or*
> *else they might be the* Overseers *of the 70,000* איש סבל Ish
> Sabbal, *Men of Burden, or Labourers, who were not Masons*
> *but served the 80,000* איש חצב Ish Chotzeb, *Men of Hewing,*
> *called also* גבלים Ghiblim, *Stone Cutters and Sculpturers ;*
> *and also* בני Bonai, *Builders in Stone, part of which belong'd*
> *to* Solomon, *and part to* Hiram, *King of Tyre,* 1 Kings v. 18.[11]

There are many other examples of Anderson citing the work and ideas of early philosophers, historians, and manuscripts. Among his citations are:

1) The Cooke MS (c. 1450).[12]

2) Diodorus Siculus, a first-century Greek historian who was the author of *Bibliotheca Historica*.[13]

3) Pliny the Elder, a first-century Roman and author of *Naturalis Historia*.[14]

4) The Venerable Bede, an eight-century theologian.[15]

5) Petrus Gyllius, a sixteenth-century French scientist.[16]

11   Anderson, *Constitutions* (1723), 10.

12   Ibid., 34.

13   Anderson, *New Book of Constitutions* (1738), 6.

14   Ibid., 36.

15   Ibid., 92.

16   Ibid., 44.

6) John Marsham[17] and James Ware,[18] noted seventeenth-century historians.

7) Inigo Jones and John Webb's eighteenth-century study of Stonehenge.[19]

The breadth of these references clearly demonstrates that Anderson devoted a substantial amount of time consulting the work of early historians, theologians, philosophers, and others. This supports the thesis that Anderson viewed his work to be a serious endeavor and that he exerted a real effort to produce a comprehensive testament to Masonry. It may be convincingly argued that Anderson's intention was to perpetuate the broad spectrum of Masonic legend that had existed over the ages yet still find iterations of Masonic culture within the accepted history of his time. The argument that the Traditional History was merely propaganda is difficult to support in light of the amount of research and effort invested by Anderson.

Freemasonry as a Sacred Institution

Another element of Anderson's *Constitutions* which demonstrates the sincerity with which he engaged Freemasonry was his view of Craft lineage and iconography as a sacred system. He clearly believed that certain parts of Craft practice were to be left to the sanctuary of the tiled lodge and that although the *Constitutions* were a valuable resource for Freemasons, the Craft's true purpose could not be written, or explained, openly. Exploring statements made by him in both the 1723 and 1738 editions, one can begin to understand that Anderson considered the Craft to be a sacred institution reserved for initiates only. Multiple state-

17   Ibid., 18.
18   Ibid., 91.
19   Ibid., 60. The nature of Stonehenge remained a topic of some fascination for the early Freemasons, as demonstrated by the work of William Stukeley.

ments in both editions of the *Constitutions* can be consulted to confirm this.

In the opening lines of the Traditional History, Anderson gives the foundation of Craft lineage. Beginning with Adam, he solidifies the mythopoetic history of the Craft as Divine and as old as Man himself:

> ADAM, our first Parent, created after the Image of God, *the great Architect of the Universe*, must have had the Liberal Sciences, particularly *Geometry*, written on his Heart; for even since the Fall, we find the Principles of it in the Hearts of his Offspring, and which, in process of time, have been drawn forth into a convenient Method of *Propositions*, by observing the Laws of *Proportion* taken from *Mechanism*: So that as the *Mechanical Arts* gave Occasion to the Learned to reduce the Elements of *Geometry* into Method, this noble Science, thus reduc'd, is the Foundation of all those Arts, (particularly of *Masonry* and *Architecture*) and the Rule by which they are conducted and perform'd.[20]

As valuable as the *Constitutions* were to be to early Freemasons, Anderson clearly recognized that there were parts of Freemasonry to be maintained as highly esoteric and reserved for the tiled lodge. In several sections of the Traditional History, Anderson refers to aspects of the Craft system as being so sacred that they cannot, and should not, be put into writing. For example, he writes the following concerning the dispersion of the Science and Art:

> In these Parts, upon the *Tygris* and *Euphrates*, afterwards flourish'd many learned *Priests* and *Mathematicians*, known by the Names of CHALDEES and MAGI, who preserv'd the good Science, *Geometry*, as the KINGS and *great Men* encourag'd the *Royal Art*. But it is not expedient to speak

20   Anderson, *Constitutions* (1723), 1–2.

more plain of the Premises, except in a *formed Lodge.*[21]

When referencing the building of Solomon's Temple, he states:

> But leaving what must not, and indeed cannot, be com-
> municated by Writing, we may warrantably affirm, that
> however ambitious the *Heathen* were in cultivating of the
> *Royal Art*, it was never perfected, until God condescended
> to instruct his *peculiar People* in rearing the above-men-
> tion'd stately Tent....[22]

Anderson believed that the secrets of Freemasonry should
remain exclusive. Such things were to be communicated only
within the tiled lodge room, and some, it seemed, could only be
experienced. He further believed that the lessons of the degrees
were designed to instruct the Craftsmen in the attainment of esoteric wisdom. In the below statement, he references the "Key of
a Fellow Craft" as being necessary to understanding the process
of communication within the Craft:

> But neither what was convey'd, nor the Manner how, can be
> communicated by writing; as no Man indeed can understand
> it without the Key of a Fellow Craft.[23]

In "Charge IV. *Of* MASTERS, Wardens, Fellows, *and Apprentices,*" Anderson explicitly states that the process of promotion
in the Craft is based on true worth and merit alone. In outlining
what constituted this merit, he wrote:

> It is impossible to describe these things in writing, and
> every Brother must attend in his Place, and learn them in

21   Ibid., 4–5.
22   Ibid., 13.
23   Ibid., 29.

a way peculiar to *this Fraternity*.[24]

One may propose that this part of the Charges was simply Anderson's way of noting that *je ne sais quoi* a lodge sought in its leaders. However, given the context here outlined, it seems more likely that this is Anderson's way of communicating the presence of another secret.

On this theme, one of the most profound statements Anderson ever made within an official Grand Lodge document was in his 1738 edition of the *Constitutions*. At the end of his message to the reader he makes the following declaration:

> Most regular societies have had, and will have, their own *Secrets*; and, to be sure, the *Free-Masons* always had theirs which they never divulged in *Manuscript*; and therefore cannot be expected in *Print*: Only, an expert Brother, by the true Light, can readily find many useful Hints in almost every Page of this Book, which *Cowans*, and Others not Initiated, cannot discern.... But the *History* here chiefly concerns MASONRY, without meddling with other Transactions, more than what only serves to connect the *History* of MASONRY, the strict Subject of this Book. It is good to know WHAT NOT TO SAY! Candid *Reader*, farewell.[25]

Interestingly, this might have been his last farewell to the Brethren, at least in an official capacity: This message was dated November 4th, 1738, only six months before his death. The *Constitutions* are the work of a man who had a love for Freemasonry, and who held its hidden mysteries as inviolable. As the *Constitutions* represent the official word, as it were, from the "Premier" Grand Lodge, Anderson's work represents the true Masonic ethos of the day.

24 Ibid., 51.
25 Anderson, *New Book of Constitutions* (1738), ix.

Further, the way in which Anderson wrote about the Fraternity casts doubt on what has been called the "hired pen" theory.[26]
The theory holds that James Anderson was simply brought in to
write the 1723 *Constitutions* because of his experience derived
from writing and publishing sermons. The passion with which
Anderson describes the Craft calls the theory into question. *Constitutions* reads like a document rendered by a man with a sincere
love of the Fraternity and not as a merely commercial project. Additionally, it seems unlikely that a man without a deep emotional
connection to the Fraternity would be able to comprehend and so
succinctly capture the essence of Masonic secrecy.

Anderson's Last Great Statement?

James Anderson wrote several non-Masonic works. Although
some of them may contain little content bearing directly upon
the Fraternity, there is good reason to explore them to gain deeper understanding of the author. Of Anderson's major works, his
best known was *Royal Genealogies; or, the Genealogical Tables of
Emperors, Kings, and Princes, from Adam to These Times*. But one
of his lesser known works is *News from Elysium, or Dialogues of
the Dead, between Leopold, Roman Emperor, and Louis XIV, King
of France*. This work presents imagined dialogues between the
spirits of men of great station in Europe, now residing together
in the Underworld. Published shortly after Anderson's death in
1739, *News from Elysium* should draw special attention from the
Freemason, but has been all too often overlooked and in at least
one instance cast aside as entirely unimportant.[27]

26 See Prescott, "The Publishers of the 1723 Constitutions," 147–62.
27 Masonic scholar Chetwode Crawley referred to the text as
    "densely, darkly, desperately dull"—see his article "Rev. Dr.
    Anderson's Non-Masonic Writings," 35. However, Crawley
    evidently did not notice the Masonic language in the section of
    Elysium under discussion here.

Mercury, cast as the "Secretary," or messenger, arrives monthly, giving report of the state of affairs in what was then present day London. In a conversation between King Charles v and Francis i, the two engage in a rather energetic dialog concerning the ephemeral nature of temporal or earthly things. Charles makes the argument that the "Teeth of Time" shall always prevail and that the Divine, or spiritual pursuits of man are what the ancients believed would prevail beyond death. Consider this excerpt:

FRANCIS

Indeed, I must own my pleasure and happiness, tho' perhaps not so great as yours, is not to be changed with all the Splendor of the upper *World*. Nevertheless I can't comprehend how you can justly blame the Things and Transactions of the Earth in general, and charge them with such Inconsistency, reducing all to nought: For you know there are some Things there that last long enough, and which you can't annihilate, viz. the Pleasure of being adorned with *Crown* and *Scepter*, to govern so many Millions of Men, to prescribe them Laws, to fight bloody Battels, and gain Victories, to conquer strong Towns and whole Provinces, and to reduce them so low, that all the Lives and Properties of the Inhabitants entirely depend on the arbitrary Will and Pleasure of the *Conqueror*. In short, the State and Condition of a Free, Independent, and Sovereign Prince, who can have every Thing his Heart Covets, is far from being vain and miserable; but on the contrary, he that lives in such a State upon Earth is rather to be esteemed happy.

CHARLES

What do I hear! Do you still defend the Vanities of the World after having been almost two *Centuries* in the *Empire* of *Death*? I must needs affirm again, that all the splendid Things of the upper World are nothing in Comparison of an happy *Eternity*; considering that *earthly* Happiness is only imaginary, not real, and of no Duration… But the Mortals themselves can well explain the Inconstancy of temporal Affairs, and prove that there is no Defence against it, even by indisputable Evidence every where upon Earth, besides the Instances we have in *holy Writ*. Where is the great *City* and *Tower* of BABEL, that was erected by the most of *Noah's* Off-spring, join'd together to make to themselves a Name, and to prevent their Dispersion, of both which they were miserably Disappointed? Where are all the great Cities built by NIMROD and his Successors? Where is the *Navigation* of the PHENICIANS, the *Scepter* and *Law-giver* of JUDAH, the holy and magnificent *City* and *Temple* of JERUSALEM, whose Description transcended human skill? Where are the *Institutions* of MOSES, and his costly Way of Worship, now observed? […] Nay, those Things that were most durable, were torn at last by the Teeth of Time; for, excepting one or two of the *Pyramids* of *Egypt*, (which stood when we reigned upon *Earth*) where are the *Seven* WONDERS of the World… I say, where are all these, and many more such Erections, that the Founders thought must have remain'd for *Eternity*? They are overturn'd by Time, without leaving scarce a Vestige of their Glory; and the curious Traveller beholds their confused Ruins, if any left, with full Conviction of what I have now asserted…. Therefore, *dear* FRANCIS, you must yield this Point, and agree with me, that nothing upon Earth is fully satisfactory and durable; but that the Wheel of Time has a perpetual Rotation, which renders all Things inconstant.

FRANCIS

Quelle Philosophie! ["What a philosophy!"] I own indeed you judge aright in the main; nevertheless, you must also own, it appears by the frequent Accounts brought us from the *Earth*, that several Sciences and Arts are there much improv'd since our Time…. As for *Religion*, I perceive, since our Demise, the different *Parties* have excited each other to hard Study, so that now they have a greater Number of learned *Divines*, and the *Theory* of Religion is certainly very much improv'd, tho' I cannot say the *Practice* of it is, *unless with a few Spiritual and heavenly people in Corners*. Therefore, *Dear* CHARLES, don't blame Changes in general, without Exception, because several of 'em are for the Houour of the present Age.

CHARLES

I grant it, Sir, but pray let me tell you that many noble Sciences and Arts are now entirely lost, or lye obscure in a few Hands; for besides all that, all the Men upon Earth put together, come far short in *Astrology* of the meanest Student in old *Egypt* and *Chaldea*, (which ancient noble *Science* the modern *Mathematicians* despise, without knowing it) where *Astronomy* also was first cultivated; have the Mortals now any *Physician* to be compared to HIPPOCRATES, GALENUS, PARACELSUS, or other learned *Ancients*, whose Writings instruct and wisely direct the most learned *Moderns*? Which is the Reason that so few of 'em have rose to Honour and Wealth purely by their great Skill in *Physick*, but chiefly by Politicks or Poetry, or the Influence of *Women* or *Apothecaries*, or by some other lucky Hits that the *Ancients* had no Leisure nor Inclination to mind: No Wonder therefore, that such great Shoals of Diseased arrive daily on our Coasts, where they are happily deliver'd from *Physick* and Physicians. Nor have we yet heard of any *modern* Poets and Historians (except a very few miraculous Men) that have justly imitated the *Ancients*, far less able to rival and excel them. And where upon Earth can now be found an APELLES or a VITRUVIUS, or such Carvers, Sculpturers,

Architects, Painters, as those formerly renown'd in *Egypt,*
Syria, Greece, Sicily, and *Rome*; far less any worthy to carry
the Tools of King *Solomon*, King *Hiram*, *Hiram Abiff*, and
the most excellent Artists of *Nebuchadnezzar,* and other
Asiaticks? Nay, an ingenious Architect lately arriv'd here, assured PALLADIO, that the Mortals have not been able even
to improve his Designs, and that their highest Ambition is
to imitate the *Ancients*. In short, we daily hear that men are
not so grave and studious as even in our Time, but rather
comical and fantastick, the *Statesmen*, the *Lawyers*, and
Clergy not excepted, and *Self-Conceit* so generally prevailing, it follows that true Wisdom and Prudence retire into
Corners, and are only to be found among a few, perhaps
not the most regarded, of Mankind.[28]

This work as a whole, but specifically the above conversation between King Charles v and Francis i, provides a glimpse
into Anderson's thoughts at a time when his life was nearing its
end. In this context, it is natural that he would have been contemplating his impending death, and all of the things he had
experienced in life. Of course, this includes his endeavors within
Freemasonry.

Anderson clearly identifies with King Charles that the vanities of life on Earth are inferior to the glory of everlasting life
beyond the grave; this could be understood to represent his own
feelings on life and death. Charles' assessment of culture is in
stark contrast to that proposed by Francis. Although somewhat
pessimistic, it gives those studying Anderson a good idea as to
his feelings about society's engagement in the arts and sciences as well as the current state of divine philosophy, contrasting
how Anderson's contemporaries studied the Mysteries against
the methodology of the ancients. Francis claims that the progression of these things in the course of history had been a benefit

28   Anderson, *News from Elysium*, 60–66.

to society, whereas Charles is determined to convince him that what may be considered advancements in the arts and sciences still pales in comparison to that of the ancients, claiming that "true Wisdom and Prudence retire into Corners, and are only to be found among a few, perhaps not the most regarded, of Mankind." There also appears a parallel to the rather bleak idea that men are more inclined toward the mundane aspects of regulatory practice than the scientific or spiritual aspects behind it. As noted above, through Charles, Anderson states:

> In short, we daily hear that men are not so grave and studious as even in our Time, but rather comical and fantastick, the *Statesmen*, the *Lawyers*, and *Clergy* not excepted, and *Self-Conceit* so generally prevailing, it follows that true Wisdom and Prudence retire into Corners, and are only to be found among a few, perhaps not the most regarded, of Mankind.

Compare this with a footnote from the 1723 *Constitutions*:

> *...as many in all Ages have been more curious and careful about the* Laws, Forms, *and* Usages *of their respective Societies, than about the* ARTS *and* SCIENCES *thereof.*[29]

There are several points to consider in these excerpts. First is that the search for wisdom is a labor undertaken by a few, and not necessarily by men of high social status or civil rank. From his work in *Constitutions*, Anderson illustrates his belief that the mysteries of Masonry provide a path toward such wisdom. Secondly, Anderson is sharing, at least in the footnote of the *Constitutions*, in a common sentiment read throughout Masonic writing of the 1730s.

In his footnote, he is referring to the introduction of Gothic

29   Anderson, *Constitutions* (1723), 29.

building and that the regulatory processes of lodges were transmitted by tradition but the preservation of the Augustan style of
architecture had been lost due to the neglect of the true science
of Masonry. This was a prevalent idea among Masonic writers of
the time, one example being Charles Leslie's *Masonry: A Poem*,
wherein he provides a poetic exclamation of the revival of the
Augustan style of architecture to correlate directly with the restoration of Freemasonry:

> And now, once more, attracts the wond'ring eye,
> With nature and long lost simplicity.
> The beautiful *Augustan* stile revives,
> Skill executes what just design contrives;
> Now lovely Order claims its ancient rule,
> And methodizes the consenting whole;
> Order, which strength and elegance imparts,
> The law of nature, and the soul of arts.[30]

Twice Anderson uses the term "Corners," in the second
paragraphs from both Francis and Charles. While there is no
evidence of this term being previously used as a synonym for
Freemasonry, there are clues in Masonic ritual that may give us
license to consider it in those terms. For instance, in the 1727 exposure, *A Mason's Confession*, steps of the various degrees are di-
agrammed out as perpendicular lines, thereby forming corners.[31]
Additionally, the Wilkinson MS (c. 1730), features this exchange:

> Q. What is the form of your Lodge?
> A. An Oblong Square[32]

---

30   Leslie, *Masonry: A Poem*, 12.
31   Anon. "A Mason's Confession." In Carr *&* Jones, *Early Masonic
     Catechisms*, 101.
32   Anon. "Wilkinson MS." In Carr *&* Jones, *Early Masonic Catechisms*,
     130.

The exposure *Masonry Dissected* (1730) has a similar description:

> Q. What Form is the Lodge?
> A. A long Square.[33]

Where one has squares, one has corners. These examples are to say nothing of the ubiquity of the square as a working tool in Freemasonry. All of these references therefore provide the rationale for the reader to assume "corners" to be a veiled reference to the Fraternity.

It is also interesting to note Anderson's use of the term "Travellers," in Charles' first paragraph. Anderson also employed this term in the Traditional History to describe Masons after the building of King Solomon's Temple. There are several examples of this throughout the 1738 *Constitutions*. For instance, after the building of King Solomon's Temple, Craftsmen would return to their homeland and spread the divine architectural style employed at the building of the Temple:

> ...when true compleat *Masonry* was under the immediate Care and Direction of Heaven; when the NOBLE and the Wise thought it their Honour to be the Associates of the ingenious Craftsmen in their well form'd *Lodges*; and so the Temple of JEHOVAH, the one true God, became the just Wonder of all *Travellers*, by which, as by the most perfect Pattern, they resolved to correct the *Architecture* of their own Countries upon their return.[34]

Also, we find:

> But SOLOMON's Royal Race, the Kings of *Judah*, succeed-

---

33   Pritchard, *Masonry Dissected*, 12.
34   Anderson, *New Book of Constitutions* (1738), 15.

ed him also in the GRAND MASTER's *Chair*, or deputed
the High Priest to preserve the *Royal Art*. [...] SOLOMON's
Travellers improved the *Gentiles* beyond Expression.[35]

Again:

> There the old Temple of Diana, built by some *Japhe-*
> *tites*...by the Direction of Dresiphon and Archiphron, the
> Disciples of *Solomon's* Travellers....[36]

Therefore, Anderson solidifies the use of the term "Travellers"
not in the sense of a mere wanderer but rather as a title, given to
a Mason after the building of Solomon's Temple, perpetuating
divine architecture.

Anderson also provides parallels between some of his historical references in the *Constitutions* and *Elysium*; specifically
of note are his reference to Nimrod and the Tower of Babel. In
Elysium, Anderson speaks of the Tower of Babel and the succession of builders from Nimrod as something lost yet desired:

> Where is the great *City* and *Tower* of BABEL, that was erect-
> ed by the most of *Noah's* Off-spring, join'd together to make
> to themselves a Name, and to prevent their Dispersion, of
> both which they were miserably Disappointed? Where are
> all the great Cities built by NIMROD and his Successors?

This parallels Anderson's use of Nimrod and Babel in the
Constitutions. Anderson uses the Tower as a demarcation point
in the Traditional History of the beginning of the Great Dispersion, an important legend in English Freemasonry. In "The
Master's Song," Anderson included the following verse:

35   Ibid., 17.
36   Ibid., 17–18.

THUS when from BABEL they disperse
In Colonies to distant Climes,
All *Masons true*, who could rehearse
Their Works to those of after Times;
King NIMROD fortify'd his Realm,
By Castles, Tow'rs, and Cities fair;
MITZRA'M, who rul'd at *Egypt's* Helm,
Built *Pyramids* stupendous there.[37]

And in the 1738 *Constitutions*:

NIMROD the Son of *Cush*, the Eldest Son of *Ham*, was at
the Head of those that would not disperse; or if they must
separate, They resolved to transmit their Memorial illus-
trious to all future ages; and so employed themselves under *Grand Master* NIMROD, in the large and fertile Vale of
Shinar along the Banks of the *Tygris*, in building a great
and Stately *Tower* and *City*, the largest Work that ever the
World saw...and soon fill'd the Vale with splendid Edifices; but They over-built it, and knew not when to desist
'till their Vanity provoked their Maker to confound their
Grand Design, by confounding their *Lip* or Speech. Hence
the City was called Babel *Confusion*. Thus they were forced
to disperse about 53 Years after they began to build...when
the General MIGRATION from Shinar commenced.[38]

As stated above, to understand an intent, is to understand a
world-view and embrace the idea that when a man should write
or speak of an important part of his life that there must be some
merit in his purpose. It would be difficult to argue that *News from
Elysium* was conceived as a Masonic treatise. Yet the excerpted
dialogue between Charles and Francis abounds with Masonic

37   Anderson, *Constitutions* (1723), 76.
38   Anderson, *New Book of Constitutions* (1738), 5.

allusions: his profound statement regarding Wisdom and Virtue; his invocation of the three Grand Masters; his use of the term "corners" to describe the place where these objects lie; his use of the appellation "curious Traveller"; his reference to the sons of Noah, Babel and Nimrod. These statements might lead us to consider that *News from Elysium* is related to his assessment of the nature of Freemasonry in "modern" society and that his intentions were of a purely human and emotional context. The parallels between statements made in both the *Constitutions* as well as *Elysium* demonstrate that the Traditional History was, to Anderson, not only a means to tell a legendary history of the Freemasons, but that it might also help illustrate the more civil affairs of society.

Conclusion

It is unknown, of the *Constitutions* of 1738 and *News from Elysium*, which was written first. Anderson's statement to the reader in the *Constitutions* of 1738 is dated November 4th, 1738, and *Elysium* was published shortly after Anderson's death on May 25th, 1739. Regardless, Anderson's clarity in purpose and his rhetoric make it clear how he was thinking about the Craft and its place—not only among Masons, but among Society as well. His inclusion of allegorical statements regarding the Craft in a non-Masonic work, written possibly very close to his death, implies that he felt deeply concerned about the state of society in London at the time, and Freemasonry's place in it. More specifically, his allegorical statement that "true Wisdom and Prudence retire into Corners" tells us that around the time of his death, Anderson believed that Freemasonry could be considered a sanctuary. In other words, amid a somewhat chaotic political, religious and social spectrum in London, the fraternity could provide refuge for a collection of men who valued the mysteries of antiquity over materialism and ephemeral authority. It appears to be a "last word," if you will, on the state of social awareness around the arts and sciences and the preservation of ancient wisdom. In *Elysium*, a non-Masonic work, Anderson states quite clearly that he felt the preservation of such matters was only found within "Corners," which this author has argued can be interpreted as an allusion to Freemasonry.

In an ideological sense, this gives the impetus to consider the present, and how Freemasonry relates to society today. Three centuries after the creation of the Premier Grand Lodge, society is still swept up in political, religious, and social discord. Anderson might well have recommended Freemasonry now as a way of finding wisdom, strength, and beauty amid the confusion. Many modern Masonic writers, however, tend to minimize the ideology apparent in Anderson's writings.

As noted above, because Anderson was writing for the Premier Grand Lodge, his words can be seen as reflecting the prominent Masonic ethos of the time. While the evidence of this period which illustrates this ethos had largely been dismissed, this is beginning to shift. This has resulted in a growing understanding of how Freemasonry was perceived and practiced by its founders. This, in turn, has given rise to some contemporary Freemasons seeking a restoration of authenticity and Masonic idealism to their Masonic practice. Masonic students of today must embrace what was bequeathed to them by early Masonic forefathers if they are to engage Masonic study in the true Light of the men responsible for its development. A reassessment of the works of James Anderson is a logical and important component of that restoration.

Bibliography

Anderson, James. *The Constitutions of the Freemasons, Containing the History, Charges, Regulations, &c. of that most Ancient and Right Worshipful Fraternity.* London: William Hunter, 1723.

—. *The New Book of Constitutions of the Antient and Honourable Fraternity of Free and Accepted Masons, Containing Their History, Charges, Regulations, &c.* London: Richard Chandler, 1738.

—. *News from Elysium, or Dialogues of the Dead, between Leopold, Roman Emperor, and Louis XIV, King of France.* London: J. Cecil, 1739.

Anonymous. *A Mason's Confession.* In Carr & Jones, Eds. *Early Masonic Catechisms.* London: Quatuor Coronati, 1975: 99–107.

—. "Wilkinson MS." In Carr & Jones, Eds. *Early Masonic Catechisms.* London: Quatuor Coronati, 1975: 108–51.

Bancks, Jonathan. *Proposals for Printing by Subscription, Miscellaneous Works, in Verse and Prose, of Mr. John Bancks.* London: Mr. Ares's Printing House, 1737.

Carr, Harry & Jones, G.P., Eds. *Early Masonic Catechisms.* London: Quatuor Coronati, 1975.

Crawley, W.J. Chetwode. "The Rev. Dr. Anderson's Non-Masonic Writings." *Ars Quatuor Coronatorum* 18 (1905): 28–42.

Edwards, Lewis. "Anderson's Book of Constitutions of 1738." *Ars Quatuor Coronatorum* 46 (1933): 357–430.

Leslie, Charles. *Masonry: A Poem.* Edinburgh: W. Sands, 1739.

Prescott, Andrew. "The Publishers of the 1723 Constitutions." *Ars Quatuor Coronatorum* 121 (2008): 147–62.

Pritchard, Samuel. *Masonry Dissected.* London: J. Wilford, 1730.

Smith, William. *The Book M: Or, Masonry Triumphant.* Newcastle upon Tyne: Leonard Umfreville and Co: 1736.

Stevenson, David. "James Anderson: Man & Mason." *Heredom: The Transactions of the Scottish Rite Research Society* 10 (2002): 93–138.

Freemasonry, the London Irish, and the Antients Grand Lodge

RIC BERMAN

*A*himan Rezon, first published in 1756 by Laurence Dermott,[1] the Antients' Grand Secretary,[2] was more than a set of rules and regulations. As Samuel Spencer, the author of *A Defence of Free-Masonry* and Dermott's counterpart at the Grand Lodge of England noted:

> I cannot help observing, that Mr Dermott has not compiled his Book for the Use of Masons only, but also for such as may be inclined to be initiated into their Mysteries, whom he assures (in order to draw them into his Society) that he has made FREE MASONRY (both Ancient and Mod-

1   Laurence Dermott (1720–1791), Grand Secretary of the Antients Grand Lodge from 1752 until 1770, Deputy Grand Master from 1771 until 1777 and again from 1783 until 1787.

2   There is a dispute over whether "Antients" Freemasonry should be written as "Antients" or "Ancients." Both forms of spelling were in use in the eighteenth century. The former has been used throughout this paper other than where the spelling differs in a direct quotation.

ern) his constant Study for twenty Years past.[3]

Spencer was correct to be worried. Dermott's strengths were wit and intelligence allied to a formidable devotion to the Antients, and *Ahiman Rezon* epitomised the application of Dermott's marketing prowess to Freemasonry. Dermott had the confidence and nous to use satire in order to promote Antients Freemasonry. More worryingly for Spencer, he succeeded in positioning the Antients as accessible, attractive and a legitimate organisation that adhered to the "ancient landmarks" of the order.

Dermott begins *Ahiman Rezon* with a conversational note in which he explains that he had been "fully determined to publish a History of Masonry," and to achieve this end had "purchased all or most of the Histories, Constitutions, Pocket-Companions and other Pieces (on that Subject) now extant in the English tongue," and furnished himself with "a Sufficient Quantity of Pens, Ink and Paper" so as to "trace Masonry not only to Adam in his sylvan Lodge in Paradise but to give some Account of the Craft even before the Creation." Dermott adds to the irony with a humorous apology that although he had written the first volume of his comprehensive new history in only a few days, he later "fell to dreaming" and on waking found that all his work, including the section covering "several years before the Creation," had been destroyed:

> a young puppy that got into the room while I slept, and seizing my papers, ate a great part of them, and was then (between my legs) shaking and tearing the last sheet...I looked upon it as a bad Omen and my late dread had made so great an impression on my mind that superstition got the better of me and called me to deviate from the general

3   *A Defence of Free-Masonry.*

custom of my worthy predecessors otherwise I would have published a History of Masonry; and as this is rather an accident than a designed fault, I hope that the reader will look over it with a favourable eye.[4]

It may not have been the first iteration of "a dog ate my homework," but the self-deprecation and light-hearted style was looked on as a welcome contrast to the worthy missives issued by the rival Grand Lodge of England.

Laurence Dermott had been appointed Grand Secretary of the Antients Grand Lodge on 5 February 1752,[5] a year after its establishment, and quickly became its driving force. He was born in Ireland in Co. Roscommon in 1720 and subsequently moved to Dublin where his grandfather[6] owned a merchant trading house.[7] Dermott's father, Thomas,[8] was also a Baltic merchant, trading from New Row, south of the Liffey, around a hundred yards from his father's premises at Usher's Quay on the north bank.

4   Dermott, *Ahiman Rezon*, vi-xvi.

5   J.R. Dashwood (ed), *Early Records of the Grand Lodge of England According to the Old Institutions*, Quatuor Coronaturum Antigrapha, volume 11 (Margate & Sittingbourne: Quatuor Coronati Lodge, 1958), esp. 8. There are no complete biographies of Laurence Dermott; however, cf., Ric Berman, *Schism: The Battle that Forged Freemasonry* (Brighton: Sussex Academic Press, 2013); Witham Matthew Bywater, *Notes on Laurence Dermott* (London, 1884); and Dudley Wright (rev.), *Gould's Freemasonry Throughout the World* (New York: Charles Scribener's Sons, 1936), 2:145–95.

6   Christopher Dermott (d. 1721).

7   J.H. Lepper & P. Crossle, *History of the Grand Lodge of Free and Accepted Masons of Ireland* (Dublin: Lodge of Research cc, 1925), 236–42. See also *Daily Gazetteer*, 8 December 1738, which notes the loss of "warehouse and a large quantity of paper belonging to Mr Dermott," the consequence of a fire at Usher's Quay in Dublin.

8   Thomas Dermott (b. 1699).

Dermott was initiated into Lodge № 26 in 1741 and became its Master in 1746.[9] He travelled to England the following year, working in London as a journeyman painter[10] for James Hagarty, a Past Master of Antients Lodge № 4 and chairman of the Grand Committee that later appointed Dermott Grand Secretary.[11]

Dermott's marriages, his son's Church of England baptism, and his burial at St. Olave's in Southwark indicates that he was a Protestant. Other family members in Ireland shared the same faith, among whom several are buried in the graveyard of St. Nicholas Without in Dublin.[12] But the family also had a Catholic branch. Laurence's uncle, Anthony,[13] who inherited the warehouse at Usher's Quay, was one of three signatories to a letter of thanks "on behalf of the Roman Catholics of Ireland" following legislation allowing greater religious toleration in Ireland;[14] he also signed a similar epistle "on behalf of His Majesty's dutiful and loyal subjects, the Roman Catholics of Ireland" addressed to the Duke of Portland, then Lord Lieutenant of Ireland.[15]

Anthony and his siblings were not the first nor the only Catholics in the Dermott family; there had been others in earlier gen-

9   Berman, *Schism*, 13–45.

10 Dermott states in the Antients' minutes that "he was obliged to work twelve hours in the day for the Master Painter who employed him." *Quatuor Coronati Antigrapha* 11(1958):30; 13 July 1753.

11 Dermott succeeded John Morgan, who resigned in February 1752, having been "appointed to office on board one of His Majesty's ships [with] orders to prepare for his departure." (Minutes of the Antient Grand Lodge, 5 February 1752)

12 St. Nicholas Without was within the Church of Ireland, i.e., Protestant.

13 Anthony Dermott (1700–1784).

14 *Parker's General Advertiser and Morning Intelligencer*, 23 May 1782.

15 *Parker's General Advertiser and Morning Intelligencer*, 24 September 1782; *Morning Herald and Daily Advertiser*, 25 September 1782, et al.

erations.[16] Indeed, it was the family's Protestantism that was more remarkable, albeit that Catholic families with assets or estates to protect often converted for commercial and political reasons. Religion nonetheless appears to have been a relative non-issue for Dermott. He associated with many different faiths in his role as Grand Secretary, and under his tenure the Antients were as tolerant as the Moderns, with a membership that included Catholics, Jews, and Quakers alongside both Conformist and Nonconformist Protestants.[17]

There is limited information on Dermott in London until 1752, when the Antients' General Register lists his address in London as Butler's Alley in Moorfields.[18] The area was one of many slums, a "rookery" in eighteenth-century slang, packed with tenements, brothels, taverns and gin shops. Pope described the area accurately as a "powerful image of shabbiness of way of life [and] morals."[19]

Despite dreadful living conditions, numerous migrants—among them many who would later join Antients Freemasonry—were aspirational, driven to better themselves and succeed in London. Dermott was one of them, and the seeds of his financial achievements were sown in the publishing success of *Ahiman Rezon*, and in his marriages, two of which brought significant income and wealth.

Dermott's first marriage to a Susanna Neale is unrecorded other than in parish records,[20] but his second, six years later, to "Mrs. Mary Dwindle, Mistress of the Five Bells Tavern be-

16 Berman, *Schism*, 22-23.
17 Ibid., chapter 3.
18 *Registers of the Grand Lodge of the Antients 1751–1813* ('*General Register*'), Volume A: Library & Museum of Freemasonry, London.
19 Valerie Rumbold, ed., *Alexander Pope: The Dunciad in Four Books* (Harlow, UK: Pearson, 2009), 4.
20 20 January 1759.

hind the New Church in the Strand" captured the interest of the press.[21] The Five Bells was a substantial business with pretensions to the upper end of the market offering a blend of food, drink and lodging, as well as several large function rooms.[22] Dermott knew it well: the Antients' Grand Committee had met at the Five Bells since 1752 and Dermott's mail was addressed to him care of the tavern.[23]

Mary Dermott died unexpectedly in February 1766 within six months of the marriage.[24] And, less than a year later, Dermott married for a third time:

> On Saturday last was married Mr. Dermott, Master of the Five Bells Tavern in the Strand, to Mrs. [Elizabeth] Merryman, relict of the late Mr. Merryman, an eminent wine merchant in Prince's Street, Tower Hill.[25]

Her previous husband, the late John Merryman, would have been known to Dermott: he was another Antients Freemason, № 594 in the General Register of members. The marriage endowed Dermott with a thriving vintner's business and a new home in King Street, Tower Hill. It also allowed Dermott to purchase a small country property at Mile End, then a hamlet east of the City of London in semi-rural Middlesex.

21   *Public Ledger*, 29 November 1765. Spelt variously as "Windall," "Windle," "Windel," and "Windell." See also, *St James's Chronicle or the British Evening Post*, 27 – 29 December 1763.

22   Cf., for example, *General Advertiser*, 19 February 1752 and 4, 7, 9, 11 March 1752; and *Daily Advertiser*, 21 January 1752; *London Daily Advertiser*, 9 April 1752; *London Gazette*, 12 – 16 June 1759, et al.

23   *QCA XI*: "Mr Dermott, Secretary to the Grand Lodge of Free and Accepted Masons at the Five Bells in the Strand."

24   *London Chronicle*, 27 February–1 March 1766; also, *London Evening Post*, 27 February 1766.

25   *London Evening Post*, 15–18 November 1766; cf., also, *Public Advertiser*, 19 November 1766.

Dermott's growing affluence is confirmed by his charitable donations and financial contributions to Antients Grand Lodge. In 1766, he donated five guineas to pay the debts of a Freemason held at Newgate Prison and a further £10 to the Grand Charity. And in 1767 following his third marriage, he paid for a Grand Master's throne "which cost in the whole £34,"[26] a vast sum.

But not everything was derived from his wives. From the late 1750s, Dermott had another source of income: the royalties from *Ahiman Rezon*. Dedicated to the Earl of Blessington, a respected Irish peer described by Dermott as "a father to the fraternity," *Ahiman Rezon* had been published privately in 1756. Its success led to five later editions in England and even more elsewhere.[27] The main text was drawn from Spratt's Irish *Constitutions*,[28] which was itself based on Anderson's rewritten 1738 *Constitutions*.[29] *Ahiman Rezon* was hugely popular and published and purchased across the English-speaking world. At least twenty editions were published in Ireland, with others in North America, where it became the basis for the constitutions of seven American states. Special editions of the work in the eighteenth century were published by four Grand Lodges: Pennsylvania, 1783; Nova Scotia, 1786; Virginia, 1791; and Maryland, 1797; with more published in the nineteenth century, including editions issued by the Grand Lodges of South Carolina and Georgia.

Although *Ahiman Rezon* was in part a set of constitutions, it

26   Robert F. Gould, *The History of Freemasonry: Its Antiquities, Symbols, Constitutions, etc.* (New York: John C. Yorston & Co., 1884), 3:188.

27   Dermott, *Ahiman Rezon*.

28   Edward Spratt, *The New Book of Constitutions of the Most Ancient and Honourable Fraternity of Free and Accepted Masons* (Dublin: Spratt, 1751).

29   James Anderson, *The New Book of Constitutions of the Most Ancient and Honourable Fraternity of Free and Accepted Masons* (London: Ward & Chandler, 1738).

was also promotional, pushing and publicising the greater antiquity and superiority of Antients' ritual versus that of the rival
Moderns. Dermott used later editions of the book to emphasise
the Masonic pacts that had been put in in place between the
Antients and the Grand Lodges of Ireland and Scotland, arguing
that this confirmed the Antients' claim to Masonic pre-eminence
in England.

The book's impact was considerable, and its anti-establishment flavor was one of the reasons why Antients Freemasonry
took off in the Americas and why it was later considered a systemic if not existential threat by the Grand Lodge of England.
Dermott's achievements in building the Antients into a national
and international force made him—in Moderns' circles—"the
best-abused man of his time."[30] He was also subjected to insults
after his death, and it became commonplace for him to be vilified
by Victorian and later historians. William Laurie wrote disin-
genuously that "much injury has been done to the cause of the
Antients...by the unfairness with which [Dermott]...has stated
the proceedings of the Moderns, the bitterness with which he
treats them and the quackery and vainglory with which he displays his superior knowledge."[31] Albert Mackey wrote in a similar
vein that Dermott "was sarcastic, bitter, uncompromising and
not altogether sincere or veracious,"[32] although he admitted that
"in intellectual attainments [Dermott] was inferior to none of his
adversaries."[33] Robert Gould complained that Dermott had been

---

30 Wright, *Gould's History of Freemasonry Throughout the World*,
    2:154.

31 William Alexander Laurie, *The History of Free Masonry and the
    Grand Lodge of Scotland* (Edinburgh: Seton & MacKenzie, 1859),
    fn., 60.

32 Albert G. Mackey, *An Encyclopædia of Freemasonry and Its
    Kindred Sciences*, 214.

33 Ibid.

an "unscrupulous writer [but] a matchless administrator."[34] William Hughan decried *Ahiman Rezon* as "absurd and ridiculous."[35] And Henry Sadler observed that Dermott's work was "comical," "ridiculous," and "scarcely worth a moment's thought."[36]

Many commentators have viewed the antagonism between the Antients and Moderns as a function of a dispute over Masonic ritual. Unfortunately, this view is not supported by the evidence. Although differences in ritual were singled out (somewhat self-servingly) by Dermott as the key differentiator between Moderns and Antients, and the argument as to who had the greater Masonic legitimacy was sustained for more than half a century on that basis, the actual differences in ritual were relatively few. And in this regard at least, Samuel Spencer's comments are broadly correct:

> And notwithstanding his Assertion, that the Lodges in the Country, particularly in Scotland and at York, kept up their ancient Formalities, Customs and Usages, without Alteration, Adding, or Diminishing, to this Hour (from whence he concludes them to be the most Ancient.) It must be acknowledged, that as Masonry must not be written, and has been handed down by oral Tradition only, for so many Ages, that it doubtless has received several Alterations, according to the Customs and Manners of the several Countries it has passed through, and I am sure, that every ingenuous Mason, both Ancient and Modern (Terms which I am obliged to use to be understood) will likewise acknowledge that Masonry in general has received no little Alteration

34   Wright, *Gould's Freemasonry Throughout the World*, 2:151.
35   William James Hughan, *Memorials of the Masonic Union*, revised edition (Leicester, 1913), 8.
36   Henry Sadler, *Masonic Facts and Fictions* (London: Diprose & Bateman, 1887), 110–12.

within these twenty Years, though the old Landmarks are nevertheless preserved.[37]

Dermott stressed that the Antients had the more traditional approach to Freemasonry and benefited from long-established roots that went back to the Cabala—"the Masons at Jerusalem and Tyre were the greatest Cabalists then in the World"[38]—and to the Hebrew texts.[39] His statement that, in contrast to the Premier Grand Lodge, the Antients kept "the ancient landmarks in view,"[40] justified and underlay his portrayal of the original Grand Lodge of England as usurpers and Moderns.

Eighteenth-century Masonic ritual was based on an oral tradition and working varied from country to country, regionally, and from lodge to lodge. Not only was there little uniformity, but many lodges had developed their own styles, including the introduction of "side orders" and higher degrees, not least because they earned the lodge additional fees.[41]

Among the Antients' more substantive complaints was that "in or about 1739"[42] the tokens and words that were an accepted form of Masonic recognition in the first and second degrees were transposed. This is accurate. The alterations had been introduced by the Grand Lodge of England supposedly to prevent entry by those whose knowledge of Masonic working had been gleaned from public exposés, the most prominent of which was Prichard's *Masonry Dissected*,[43] a book so popular that it was reprinted

---

37   Spencer, *A Defence of Free-Masonry.*
38   Dermott, *Ahiman Rezon* (1756), xiv.
39   Ibid., 43–50.
40   Ibid., Dedication.
41   Berman, *Schism*, 13–44.
42   *Quatuor Coronatorum Antigrapha*, Volume 10 (Margate: Quatuor Coronati Lodge, 1913), fn (a), 259.
43   Samuel Prichard, *Masonry Dissected* (London: J. Wilford, 1730).

three times within two weeks of its publication. But while Masonic impostors may have been a concern, and there is no doubt that there were unauthorized "irregular" lodges that carried out initiations as a money-making exercise, Grand Lodge's principal concerns were, first, to retain their position of authority as the sole arbiter and controller of English Freemasonry, and, second, to exclude those they did not wish to welcome into what was in effect a collection of upper middling private clubs.

The issue of control over Freemasonry had been addressed as early as 1723. Grand Lodge resolved that it would not recognise any new lodge in or near London without it having been regularly constituted by Grand Lodge itself, nor would the Master and Wardens of any such lodge be permitted entry to Grand Lodge.[44] This was reinforced the following year with a second resolution:

> That no Brother belonging to any Lodge within the Bills of Mortality be admitted to any Lodge as a Visitor unless personally known to some Brother of that Lodge where he visits, and that No Strange Brother however Skilled in Masonry be admitted without taking the Obligation over again, unless he be Introduced or vouched for by Some Brother known to, and approved of by the Majority of the Lodge.[45]

And with a third:

> That if any Brethren shall meet Irregularly and make Masons at any place within ten miles of London the persons present at the making (the New Brethren excepted) shall

44   William J. Songhurst, ed., *The Minutes of the Grand Lodge of England, 1723–1739* (London: Quatuor Coronati Lodge, 1913), 54; 25 November 1723.
45   Ibid., 56; 19 February 1724.

not be admitted even as Visitors into any Regular Lodge whatsoever unless they come and make Such Submission to the Grand Master and Grand Lodge as they shall think fit to impose upon them.[46]

Allied to the problem of admitting the un-vetted was a concern that such members would be an imposition on individual lodge charities and on the Grand Charity's own funds. Desaguliers made the point directly in 1729 when he "took notice of some Inconveniencies which might attend this general Charity and particularly recommended that they should admit no person into the Society who can be supposed to come in for the sake of the Loaves, and that none shall be entitled to the same who are not regular and are Contributors thereto."[47] This was pursued the following year with another resolution: "In order to prevent the Lodges being imposed upon by false Brethren or Imposters, no person whatsoever should be admitted into Lodges unless some member of the Lodge then present would vouch for such visiting Brothers."[48]

The issue remained a major concern throughout the 1730s. In 1735, for example, the Grand Master

took notice (in a very handsome speech) of the Grievance of making extraneous Masons in a private and clandestine manner, upon small and unworthy Considerations, and proposed that in Order to prevent that Practice for the future NO person thus admitted into the Craft, nor any that can be proved to have assisted at such Makings shall be capable either of Acting as a Grand Officer on Occasion or even as an Officer in a private Lodge, nor ought they to

46   Ibid., 59; 21 November 1724.
47   Ibid., 105; 21 July 1729.
48   Ibid., 136; 15 December 1730.

have any part in the General Charity which is much impaired by this clandestine Practice. His Lordship secondly proposed that since the General Charity may possibly be an Inducement to certain Persons to become Masons merely to be admitted to the Benefit thereof, That it be a Resolution of the Grand Lodge that the Brethren subscribing any Petition of Charity should be able to certify that they have known the Petitioner in reputable or at least tolerable Circumstances.[49]

And in 1736—heading the order of business—was a proposal that, with limited exceptions, "none be admitted to any future Quarterly Communication except such Masons as appear in the Character of and are the known to declared Members of the Grand Lodge."[50]

It is self-evident that the eighteenth-century English establishment was class conscious. And given the level of indigence among recent émigrés and a more general bias against papists, it was also anti-Irish. Although other factors were involved,[51] the rejection by Grand Lodge of the Master and Wardens of an Irish lodge carrying a deputation from Lord Kingston,[52] a Past Grand Master of England and the then Grand Master of Ireland, can be understood best in the context of Grand Lodge's desire to exclude those deemed poor or socially inferior, or both.

In his introduction to the Quatuor Coronati-published *Minutes of the Grand Lodge of England, 1723–1739*, Songhurst excuses Grand Lodge's decision to rebuff the Irish delegation with the explanation that there was no "fraternal intercourse" between An-

49 Ibid., 251, 31 March 1735.
50 Ibid., 268, 6 April 1736.
51 Berman, *Schism*, 15–16.
52 Songhurst, *Minutes of the Grand Lodge of England, 1723–1739*, 260, 11 December 1735.

tients and Moderns.[53] In a footnote he goes further, commenting that the decision not to admit the delegation "seems to point to alterations having been made which prevented inter-visitation."

We know that the premier Grand Lodge was not recognised either in Ireland or Scotland, though both maintained fraternal correspondence with the Antients. Recognition by the Grand Lodges in the sister kingdoms, and a union with the Grand Lodge of the Antients only became possible after the resolution passed by the Moderns in 1809 "that it is not necessary any longer to continue in force those measures which were resorted to in or about the year 1739 respecting irregular masons, and do therefore enjoin the several lodges to revert to the ancient land marks of the Society."[54]

Songhurst's argument is incorrect as a matter of fact. The Antients Grand Lodge was not formed until 1751, sixteen years after the Irish delegation was turned away. And there was no formal break in the Masonic relationship between the Grand Lodges of Ireland and England until 1758, twenty-three years later—it was only at that time that the Antients Grand Lodge was recognised by Dublin as the only legitimate grand lodge in England. Additionally, the Grand Lodge of Scotland did not recognise the Antients as the exclusive governing body for Freemasonry in England until 1773, the year that the 3rd Duke of Atholl was simultaneously Grand Master of the Antients and Grand Master-elect of the Grand Lodge of Scotland.

Songhurst and others also cleaved to a belief that alterations in Masonic ritual prevented inter-visitation and thus help to explain the exclusion of the Irish. There were two principal sets of changes to Masonic working in the first half of the eighteenth century. In the early 1720s, many scholars theorize that an inner circle at English Grand Lodge, led by the Rev. Dr. J.T. Desaguliers

53   Ibid., v.
54   Ibid., 259–60.

and George Payne, altered the wording of the Charges among other reasons to promote religious tolerance. Lodge meetings were also developed to incorporate Enlightenment themes, including educational lectures. However, far from preventing inter-visitation, the changes, combined with the well-publicised patronage of the Whig aristocracy and gentry, made Freemasonry considerably more, not less popular, and encouraged emulation in Ireland and Scotland.[55]

A second raft of changes was introduced in the late 1730s, some four years after the Irish deputation had been barred, and it is these that are commonly seen as the *casus belli* that kicked off over half a century of Masonic acrimony.[56] But what the Antients criticised and held to be "innovative ritual" and "the discard...of the old unwritten traditions of the Order" was form more than substance. And although the ritual used by Irish and Antient Masons varied from that worked by the Moderns, the extent of that divergence was demonstrably less far-reaching than some researchers have supposed.

Another complaint was that the Saint Days of St. John the Baptist and St. John the Evangelist had been downplayed. But given the evidence, this grievance is hard to accept. Other gripes included the omission or shortening of the catechisms attached to each degree; the absence of deacons, a significant office in Ireland; and the exclusion of additional degrees from lodge working. But the Antients' single most important protest was against the failure of the Moderns to recognise the Royal Arch degree.

Despite its recent introduction into Masonic ceremonial, the Royal Arch was championed by the Antients as a key differentiator—"the Root, Heart and Marrow of Free-Masonry"[57]—and

55   Berman, *Foundations*.
56   Lepper & Crossle, *History of the Grand Lodge of Free and Accepted Masons of Ireland*, 1:232.
57   Dermott, *Ahiman Rezon* (1756), 47.

as offering clear evidence of the Antients' greater legitimacy and adherence to ancient traditions. It is ironic that by the end of the eighteenth century what began as a fictional claim had become fact. The Royal Arch had also developed to become sufficiently popular among Freemasonry writ large that it had made inroads into Moderns Freemasonry. Its later acceptance and incorporation into the ritual agreed by the United Grand Lodge of England in the second decade of the nineteenth century cemented the union of the two rival grand lodges.

Leaving the Royal Arch to one side, one assessment of the Antients' case is given in *Hiram*, an exposé written in the mid–1760s that includes a few comparisons between the two forms of ritual. These may indicate that the Antients' argument was overstated and that Moderns' and Antients' working overlapped substantially.[58] But if differences in ritual were not the root of the dispute, we need to seek another explanation.

From the late 1730s and more especially into the 1740s and 1750s, English Grand Lodge suffered from arrogance and poor leadership, and an obsession over the need to centralise control of English Freemasonry. One of the worst offenders, but far from the only one, was John Ward, later Viscount Dudley and Ward.[59]

Ward was the first man to rise through the ranks to become Grand Master. He was an avid Freemason, a founder, then Master and later Secretary of Staffordshire's earliest recorded lodge, the Bell and Raven in Wolverhampton;[60] he was also a member of the aristocratic Bear and Harrow Lodge in London, among others. Ward had been selected to become a Grand Steward in 1732, was appointed Junior Grand Warden and Senior Grand

58 Anonymous ["A member of Royal Arch"], *Hiram: or the Grand Master-Key* (London: W. Griffin, 1764). See pages 31 34n.

59 John Ward was created Lord Ward, Baron of Birmingham in 1740. He was appointed GM (1742–1744), following his elevation to the peerage.

60 Constituted 28 March 1732.

Warden (1732–1734), and sat as Deputy Grand Master thereafter (1735–1737).[61] In 1742, having succeeded his cousin to become the 6th baron Ward of Birmingham he was selected as the Grand Master of the Premier Grand Lodge.

Ward's estates in Staffordshire were at the centre of what became known as the "black country" and contained some of England's largest and most profitable coal mines. He was elected the member of parliament for Newcastle-under-Lyme in 1727 but lost the seat in 1734,[62] which would have been a major disappointment given that his father had sat as an MP for Staffordshire from 1715 until his death.

Politically, Ward tended to the Tory opposition, and before the 1745 Rising was associated with the Jacobite cause, his name communicated to the French as an ostensible supporter. Ward's political activities reflected a self-interested desire to safeguard his property and financial assets. He spoke in the Commons only once, on 18 May 1733, and only in relation to his own estate:

> a Complaint being made to the House, that Jonah Perse-house, of Wolverhampton, in the County of Stafford, John Green, William Mason, Daniel Mason, Thomas Mason, William Goston, Samuel Mason and Benjamin White-house, of Sedgeley, in the said County, having sunk a coal pit adjoining to the Estate of John Ward, esquire, a member of this House, have entered upon his said estate, and taken coals therefrom; in breach of the Privilege of this House.[63]

---

61   Weymouth did not attend Grand Lodge as Grand Master other than at his installation; John Ward deputised.

62   *Weekly Journal or British Gazetteer*, 17 February 1728. Ward's father, William, had been MP for Staffordshire from 1710 to 1713 and again in 1715 until his death.

63   *Journals of the House of Commons*, Seventh Parliament of Great Britain: 6th session, 155, *18 May 1733*.

Ward also pursued a self-interested line in the House of Lords, supporting and promoting road construction.[64] During this period the revenues from the Dudley and Ward estates increased more than fivefold.[65] Ward's resources were however mainly expended in self-promotion, and the development of his Staffordshire mines took second place to the demolition of the family's mediaeval mansion at Himley and its replacement with a vast Palladian house in ornamental grounds, an exercise which required the relocation of the local village. Ward's London townhouse was in fashionable Upper Brook Street, Mayfair, where he owned two houses. But they too were insufficiently grand for Ward's taste and in the 1750s he financed the construction of Dudley House, a Park Lane palace that was completed in 1757.[66]

Ward believed that wealth and property marked a gentleman, a view that explains in part his approach as Grand Master. Ward held that the function of the Grand Master was to maintain and enhance the authority of Grand Lodge, and thereby his own stature and authority. Ignoring developments in society more widely, Ward epitomised the unreconstructed agricultural landed interest to which his mining activities were simply an adjunct. His coal and iron revenues provided the means to fund an ostentatious lifestyle, not to construct a commercial enterprise.

Under Ward's stewardship, Grand Lodge became increasingly arrogant and self-obsessed. And Masonic disaffection became so

---

64   Cf. for example, *Journals of the House of Lords*, Ninth Parliament of Great Britain: 3rd session, 464, *21 March 1744*; 5th session, 51, *24 February 1747*; 6th session, 93, *3 April 1747*; Tenth Parliament of Great Britain: 1st session, 220, *26 April 1748*; and General Index, vols. 20–35, 855.

65   Cf., George J. Barnaby, "Review: The Economic Emergence of the Black Country by T.J. Raybould," *Economic History Review*, 27.3 n.s. (1974): 475–76.

66   F.H.W. Sheppard, *Survey of London* (London: English Heritage, 1980), volume 40, 210–21. The new building was constructed on land to the rear of numbers 30–36 Upper Brook Street.

considerable that by the end of the 1740s around forty, almost a quarter of London's lodges, had been expelled and erased from the Grand Register, while others chose to remain independent.

Ward was followed as Grand Master by Thomas Lyon, Earl of Strathmore, and James Cranstoun, 6th Lord Cranstoun, both of whom continued with Ward's policies and compounded Masonic dissent, and by William Byron, 5th Lord Byron. Byron's installation as Grand Master was the low point of what has been characterised as an extended period of "Masonic Misrule."[67] Although he promised that "he would to the utmost of his power promote the benefit of the Craft," Byron was present in Grand Lodge on only one occasion after his installation: on 16 March 1752, when he proposed that Lord Carysfort be installed as his successor. During the intervening five years, English Freemasonry would fall under the domain of Byron's inadequate Grand Officers. The absence of a noble Grand Master resulted in muted press coverage and limited public interest. The five-year gap in leadership set a seal on English Freemasonry's mid-century decline. It also encouraged the formation of an Irish-led rival— namely, the Antients.

Dermott's *Ahiman Rezon* attacked the Moderns, with Dermott deploying ridicule and poking fun at his rivals. He joked (arguably correctly) that the Moderns were more interested in dining and drinking, and that they considered it:

> expedient to abolish the old custom of studying geometry in the lodge and some of the young brethren made it appear that a good knife and fork in the hands of a dextrous brother (over the right materials) would give greater satisfaction and add more to the rotundity of the lodge...from this improvement proceeded the laudable custom of charging to a public health to every third sentence that is spoke in

67   Berman, *Schism*, 118–58.

the lodge.[68]

He also accused the original Grand Lodge of being interested only in form, not substance:

> There was another old custom that gave umbrage to the young architects, i.e. the wearing of aprons, which made the gentlemen look like so many mechanics, therefore it was proposed, that no brother (for the future) should wear an apron. This proposal was rejected by the oldest members, who declared that the aprons were all the signs of masonry then remaining amongst them and for that reason they would keep and wear them. It was then proposed, that (as they were resolved to wear aprons) they should be turned upside down, in order to avoid appearing mechanical. This proposal took place and answered the design, for that which was formerly the lower part, was now fastened round the abdomen, and the bib and strings hung downwards, dangling in such manner as might convince the spectators that there was not a working mason amongst them. Agreeable as this alteration might seem to the gentlemen, nevertheless it was attended with an ugly circumstance: for, in traversing the lodge, the brethren were subject to tread upon the strings, which often caused them to fall with great violence, so that it was thought necessary to invent several methods of walking, in order to avoid treading upon the strings.[69]

The Moderns reacted badly to Dermott's insults and jests, and their retaliation—*A Defence of Freemasonry*—was published in 1765, a year after the launch of the expanded second edition of *Ahiman Rezon*. Advertisements noted that it contained "a refuta-

68   Dermott, *Ahiman Rezon* (1764), xxx–xxxi.
69   Ibid.

tion of Mr Dermott's ridiculous account of that ancient society,"[70] but it failed in that objective and arguably harmed the Moderns' case. Not only were there substantial errors of fact but the pamphlet displayed a painful bias.

Samuel Spencer, the author of *A Defence of Freemasonry*,[71] was the Grand Secretary of the Moderns Grand Lodge and known for his anti-Antients views. He once proclaimed that "our Society is neither Arch, Royal Arch or Antient."[72] But *A Defence* is not restricted to arguing against Antients Freemasonry per se. The core issue becomes clear near the end of the pamphlet with a vicious diatribe against the London Irish who constituted the majority of Antients' members. The details of a three-hour lecture by "a red hot hibernian," and the denigration of a chairman[73] who, too poor to pay the full lodge fee, offers five shillings in cash and five via an IOU, is an exercise in condescension. And Spencer's disdain for the Antients' "customs and ceremonies" is extended to their members, described as a "disgrace to society," men "with scarcely a coat or shirt to their backs...sat in ale houses...hooting and hollooing."[74]

Spencer's anti-Irish stance was mirrored elsewhere in a Grand Lodge of England dominated by senior members of the magistracy and other members of the establishment. For many there would have been a direct if not axiomatic link between Irish immigration, crime, and disorder.[75] There was at the time an almost universal belief in Irish criminality and in the applicability of the Irish stereotype of feckless, drunken and criminal. Negative

70   *Gazetteer and New Daily Advertiser*, 21 September 1765, et al.
71   *A Defence of Free-Masonry*.
72   Berman, *Schism*, 44. Cf. also Sadler, *Masonic Facts and Fictions*.
73   A porter, one half of the pair who would transport a passenger by sedan chair.
74   *A Defence of Free-Masonry*.
75   Roger Swift, "Heroes or Villains?: The Irish, Crime, and Disorder in Victorian England," *Albion*, 29.3 (1997): 399–421.

press comment was mirrored in Old Bailey Court Reports, both of which set out the prejudice suffered by the Irish, with "Irish bog-trotting dog" one of the less offensive epithets.[76]

The Irish were viewed as a caricature by the eighteenth-century English establishment, including many within the Grand Lodge of England and its constituent lodges. Their concern regarding the admission of Irishmen to English Freemasonry was genuine, with the Irish held to be the antithesis of the deserving poor and a threat to the viability of the Grand Charity.

Providing support to indigent Freemasons may have been a tenet of lodge life for many years, but anti-Irish prejudice led to the exclusion of the Irish, not least by insisting that a recipient be a member of a recognised lodge for at least five years and of acceptable prior financial standing.[77] And there were other bars. It was only in the 1750s that Grand Lodge allowed the Charity Committee "to relieve any foreign indigent brother," but only "after due examination."[78] And even then, as Spencer put it, "[the Irish] have no right to partake of our charity." Indeed, *A Defence* mocked the Antients in this regard with the observation that "contributions to their charity are not voluntary, but obligatory, and every member of a lodge is obliged to contribute monthly or weekly, a small sum."[79]

A second factor underlying English Freemasonry's condescension towards the Irish was the influence of members of the Westminster, Middlesex, and City magistracy. Judicial statistics were not disaggregated by nationality prior to the 1860s, but in

76 *Proceedings at the Sessions of Peace, Oyer and Terminer, for the City of London, and County of Middlesex*, 234.

77 The Grand Lodge of England *Minutes* for 23 July 1740 offers an example of an application for charity that was rejected because the petitioner had less than five years membership of a regular lodge.

78 Grand Lodge of England *Minutes*, 30 November 1752.

79 *A Defence of Free-Masonry.*

the late nineteenth century the Irish were up to five times more likely to be prosecuted and convicted for offences when compared to the English and Welsh.[80] The statistic is supportive of anecdotal evidence from eighteenth-century press reports and provides an indication of what would have been current at that time. Public and private attitudes were not dissimilar, and there had been no fundamental changes to the nature of the judiciary.[81]

The magistrates' court was the establishment's front line, with magistrates empowered to penalise severely (and thus deter) offences against property and the person, punish disorder and uphold constitutional law. And, within London, a quarter of the magistracy, perhaps more, were Freemasons.[82] Many held positions of authority within Grand Lodge. Earl Cowper, the Lord Chancellor's nephew, William Cowper, the Clerk to the Parliaments, was a former Grand Secretary and Deputy Grand Master.[83] He chaired the Westminster magistrates' bench from 1723 to 1727, and the Middlesex bench from 1729 to 1730 and 1733. Cowper's address to his judicial colleagues underlined their obligation "to uphold the honour, the dignity, and the majesty of the state," and that whoever worked against approved law "should be treated as, a subverter of peace, order and good government...and an Enemy to human society."[84]

80 Cf. *House of Commons Parliamentary Papers, Judicial Statistics, England & Wales, 1858*, Part 1, pp xxii–xxiv, and *1859*, Part 1, xxv. Irish prisoners represented over 13% of the total prison population in 1858 and more than 14% in 1859. A prisoner's place of birth was recorded for the first time in 1857. The data did not account for second and third generation Irish, thus the true figure would have been substantially higher.

81 Berman, *Schism*, 105–17.

82 Berman, *Foundations*, 64–97.

83 William Cowper (d. 1740), Clerk to the Parliaments, DGM, 1726; GS 1723–1727.

84 William Cowper, *The Charge delivered by William Cowper, Esq., at the Sessions of the Peace and Oyer and Terminer, for the County*

Nathaniel Blackerby, a colleague from the Horn Tavern lodge, was elected chair of the Westminster bench in 1738.[85] He had also served as Deputy Grand Master and was the first Grand Treasurer of Premier Grand Lodge. Blackerby's address to the Westminster bench on his election also enjoined his colleagues to "exert yourselves for the preservation of the laws of your country... [such that] every man enjoys the fruits of his labour, his liberty, his property."[86] His words echoed Cowper's, who had in turn charged his judicial colleagues on the bench to be "vigilant to detect and produce to punishment [those who] attempt the subversion of the great basis upon which stands all that is or can be dear to England and Protestants... our religion, our liberty and our property."[87]

Alongside Cowper and Blackerby, sat George Carpenter[88] and Charles Delafaye, the government's anti-Jacobite spymaster;[89] and among a number of other prominent Masons in the 1730s and 1740s were Sir Thomas de Veil, Henry Norris, Richard Gifford, Richard Manley and Clifford William Philips, all exacting magistrates. De Veil was a Past Master of William Hogarth's lodge at the Apple Tree tavern. He was satirised by Hogarth in *Night*, shown, hypocritically drunk, in Masonic regalia on his way home from a lodge meeting.[90] De Veil sat on both the Mid-

    of Middlesex (London, 1730), 5–6.

85   John Chamberlayne, *Magnae Britanniae*, (1736), 160; *Daily Gazetteer*, 6 April 1738. Blackerby was first appointed to the bench in 1719.

86   Nathaniel Blackerby, *The Speech of Nathanial Blackerby* (London, 1738), 18.

87   *Pasquin*, 17 January 1723.

88   Hon. Colonel George Carpenter (c. 1694–1749), later 2nd baron Carpenter of Killaghy, MP, Grand Warden (1729).

89   Charles Delafaye (1677–1762).

90   Marie Mulvey-Roberts, "Hogarth on the Square: Framing the Freemasons," *Journal for Eighteenth Century Studies*, 26.2(2003):

dlesex and Westminster benches, and established the first formal
magistrate's court in 1739 at Bow Street. His pro-government
approach was such "that the government turned to de Veil whenever it needed a magistrate's services."[91] As a reward, he was made
a colonel in the Westminster militia, given sundry sinecures and,
in 1744, invested a knight. At the time of his death he had become
the administration's principal "go-to" magistrate in London.

Antients Freemasonry thrived in part because of the prejudice
of the Premier Grand Lodge. Under Dermott's leadership and
guidance, the Antients traded on a combination of greater utility
and inclusivity, and superior antiquity. This was underlined in
the second edition of *Ahiman Rezon* where the "Philacteria for
such gentleman as may be inclined to become Free-Masons"[92] set
out a catechism which captured the perception of the Antients
as superior Masonic beings:

> *Quere* 1st. *Whether free masonry, as practiced in antient
> lodges, is universal?*
> *Answer:* Yes.
>
> 2d. *Whether what is called modern masonry is universal?*
> *Answer:* No.
>
> 3d. *Whether there is any material difference between antient
> and modern?*
> *Answer:* A great deal, because an antient mason can not
> only make himself known to his brother but in cases of
> necessity can discover his very thoughts to him, in the pres-

251–70. *Night*, part of *Four Times of the Day*, was completed in
1736 and published in 1738. Cf. also Philip Sugden, "Sir Thomas
de Veil (1684–1746)," *ODNB*.
91   Sugden, "Sir Thomas de Veil."
92   Dermott, *Ahiman Rezon* (1764), xvii.

ence of a modern, without being able to distinguish that
either of them are free masons.

4th. *Whether a modern mason may with safety communicate all his secrets to an antient mason?*
Answer: Yes.

5th. *Whether an antient mason may with the like safety
communicate all his secrets to a modern mason without further ceremony?*
Answer: No. For as a Science comprehends an Art (though
an artist cannot comprehend a science) even so antient
masonry contains everything valuable amongst the modern, as well as many other things that cannot be revealed
without additional ceremonies.[93]

9th. *Whether the present members of modern lodges are
blameable for deviating from the old land marks?*
Answer: No. Because the innovation was made in the reign
of king George the first, and the new form was delivered as
orthodox to the present members.

10th. *Therefore as it is natural for each party to maintain
the orthodoxy of their masonical preceptors. How shall we
distinguish the original and most useful system?*
Answer: The number of antient masons compared with the
moderns being as ninety-nine to one proves the universality of the old order....[94]

What Dermott held out as fact was, of course, opinion. But it
nevertheless set down a powerful polemical rationale to join the

93   Ibid., xxv–xxvi.
94   Ibid., xxvi–xxvii.

Antients, or convert from Moderns Freemasonry. Dermott's gaze was also directed overseas, especially to British and Irish colonists in the Americas whose "right worshipful and very worthy gentlemen" were singled out for mention and flattery.

Bolstered by a growing lower middling membership, the Antients expanded their numbers in London. Antients Grand Lodge may have been formed only in 1751 at the head of a small group of five predominantly Irish lodges, but while the Moderns went into retreat, with lodges expelled and erased, membership of the Antients climbed. By 1752, the number of Antients' lodges had risen to thirteen; the following year there were thirty; and a year later almost forty. Within three decades, the number would exceed 200, with seventy-five in London, around eighty across provincial England and some fifty overseas. And by the 1800s, there would be over 500. Other Antients lodges were warranted by overseas grand lodges who had themselves been warranted by the Antients Grand Lodge in London, not least the "Brethren at Philadelphia," who switched allegiance from the Moderns and whose new warrant was granted in 1759.[95] The Antients were especially successful in establishing lodges in the newly emerging centres of population—whether in Britain or elsewhere—and can be traced along the canals and later railways that bisected the home nations, many of which were built using Irish labour. Mass emigration from Ireland became a fact of life, with some half a million leaving for America, Europe and Britain—the last described distressingly as "the nearest place that wasn't Ireland."[96]

Irish migration to Britain had in the past been seasonal but a series of harsh winters and the famines that followed, combined with ever more restrictive anti-Irish trade legislation, altered

95   Ric Berman, *Loyalists and Malcontents* (Old Stables Press, 2015), Preface.

96   Ruth-Ann Harris, *The Nearest Place That Wasn't Ireland: Early Nineteenth Century Labor Migration* (Iowa: Iowa State University Press, 1994).

the paradigm and promoted mass migration from Ireland. The émigré Irish came to England in their tens of thousands. They settled in the main entry ports and in the towns and cities of what would emerge as Britain's industrial heartland, but most especially they settled in London. Precise numbers are unavailable—census data only begins in the nineteenth century—but in the 1750s and 1760s the number of London Irish migrants would have been in the mid-tens of thousands.

Living conditions for most émigrés were squalid, and life was short. But this was not universal. A minority climbed the social and financial ladder, their success built on networks of Irish-owned tenement houses, chop houses, and gin and ale shops, and on the supply of services, with many becoming skilled tradesmen or professionals, apothecaries, lawyers and doctors.

London's rookeries were a font of aspiration and entrepreneurialism, and many London Irish broke free of poverty's constraints. Antients Freemasonry was populated largely from this layer of lower middling and middling society, evidence for which is seen in the nature of those who joined, the fees they paid and the charity they donated.[97] The Antients' General Registers, the early membership records, contain details of occupation and address. Some 5% of members are categorised as "gentlemen;" more than 10% as professionals, including apothecaries, attorneys, goldsmiths, silversmiths and medical practioners; and almost a quarter as skilled artisans, including clock and watchmakers, bookbinders and printers. And many, perhaps most, of those that appear in the Registers as tradesmen—carpenters, painters, tailors, wig-makers and weavers—were not employees but employers. An eighteenth-century business owner would usually be described by the underlying service he provided—a painter, for example—rather than as the owner of a decorating business.

One of the more important drivers behind the success of An-

97   Berman, *Schism*, 45–104.

tients Freemasonry was the organisation's provision of practical mutual support, something fundamental to all émigrés, whether leaving for England or the Americas. The minutes of Antients' lodge meetings demonstrate the widespread application of financial aid within the local community, including assistance to the ill, unemployed and families of deceased members. The Antients also issued membership certificates that acted as proto-passports, identifying the holder as someone entitled to access the mutual support network of Antients Freemasonry in Britain, Ireland and overseas. They were a means to access Freemasonry's mutual support structure and assisted itinerant workers to find employment. This was also the case for those headed overseas, whether returning to Ireland or making a new life in the Americas and Caribbean. The minutes of Lodge № 20, the Hampshire Hog in Goswell Street, for 2 September 1754, record Bro. Blunt's request for a membership certificate "as he is going to Jamaica." The certificate was granted, "received honourably, as he has paid all his dues in our lodge."[98] And the following year Samuel Galbraith, the Senior Warden, introduced Thomas Dowsett as a joining member, proving Dowsett "worthy of being a member" by means of "his certificate from № 218, Ireland."[99]

The evidence of the Antients' General Registers and Minutes dismisses the image of the feckless Irish and speaks instead to a nuanced view of social ambition, self-help and, above all, economic aspiration. Antients Freemasonry under Dermott developed to become an effective friendly society as well as a fraternal association bound by ritual.

As Antients Freemasonry expanded across England and Britain's overseas colonies, it posed a challenge to the authority of the Moderns and to that of the British establishment. And by the 1770s, the potentially seditious nature of Antients Freemasonry

98   Ibid., 60–64.
99   Ibid.

had become embedded in its literature. Dermott's frontispiece
to the 1778 edition of *Ahiman Rezon* featured a design that reflected the marginalisation of the Moderns in favour of the now
conjoined Irish, Scottish, and Antients branches:

> The three figures upon the dome represent the great mas-
> ters of the tabernacle… The two crowned figures with that
> on their right hand represent the three great masters of the
> holy temple at Jerusalem. The three figures on the left hand
> represent the three great masters of the second temple at
> Jerusalem.
>
> The three columns bearing Masons aprons with the
> arms of England, Ireland and Scotland and supporting the
> whole fabric, represents the three Grand Masters…who
> wisely and nobly have formed a triple union to support
> the honour and dignity of the Ancient Craft, for which
> their Lordship's names will be honoured and revered while
> Freemasonry exists in these kingdoms.[100]

There are few direct references to the Antients in the minutes
of the Grand Lodge of England, but a resolution passed on 29
November 1754 under the auspices of the Marquis of Carnarvon,
the then Grand Master, hit the subject head on, resolving that

> if any mason shall attend, tyle or assist as tyler at any meet-
> ings or pretended lodges of persons calling themselves ma-
> sons not being a regular constituted lodge acknowledging
> the authority of our Rt. Worshipful Grand Master and
> conforming to the Laws of the Grand Lodge, he shall be
> forever incapable of being a tyler or attendant on a lodge

100 Dermott, *Ahiman Rezon*, 3rd ed. (1778), "Explanation of the
     Frontispiece."

or partaking of the General Charity.[101]

In short, the response of the Moderns to the challenge posed
by the Antients was to rule that no Antients Freemason would
be able to access charity funds nor be allowed to serve as a lodge
attendant or tyler, a role frequently undertaken by indigent Freemasons, and that they would be excluded from "regular," that is,
Moderns, lodge meetings.

The ruling was put to the test six months later, when the Master and Wardens of the Ben Johnson's Head were summoned to
Grand Lodge to answer the charge that they had met as an Antients lodge. They responded by arguing that as private persons
they had the right to meet in any manner they saw fit. Thomas
Manningham, the acting Grand Master, asked that they put forward a proposal to settle the issue and, "after some debate about
the question to be proposed," a suggestion was tabled that "the
Members of the Lodge at the Ben Johnson's Head be permitted to
meet independent of their Constitution from this Society under
the Denomination of a Lodge of Ancient Masons."[102]

The resolution was denied virtually unanimously, only two
lodges voting in favour: that of the Ben Johnson's Head and a delegation from the Fish and Bell in Soho. The Ben Johnson's Head
having been invited to "refrain from their said irregular Meetings [and] reconcile themselves to Grand Lodge," the minutes
continue that the request was "without effect" and accordingly
"a question was then put, that the lodge Nº 94, held at the Ben
Johnson's Head in Pelham Street, Spitalfields, be erased from the
Book of Lodges and that such of the Brethren thereof who shall
continue those irregular Meetings be not admitted as Visitors
in any Lodge." The resolution was carried "almost unanimously,

101 *Grand Lodge of England Minutes*, 29 November 1754.
102 Ibid., 24 July 1755.

with the same Brethren as above only dissenting."[103]

The Fish and Bell, Soho, the only lodge to support the Ben Johnson's Head, was one of the four founding lodges and had met previously at the Apple Tree Tavern.[104] It was also one of a number of older lodges that had not modified their ritual to comply with the new form approved by Grand Lodge. Their resistance to diktat was shared by others, including the Horn Tavern, the senior founding lodge, which had ceased to be recognised as a regular lodge by Grand Lodge and stood erased until 1751.

Dermott used the Ben Johnson's Head incident as a means to heap abuse and derision on the Moderns. The episode was detailed at length in the third edition of *Ahiman Rezon* in a passage designed explicitly to show the Moderns in an unfavourable light and underscore the superiority of Antients Freemasonry:

> [The Ben Johnson's Head was] composed mainly of Antient Masons, though under the Modern Constitution. Some of them had been abroad and received extraordinary benefits on account of Antient Masonry. Therefore they agreed to practice Antient Masonry on every third lodge night. Upon one of those nights some Modern Masons attempted to visit them but were refused admittance; the persons so refused laid a formal complaint before the Modern Grand Lodge...[who] ordered that the Ben Johnson's Head should admit all sorts of Masons without distinction. And upon non-compliance to that order, they were censured.[105]

Quoting from a pamphlet, Dermott assured his readers had been issued by Ben Johnson's Head, he argued that the "injustice" to the Ben Johnson's Head was due to the Moderns' ignorance

---

103 Ibid.
104 Now Fortitude and Old Cumberland, № 12.
105 Dermott, *Ahiman Rezon*, 3rd edition, xvi–xvii.

of true Freemasonry, comparing the Moderns' understanding to that of "a blind man ... in the art of mixing colour." Finally, and notwithstanding that it conflicted with his earlier remarks, Dermott stated with some irony that the members of the Ben Johnson's Head had not even been Antients Freemasons, although "(from [his] personal knowledge and public report) they were persons of the most amiable character as men and masons."[106]

The incident offers another demonstration of Dermott's skill in positioning Antients Freemasonry so that it would be perceived as the more attractive of the two Masonic organisations while simultaneously trashing the Moderns and encouraging the recruitment of new members to the Antients.

Dermott emphasised that it was Antients Freemasonry that provided effective Masonic benevolence, even when members were overseas: members of Ben Johnson's Head "had been abroad and received extraordinary benefits on account of Antient Masonry." He drew attention to the Antients' possession of superior ritual, arguing that the Ben Johnson's Head was correct to refuse admittance to lesser qualified Moderns Freemasons. And he inferred that the Moderns Grand Lodge was both dictatorial and ignorant: their decision to order the admittance of "all sorts of Masons without distinction" confirming an absence of knowledge as to the "true" nature of Freemasonry.

Disparagement of the Moderns remained a constant theme of Dermott's terms in office. Even in 1772, twenty years after having been appointed Grand Secretary, he persisted: one example being the leaking to the press of a letter from the Duke of Atholl:

> The duke thanked them for the great honour they had conferred upon him by continuing him Grand Master for the year ending and he likewise acquainted them that he was of opinion (and it is the opinion of the Society in general)

106   Ibid., xviii.

> *the Modern Masons are acting entirely inconsistently with*
> *the antient customs and principles of the craft.*[107]

By this point the two rival grand lodges had warred for two decades. The Moderns' complaint against Ben Johnson's Head was in essence that it was a threat to the reputation and authority of the Moderns: "Brethren [were] Forming and Assembling under the denomination of a Lodge of Ancient Masons who as such considered themselves as independent of this Society and not subject to our Laws or the Authority of our Grand Master." This was not only "contrary to our Laws" but "a great Insult on the Grand Master & the whole Body of Free & Accepted Masons." Compounding the problem, they "introduce into the Craft the Novelties & Conceits of opinionative Persons & to create a Belief that there have been other Societies of Masons more Ancient than that of this Ancient & Honourable Society."[108]

By the 1760s, the Moderns were sufficiently distressed at their deteriorating position that they attempted to secure their authority via an application to Parliament for a Charter of Incorporation "in order to annihilate the Society who styled themselves Antient Free Masons." They failed, and the follow-up, an attempt to assert their superiority by constructing a Grand Hall in London had the unintended consequence of alienating many formerly loyal masons in provincial England to whom they turned for funding.

But it was America that would prove a more defining battlefield, with the split in American Freemasonry between the Moderns and Ancients accentuated as in England by politics and social class. The Masonic feud may have commenced in

107 *Middlesex Journal or Chronicle of Liberty,* 9–11 April 1772. Author's italics.

108 J.R. Dashwood, Ed., *The Minutes of the Grand Lodge of Freemasons of England 1740–1758* (Margate: Quatuor Coronati Lodge, 1960), 20 March 1755.

Philadelphia but it spread quickly across the thirteen colonies. As on the other side of the Atlantic, the "essential dividing line [was]... the social barrier between those who could claim honor and gentility and those who could not."[109] The Antients' broader and more aspirational membership held the key to its popularity in America, and to its later growth.[110] After all, members of any elite are limited in number by definition. And the Moderns were no exception.

Although the divide between Moderns and Antients Freemasonry has been interpreted as a schism over Masonic ritual and tradition, it was in reality a product of more significant social factors, the most important of which was the changing composition of eighteenth-century society in Britain and America and, in particular, the development of the aspirational lower middling.

Under Dermott, Antients Freemasonry reflected and sometimes led the social and economic changes taking place elsewhere. And by extending sociability beyond the gentry and upper middling, Dermott created an organisation whose networking and social welfare functions were as important as its ritual, if not more so.

Bibliography

Anderson, James. *The New Book of Constitutions of the Antient and Honourable Fraternity of Free and Accepted Masons, Containing Their History, Charges, Regulations, &c.* London: Richard Chandler, 1738.

Anon. ["A member of Royal Arch"]. *Hiram: or the Grand Master-Key.*

109 Steven C. Bullock, *Revolutionary Brotherhood: Freemasonry and the Transformation of the American Social Order, 1730–1840* (Chapel Hill, N.C.: University of North Carolina Press, 1996), 65–67.

110 Berman, *Loyalist & Malcontents*, esp. Appendix Two.

London: W. Griffin. 1764.

Barnaby, George J. "Review: The Economic Emergence of the Black Country by T. J. Rambould." *Economic History Review.* Vol. 27, No. 3 (1974): 475–76.

Berman, Ric. *The Foundations of Modern Freemasonry: The Grand Architects, Political Change and the Scientific Enlightenment, 1714– 1740.* Brighton: Sussex Academic Press, 2015.

———. *Loyalists and Malcontents: Freemasonry & Revolution in the Deep South.* Oxfordshire: Old Stables Press, 2015.

———. *Schism: The Battle the Forged Freemasonry.* Brighton: Sussex Academic Press, 2013.

Blackerby, Nathaniel. *The Speech of Nathaniel Blackerby.* London, 1738.

Bullock, Steven C. *Revolutionary Brotherhood: Freemasonry and the Transformation of the American Social Order, 1730–1840.* Chapel Hill, N.C.: University of North Carolina Press, 1996.

Bywater, Witham Matthew. *Notes on Laurence Dermott.* London: privately printed, 1884.

Cowper, William. *The Charge Delivered by William Cowper, Esq. at the Sessions of the Peace and Oyer and Terminer, for the County of Middlesex.* Printed for J. Stagg, 1730.

Daily Advertiser, January 21, 1752.

Daily Gazetteer, April 06, 1738.

Daily Gazetteer, December 08, 1738.

Dashwood, J.R., Ed. *The Minutes of the Grand Lodge of Freemasons of England 1740–1758.* Margate: Quatuor Coronati Lodge, 1960.

———. *Quatuor Coronatorum Antigrapha, Vol. 11.* Margate & Sittingbourne: Quatuor Coronati Lodge, 1958.

Dermott, Laurence. *Ahiman Rezon: Or, A Help to a Brother.* London: James Bedford, 1756.

———. *Ahiman Rezon: Or, A Help to a Brother.* London: Robert Black, 1764.

———. *Ahiman Rezon: Or, A Help to a Brother.* London: James Jones, 1778.

Gazetteer and New Daily Advertiser, September 21, 1765.

General Advertiser, February 19, 1752.

General Advertiser, March 4, 1752.

General Advertiser, March 7, 1752.

General Advertiser, March 9, 1752.

General Advertiser, March 11, 1752.

Gould, Robert. *Gould's History of Freemasonry Throughout the World, Vol. II.* New York: Charles Scribner's Sons, 1936.

————. *The History of Freemasonry: Its Antiquities, Symbols, Constitutions, etc. Vol. III.* New York: John C. Yorston & Co., 1884.

Harris, Ruth-Ann. *The Nearest Place that Wasn't Ireland: Early Nineteenth Century Labor Migration.* Iowa: Iowa State University Press, 1994.

Hughan, William James. *Memorials of the Masonic Union.* Revised edition. Leicester: Johnson, Wykes, & Payne, 1913.

House of Commons Parliamentary Papers, Judicial Statistics, England & Wales, 1858.

House of Commons Parliamentary Papers, Judicial Statistics, England & Wales, 1859.

Journal for the House of Commons. Seventh Parliament of Great Britain, 6th Session.

Journal for the House of Lords. Ninth Parliament of Great Britain, 3rd Session.

Journal for the House of Lords. Ninth Parliament of Great Britain, 5th Session.

Journal for the House of Lords. Ninth Parliament of Great Britain, 6th Session.

Journal for the House of Lords. Tenth Parliament of Great Britain, 1st Session.

Laurie, William Alexander. *The History of Free Masonry and the Grand Lodge of Scotland.* Edinburgh: Seton & MacKenzie, 1859.

Lepper, J.H. & Crossle, P. *History of the Grand Lodge of Free and Accepted Masons of Ireland.* Dublin: Lodge of Research CC, 1925.

London Chronicle, February 27–March 01, 1766.

London Daily Advertiser, April 09, 1752.

London Evening Post, February 27, 1766.

London Evening Post, November 15–18, 1766.

London Gazette, June 12–16, 1759.

Mackey, Albert G. *An Encyclopædia of Freemasonry and Its Kindred Sciences*. Philadelphia: Moss & Co., 1874.

Middlesex Journal or Chronicle of Liberty, April 9–11, 1772.

Morning Herald and Daily Advertiser, September 25, 1782.

Mulvaney-Roberts, Marie. "Hogarth on the Square: Framing the Freemasons." *Journal for Eighteenth Century Studies*. Vol. 26, No. 2 (2003): 251–70.

Parker's General Advertiser and Morning Intelligencer, May 23, 1782.

Parker's General Advertiser and Morning Intelligencer, September 24, 1782.

Pasquin, January 17, 1723.

Pritchard, Samuel. *Masonry Dissected*. London: J. Wilford, 1730.

Proceedings at the Sessions of Peace, Oyer and Terminer, for the City of London, and County of Middlesex, on the Wednesday the 3d, Thursday the 4th, Friday the 5th, and Saturday the 6th of September. In the 14th Year of His Majesty's Reign. London: T. Cooper, 1740.

Public Advertiser, November 19, 1766.

Public Ledger, November 29, 1765.

Registers of the Grand Lodge of the Antients 1751–1813, Volume A. Library and Museum of Freemasonry, London.

Rumbold, Valerie. *The Dunicad in Four Books*. Revised Edition. Harlow: Pearson, 2009.

Sadler, Henry. *Masonic Facts and Fictions*. London: Diprose & Bateman, 1887.

Sheppard, F.H.W. *Survey of London, Vol. XL*. London: English Heritage, 1980.

Songhurst, William J. Ed. *Minutes of the Grand Lodge of England, 1723–1739*. London: Quatuor Coronati Lodge, 1913.

————. *Quatuor Coronatorum Antigrapha, Vol. 10*. Margate & Sitting-bourne: Quatuor Coronati Lodge, 1913.

Spratt, Edward. *The New Book of Constitutions of the Most Ancient and Honourable Fraternity of Free and Accepted Masons*. Dublin: Edward Bate, 1751.

[Spencer, Samuel]. *A Defence of Free-Masonry, As Practiced in the Regular Lodges, Both Foreign and Domestic, Under the Constitution of the English Grand-Master*. London: Flexney & Hood, 1765.

St. James Chronicle or the British Evening Post, December 27–29, 1763.

Sugden, Phillip. "Sir Thomas de Veil (1684–1746)." *Oxford Dictionary of National Biography*.

Swift, Roger. "Heroes or Villains?: The Irish, Crime, and Disorder in Victorian England." *Albion*. Vol. 29, No. 3 (1997): 399–421.

Weekly Journal or British Gazetteer, February 17, 1728.

"Genius of Masonry"

The Preservation of Masonic Tradition in the Songs of the Freemasons

NATHAN A. ST. PIERRE

THROUGHOUT THE HISTORY of the Freemasons, music has held a place of honor in the fraternity. As a discipline, it was first described Masonically within the Cooke MS of the Old Charges of the Order, which dates to c. 1450:

> Musik that techith a man the crafte of song in notys of voys and organ & trompe and harp and all othur pteynyng to hem.[1]

As the fraternity continued through the centuries, into the early 1700s, music maintained its literal meaning, but also took on a symbolic one as well, a "speculative" compliment to the "operative" definition. As a result, music became a source for philosophical discussion related to the nature of harmony both natural and metaphoric, and a tool for uniting a far-reaching brotherhood into a common culture with shared ideals. In Benjamin Cole's *A Book of the Antient Constitutions of the Free and*

---

1 Cooke MS, lines 69–72.

Accepted Masons (1728), the importance of the quadrivium was established:

> The fourth is Arithmetic, which teacheth a man to reckon or account all manner of Numbers &c.

> The fifth is Geometry, which teacheth the Mensuration of lines, Superficies, Solids, &c. which Science is the Basis of Masonry.

> The Sixth Science is called Musick which teacheth ẙ Proportions Harmony & Discords of Sounds &c. which qualifies a man in the art of singing, Composing Tunes, and playing upon divers Instruments, as the Organ, Harp, &c.

> Lastly, the Seventh Science is called Astronomy, which teacheth the motions of the Luminaries, Planets, Fix'd Stars, &c. & to Measure their Magnitudes, & Determine their Distances.[2]

This is important because it firmly notes that the purpose of Music among the Freemasons was twofold: a) understanding proportion and harmony had metaphoric applications beyond the creation of pleasant sounds, and b) men should be "qualified" in the art of singing. Music was not meant for the talented to perform for audiences, but rather for all Masons to perform as a group. This occurred most frequently, although not exclusively, during the feasts that followed the "grave business" of the lodge.[3] Making music collectively was part of their culture. As such, the musical culture of the Freemasons can be studied as any other culture.

2   Cole, *Ancient Constitutions*, 4–5.
3   See Anderson, *Constitutions*, 84.

The purpose of the current study will be to establish a theo-
retical framework based on the notions of Bruno Nettl's music
"in-or-as culture"; the beliefs of folklorists such as Cecil Sharp
and Alan Lomax regarding the preservation of authentic cultures; and Eric Hobsbawm's theory of "invented tradition." This
framework will serve to demonstrate that the song material of
the eighteenth-century Freemasons served as a repository for a
genuinely invented tradition through which these Masons preserved their most important ideals, legends, values, and philosophy.

Masonic Musical Culture

It has been said that the creation of group identity happens, at
least in part, through creation and preservation of song material
within said group.[4] This calls to mind the research of Alan Lomax who stated that "a song style, like other human things, is a
pattern of learned behavior, common to the people of a culture.
Singing is a specialized act of communication, akin to speech, but
far more formally organized and redundant."[5] As a specialized
act of communication, it is meant to be shared; its redundancy
leads to memorization, which aids in the oral transmission of the
culture. According to Lomax, "the chief function of song is to express the shared feelings and mold the joint activities of some human community."[6] The Freemasons were no different than other
groups or cultures in this regard. As Katherine Campbell stated,
"song played an important role from the time of [Freemasonry's]
formalization in the early eighteenth-century, and song was also
likely involved even in the informal freemasonry that is known

4   Campbell, "Masonic Song in Scotland," 88.
5   Lomax, *Folk Song*, 3.
6   Ibid., 3.

to have taken place earlier in Scotland within taverns and the like and in the convivial activities that accompanied proceedings."[7] A study of Masonic songs, therefore, would be a study of Masonic culture. Ethnomusicology can be defined as "the study of music in its cultural context."[8] However, studying music "in" a culture only provides one perspective; studying music "as" culture provides another. To truly understand the music of a people, one should aim to show music in-or-as culture.[9] Bruno Nettl's theory of music-in-or-as culture suggests that the music of a people might reflect certain central values of a culture. Music in-or-as culture implies a relationship between music and the people who make it.[10] As part of the music in-or-as culture paradigm, this study will, at least in part, examine the relationship between the eighteenth-century Freemasons and their songs.

Cultural Preservation

Part of the music in-or-as culture relationship involves the use of songs to preserve cultural values and/or traditions. If it can be said that the written word preserves knowledge, it can also be said that the complex symbolic structure of music can "preserve and expand a life-style."[11] This preservation of culture was the primary aim of the folklorists in the early twentieth-century, the most influential of whom was Cecil Sharp. Sharp and his contemporaries believed that "authentic" traditions were "dying out" and it was the role of folklorists and song collectors to preserve them as authentically and as frequently as possible before

7   Campbell, "Masonic Song in Scotland," 88.
8   Nettl, *The Study of Ethnomusicology*, 231.
9   Ibid., 236.
10   Ibid., 222.
11   Lomax, *Folk Song*, 6.

these cultures were further corrupted by industrialization and urbanization.[12] This "dying out" was considered to be a problem of paramount importance. Alan Lomax said:

> to a folklorist the uprooting and destruction of traditional cultures and the consequent grey-out or disappearance of the human variety presents as serious a threat to the future happiness of mankind as poverty, overpopulation, and even war.[13]

Given the vast international expansion of Freemasonry in the eighteenth century, it is unlikely that members of the fraternity predicted any collapse. While it is true that some men, such as the Irish Mason Fifield D'Assigny and, a generation later, the English Mason William Preston, observed weaknesses developing within Freemasonry, the 1700s were surely a time for optimism regarding the future of Freemasonry.[14] Perhaps it was this confidence in the longevity of their institution that prompted the Freemasons to publish hundreds of their songs and poems in a large number of song collections, histories, exposures, and other publications in the 1700s and early 1800s. It would likely surprise Masons of the eighteenth century to find that, generally speaking, the singing of Masonic songs is no longer an important part of the lodge experience in the twenty-first century. Additionally, the commingling of Late-Renaissance mysticism with Enlightenment philosophy—a feature of many early lodges—are also topics no longer frequently discussed. In short, there has been a "dying" or "grey-out" of Masonic culture, and contemporary scholars should be grateful to these early Masons for preserving their songs in print. With

12   Pegg et al., "Ethnomusicology."
13   Lomax, *Folk Song*, 4.
14   See D'Assigny, *Serious and Impartial Enquiry*; See also, Preston, *Illustrations*.

access to that body of work, research can now more fully examine the traditional values and philosophies of the Order and attempt to document how they have changed over time.

Invented Tradition

Since the song material of the Freemasons can be considered a window through which to view the traditional practices and beliefs of the fraternity, it is important to fully grasp the nature of tradition. According to Bruno Nettl:

> The way in which a tradition is passed on is called "transmission," and the two terms are sometimes used, informally and perhaps colloquially, to emphasize two sides of the character of a culture or indeed of a music—its stability on the one hand, its tendency to change on the other.[15]

It is important to note that both "stability" and "tendency to change" are mentioned here because these concepts will feature prominently in the ideas of Eric Hobsbawm, one of the leading theorists on the nature of tradition. Hobsbawm's greatest contributions to this field were his theories regarding the "invention of tradition." Hobsbawm wrote that "'traditions' which appear or claim to be old are often quite recent in origin and sometimes invented."[16] He also stated that these invented traditions usually belong to three types:

a) those establishing or symbolizing social cohesion or the membership of groups, real or artificial communities;

b) those establishing or legitimizing institutions, status or relations of authority;

15   Nettl, "Types of Tradition," 3.
16   Hobsbawm & Ranger, *Invention of Tradition*, 1.

c) those whose main purpose was socialization, the inculcation of beliefs, value systems and conventions of behavior.[17]

Hobsbawm described Freemasonry as an "earlier invented tradition of great symbolic force."[18] To counter the negative connotation that "invented tradition" carries, Hobsbawm states:

> the strength and adaptability of genuine traditions is not to be confused with the "invention of tradition." Where the old ways are alive, traditions need be neither revived nor invented.[19]

There are strong connections between the "stability" and "tendency to change" mentioned by Nettl and the "strength" and "adaptability" mentioned by Hobsbawm. What is unclear, however, is what exactly establishes a "genuine tradition?" How much "adaptability" is allowed before a genuine tradition becomes "invented?" For that matter, how long must an invented tradition have "stability" before it becomes "genuine?"

An important idea moving forward is that a tradition can be invented and still be sociologically important.[20] To illustrate this further, the concepts of "Folk Music" and "Art Music" are themselves recent constructions that have "portrayed themselves as timeless categories"; therefore even these music genres can be considered invented traditions.[21] Their usefulness in the discourse, however, does not change. It also could be a logical assumption that all traditions were invented at some point. Therefore, whether or not Freemasonry is an invented tradition is much less important than the fact that it is a tradition that has

17   Ibid., 9.
18   Ibid., 6.
19   Ibid., 8.
20   Hetherington, *Badlands of Modernity*, 87.
21   Gelbart, *Invention of Folk Music*, 6.

been transmitted through ritual and song.

A Brief History of the Masons

Nettl said, "study of music in or as culture ... requires a conception (going now beyond definition) of culture, and a conception of music for juxtaposition."[22] To provide this conception of culture, one must be familiar with the self-identity and history of early Masons. Often Grand Lodges, as well as some individual Masons, offered their own printed histories in the early Masonic publications. James Anderson's *The Constitutions of the Free-Masons* (1723), or, as it is more commonly known, Anderson's *Constitutions*, began with a printed history that traced Masonry from Adam through Noah, Moses, and other biblical figures to Egypt, Greece, Rome, and finally to the English and Scottish kings.[23] Malcolm Davies referred to this as the "mythopœic history;"[24] it is also widely known in Masonic scholarship as the "Traditional History." One of the earliest Masonic songs, "The Master's Song: Or the History of Masonry," was a twenty-eight-verse adaptation of this Traditional History. It begins:

> Adam, the first of humane Kind
> Created with GEOMETRY
> Imprinted on his Royal Mind,
> Instructed soon his progeny
> CAIN and SETH, who then improv'd
> The lib'ral Science in the Art
> Of ARCHITECTURE, which they lov'd

22   Nettl, *Study of Ethnomusicology*, 222.
23   Anderson, *Constitutions of the Free-Masons*, 1–45.
24   Davies, "Muse of Freemasonry," 95.

And to their Offspring did impart[25]

In 1756, another Masonic publication, *Ahiman Rezon: or A Help to a Brother*, by Lawrence Dermott, offered another mythopœic story in which the author attempts to write an even more thorough history of Masonry than that of Anderson and subsequent writers, dating the Craft to before the creation itself. In this story, when Dermott finishes his history, and is quite pleased with the results, he falls asleep. While he slumbers, he is visited by four sojourners from Jerusalem who bring him to the High Priest of the Hebrew Temple. The High Priest tells Dermott that his history is still incomplete and offers him further enlightenment. Dermott is then awakened by a "young Puppy that (got into the Room while I slept, and, seizing my Papers, eat a great Part of them, and) was then (between my legs) shaking and tearing the last Sheet of what I had wrote."[26]

Given these elaborate mythopœia, it is easy to see why Hobsbawm would consider Freemasonry to be an invented tradition, but the actual history of Masonry is easier to trace. The earliest written record of Masonry is the Regius Poem within the Halliwell MS, which is dated between 1385 and 1445. It serves as a set of rules for the governance of Masons, discusses their secrets, and traces their history to king Athelstan in the year 925 CE.[27] The word "Freemason" itself can be traced to the fourteenth century and either applied to workers in "freestone" (i.e., "freestone masons") or used to refer to the ability of those artisan workers to move freely to wherever there was work to be done—a luxury not afforded to most in feudal societies.[28] It is in this world that the guild system emerges. There is evidence of these guilds as far

25   Anderson, *Constitutions*, 75.
26   Dermott, *Ahiman Rezon*, xvi.
27   Davies, *Masonic Muse*, 20.
28   Davies, *Masonic Muse*, 20.

back as the fourteenth century, but it is in 1481 that the Company of Masons were granted their constitution. The company had the offices of Master and Warden (two offices still in use in Masonic lodges) and a uniform manner of dress for members.[29] The Company of Masons, and other Masonic guilds like it, operated by a set of "charges" which were essentially rules by which they were governed. The Regius Poem can be considered an example of these charges, but the earliest set of charges with an exact date comes from 1583. These charges would have been read or recited each time a new member was admitted to the lodge.[30] This can be seen as an early initiation ritual for new Masons. From the sixteenth and seventeenth centuries there exist records of members of lodges who were not actual stone workers. Often, these were architects from wealthy families who worked intelligently from plans and drawings, but did not work on actual stone. Also among these "Speculative Masons" were members of the Society who did not work with stone even on an intellectual level. Some important Speculative, or symbolic, Masons include Elias Ashmole and Sir Robert Moray, the latter of whom was to be a crucial figure in the establishment of the Royal Society.[31]

On June 24th, St. John the Baptist's Day, 1717, four of the symbolic lodges in London, who met in close proximity to each other, united to form the first Grand Lodge. For historical clarification, this organization was later variously described as the "Premier" or "Modern" Grand Lodge of England, in order to distinguish it from other groups. By 1723 (when Anderson's *Constitutions* was published) there were fifty lodges in the Grand Lodge, and by 1750 that number had grown to almost 200.[32] In 1751, a number of the lodges that had not united under, or had been recognized

29   Davies, *Masonic Muse*, 20–21.
30   Davies, *Masonic Muse*, 21.
31   Davies, *Masonic Muse*, 21.
32   Davies, *Masonic Muse*, 22; MacNulty, *Freemasonry*, 70.

by, the Grand Lodge of England formed a rival Grand Lodge called "The Most Antient and Honourable Society of Free and Accepted Masons."

Masonic author W. Kirk MacNulty, F P S, wrote that this new Grand Lodge referred to themselves "as the 'Antients,' because they kept to old practices, they dubbed the older, original Grand Lodge 'Moderns' because of its innovations."[33] These two Grand Lodges would remain rivals until 1813 when they merged to form the United Grand Lodge of England.[34] Despite the fact that there was an often bitter rivalry between these two Grand Lodges, the importance of music and song seems to be one concept on which they agreed. Printed song material from the eighteenth century reveals that there was a great deal of uniformity between the Antients and Moderns in terms of musical performance practice prior to their union in 1813.[35]

The Creation of Song

The way the Masonic songs were created also provides insight into the culture, or perhaps more accurately, deeper understanding of the life and times in which they were written. Songs by their very nature are part of the oral tradition. This is because even if they are written down, they still require oral tradition for transmission.[36] Now while the concept of "oral tradition" itself is an eighteenth-century construct,[37] in music it "refers to those aspects of music that are passed down by humans teaching one

---

33   MacNulty, *Freemasonry*, 70–71.

34   MacNulty, *Freemasonry*, 71.

35   Pink, "When They Sing," 4.

36   McLucas, *Musical Ear*, 2.

37   Gelbart, *Invention of Folk Music*.

another the art form."[38] Anne Dhu McLucas has argued that all musical performance, because it is taken in aurally, is part of oral tradition.[39] McLucas also stated that, while we can read about performance practices, "there is no way to find out what a single song actually sounded like before the era of recorded music."[40] In other words, the singing of a song is ephemeral; but, the song itself endures, provided it is written down, as so many Masonic songs were. Further to McLucas's point, each performance of a song is a recreation from memory. Therefore, within an oral tradition *not* supplemented by a written record, unmemorable songs die.[41]

The notion of memorability was important in the minds of the Masonic songwriters. There was a very different understanding of "art" and of "genius" in eighteenth-century society than existed in later periods. The concept of "art" was more closely tied to "artifice" than to the created work of an artistic genius as it is now.[42] Even the concept of "genius" itself was defined differently. The term "genius" seemed to have more to do with internal inspiration.[43] Songs could be considered "flights of genius" but were not considered art.[44]

This concept has been demonstrated in the Masonic song "Of Masonry: An Ode" (1737) by John Bancks:

> GENIUS of MASONRY! descend,
> In mystic Numbers while We sing;
> Enlarge our Souls, the CRAFT defend,

---

38   McLucas, *Musical Ear*, 2.
39   McLucas, *Musical Ear*,
40   McLucas, *Musical Ear*, 47.
41   McLucas, *Musical Ear*, 47.
42   Gelbart, *Invention of Folk Music*, 191.
43   Gelbart, *Invention of Folk Music*, 191
44   Gelbart, *Invention of Folk Music*, 192.

And hither all Thy Influence bring;
With social Thoughts our Bosoms fill,
And give Thy Turn to every Will.[45]

Another example, this one from William Smith's *Pocket Companion*, appeared in 1735, and invoked the inspiration that created Egypt, Syria, and Babylon:

Guardian Genius of our Art divine,
Unto thy faithful Sons appear;
Cease now o'er Ruins of the *East* to pine,
And smile in blooming Beauties here.

Egypt, *Syria*, and proud *Babylon*,
No more thy blissful presence claim;
In *Britain* fix thy ever-during Throne,
Where Myriads do confess thy Name.[46]

When it came to songwriting in the eighteenth century, originality was sometimes actually discouraged. Benjamin Franklin, in a 1765 letter to his brother, Peter, chided him for composing a ballad that could not be set to any commonly known tune saying, "Had you fitted it to an old one, well known, it must have spread much faster than I doubt it will do from the best new tune we can get compos'd for it."[47] Many songbooks from this period, not only Masonic ones, feature texts labeled with "to be sung to the tune of…."[48] This practice is derived from *contrafactum* (i.e., taking an existing tune and imposing new text onto it), which was a popular compositional technique from

45   Bancks, *Proposals for Printing*, 31.
46   Smith, *Pocket Companion*, 78–79.
47   McLucas, *Musical Ear*, 84.
48   McLucas, *Musical Ear*, 83.

Medieval music through the Renaissance that continued into the eighteenth century where it mixed with parody.[49] To take an already existing tune from one source and superimpose new text was common practice in numerous centuries. For instance, in vaudeville acts of the late-nineteenth and early-twentieth-centuries, when a tune was not popular during its first incarnation, songwriters would "frequently adapt a second or even third set of lyrics to the original tune. They would retain the timbre of the superseded words, but in turn a new timbre could result from a more popular newer set of words."[50] It is precisely in this musical practice that the Masons composed much of the song material that was to become part of their tradition.

Some scholars search for symbolic meaning or hidden secrets within the works of famous composers who were also members of the fraternity, such as Mozart, Haydn, and Sibelius. In some cases, the generally-accepted presence of Masonic symbolism in this music might even be exaggerated.[51] However, when it comes to the Masonic songs, there is little evidence that there is any hidden Masonic symbolism in the music since most of the songs are *contrafacta*.[52] The melodies were taken from folk songs, theater songs, and popular songs of the day. These song styles were used because, as Campbell advises, they "made the songs accessible to people, whether or not they could read staff music notation. To people already familiar with the tunes in an oral context, this method offered the chance for immediate performance."[53] Theater, and especially musical theater, was an important part of eighteenth-century culture since it had not yet become a source

49   Falck & Picker, "*Contrafactum*."
50   Davies, *Masonic Muse*, 146.
51   Buch, "Die Zauberflöte," 193.
52   Davies, "Freemasonry and Music," 499.
53   Campbell, "Masonic Song in Scotland," 96.

of entertainment only for the élite,[54] and melodies that were "played on stage, especially by popular entertainers, were particularly memorable and encores were frequently requested."[55] It is interesting to note the egalitarian appeal of musical theater at this time, as it relates to the Masonic belief of equality among men. It seems then, whether the subtext was intentional or not, that *contrafacta* songs were, as a concept, supportive of the Masonic belief of "meeting on the Level."

Perhaps the earliest explicit example of this musical practice is found in the 1755 work, *A Choice Collection of Songs to be Sung by Free-Masons.* This work presents several songs that had earlier been in print, but with the addition of naming the tune by which the songs could be sung. For instance, "The Secretary's Song" was originally published in the second edition of Anderson's *Constitutions* in 1738. When it was reprinted in the *Choice Collection,* it specified that it was to be sung to the tune of "To You Fair Ladies Now at Land."[56] Another example is the song beginning, "We'll have no idle prating…." Appearing as early as 1730, in Farmer's *A New Model,* this song was there said to have been sung at a "Bacchanalian Banquet of Free Masons," but without a tune specified. When it appeared in the *Choice Collection,* the tune is identified as belonging to "Beggar Lasses."[57]

The earliest known Masonic song was first printed as "The Free Mason's Health," and was "inserted in *The Bottle Companions,* an undated collection of engraved sheets of music."[58] This folio appeared in 1709. The song would later become far better known as "The Enter'd 'Prentices Song," and was practically ubiquitous in the Masonic publications of the eighteenth century.

54   See Levine, *Highbrow/Lowbrow.*

55   McLucas, *Musical Ear,* 91.

56   Anderson, *New Book,* 210; Anon., *Choice Collection,* 21.

57   Farmer, *A New Model,* 23; Anon., *Choice Collection,* 28.

58   Knoop, Hamer & Jones, *Early Masonic Pamphlets,* 36.

This song was included in the first widely published collection of Masonic songs, which featured in James Anderson's *Constitutions*. This book was the first official Masonic publication after the creation of the Grand Lodge of England. Anderson's *Constitutions* also featured three other songs: "The Master's Song," "The Warden's Song," and "The Fellow Craft's Song." The presence of these four songs, and the fact that notation was included to ensure uniformity in performance,[59] show the important place these songs must have had in early Masonic practice. As noted above, "The Enter'd 'Prentices Song" was widely published. So too was "The Fellow Craft's Song," in both Masonic and non-Masonic songbooks of the time. In fact, these songs were so well known in English society that irritated parodies of them appear as early as 1725. In that year, *The London Journal* printed a lampoon of the "Enter'd 'Prentices Song":

> Good People give ear.
> And the truth shall appear,
> For we scorn to put any grimace on:
> We've been lamm'd long enough.
> With this damn'd silly stuff,
> Of a Free and an Accepted Mason[60]

This is likely because, in keeping with common musical practices, the melodies were simple and the "song texts were straightforward to sing, using commonly available musical settings that required no more musical resources than just the voices of those present."[61]

It was assumed that Masons reading these song texts would be familiar with a large repertoire of melodies in various meters,

---

59   Anderson, *Constitutions*, 75–90.
60   Pink, "When They Sing," 7.
61   Ibid., 4.

or at least that there would be someone in the lodge who could teach them given the human-to-human nature of oral tradition. For this reason, there are many Masonic songs where no tune title is indicated. Katherine Campbell wrote that this was likely due to the fact that many familiar melodies could fit the meter of the song text and performers "could simply draw on any tune they knew that fitted the words."[62] This is consistent with the observations of Malcolm Davies, who identified at least three melodies to which the opening ode "Hail, Eternal! by Whose aid" has been sung by Masons.[63]

Taxonomy of Masonic Songs

Malcolm Davies described Masonic songs, apart from the composed odes, cantatas and the music of Mozart and Haydn, as being mainly toasts, drinking songs, and mythopœic history.[64] This categorization is insufficient and other scholars have been more thorough in their organization. Andrew Pink, while studying the eighteenth-century songs for performance purposes, also attempted to create an organizational model for the song material.[65] Pink determined that the songs were either used for formal use at the end of a "lecture" (i.e., work in the Masonic Degrees) or during a lodge meal. The former he refers to as "formal-liturgical" use and the latter "formal-convivial" use.[66] Katherine Campbell found similar categories in her study of Scottish Masonic songs. For Campbell, "in general, two types of song can be observed: formal songs dealing with the history of Freema-

---

62   Campbell, "Masonic Song in Scotland," 96.
63   Davies, "Freemasonry and Music," 504.
64   Davies, "Muse of Freemasonry," 95.
65   Pink, "When They Sing," 1.
66   Ibid.

sonry, its principles, and so on, sometimes of an anthem-like nature, and more informal material of a drinking song variety."[67] Andreas Önnerfors identified four categories: a) functional to accompany lodge rituals, b) convivial to provide entertainment, c) internally edifying to praise Masonic virtues, and d) externally demarcating to counter the "Othering" that was occurring regarding the Masons from the outside.[68] This "Othering" had to do with the way the outside world saw Masonry and was the attempt of the members to prove the excellence and necessity of the Order.[69] From Anderson's *Constitutions*, "The Master's Song: Or, the History of Masonry" and "The Warden's Song: Or, Another History of Masonry" can both be considered internally edifying and convivial, in that they celebrate the mythopœic history of the fraternity while pausing for toasts between various verses. The "Fellow-Crafts Song" and "The Enter'd 'Prentices Song" can be considered functional because of their use after lectures on the initiation degrees of the same names.[70] Examples of each of Önnerfors' levels can be found in Table 1.

Music in the Lodge

It is a natural progression to then here address the manner in which the songs were used in the lodge. Songs and other forms of music were not officially specified as part of the Masonic rituals, but song use outside of the ritual is suggested in many of the texts. For instance, Anderson's 1723 *Constitutions* advises that the "Enter'd 'Prentices Song" is "To be sung when all *grave Busi-*

---

67   Campbell, "Masonic Song in Scotland," 88.

68   Önnerfors, "You Will Prise Our Noble Companionship," 137.

69   Ibid., 136.

70   Campbell, "Masonic Song in Scotland," 3.

Table 1

Examples of Andreas Önnerfors' Levels of Masonic
Songs Selected by the Author

Song Title	Level
The Fellow-Crafts Song[A] The Enter'd Prentice's Song[B] The Warden's Song, at Closing the Lodge[C]	Functional ('liturgical')
Arise, Gentle Muse, and Thy Wisdom Impart[D] Hark! The Hiram Sounds to Close[E] With Harmony and Flowing Wine[F]	Convivial
Of All Institutions to Form Well the Mind[G] A Mason is Great and Respected[H] A System More Pure Ne'er Was Modell'd by Man[I]	Internally Edifying
Blest Masonry! Thy Arts Divine[J] On You Who Masonry Despise[K]	Externally Demarcating

A   Anderson, *Constitutions*, 83.
B   Anderson, *Constitutions*, 84.
C   Anon. [Spencer], *Defence of Free-Masonry*, 54.
D   Hale, *Social Harmony*,1.
E   Jones, *Masonic Miscellanies*, 110.
F   Dermott, *Ahiman Rezon*, 151–52
G   Dermott, *Ahiman Rezon*, 134–35.
H   Anon. [Spencer], *Defence of Free-Masonry*, 54–55.
I   Jones, *Masonic Miscellanies*, 9–10.
J   Jones, *Masonic Miscellanies*, 13.
K   Anon., *Prologue, and an Epilogue. And Songs*, 6–7.

ness is over, and with the MASTER's *Leave*."[71] Malcolm Davies described the musical practice with:

> Typically, there might be an opening and closing hymn that becomes standard usage within a lodge or group of lodges. Other instrumental or vocal music may be added at various moments in the ritual. Processions and some ritual actions may be accompanied by music. The use of specific pieces for designated parts of rituals may also be suggested or even required by a Grand Lodge or governing body.[72]

Songs were more commonly sung at the lodge meal following the meeting or ritual. Toasts and songs were closely associated with one another where "a certain song required a certain toast; a certain toast required a certain song."[73] This established formality during the conviviality of the meal time and moderated the drinking.[74] This serves as evidence to counter some recent scholarship that has implied that the purpose of the songs was to drink to intoxication.[75] The singing of songs both after ritual and as part of the conviviality of the meal provided new and existing members with important lessons and reaffirmations regarding the Craft of Masonry. According to Andreas Önnerfors, "By combining text with music and repeatedly (we may even call it ritual) in singing [sic], the text message was established as a powerful means of masonic education."[76]

71   Anderson, *Constitutions*, 84.
72   Davies, "Freemasonry and Music," 497.
73   Pink, "When They Sing," 6.
74   Ibid.
75   See Morrison, "Making Degenerates into Men."
76   Önnerfors, "You Will Prise Our Noble Companionship," 135.

Recurring Song Themes

Malcolm Davies drew a close analogy, comparing Masonic songs to the music of a church congregation. Davies believed that by examining hymnbooks one can learn about theology, and by examining the Masonic songs one can learn about Masonic philosophy.[77] When looked at in this way, many recurring themes emerge. The tracking and description of all those themes would be a book unto itself and is beyond the scope of this study. However, to continue the examination of Masonic song in-or-as Masonic culture a few of the important themes will be discussed: a) Freemasonry and Its Virtues, b) the Lodge as Holy Ground, c) Mason's Secret Art, and d) God as Architect of the Universe.

FREEMASONRY AND ITS VIRTUES

Songs that praise the fraternity and build up the Order fit into both the "internally edifying" and the "externally demarcating" domains. Songs in these domains include "The Master's Song" that traces the lineage of Masonry back to Adam as well as songs such as "You People who laugh at Masons draw near" which counters potential opponents by stating that the "Noble Art" comes directly from God:

> You People who laugh at Masons draw near,
> Attend to my Ballad without any Sneer;
> And if you'll have Patience you soon shall see,
> What a fine Art is Masonry.
> There's none but an Atheist can ever deny,
> But that this great Art came first from on high;
> Since God himself I'll prove for to be,

77 Davies, *Masonic Muse*, 339.

The first great Master of Masonry[78]

Though these songs seem to describe a perfect society that the fraternity can never become, "the ideal being portrayed was highly desirable. It was a paradigm worth aiming at. There was perhaps a feeling amongst the early masonic poets that if you describe the ideal and long for it, then it will inevitably become reality."[79]

LODGE AS HOLY GROUND

For some Masons, the foremost function of the lodge was to serve as a holy place. For some Masonic songwriters, the lodge represented "a microcosm of an ideal world."[80] Perhaps the earliest reference in song to the lodge as sacred or holy ground comes in "The New Fairies: Or, the Fellow-Craft's Song" published in 1731. The song tells a story of a ring of fairies who, despite not being "free," subversively sneak into a Masonic lodge room. It begins:

> COME all ye Elves *that be,*
> *Come follow, follow me,*
> *All ye that* Guards *have been*
> *Without, or serve within:*
> *Come sing for Joy, thro' us 'tis found,*
> *That all this* Lodge *is* sacred Ground[81]

---

78   Anon., *Prologue, and an Epilogue,* 4.

79   Davies, *Masonic Muse,* 208.

80   Ibid., 222.

81   Anon., *Curious Collection,* 1; for earlier version of this song, cf. Cole, *Antient Constitutions,* 57; cf. Farmer, *New Model,* 19-21.

Another instance where the lodge is shown as holy ground is in the song with the incipit "Once I was blind and cou'd not see," which describes Divine Providence leading the narrator to a friend who brings him to the lodge:

> All Stumbling Blocks he took away,
> That I might walk secure;
> And brought me long e'er Break of Day,
> To Wisdom's Temple-Door;
> Where there we both Admittance found,
> To mystic Paths on hallow'd Ground.[82]

THE MASON'S SECRET ART

Secrecy is one of the central features of Freemasonry.[83] Davies connected these secrets to the practices of the Masonic guilds when he wrote:

> the idea of hidden knowledge was of course one of the main attributes of Freemasonry from its operative days, when the skills of the "mystery" of building in stone were guarded and passed on from generation to generation. It had this in common with many trades…the idea of the secrets of the trade was taken over into speculative masonry at its inception.[84]

An illustration of this is "Hail secret Art!":

Hail secret Art! by Heav'n design'd

82   Dermott, *Ahiman Rezon*, 158.
83   Davies, *Masonic Muse*, 223.
84   Ibid.

> To cultivate and cheer the Mind;
> Thy Secrets are to all unknown,
> But Masons just and true alone.
> [...]
> No human Eye thy Beauties see,
> But Masons truly just and free;
> Inspir'd by each heav'nly Spark,
> Whilst Cowans labour in the Dark.[85]

The secrecy of the Masons is something that led to outside attacks also. Sometimes these attacks came in the form of various *exposures* which proliferated in the early- to mid-eighteenth-century. These exposures sought to make the private rituals and modes of recognition of the Masons available to all, but there is some suggestion that the more reliable exposures were actually used and studied by the lodges as handbooks for the rituals.[86] In some cases these publications were simply "unofficial printed rituals" that were intended to create uniformity among the English lodges.[87] Some Masonic songs even seem to allude to this. For example:

> Some Folks have with curious Impertinence strove,
> From Free-Masons Bosoms their Secrets to move,
> I'll tell why in vain their Endeavours must prove,
> Which Nobody can deny, &c.

> Of that happy Secret when we are possess'd,
> Our Tongues can't explain what is lodg'd in our Breasts,
> For the Blessing's so great it can ne'er be express'd.

85   Dermott, *Ahiman Rezon*, 119–120.
86   Davies, *Masonic Muse*, 224.
87   Pink, "When They Sing," 3.

Which Nobody can deny, &c.[88]

Another example:

> On you who *Masonry* despise
> This Council I bestow,
> Don't ridicule, if you are wise,
> A Secret you don't know;
> Your selves you banter, but not it;
> You shew your Spleen, but not your Wit.
> With a fa, la, la, &c.[89]

Because the secrets are believed to be of divine origin (i.e., sacred), their preservation even extends to the supernatural. Returning to "The New Fairies: Or, the Fellow-Craft's Song," despite the subversive nature of these elves unlawfully gaining admission into the Masonic lodge, they do not report what they saw:

> *Yet what we* hear and *see*
> *In Lodges where we be,*
> *Not* Force *nor offer'd* Gold
> *Can Masons* Truths unfold;
> *Besides, the* Craft *we love, not* gain,
> *And* Secrets *why should we* profane?[90]

GOD AS ARCHITECT OF THE UNIVERSE

Belief in God has been an essential part of Masonic tradition at least since the time of the Old Charges. This medieval Masonic

88   Anon., *A Prologue, and an Epilogue*, 10.
89   Ibid., 6.
90   Anon., *Curious Collection*, 9.

religiosity was specifically Christian. This changed with the formation of the Premier Grand Lodge, when God was referred to
by the more universal appellation, *"the Great Architect of the Universe."*[91] While it is not true that this title displaced (or even was
intended to displace) Christian references within Freemasonry,
the opportunity for a more inclusive religious pluralism was
made explicit in the charge *"Concerning* GOD *and* RELIGION:"

> ... 'tis now thought more expedient only to oblige them to
> that Religion in which all Men agree, leaving their particu-
> lar Opinions to themselves... by whatever Denominations
> or Persuasions they may be distinguish'd.... [92]

References in many Masonic songs to God are kept purposefully vague to allow members of varying denominations
to impose their own perception of the creator.[93] To illustrate
this point, attention is again called to "You People who laugh at
Masons draw near." Earlier it was established that this text refers
to Masonry as coming from "The Almighty God" but further
verses demonstrate how the Almighty is an architect creating
the universe:

> He took up his Compass with masterly Hand,
> He stretch'd out his Line and he measure'd the Land;
> He laid the Foundation of Earth and Sea,
> By the first Rules of Masonry[94]

The creation myth referenced here is Jewish, with architectural language drawn from Job 38:4–5. However, the phrasing of

---

91   Anderson, *Constitutions*, 1.
92   Ibid., 50.
93   Davies, *Masonic Muse*, 228.
94   Anon., *Prologue, and an Epilogue*, 5.

the song allows all those singing or hearing to imagine their own understandings of deity being characterized in this mythopœic story. Another example has the incipit "Come lend me your ears, loving brethren, a while:"

> When to this confusion no end soon appear'd,
> The sov'reign Grand Master's word sudden was heard:
> Then teem'd mother Chaos with maternal throes!
> And so the grand lodge of this world arose.

> Then heaven and earth with jubilee rung,
> And all the creation of masonry sung.
> But, lo! to adorn and complete the gay ball,
> Old Adam was made the grand master of all.[95]

Another example portrays the creator not as an architect, but as an artist:

> When Earth's Foundation first was laid,
> By the Almighty Artist's Hand;
> It was then our perfect, our perfect Laws were made,
> Establish'd by his strict Command.
> Hail, mysterious! Hail, glorious Masonry,
> That makes us ever great and Free[96]

Though these are just a few examples, it is clear that song-writers within the fraternity used their talents to render concepts of Masonic philosophy and religiosity into their chosen medium: the song. In doing so, and particularly through publication of these labors, Masonic songwriters contributed to the preservation of the shared value system and mythology of the

95   Anon., *Free Masons Pocket Companion*, 219.
96   Dermott, *Ahiman Rezon*, 137.

eighteenth-century fraternity.[97]

Need for Further Study

One challenge to further study in this area may be the general shift away from sincerity and seriousness within Freemasonry amid shifting attitudes within the larger scene of twentieth-century fraternalism. In many ways, fraternalism morphed into a parody of itself through theatrical spectacles simply for the sake of spectacle, the creation of fraternal orders based on animals, and derisive, fictionalized representations in popular culture. Where there is a lack of seriousness, there is no impetus to consider a thing seriously. Consequently, there is now a significant discrepancy that exists between the public face of contemporary Masonry and the traditional portrait illustrated by the surviving documents of the dawn of the Grand Lodge era.[98] Andreas Önnerfors identified the Masonic songbooks as a largely "untapped" resource for Masonic scholarship.[99] If these documents are studied, by Masonic and non-Masonic scholars alike, it will more clearly articulate the genuinely-invented tradition of Freemasonry. The term "genuinely-invented tradition" is used because the mythopœic history and philosophy published in the eighteenth-century songbooks is a more genuine representation of the original values of the Order than the evolved traditions, pageantry, and social mundanity of contemporary Freemasonry. In other words, the best means of understanding early Freemasonry is to study the early Masonic works, of which these songs are an integral part.

Further research is needed in the area of textual content anal-

---

97   Davies, *Masonic Muse*, 203.
98   Kilde, "Spectacle of Freemasonry," 377.
99   Önnerfors, "You Will Prise Our Noble Companionship," 135.

ysis. There are hundreds of Masonic songs from the eighteenth century published in both Masonic and non-Masonic songbooks. As Malcolm Davies said, "these songs can be seen as an expression of Masonic thought."[100] Davies also believed that these songs "more perhaps than any other Masonic source, demonstrate the development of the ideals of Freemasonry."[101] These texts could be examined to identify all the common themes, illuminate allusions to other song material, and more clearly document the mythopœic history and philosophy of the fraternity.

Conclusions

Ancient documents such as the Halliwell MS and Cooke MS outlined that operative lodges held themselves to charges for governance, and were nested within a mythopœic history. As the Craft developed initiation rituals and a richer symbolic lexicon, non-Masons joined lodges for their speculative content. With increasing frequency, these "Accepted" Masons joined lodges, and by the beginning of the early Grand Lodge era, operative lodges became a rarity. Still, there were core themes in the Masonic narrative that remained in the lodges of the 1700s. But something new developed alongside these medieval beliefs: a body of Masonic songs was crafted that represented the shared values of the society. In this way, the Masonic songs can be viewed as music in-or-as culture. This music in-or-as culture represents a genuinely-invented tradition where the highest ideals of the institution, the mythology, and the principal tenets are shared and preserved for use among the participants, in perpetuity. In the words of Malcolm Davies, "the words and ideals express a longing for improving the individual and society in general. This

100 Davies, *Masonic Muse*, 33.
101 Davies, *Masonic Muse*, 238–39.

longing for improvement was decidedly one of the central tenets of eighteenth-century Freemasonry."[102]

Bibliography

Anderson, James. *The Constitutions of the Freemasons, Containing the History, Charges, Regulations, &c. of that most Ancient and Right Worshipful Fraternity.* London: William Hunter, 1723.

————. *The Constitutions of the Freemasons. Containing the History, Charges, Regulations, &c. of that most Ancient and Right Worshipful Fraternity.* Philadelphia: Benjamin Franklin, 1734.

————. *The New Book of Constitutions of the Antient and Honourable Fraternity of Free and Accepted Masons, Containing Their History, Charges, Regulations, &c.* London: Richard Chandler, 1738.

Anonymous. *A Curious Collection of the Most Celebrated Songs in Honour of Masonry.* London: B. Creake, 1731.

————. *A Prologue, and an Epilogue, and Songs, Spoken and Sung to the Antient and Rt. Worshipful Society of Free-Masons, at the Theatre-Royal, on Thursday November the 29ᵗʰ, 1733, being Mr.* GRIFFITH's *Benefit.* Dublin: Geo. Faulkner, 1734.

————. *The Free Masons Pocket Companion.* Glasgow: Joseph Galbraith, 1765.

Baker, P. G. "'Night into Day': Patterns of Symbolism in Mozart's The Magic Flute." *University of Toronto Quarterly.* Vol. 49, No. 2 (1979): 95–116.

Bancks, Jonathan. *Proposals for Printing by Subscriptions, Miscellaneous Works, in Verse and Prose, of Mr. John Bancks.* London: Mr. Ares's Printing House, 1737.

Buch, David J. "Die Zauberflöte, Masonic Opera, and Other Fairy Tales." *Acta Musicologica.* Vol. 76, No. 2 (2004): 193–219.

Burns, Robert. *Poems, Chiefly in the Scottish Dialect.* Philadelphia: Pe-

---

102   Ibid., 239.

ter Stewart & George Hyde, 1788.

Campbell, Katherine. "Masonic Song in Scotland: Folk Tunes and Community." *Oral Tradition.* Vol. 27, No. 1 (2012): 85–107.

[Cole, Benjamin]. *A Book of the Ancient Constitutions of the Free & Accepted Masons.* London: Benjamin Cole, 1728.

Cole, Benjamin. *The Antient Constitutions of the Free and Accepted Masons, Neatly Engrav'd on Copper Plates.* London: B. Creake, 1731.

D'Assigny, Fifield. *A Serious and Impartial Enquiry Into the Cause of the Present Decay of Free-Masonry in the Kingdom of Ireland.* Dublin: Edward Bate, 1744. In Williams, Louis & Cerza, Alphonse, Eds. *D'Assigny.* Bloomington: The Masonic Book Club, 1974: 19–48.

Davies, Malcolm. "Freemasonry and Music." In Bogdan, Henrik & Snoek, Jan, Eds. *Handbook of Freemasonry.* Leiden; Boston: Brill Academic, 2014: 497–522.

———. *The Masonic Muse: Songs, Music and Musicians Associated with Dutch Freemasonry, 1730–1806.* Koninklijke Vereniging voor Nederlandse Muziekgeschiedenis, 2005.

———. "The Muse of Freemasonry: Masonic Songs, Marches, Odes, Cantatas, Oratorios and Operas, 1730–1812." In Stewart, Trevor, Ed. *The Canonbury Papers, Volume 2: Freemasonry in Music and Literature.* London: Canonbury Masonic Research Centre, 2005: 85–104.

Dermott, Laurence. *Ahiman Rezon: Or, A Help to a Brother; Shewing the Excellency of Secrecy, and the First Cause, or Motive, of the Institution of Free-Masonry.* London: James Bedford, 1756.

Eyer, Shawn. "'And Hinder Not Music': The Role of Music and Song in Traditional Freemasonry." *Philalethes: The Journal of Masonic Research and Letters* 67(2014): 110–24.

Falck, Robert, & Picker, Martin. "*Contrafactum.*" Grove Music Online. Oxford University Press, n.d.

Falck, Robert & Rice, Timothy, Eds. *Cross-Cultural Perspectives on Music.* Toronto ; Buffalo: University of Toronto Press, 1983.

Farmer, Peter. *A New Model for the Rebuilding of Masonry on a Stronger Basis Than the Former.* London: J. Wilford, 1730.

Gelbart, Matthew. *The Invention of "Folk Music" and "Art Music":
Emerging Categories from Ossian to Wagner*. Cambridge, UK ; New
York: Cambridge University Press, 2007.

Hale, Thomas. *Social Harmony Consisting of a Collection of Songs and
Catches in Two, Three, Four and Five Parts, from the Works of the
Most Eminent Masters: To Which Are Added Several Choice Songs
on Masonry*. Cheshire: Hale & Sons, 1763.

Hetherington, Kevin. *The Badlands of Modernity: Heterotopia and Social Ordering*. International Library of Sociology. London: Routledge, 1997.

Hobsbawm, Eric, & Terence Ranger, Eds. *The Invention of Tradition*.
Cambridge: Cambridge University Press, 1992.

Jones, Stephen. *Masonic Miscellanies, in Poetry and Prose*. London:
Vernor & Hood, 1797.

Kilde, Jeanne Halgren. "The Spectacle of Freemasonry." *American
Quarterly*. Vol. 50, No. 2 (1998): 376–96.

Knoop, Douglas, Hamer, Douglas, & Jones, G.P., *Early Masonic Pamphlets*. Manchester: Manchester University Press, 1945.

Levine, Lawrence W. *Highbrow/Lowbrow : The Emergence of Cultural
Hierarchy in America*. Cambridge, Ma.: Harvard University Press,
1990.

Lomax, Alan, Ed. *Folk Song Style and Culture*. New Brunswick, N.J:
Transaction Publishers, 1978.

MacNulty, W. Kirk. *Freemasonry: A Journey Through Ritual and Symbol*. New York, N.Y: Thames & Hudson, 1991.

McLucas, Anne Dhu. *The Musical Ear: Oral Tradition in the USA*.
Farnham, England; Burlington, Vt.: Ashgate Publishing, Ltd., 2010.

Morrison, Heather. "'Making Degenerates into Men' by Doing Shots,
Breaking Plates, and Embracing Brothers in Eighteenth-Century
Freemasonry." *Journal of Social History*. Vol. 46, No. 1 (2012): 48-65.

Nettl, Bruno. *The Study of Ethnomusicology: Thirty-One Issues and
Concepts*, 2nd Edition. Urbana: University of Illinois Press, 2005.

———. "Types of Tradition and Transmission." In Falck, Robert &

Rice, Timothy, Eds. *Cross-Cultural Perspectives on Music*. Toronto ; Buffalo: University of Toronto Press, 1983: 3–19.

Önnerfors, Andreas. "'You Will Prise Our Noble Companionship': Masonic Songbooks of the Eighteenth Century—An Overlooked Literary Sub-Genre." In Stewart, Trevor, Ed. *The Canonbury Papers, Volume 2: Freemasonry in Music and Literature*. London: Canonbury Masonic Research Centre, 2005: 135–50.

Pegg, Carole, Helen Myers, Philip V. Bohlman, & Martin Stokes. "Ethnomusicology." Grove Music Online. Oxford University Press, n.d.

Pink, Andrew. "When They Sing: The Performance of Songs in eighteenth-Century English Lodges." In Stewart, Trevor, Ed. *The Canonbury Papers, Volume 2: Freemasonry in Music and Literature*. London: Canonbury Masonic Research Centre, 2005: 1–15.

Preston, William. *Illustrations of Masonry*. London: J. Williams, 1772.

Smith, William. *A Pocket Companion for Free-Masons. Deus Nobis Sol & Scutum. Dedicated to the Society*. London: E. Rider, 1735.

[Spencer, Samuel]. *A Defence of Free-Masonry, As Practiced in the Regular Lodges, Both Foreign and Domestic, Under the Constitution of the English Grand-Master*. London: Flexney & Hood, 1765.

Stewart, Trevor, Ed. *The Canonbury Papers, Volume 2: Freemasonry in Music and Literature*. London: Canonbury Masonic Research Centre, 2005.

Thomson, Katharine. *The Masonic Thread in Mozart*. London: Lawrence & Wishart Ltd, 1977.

Williams, Louis & Cerza, Alphonse, Eds. *D'Assigny*. Bloomington: The Masonic Book Club, 1974.

The Grand Lodge of All England Held at York

An Independent Grand Lodge in England in the Eighteenth Century

DAVID HARRISON

Y ORK, KNOWN AS EBORACUM in Roman times, was the
capital of the province of Britannia Inferior, the northern part of Roman Britain, and the city played a vital
role in the history of the Roman Empire when Constantine the
Great was proclaimed Emperor by the troops based in the fort in
306 AD.[1] After the decline of Roman Britain, the old Roman fort
became the centre for King Edwin of Northumbria in the early
seventh century. By the ninth century, the city was the centre of
the Vikings, and their name for the city—Jórvik—later became
reduced to York following the Norman Conquest. So York, in
effect, had been the capital of northern England from the Roman
era, through the Anglo-Saxon and Viking periods.

With this in mind, it is understandable that during the eighteenth century, the York Grand Lodge celebrated its indepen-
dence from the London Premier Grand Lodge, basing its ancient

1   See Frere, *Britannia*, 184.

foundation on the tradition that the Anglo-Saxon Prince Edwin held the first Assembly of Masons in York in 926 AD. There is no existing evidence for Prince Edwin's York Masonic Assembly, and many Masonic writers and historians, such as Arthur Edward Waite, FPS, dismissed the event as pure legend. Waite did acknowledge that a Prince Edwin existed in relation to King Athelstan, dating to around the time of the early tenth century, as there was an Edwin who appeared as a witness to Athelstan's signature on an extant charter at Winchester. The Anglo-Saxon scribe Bede does write of King Edwin of Northumbria being baptised at York Cathedral in 627 and mentions the rebuilding which took place at this time. Indeed, it is this reference that may have influenced Dr. Francis Drake when he presented a date "about the Six Hundredth Year after Christ" for Edwin as "Grand-Master" in York, when he gave his famous speech at the Merchant Adventurers' Hall in 1726.[2] Drake was presenting King Edwin as the great Anglo-Saxon ruler of All England, harkening back to a time when Northumbria was a powerful Anglo-Saxon kingdom, a kingdom that spawned other mighty leaders during the seventh century such as King Oswald.[3] This is the vision that Drake held when he put forward the title of *the Grand Lodge of all England*—a nomenclature that reflected powerful ancient roots, not just in Freemasonry but in the history of York itself.[4]

The stance of the York Grand Lodge was clear: York was the ancient northern capital, and they had an ancient right as a Grand Lodge. Francis Drake reiterated this stance when he wrote *Eboracum*, a somewhat hefty book of around 800 pages with the rather long subtitle of *The History and Antiquities of the City of York, from its Original to the Present Time; together with the History of the Cathedral Church and the Lives of the Archbishops of*

2   Eyer, "Drake's Oration of 1726 with Commentary and Notes," 23.
3   Cryer, *York Mysteries Revealed*, 234–35.
4   Harrison, *York Grand Lodge*, 15–16.

that See, which was finally published in 1736. There were 540 sub-scribers—a number of whom were members of the York Grand Lodge; good old local Masonic networking providing some fine support. Elements of the work reflected the themes found in his speech to the Merchants Adventurers' Hall ten years earlier, with the importance of the history of York—architecturally and culturally—being strongly put forward throughout. York was a cultural rival to London, and for Drake, there was no doubting that.

Indeed, Drake confidently guaranteed his readers that "There is no place out of *London*, so polite and elegant to live in as the *city of* York."[5] The work also criticized how London came into prominence under William the Conqueror, Drake writing how York was ravaged under the "Tyrant" who subjected his own people to "the greatest slavery"; the once superior Roman city becoming the second city of the kingdom—a theme that was certainly reflected in the treatment of the York Grand Lodge by its London rival.[6] York was indeed a thriving cultural center of the north; during the eighteenth century York becoming renowned for its Georgian architecture and its cultured social scene became attractive to the visiting Scottish nobility. The York races became an important attraction, the ancient city having many fine Inns to accommodate visitors, and it cultivated an intellectual scene, with scientists such as John Goodricke, artists such as Thomas Beckwith, actors such as Tate Wilkinson and Bridge Frodsham, and writers such as Dr. Francis Drake and Dr. John Burton.[7]

The York Grand Lodge attracted many writers after its demise at the close of the eighteenth century in an effort to investigate its

5   Drake, *Eboracum*, 241.

6   Drake, *Eboracum*, 86–87; For a discussion on Drake's portrayal of William the Conqueror as a villain and how York was destroyed and struggled to rebuild its fortunes, see Sweet, "History and Identity," 18.

7   Harrison, *York Grand Lodge*, 45–57.

origins and mysteries, these writers doing much to inspire later Masonic researchers. One such writer was Godfrey Higgins, a Freemason, social reformer and radical writer of religious works, the most renowned of these works being *Anacalypsis*, which was published posthumously in 1836. Higgins was a member of the prestigious London-based Prince of Wales Lodge, which boasted such members as Prime Minister George Canning and, of course, the Prince of Wales. He had visited the last Grand Secretary of the York Grand Lodge—owner of the York Chronicle, William Blanchard—and mentions in *Anacalypsis* that he had seen certain documents, particularly describing the "Old Charges" that would later become known as the York MS № 1. He discusses how it was written on the back of the parchment roll that Francis Drake had presented to the York Grand Lodge, and that it had been found in Pontefract Castle, Higgins also putting forward that there was a tradition that the lodge records were sent to the castle during the Civil Wars.

Higgins also stated that he had passed the documents on to the Duke of Sussex, who was the Grand Master of the United Grand Lodge at the time of his writing, though it appears that it was only a copy that was presented to the Duke, as the original manuscript is still kept in York. According to William James Hughan in his *Old Charges*, a copy of the York MS № 1 was made around 1830 by order of Freemason William Henry White, the Grand Secretary of the time, but not being a perfect copy, another was copied by Freemason Robert Lemon, Deputy Keeper of State Papers, and was presented to the Duke of Sussex. Both transcripts are still preserved, likewise a letter from the latter gentleman to the Duke, dated September 9, 1830, states that "it might be interesting to collate the transcript, said by [William] Preston to be in the possession of the Lodge of Antiquity, with that from which the above is made."[8]

8   Hughan, *Old Charges*, 5–6; William Preston had founded the

Putting forward that the York Grand Lodge had older and more mystical origins, Higgins enigmatically stated that "the presumption was pretty strong" that the Druidical Lodge—a lodge that came under the sway of the York Grand Lodge that had been based in Rotherham—was the same as the Culdees. He goes further to link the Masons of York to India,[9] and his comments on the York Grand Lodge, and his visit to Blanchard, were later discussed by Arthur Edward Waite.[10] More recently, historian Andrew Prescott remarked that Higgins may have been an influence on Richard Carlile's version of the Masonic ritual which was published in his early nineteenth century exposé *Manual of Freemasonry*.[11] Other writers that visited William Blanchard, who became the last surviving member of the York Grand Lodge, included William Hargrove, who in 1819, claimed to have been shown documents that had once belonged to the York Grand Lodge by Blanchard, including the now lost final minute book of 1780–1792. Hargrove wrote the renowned *History and Description of the Ancient City of York*, published in 1818. His visit to Blanchard and the documents he witnessed were referred to by later prominent Masonic writers such as Robert

Grand Lodge of England South of the River Trent in 1779, a Grand Lodge that aligned itself under the Grand Lodge of All England held at York.

9   The York MS № 1 is still in the possession of the York Lodge; See Higgins, *Anacalypsis*, 767–70.

10   Arthur Edward Waite, FPS, stated that Blanchard had given "all the books and papers" of the York Grand Lodge to William Hargrove, and that Godfrey Higgins from Doncaster, sometime before 1836, went to York and "applied to the only survivor of the Lodge who shewed me, from the documents which he possessed, that the Druidical Lodge, or Chapter of Royal Arch Masons, or Templar Encampment was held for the last time in the Crypt [of the Cathedral at York] on Sunday, May 27th, 1778." See Waite, *Secret Tradition*, 50–51.

11   See Prescott, "Hidden Currents of 1813," 31–32.

Freke Gould in his widely read *History of Freemasonry*,[12] and by the aforementioned Arthur Edward Waite, who both continued to research the importance of the York Grand Lodge.

Medieval Masons in York

Being an ancient city, York was a traditional centre for Christian worship, with Christian activity at the site of the Minster in York dating back at least to Anglo-Saxon times; the chronicler Bede mentioning that King Edwin of the Northumbrians was baptized there in 627.[13] This was probably a wooden structure erected on the site, but a stone building was completed later. The church itself was built on the site of the old Roman headquarters of the city, and after being damaged during William the Conqueror's "Harrying of the North" in 1069, rebuilding occurred and, around 1230, construction began on a glorious Gothic structure that was only finally completed in 1472. The subsequent Reformation and Civil War took its toll on the Minster, and it was not until the nineteenth and twentieth centuries that extensive repair work was carried out.

Such extensive building work at York Minster during the medieval period demanded the long-term presence of operative stone masons, and indeed, there are records of such masons, such as Master Mason William de Hoton, Jr., who was the draughtsman of the full-size setting of an aisle window on the plaster floor of the York tracing house. William de Hoton junior had followed his father William de Hoton, Sr., as a Master Mason, both working on the building of the Minster during the fourteenth century. Other Master Masons are listed throughout the Gothic rebuilding phase of the Minster, such as Thomas

12   Gould, *History of Freemasonry*, 2:419.
13   John Marsden, *Illustrated Bede*, 16.

de Pakenham in the 1340s and William Hyndeley at the end of the fifteenth century. These all appear in the York Minster Fabric Rolls, the rolls revealing an account of the expenses paid during the building work at the Minster.

Certain rolls also present a unique insight into the hierarchal structure and the rules of the operative masons; such as when:

> the principal and second masons, who are called their masters, and the carpenter…who have been received by the Chapter, and will be received in perpetuity, shall swear in the presence of the Chapter, that they shall perform the ancient customs written below by means of the other masons, carpenters and other workmen, and they shall be faithfully observed….[14]

The masons would thus go to the chapter and swear to observe rules to ensure punctuality, order and the finest workmanship.[15] As early as 1349, a mason's lodge is mentioned in relation to the building of the Minster; the lodge being a workshop where the masons could cut and dress the stone for use in constructing the building.[16] This lodge would also be a place where the masons could eat, drink, and rest, and they could discuss and plan their work; in 1349 for example, the records of the Minster list the tools of the lodge; a "magna kevell" is recorded, along with "mallietes,"

---

14   Raine, *Fabric Rolls of York Minster*, 171–72; See also Neville Barker Cryer, *York Mysteries*, 82. Cryer comments on the masons' lodge at York Minster and how it was used, presenting a brief translation of the Latin from the Rolls.

15   Raine, *Fabric Rolls of York Minster*, 171 and 181.

16   Raine, *Fabric Rolls of York Minster*, 17; See also Cryer, *York Mysteries*, 82–83 and 125–26; Knoop & Jones, *Genesis of Freemasonry*, 37. Knoop and Jones also discuss the lodge at York Minster based on Raine's work on the Fabric Rolls.

"chisielles," a "compass," and "tracyngbordes."[17] The use of aprons and gloves are also mentioned in the Rolls, with "setters" John Taillor and John Bultflow being given money for two skins from which to make aprons and 18d. for ten pairs of gloves.[18]

Despite the completed structure of the Minster being consecrated in 1472, work continued for a number of years on the fabric, with Master Mason William Hyndeley for example designing a rood screen. Other building around York also demanded operative masons, such as the Bedern—part of the College of the Vicars Choral—which was completed in the fourteenth century, and of course the city walls, the castle, and the many other medieval churches within York, all requiring both building and maintenance work by skilled stone masons.

It was within this culture of civic building in York that certain masons took on important roles in the service of their community, such as Robert Couper who was admitted a freeman in 1443 and was then appointed Chief Mason to the Corporation. He was also the leading mason in the building of the Guildhall. It is clear that masons were essential to the medieval development of York, and even when we reach the Tudor period, these craftsmen were still serving important offices for the community, such as carver Thomas Drawswerd, who became a freeman in 1496, Chamberlain in 1501, Sheriff in 1505, alderman in 1508, member of Parliament for York in 1512, and Lord Mayor in 1515 and also in 1523.[19]

Between 1558 and 1563, a group of English laws called the "Statute of Artificers" was passed by the government of Elizabeth I, regulating the supply of labour, setting wages for certain

17   Raine, *Fabric Rolls of York Minster*, 17. In his *York Mysteries*, Cryer incorrectly puts this year as 1399.
18   Raine, *Fabric Rolls of York Minster*, 50.
19   For a list of Sheriffs and Lord Mayors of York, see Hargrove, *History and Description*, 319–20; See also Raine, 91–2 and 97, where he is described as "magistri Drawswerd."

classes of worker, and disallowing apprentices to look for work outside their parish, effectively restricting the free movement of workers. For the masons, this was particularly difficult, as they were restricted in travelling to other areas to repair and maintain churches and other buildings. Other trades could still survive by serving their community; the Glovers, Brewers, and the Smiths, for example, could ply their trade from a fixed location within the town or city, but those crafts relating to the specialist building trades who depended on travelling to other areas, were restricted. In effect, the powers held by the craft guilds were transferred to the English state.

The effects of the Reformation led nineteenth-century Masonic historians, such as W.H. Rylands to comment that:

> The Reformation had a disastrous effect on the system upon which the guilds of Masons were based. The whole was changed. It is not surprising, therefore, to find that many of the operative lodges died out, and the members for the most part were probably scattered over the whole country. Some, however, as independent bodies, survived the storm, and lasted for a considerable period. Of course their use for ruling the trade generally of a district or town had largely, if not entirely, passed away. The speculative element lasted, and, in some instances at least, if they did not take entire possession of the lodge, they appear to have assisted in keeping it alive.[20]

The entries of masons as freemen in Chester for example seem to support this, with no masons appearing as freemen from the 1520s until the late 1650s. With the admission being based on whether their father was a freeman or apprenticeship, and with the cost of the privileges attached to the enfranchisement, the

20   Rylands, "Freemasonry in Lancashire & Cheshire," 135–6.

masons' absence from the Freemen Rolls during this 130-year period certainly reflects a downturn in demand for the trade in Chester, a downturn which would have affected the number of masons working in the area. Masonic historian Neville Barker Cryer in his work on York lodges during this period has also stated that there was an "almost complete demise of the local building site lodges between 1530 and 1630."[21] Though in York during this period, despite a handful of masons who became freemen, including a small number who were listed as "free-maysons," the trade decayed, and as Cryer stated in *York Mysteries Revealed* (2006), "the list of working masons began to diminish after 1540," on the whole due to the fact that the religious centres such as the abbeys and the chantry chapels closed.[22]

However, the stonemasons' trade certainly seems to have recovered after the Civil War period as both in Chester and in York there were applications made by the masons for a new charter for a stonemasons' guild. In both cases, the municipal authorities referred to the fact that there was already an existing body for the masons; however, the operative masons managed to put across a strong case that the existing masons guilds were not adequate and, in York in 1673, and in Chester in 1691, the stone masons were authorised to combine with the Bricklayers, and the Carpenters.[23] Similarly, in Canterbury, around 1680, the Joiners, Carpenters, Carvers, Masons, and Bricklayers were all

21 Cryer, "The Grand Lodge of All England at York and its Practices."
22 Cryer, *York Mysteries*, 163-64 and 179–80. Cryer refers to a relatively small list of seven men listed as either "freemaysons" or "masons," compiled by G.Y. Johnson that became freemen of York between 1619 and 1691. Cryer suggested that by 1700, the non-operatives had used the new name of "freemayson" while the operatives had reverted to being called "mason."
23 Cryer, "The Grand Lodge of All England at York and its Practices." See also Cryer, "Restoration."

incorporated into one body.[24]

A similar occurrence can also be seen in London in 1677, when the Masons Company was formally incorporated by Royal Charter, which gave:

> ...all and singular Masons Freemen of our said Citty of London or Westminster in the Suburbs of the same Citties or seaven Miles Compasse of the same on every side thereof by virtue of these psents shalbe one Body Incorporate and politick in deed and in name by the Name of Master Wardens Assistants and Community of the Art or Mistery of Masons of the Citty.[25]

The masons certainly seemed to have recovered after the Civil War in Chester, York, in Lymm near Warrington, and especially in London, where the building of St. Paul's Cathedral under Sir Christopher Wren created a revival in the trade.[26]

Masonic historians Knoop and Jones in their work, *The Genesis of Freemasonry* (1947), commented that it was "likely...that [the Old York Lodge] or some other lodge existed at York before 1705."[27] In referring to a copy of the Old Charges called the Levander York MS, which dates to c. 1740, and is handwritten on the flyleaves of a copy of Anderson's 1738 edition of the *Constitutions*, signed at the end "From York Lodge—copy'd from the

24 Rylands, "Freemasonry in Lancashire & Cheshire in the Seventeenth Century," 136.

25 The original charter of 1677 granted by Charles II was confiscated by James II, who replaced it with a charter of his own in 1686. The Masons Company preferred the original charter, and an exemplification of the original grant was obtained under the Privy Seal of Queen Anne in 1702, in which the whole text of the Charles II charter was recited.

26 See Harrison, "Lymm Freemasons," 169–90.

27 Knoop & Jones, *Genesis of Freemasonry*, 154.

Original... in the Year 1560," they point out that as the original is lost, it is unsafe to use as evidence of an existing lodge at that time. However, they ascertain that if the York Lodge did exist in 1560, it would have been operative.[28] It was within the culture of building that operative masonry in York developed, and we must now examine the early evidence of speculative Freemasonry in York.

The Early References of Speculative Freemasonry at York

The earliest possible reference to non-operative or speculative Freemasons in Yorkshire was mentioned by Masonic historian Neville Barker Cryer in his book *York Mysteries Revealed*, where he identified two men who were named in an introduction to a version of the "Old Charges" written on a manuscript entitled the York MS № 1, dated to c. 1600. The introduction reads:

> An Anagraime upon the name of Masonrie
> William Kay to his friend Robt Preston
> Upon his Artt of Masonrie as Followeth[29]

Cryer put forward that the two men mentioned in the document were two local Freemen from York; William Kay who was accepted as a spurrier in 1569, and Robert Preston who was accepted as a fishmonger in 1571, suggesting that they were at least interested in and involved with "Masonrie."[30] The manuscript is certainly a very important and intriguing document, especially when analysing the wording of the anagram which states "Upon

28   Knoop & Jones, *Genesis of Freemasonry*, 154–55.
29   York MS № 1, Duncombe Place, York.
30   Cryer, *York Mysteries*, 156–57.

his Artt of Masonrie," suggesting that the Robert Preston mentioned in the manuscript was certainly interested in the "Artt" in
some form. Michael Baigent however, who wrote the rather sen-
sationalist foreword to Cryer's book, was less cautious and erro-
neously stated that these men had actually joined a lodge in York,
when there is no actual mention of them being in a York-based
lodge at all.[31] These two men were connected with each other in
some way to appear at the beginning of the document, but the
precise nature of their involvement with "Masonrie" remains
a mystery as there is no other supporting evidence; they were
certainly involved in the writing of these "Old Charges," perhaps
in a similar way that the Old Charges written for the lodge in
Warrington mentioned by Elias Ashmole in 1646, was compiled
by Edward Sankey, son of lodge member Richard Sankey.[32]

Moreover, the York MS Nº 1, according to a written inscription on the reverse of the manuscript, was only presented to the
York Grand Lodge in 1736 by Dr. Francis Drake, stating it had
been found during the demolition of Pontefract Castle, which
occurred after its surrender as a Royalist stronghold at the end
of the second stage of the Civil War in 1649.[33] Drake's grandfa-

31 Cryer, *York Mysteries*, vii.
32 See Hughan, *Old Charges*, 8. The version of the "Old Charges"
    written by Edward Sankey are preserved in the British Museum,
    the document being known as the Sloane MS Nº 3848.
33 For a further description of the York MS Nº1, see Hughan, *Old
    Charges*, 5–6. Hughan mentions that the document was presented
    to the York Grand Lodge by Drake in 1736, but Cryer mentioned
    that the date was 1732; see Cryer, *York Mysteries*, 156. However,
    William Hargrove in his *History and Description of the Ancient
    City of York* gives the date as 1738, which is discussed in Poole &
    Worts, "Yorkshire," 110, which suggests it could be 1736 or 1738.
    When York Lodge archivist David Taylor and I examined the
    written text on the reverse of one of the four sheets of parchment
    that comprise the MS Nº 1, the ink was faded somewhat, but we
    both agreed that the last digit looked like a six. If this is correct,
    then the manuscript was given to the Grand Lodge as late as 1736,

ther, before being ordained as a vicar, was a Royalist officer and was present during the siege, so the manuscript could have been previously kept by Dr. Francis Drake's family.[34]

For firmer evidence of non-operative Freemasonry in York, we have to look at the later seventeenth century. For example, there exists a mahogany flat rule with a date of 1663, measuring eighteen inches, now held by the York "Union" Lodge, displaying Masonic symbols and mentioning three men associated with York: John Drake, and William and John Baron.

John Drake seems to have been collated to the Prebendal Stall of Donnington in the Cathedral Church of York in October 1663, and was a cousin of Dr. Francis Drake's father; William Baron was made a Freeman grocer in 1662, serving as sheriff of York in 1677, and John Baron may have been a relative of his.[35] Again, no lodge is actually mentioned, but the evidence of the rule, the symbols, and the mention of a member of the Drake family and of a prominent Freeman of York is suggestive of a locally important gathering which certainly used the "Artt of Masonrie." Thirty years later in 1693, a parchment roll entitled the York MS Nº 4—another copy of the "Old Charges"—mentions six men who were members of a lodge in Yorkshire.[36] This version of the "Old Charges" was written by a certain Mark Kypling, who, along with the other men named, have been associated with the Tees Valley in the North Riding.[37]

and was thus still very much in operation at that time.

34 Hughan, *Old Charges*, 6. Hughan mentions that the grandfather of Dr. Francis Drake wrote a diary of the siege.
35 See Cryer, *York Mysteries*, 189. For a comprehensive list of the Sheriffs and Lord Mayors of York see Hargrove, *History and Description of the Ancient City of York*, 1:327.
36 Hughan, *Old Charges*, 15–16.
37 Hughan, *Old Charges*, 15–16. For the Tees Valley associations of the six men named in the York MS Nº 4, see Cryer, *York Mysteries*, 191.

There exists a 1705 list of "Presidents" of a Masonic governing body at York, which was discussed by Gould in his *History of Freemasonry*. Also fom 1712, there exists the minutes of this old Lodge at York displayed in a manuscript entitled the York MS Nº 7, which supplies positive evidence that lodge meetings were held intermittently throughout the year at various local Inns such as Luke Lowther's Star Inn in Stonegate and John Colling's White Swan in Petergate, both of the proprietors being members of the York Lodge.[38] These lodge meetings were on the whole termed as "private lodges," but were occasionally called "General lodges" such as the one held at the house of James Boreham in Stonegate on St. John's Day on the 24th of June, 1713, or at certain times during the Christmas period as "st. Johns lodges," such as in 1716 and 1721.[39] By the time we come to the 27th of December 1725, the term "Grand Feast" is used for the first time after a procession to the Merchant's Hall and the following year, the term "Grand Lodge" is used by York for the first time.[40]

The Grand Lodge of All England Held at York

York was indeed one of the first leading localities that declared itself independent from the Premier Grand Lodge of England, and on the 27th of December 1726, during Francis Drake's speech in the Merchants Adventurers' Hall, the new title of *Grand Lodge of all England held at York* was announced. York, like its other

38   York MS Nº 7, displaying minutes of lodge meetings dating from the 19th of March 1712 until the 4th of May 1730, Duncombe Place, York. For a transcription of these minutes see Gould, *History of Freemasonry*, 2:271–74 and 2:401–404.

39   Gould, *History of Freemasonry*, 2:271–74 and 2:401–404. A St. John's Lodge meeting is also referred to on the 24th of June 1729, the festival of John the Baptist.

40   Ibid.

northern Roman city Chester, has a strong tradition of medieval mystery plays associated with the ancient city's trade guilds, and, as noted, has possible early references to "speculative" Freemasonry dating to the 1600s. Chester also has a number of early references to Freemasonry going back to the late seventeenth and early eighteenth-centuries, and like York, all featuring prominent local families, merchants and tradesmen.[41] The York Grand Lodge kept this traditional link to the Freemen merchants and tradesmen, for example a grocer named Seth Agar was made a Freeman in 1748, became Sheriff in 1760 and Grand Master of the York Grand Lodge in 1767.

Though records reveal the York Grand Lodge was only officially named as such in 1726, perhaps as a reaction to the London-based Premier/Modern Grand Lodge, Gould, in his *History of Freemasonry*, suggested that it had its foundations much earlier. He gives 1705 as a date in which the York "Grand Lodge" began, despite only meagre evidence.[42] In 1725, however, it seems the York brethren began to use the term "Grand Master" instead of "President," and a year later, they claimed superiority over the Premier/Modern Grand Lodge of 1717, thus adding legitimacy to its status and producing the absolute title of the "Grand Lodge of *all* England held at York."[43]

The Old York Lodge had been controlled by leading local gentlemen, such as Sir George Tempest Baronet, who is listed as being "President" in 1705. Other examples of this powerful élite include the Right Honourable Robert Benson, Lord Mayor of York (later Baron Bingley) who is also listed as being President in 1707, and Admiral Robert Fairfax, member of Parliament in 1713 and Mayor in 1715, who became Deputy President in 1721.

---

41   Harrison, *Genesis of Freemasonry*, 31–36.
42   Gould, *History of Freemasonry*, 2:408.
43   Gould, *History of Freemasonry*, 2:407–408; see also Whytehead, "Relics," 93–5.

The majority of the gentlemen and tradesmen involved in the Grand Lodge served in local government as aldermen, mayors, sheriffs and as members of Parliament for York and the surrounding area. Such men include Sir William Robinson who was President in 1708 and became member of Parliament for York in 1713, William Milner, who also served as a Member for York, and Edward Thompson Esq., who actually served as a member of Parliament during his time as Grand Master in 1729.[44]

This strong and close clique of powerful local gentlemen seemed to rule York Freemasonry completely in the early decades of the eighteenth century. The Freemen tradesmen within the York Grand Lodge also had family connections within Freemasonry such as Leonard Smith, who was also an operative mason. His son followed in his footsteps and also became an operative mason and a lodge member. John Whitehead, a Freeman Haberdasher who became Chamberlain in 1700 and Sheriff in 1717 was the great-great-great uncle of York Grand Lodge historian T.B. Whytehead. Other members who had relatives within the Grand Lodge include Thomas and Josiah Beckwith, George and John Palmes, and the aforementioned Francis Drake, FRS, to name but a few.[45]

Despite this seemingly harmonious image of close family ties within York Freemasonry, it is interesting that Charles Fairfax, who held Jacobite sympathies, was fined and subsequently imprisoned for recusancy in 1715. His house was searched and his gun confiscated, and he was eventually brought before Robert Fairfax (who was Mayor at the time), Sir Walter Hawksworth and Sir William Robinson, all members of the Old York Lodge. Another local gentleman present at Charles Fairfax's hearing was Sir Henry Goodricke, who married the daughter of another Old York Lodge member, Tobias Jenkyns, who happened to be

44 Ibid.
45 Ibid.

Mayor twice in 1701 and 1720. Jenkyns also served as member
of Parliament for York in 1715, beating fellow candidate and Old
York Lodge member Sir William Robinson.[46]

Francis Drake also had Jacobite sympathies, though, as far as
can be ascertained he did not become actively involved in any
agitation.[47] However, his friend and associate Dr. John Burton
did become involved in Jacobite intrigues, being imprisoned for
a time. A later visitor to the York Grand Lodge who held Jacobite
sympathies was local Catholic and Freemason William Arundell, famous for removing the skulls of executed Jacobites from
the pinnacles of Micklegate Bar in York in 1754. In his all-im-
portant speech to the Merchant Adventurers Hall in 1726, Drake
commented that "the whole Brotherhood may be called good
Christians, Loyal Subjects, and True Britons,"[48] perhaps asserting
that the York Brethren were as loyal as the staunch Hanoverian London-based Modern Brethren. Despite this assertion, it is
suspicious that the York Grand Lodge became quiet during the
1740s and 1750s, the period of the Jacobite uprising.[49]

Of all the local gentlemen involved in the York Grand Lodge,
Drake was perhaps one of the most important. Drake was the son
of a Yorkshire clergyman who had been the Vicar of Pontefract,
and became involved in Freemasonry at an early age, being a
passionate champion of the ancient traditions of the York Grand
Lodge. Drake zealously expressed the mythical links with King
Edwin's first Masonic assembly at York Cathedral.[50] Somewhat
like his southern counterpart, William Preston, Drake was a his-

---

46   Ibid.

47   Ibid.

48   Anon., *Antient Constitutions*, 20.

49   Cryer, *York Mysteries*, 267–68. Cryer certainly supports the view
     that the Jacobite Rebellion had an effect on the York Grand Lodge,
     forcing its members to cease their meetings until the political
     climate had eased somewhat.

50   Anon., *Antient Constitutions*, 20.

torian, writing a history of York which was published in 1736. Drake also presented to the York Grand Lodge the Parchment Roll of Constitutions, which had been supposedly found during the demolition of Pontefract Castle, and would have given Drake increased status within the close circle of York Masons. Indeed, even in a mid-nineteenth-century edition of Paine's *Origins of Freemasonry*, this document is mentioned in the preface of the work when the editor comments on the rebellions and rivalries within Freemasonry:

> These two lodges (London and Scotland) soon began to quarrel about precedency; each endeavouring to prove its priority by existing records of labouring masons... established many centuries before. The Yorkites, it is believed produced the oldest documents.[51]

Drake played a major role during the revival of the York Grand Lodge in 1761, being Grand Master until 1762. He died in 1771.[52]

The lack of official York Masonic records during the 1740s and 1750s has led Masonic historians of the nineteenth century, such as Gould, to suggest that the York Grand Lodge quickly went into decline. It has therefore been accepted that the York Grand Lodge became dormant during this period, but was hastily revived in 1761 when it became apparent that the Modern Grand Lodge of London had spread its influence and invaded the territory of the old York Grand Lodge. The founding of a Modern lodge by a company of actors within the city walls at a tavern called the Punch Bowl, seemed to have triggered a reaction from a small group of original York Grand Lodge Masons, who quick-

51   Paine, *Origins of Freemasonry*, 217.
52   Gould, *History of Freemasonry*, 407–408; See also Whytehead, "Relics," 93–5.

ly ejected the Modern lodge, replacing it with their own lodge.[53]

This revival of the York Grand Lodge was the result of the involvement of six original York Grand Lodge members, led by the indefatigable Francis Drake. It soon began to flourish again and over the ensuing decades had ten lodges founded under its jurisdiction. Though during the official "re-launching" of the York Grand Lodge, a number of brethren were present from the usurped Modern lodge, some of whom had actually joined the re-launched York Grand Lodge. The majority of the new lodges were located in Yorkshire, with one particularly successful lodge being found in Rotherham, called the Druidical Lodge; this is the same Lodge Higgins associated with the ascetic Culdees of the medieval British Isles (noted above). Additionally, one lodge was founded in Lancashire, and one lodge, the "Duke of Devonshire," was founded as far away as Macclesfield in Cheshire.

The Lancashire lodge, founded in 1790, was situated in Hollinwood, near the cotton producing town of Oldham, and was called the Lodge of Fortitude; this lodge was mentioned in the minutes of the Oldham-based Modern Lodge of Friendship.

The minutes also refer to various visiting brethren from the York lodge, as well as various members of the York lodge also having dual membership with the Modern lodge. These dual members were mentioned into the early nineteenth century as being active in the Lodge of Friendship.[54] The visits between the York and Modern lodges provide an insight into the relationship between Masons from different governing bodies, reminding us that despite the antagonism between Grand Lodges, Freemasons

---

53   Gould, *History of Freemasonry*, 413–15; See also Whytehead, "Relics," 96–7.

54   Visiting brethren from the Lodge of Fortitude are mentioned in the Minutes of the Lodge of Friendship № 277, on the 16th of February, 1791 to the 23rd of September 1795, and associated Fortitude brethren are mention up until 1811. Masonic Hall, Rochdale. Not listed.

from all backgrounds could still relate to each other at local level.

The York Grand Lodge had continued to include prominent local gentlemen. These included William Siddall Esq., who served as Mayor the same year he served as Grand Master in 1783, Sir Thomas Gascoigne, Bartholomew and William Blanchard, who was the last Grand Secretary and who, as noted, owned the *York Chronicle*. Blanchard was also the custodian of the minutes and documents of the York Grand Lodge after its demise, and became the main source of information for Masonic historians in the early nineteenth century. He also presented the Records of the York Grand Lodge to the York-based "Union" Lodge in 1837.[55] The York Grand Lodge continued officially until 1792, however, it may have survived into the early years of the nineteenth century, though no documents are in existence to substantiate this. The last entry in the minute book is dated the 23rd of August 1792. After this date, the surviving York Grand Lodge members, such as Blanchard, the Grand Chaplain Rev. John Parker, and the last Grand Master Edward Wolley, became increasingly involved with the "Union" Lodge, finding sympathy in a lodge which had been founded on the principles of union.[56]

The York Union Lodge was founded in York in 1777 under the Modern Grand Lodge. Some of its founders were of Antient persuasion, however, the Lodge became a bastion to the memory of the York Grand Lodge.[57] The brethren were still using the York Working of the ritual in 1822 when the lodge finally agreed to adopt the new system, as taught by the Lodge of Reconciliation, which had been set up by the United Grand Lodge. Despite this, the Union Lodge decided to continue the York Working as no

55   Benson, *John Browne*, 5.
56   See Harrison, *York Grand Lodge*.
57   The York Grand Lodge Minute Books dating from March 17, 1712 and ending August 23, 1792 are in the possession of the York "Union" Lodge. There are no Minutes, however, from 1734 to 1761.

member of the lodge had seen the new system demonstrated.[58] There is a lodge tradition that York architectural historian John Browne, who joined the Union Lodge in 1825, was a supporter of this York Working and ensured its survival. In the end, the York Grand Lodge seemed unable to compete with the might of the Modern and Antient Grand Lodges, and faded away in the opening years of the nineteenth century.[59]

The End of the York Grand Lodge and Its Legacy

Despite the end of the York Grand Lodge, York did leave a legacy, and there are still remnants of the extinct Grand Lodge existing today. Another lodge was in the process of being constituted after the Lodge of Fortitude—its Constitution being mentioned in the last ever minute entry we have of the York Grand Lodge on the 23rd of August 1792, although which lodge in particular remains a mystery. Cryer mentions that there was an opinion that this lodge could have been the Lodge of Hope in Bradford,[60] which still exists and has in its possession a version of the Old Charges, referred to as the Old York Manuscript Constitution or the Hope MS, which has been dated to c. 1680. Masonic historian William Hughan likened it to the York MS Nº 4 of 1693.[61] The Lodge of Hope, however, was constituted under the Moderns on the 23rd of March 1794, although it had originally conferred its Mark degree

---

58   Wood, *York Lodge No. 236*, 20.

59   Gould, *History of Freemasonry*, 419–21. Also see Waite, *New Encyclopædia*, 482. Gould stated that the 1780–1792 volume of minutes from the York Grand Lodge was missing at the time of his writing. As stated above, these minutes may currently be found at Freemasons Hall, York.

60   See Cryer, *York Mysteries*, 374.

61   Hughan, *Old Charges*, 12.

under the old York Manuscript Constitution.[62]

This interest in higher degrees had led Freemasons from across the Grand Lodge divide to seek out York Masonry before, an example being the lodge that had taken hold in Lancashire. This York lodge that had established itself in Lancashire, according to Cryer, was perhaps one of the last to survive out of the "York" lodges, and according to new analysis of certain documents, the lodge may have lasted at least until 1802, though as we shall see, its influence certainly lasted much longer. A committed member of the York Grand Lodge, a certain Jacob Bussey, who had served as Grand Secretary, moved to Manchester in 1779, but died unexpectedly three years later, his death being mentioned in the *York Chronicle*.[63] John Hassall, was a "York" stalwart, who had previously been a founder of the Druidical Lodge in Rotherham, had moved to Manchester after being imprisoned for debt at York Castle, and it was Hassall who was to energetically spread the influence of the York Grand Lodge west of the Pennines.

After forming a Royal Encampment of Knights Templar in Manchester in 1786, Hassall then tried to get a Craft lodge under York off the ground in Manchester, with a petition to form the lodge being forwarded to the York Grand Lodge on the 23rd of December 1787 by four men including Hassall. This came to nothing, but two of the other men that had signed the petition—Thomas Daniel and John Broad—entered into the Royal Encampment.[64] Hassall then suddenly appeared as a visitor in the Oldham-based Lodge of Friendship on the 17th of August 1790.

It seems that Hassall had been recruiting members for a new lodge under York, as the Lodge of Fortitude was founded soon

62   Waite, *Secret Tradition*, 46–7.
63   See Johnson, *Subordinate Lodges*, 133.
64   Shepherd & Lane, *Jerusalem Preceptory*, 12–13. John Broad was entered on the 17th of April 1787 and Thomas Daniel was entered on the 17th of August 1788.

after on the 27th of November, with Hassall and up to six leading brethren from the Oldham-based "Modern" lodge being involved, five of them being petitioners. Hassall certainly did not
let Masonic prejudice get in the way of his recruitment process—
both Antient and Modern Brethren being ready recruits for York
Masonry. The Lodge of Fortitude first met at The Sun, described
as being located at the "Bottom of Hollinwood," near Oldham,
the landlord of which, a certain James Taylor, had initially joined
the Lodge of Friendship on the 2nd of September 1789, becoming a "full member" on the 23rd of February, the following year.
Despite his obvious involvement in the "York" lodge, he still
visited his old lodge, with two recorded visits being on the 16th
of March 1791 (as a visitor from the Lodge of Integrity) and on
the 20th of March 1799.[65]

The five petitioners of Fortitude who came from the Lodge of
Friendship included Jonathan Raynor, an Oldham weaver and
founding member of Friendship who had been initiated into
Lodge N° 354, an Irish lodge attached to the 49th Regiment, on
the 7th of July 1781. Raynor, as we shall see, cannily kept joint
membership of both Friendship and Fortitude. Another petitioner, Isaac Clegg, who was a cotton manufacturer, was also a
founding member of Friendship, and actually served as Worshipful Master in both the lodges at the same time, being the first
to take the Chair in Fortitude. Clegg had also been a founding
member of the Manchester-based Lodge of Union N° 534 (Moderns) in 1788, along with a number of other future members
of the Lodge of Friendship.[66] A further founding member of
Friendship who was also a founding member of Fortitude was

65   List of Members of the Lodge of Friendship, N° 277, 2nd of
     September 1789. See also Pick, "The Lodge of Fortitude at
     Hollinwood," 32–37.
66   See Lane's *Masonic Records*. The Lodge of Union N°534 was
     constituted on the 27th of September 1788, but was named the
     Union Lodge in 1792.

tailor Samuel Brierley, though unlike Raynor and Clegg, he resigned from Friendship. Painter Henry Mills, also resigned from
Friendship to serve as the first Senior Warden in Fortitude, but
continued to visit his old lodge, as did weaver John Booth, who
also resigned from Friendship.[67]

These visits from Fortitude continued to be indicated in
the minutes of the Lodge of Friendship. For example, a certain
Brother James Whitehead from Fortitude attended on the 16th of
February 1791,[68] and another entry on the 5th of June 1791, indicated that a certain John Scholfield was "Renter'd from the Lodge
of Fortitude."[69] Whitehead continued to visit Friendship, next
appearing while visiting with John Booth and William Fletcher on the 26th of August, 1795, the minutes indicating that they
were from "Hollinwood," where of course, Fortitude was based.[70]
Whitehead returned later in the year on the 23rd of September
with Fletcher and Michael Gunn, as did Booth, accompanied by
Henry Mills on the 28th of October.[71] These visits certainly point
to Fortitude still being very active throughout 1795.

Jonathan Raynor, who had been the Lodge of Friendship's
first Worshipful Master, visited Friendship on the 17th of December 1791, when he was "sencered for his bad behaviour...."[72]
Despite this behavioural lapse, he remained a prominent fig-

67 See Pick, "The Lodge of Friendship № 277 With Notes," 78–9; See
    also Pick, "Lodge of Friendship № 277; A Link," 150–51.
68 Minutes of the Lodge of Friendship, № 277, 16th of February 1791.
69 Minutes of the Lodge of Friendship, № 277, 5th of June 1791; See
    also Pick, "Lodge of Fortitude," 35.
70 Minutes of the Lodge of Friendship, № 277, 26th of August 1795;
    See also Pick, "Lodge of Fortitude," 35.
71 Pick, "Lodge of Fortitude," 35. In Pick's early paper "Lodge of
    Friendship № 277; A Link," 153, he uses the 28th of August instead
    of the 26th as the date of Whitehead's visit, and on the same page,
    he uses the year 1803 instead of 1808 for Henry Mills" Office in
    Friendship as substitute Treasurer.
72 Minutes of the Lodge of Friendship, № 277, 17th of December 1791.

ure in Friendship; he had served as Worshipful Master again in 1791 and 1795, and was always proposing candidates, though he seemed to fall on hard times, claiming relief from Friendship intermittently from November 1791, when he was advanced two guineas for the security of his watch, which was repaired and valued by another member.[73] On the 27th of August 1792, Raynor was again given relief due to his "his wife being ill a long time." His wife subsequently died, and Raynor remarried in 1793, but his hardships continued, and several monthly records appear in the Friendship cash book for his relief in early 1809.[74]

The lodge may have gradually faded away a number of years after Hassall's death in 1795, though with members still being mentioned as late as 1811, his influence may have lived on. A Moderns-aligned Royal Arch chapter called the Chapter of Philanthropy was founded on the 13th of September 1791, which met at the White Lion in Werneth, half way between Oldham and Hollinwood, and there were a number of active brethren from Hollinwood included, one of the founders being none other than Samuel Brierley. This Chapter was finally erased in 1839, and intriguingly a notebook was found and presented to the UGLE in 1963 which included the bylaws of the Lodge of Fortitude, along with the bylaws of the Royal Arch and a list of members involved in local Mark Masonry from 1790 to 1793. The list reveals eighteen local Mark members and it presents some recognisable names such as Samuel Brierley, James Taylor, John Booth and Michael Gunn, all linked to both Fortitude and Friendship.[75] One of the other members listed, a certain William Barlow, was also a member of the Knights Templar St. Bernard's Conclave that had been founded at Hollinwood on the 1st of October 1793.[76] The notebook

73   Pick, "The Lodge of Friendship Nº 277 With Notes," 77.
74   Minutes of the Lodge of Friendship, Nº 277, 29th of March 1809.
75   Pick, "Lodge of Fortitude," 35–37.
76   Pick, "Lodge of Friendship Nº 277; A Link," 81–82; And Pick,

also includes extracts from the 1802 New York edition of Thomas Smith Webb's *Freemasons' Monitor*, which could suggest that the Lodge of Fortitude was still functioning at least until that date, or at the very least insinuates that a member of Fortitude was still very interested in a variant form of Freemasonry.

The lone York Craft lodge in Lancashire which Hassall had instigated, certainly continued to have an impact on Masonry in the area, with members of the lodge being active in local Freemasonry well into the first few decades of the nineteenth century, and its members influencing the continuation of Royal Arch and Mark Masonry in Oldham and Hollinwood. Further degrees were certainly of an interest to certain members of the Lodge of Friendship, with Thomas Taylor from Friendship, for example, joining the Manchester-based Royal Encampment of Jerusalem in 1790.[77] Hassall was poorly educated, and it is a testament to his hard work that this lodge became not only one of the last bastions of the York Grand Lodge, but it firmly bridged the divide between Modern and York Masonry; Freemasons from different backgrounds working together and exploring and enjoying further degrees. The same can certainly be said of the Royal Encampment which included an eclectic mix of Masons from Antient and Modern lodges; there was a dynamic desire by keen Freemasons to search deeper into the hidden mysteries of nature and science, and to delve into a more Antient ceremony and research the higher degrees as practised by York.

"Lodge of Fortitude," 37.

77   See Shepherd & Lane, *Jerusalem Preceptory*, 54. See also The List of Membership of the Lodge of Friendship, № 277. Thomas Taylor was a founding member of the lodge.

Bibliography

The main source material that still exists on the York Grand Lodge can be located at Duncombe Place in York, and there are certain other existing lodges that hold York artefacts. The York Grand Lodge documents, which date periodically from the 19th of March, 1712 and end on the 23rd of August, 1792, are in the possession of the York "Union" Lodge № 236. The first collection of records begins on the 19th of March, 1712 and end on the 4th of May, 1730, and are to be found on a parchment roll known as Roll № 7. There is a mention of an "Original Minute Book of this (the York) Grand Lodge" which dated from 1705 to 1734, in a letter dated August 1778 from the Grand Secretary Jacob Bussey, to Bro. B. Bradley of the Lodge of Antiquity in London.

There are no minutes at all between the years 1734 to 1761, and a possible earlier document listing earlier meetings from 1705 to 1712 has disappeared. Other York Grand Lodge relics, including furniture, jewels, manuscript rolls including the various Antient Charges, the rule dating from 1663, collective letters and the original Warrant for the Lodge of Fortitude, are all held at Freemasons Hall, Duncombe Place, York, which is the current residence of the York "Union" Lodge. There is also an excellent collection of books held at Duncombe Place, dating from the eighteenth and early-nineteenth-centuries, such as the rare copy of William Preston's *Illustrations of Masonry*, and an original copy of Drake's *Eboracum*.

The minutes of the revived York Grand Lodge are also held at Duncombe Place by the York "Union" Lodge № 236. Johnson and Bramwell comprehensively catalogued the lodge's library in 1958; there are the two York Grand Lodge minute books covering 1761 to 1774 and 1774 to 1780, and the two York Grand Lodge Royal Arch minute books covering 1762 to 1772 and 1778 to 1781 respectively. There is a list of members (Manuscript Roll № 10) that includes all initiates from 1761 to 1790 and a scrap of paper that has a manuscript minute from 23rd August 1792. Quatuor Coronati member Thomas B. Whytehead (Worshipful Master in 1899), who was also editor of the *Yorkshire Gazette*, wrote several articles about the Grand Lodge of All England at York and concluded that a minute book probably existed covering the period 1782 to 1792, but its whereabouts were unknown. All subsequent research into the Grand Lodge of All England has reached a similar conclusion. There are also the lists of members & minutes of the Lodge of Friendship, № 277, dating from 1789, once based in Oldham, but now located at the Rochdale Masonic Hall. The minutes and artefacts of the Jerusalem Preceptory № 5 are held at the Manchester Masonic Hall.

Anderson, James. *The Constitutions of the Antient and Honourable Fraternity of Free and Accepted Masons. Revised Edition.* (London: J. Scott, 1756).

————. *Constitutions of the Antient and Honourable Fraternity of Free and Accepted Masons.* London: G. Kearsly, 1769.

————. *The Constitutions of the Freemasons, Containing the History, Charges, Regulations, &c. of that most Ancient and Right Worshipful Fraternity.* London: William Hunter, 1723.

————. *The New Book of Constitutions of the Antient and Honourable Fraternity of Free and Accepted Masons, Containing Their History, Charges, Regulations, &c.* London: Richard Chandler, 1738.

————. *Constitutions of the Antient and Honourable Fraternity of Free and Accepted Masons.* London: G. Kearsly, 1769.

Anonymous. *A Curious Collection of the most Celebrated Songs in Honour of Masonry.* London: B. Creake, 1731.

————. *Jachin and Boaz: Or, An Authentic Key to the Door of Free-Masonry.* London: W. Nichols, 1762.

Armstrong, John. *History of Freemasonry in Cheshire.* London: Kenning, 1901.

Ayres, Philip J. *Classical Culture and the Idea of Rome in Eighteenth-Century England.* Cambridge: Cambridge University Press, 1997.

Benson, G. *John Browne 1793–1877, Artist and the Historian of York Minster.* York: Yorkshire Philosophical Society, 1918.

British History Online. "Newspapers." *A History of the County of York: the City of York* (1961). *http://www.british-history.ac.uk/report.aspx?compid=36391.* Accessed: 19th of May 2012.

Brown, J. *Masonry in Wigan being a brief history of the Lodge of Antiquity No. 178, Wigan, originally No. 235.* Wigan: R. Platt, Standishgate and Millgate, 1882.

Crossley, Herbert. *The History of the Lodge of Probity No. 61.* Hull: M.C. Peck & Son, 1888.

Cryer, Neville Barker. "The Grand Lodge of All England at York and its Practices." *http://www.lodgehope337.org.uk/lectures/.* Accessed: 21st of July, 2009.

———. *Masonic Halls of England The North.* Shepperton: Lewis Masonic, 1989.

———. "The Restoration Lodge of Chester." Unpublished paper delivered to the Cornerstone Society, November 2002.

———. *York Mysteries Revealed.* Hersham: N.B. Cryer, 2006.

Dermott, Laurence. *Ahiman Rezon: Or, A Help to a Brother.* London: James Bedford, 1756.

———. *Ahiman Rezon, or a help to all that are, or would be Free and Accepted Masons.* London: Robert Black, 1764.

———. *Ahiman Rezon or a Help to all that are, or would be Free and Accepted Masons (with many additions).* London: James Jones, 1778.

Drake, Francis. *Eboracum or The History and Antiquities of the City of York, from its Original to the Present Time; together with the History of the Cathedral Church and the Lives of the Archbishops of that See.* London: William Bowyer, 1736.

———. *Eboracum.* York: Wilson and Spence, 1788.

Dunn, P.M. "Dr. John Burton (1710–1771) of York and his Obstetric Treatise." *Archives of Disease in Childhood: Fetal and Neonatal* 84

(2001).

Eyer, Shawn. "Drake's Oration of 1726 with Commentary and Notes." *Philalethes: The Journal of Masonic Research and Letters* 67(2014): 14–25.

Frere, Sheppard. *Britannia: A History of Roman Britain*. London: Pimlico, 1992.

Friendship Lodge № 277. List of Members. Unpublished.

Friendship Lodge № 277. Meeting Minutes. Unpublished.

Gilbert, R.A. "The Masonic Career of A.E. Waite." *Ars Quatuor Coronatorum* 99 (1986): 88–110.

Gould, Robert Freke. *The Concise History of Freemasonry*. New York: Dover Publications, 2007.

———. *History of Freemasonry*, Vol. 2. London: Thomas C. Jack, 1883.

Hallett, Mark & Rendall, Jane, Eds. *Eighteenth-Century York: Culture, Space and Society*. York: University of York, 2003

Hargrove, William. *History and Description of the Ancient City of York: comprising all the most interesting information already published in Drake's Eboracum*. York: William Alexander, 1818.

Harrison, David. *The City of York: A Masonic Guide*. Hersham: Lewis Masonic, 2016.

———. "Freemasonry, Industry and Charity: The Local Community and the Working Man." *Journal of the Institute of Volunteering Research* Vol. 5, No. 1 (2002): 33–45.

———. *The Genesis of Freemasonry*. Hersham: Lewis Masonic, 2009.

———. "The Last Years of the York Grand Lodge—Part One." *The Journal of the Masonic Society* 23(2014): 16–23.

———. "The Liverpool Masonic Rebellion and the Grand Lodge of Wigan." *The Historical Society for Lancashire & Cheshire* 160(2012): 67–88.

———. *The Liverpool Masonic Rebellion and the Wigan Grand Lodge*. Bury St. Edmunds: Arima Publishing, 2012.

———. "The Lymm Freemasons: A New Insight into Transition-Era Freemasonry." *Heredom* 19 (2011): 169–90.

———. *The Transformation of Freemasonry*. Bury St. Edmunds: Arima, 2010.

———. *The York Grand Lodge*. Bury St. Edmunds: Arima, 2014.

Harrison, David & Belton, John. "Society in Flux." *Researching British Freemasonry 1717–2017: Journal for the Centre for the Research into Freemasonry and Fraternalism* 3 (2010): 71–99.

Hawkins, David. "Membership of the "Anchor and Hope" Lodge, Bolton, 1732–1813." Unpublished paper delivered to the International Conference on the *History of Freemasonry*. May 2009.

Higgins, Godfrey. *Anacalypsis*. Stilwell: Digireads.com Publishing, 2007.

Hughan, William James. *The Old Charges of British Freemasons*. London: Simpkin, Marshall and Co., 1872.

Johnson, G.Y. "The Subordinate Lodges Constituted by the York Grand Lodge, Part I." *Ars Quatuor Coronatorum* 52 (1941): 225–68.

Johnson, G.Y. "The Subordinate Lodges Constituted by the York Grand Lodge, Part II." *Ars Quatuor Coronatorum* 53 (1942): 195–297.

Knoop, D., & Jones, G.P. *A Short History of Freemasonry to 1730*. Manchester: Manchester University Press, 1940.

———. *Early Masonic Pamphlets*. Manchester: University of Manchester Press, 1945.

———. *The Genesis of Freemasonry*. Manchester: University of Manchester Press, 1947.

———. *The Mediaeval Mason: An Economic History of English Stone Building in the Later Middle Ages and Early Modern Times*. New York: Barnes and Noble, 1967.

Lane's Masonic Records. http://freemasonry.dept.shef.ac.uk/lane/. Accessed: 9th of June, 2012.

Mackenzie, Kenneth. *The Royal Masonic Cyclopaedia*. Wellingborough: The Antiquarian Press, 1987.

Maclean, Fitzroy. *Bonnie Prince Charlie*. Edinburgh: Canongate, 1989.

Marsden, John. *The Illustrated Bede*. London: Macmillan, 1989.

Masson, John. *Statutes of the Order of Masonic Knights Templar 1853*.

Montana: Kessinger Publishing, 2010.

Morton, Albert. *A Brief History of Freemasonry in Richmond, Yorkshire, Compiled from the records of the Lennox Lodge, № 123, and other sources*. Richmond: Thomas Spencer, 1911.

Morton, Albert. *Lennox Lodge, No. 123*. Richmond: Privately Printed, 1947.

Paine, Thomas. *The Works of Thomas Paine*. New York: E. Haskell, 1854.

Parker, John. *A Sermon, Preached in the Parish-Church of Rotherham, Before the Most Worshipful Grand Master of the Most Ancient Grand Lodge of All England . . . and the Newly Constituted Rotherham Druidical Lodge of Free and Accepted Masons, December 22, 1778*. York: W. Blanchard and Co., 1779.

Pick, Fred L. "The Lodge of Fortitude at Hollinwood." *Manchester Association for Masonic Research* 53 (1963): 32–37.

———. "Lodge of Friendship № 277; A Link With The Grand Lodge Of All England, At York." *Manchester Association for Masonic Research* 21 (1931): 149–54.

———. "The Lodge of Friendship № 277 with Notes on Some Neighbouring Lodges and Chapters." *Manchester Association for Masonic Research* 23 (1933): 74–123.

Poole, H., & Worts, F.R. *"Yorkshire" Old Charges of Masons*. York: Ben Johnson & Co. Ltd, 1935.

Porter, Roy. *Enlightenment*. London: Penguin, 2000.

Pound, Ricky. "Chiswick House—A Masonic Temple?" *Brentford & Chiswick Local History Journal* 16 (2007): 4–7.

Prescott, Andrew. "The Hidden Currents of 1813." The Square, Vol. 40, No. 2 (2014): 31–32.

Preston, William. *Illustrations of Masonry*. London: Whittaker, Treacher & Co., 1829.

Provincial Grand Lodge of Mark Master Masons of Cornwall. "History of Mark Master Masons." *http://www.markmastermasonscornwall.org.uk/history-of-mark-master-masons*. Accessed: 30th of May, 2012.

Raine, J, Ed. *"Fabric Rolls of York Minster* (1360–1639, with an Appendix, 1165–1704)." *Surtees Society* 35 (1858): 174–75.

Ramsden Riley, J. *The Yorkshire Lodges: A Century of Yorkshire Freemasonry*. Leeds: Thomas C. Jack, 1885.

Rogers, Norman. "The Lodge of Sincerity, Nº 1 of the Wigan Grand Lodge." *Ars Quatuor Coronatorum* 62 (1951): 33–76.

————. "Two Hundred Years of Freemasonry in Bolton." *Manchester Association for Masonic Research* 31 (1941): 27–82.

Rosenfeld, Sybil. *Strolling Players and Drama in the Provinces 1660–1765*. Cambridge: Cambridge University Press, 1939.

Rylands, W.H. "Freemasonry in Lancashire & Cheshire in the Seventeenth Century." *Transactions of the Lancashire & Cheshire Historical Society* 50 (1898): 131–202.

Scott, C.J. "The Tradition of The Old York T. I. Lodge of Mark Master Masons: An Enquiry into Early Freemasonry at Bradford and Neighborhood, 1713–1873." *http://www.bradford.ac.uk/webofhiram/?section=york_rite&page=tradoldyork.html*. Accessed: 30th of October 2013.

Shepherd, F.C. & Lane, M.P. *Jerusalem Preceptory No. 5. Bi-Centenary History 1786–1986*. Manchester: Privately Printed, 1986.

Smith, Joseph. *A Descriptive Catalogue of Friends" Books, or Books written by the Members of the Society of Friends, commonly called Quakers*. London: Joseph Smith, 1867.

Springett, Bernard H. *The Mark Degree*. London: A. Lewis, 1968.

Sterne, Laurence. *The Life and Opinions of Tristram Shandy, Gentleman*. London: R. & J. Dodsley, 1760.

Sweet, Rosemary. "History and Identity in Eighteenth-Century York: Francis Drake's *Eboracum* (1736)." In Mark Hallett & Jane Rendall, Eds. *Eighteenth-Century York: Culture, Space and Society*. York: University of York, 2003: 14–23.

Timperley, Charles Henry. *A Dictionary of Printers and Printing*. London: Johnson, 1839.

University of Bradford. "Historical Notes Concerning the York Grand Lodge." *http://www.brad.ac.uk/webofhiram/?section=york_*

rite&page=grandyork.html. Accessed: 1ˢᵗ of February 2013.

Waite, Arthur Edward. *Secret Tradition in Freemasonry*. New York: Rebman, 1911.

Webb, Thomas Smith. *Webb's Freemason's Monitor*. Cincinnati: C. Moore, 1865.

Whytehead, T.B. "The Relics of the Grand Lodge at York" *Ars Quatuor Coronatorum* 13 (1900): 93–115.

Wilkinson, Tate. *Memoirs of His own Life*. York: Wilson, Spence and Mawman, 1790.

Wilkinson, Tate. T*he Wandering Patentee, Or A History of the Yorkshire Theatres From 1770 to the Present Time*. York: Wilson, Spence and Mawman, 1795.

Wood, Robert Leslie. *York Lodge No. 236, formerly The Union Lodge, the Bi-Centennial History, 1777–1977*. York: Privately Printed, 1977.

W___O___V____n. *The Three Distinct Knocks On the Door of the most Antient Free-Masonry*. London: H. Srjeant, 1760.

John Desaguliers

The Balance of Religion and Science

JEDEDIAH FRENCH

MODERN FREEMASONRY clothes itself in the garment of universalism. However, prior to the French Revolution, this was not necessarily the case. The origin story of the Craft reports that the founding of the Grand Lodge of England was in 1717 during the meeting at the Goose and Gridiron. It is logical to assume that membership in the Fraternity at that time was largely conditional upon adherence to the Christian faith.[1] In Germany, particularly in the latter half of the eighteenth century, intense struggles erupted as to the place of non-Christian religions within Masonic lodges. This fact alone suggests that, for early Masons, Christianity was taken as a given.

Jews in small numbers had been admitted into lodges in London and Holland in the 1730s, 40s, and 50s. At this time, there were even so-called "Jewish Lodges."[2] The existence of such

1 In part, this was due to the Christian orientation of operative guilds, as evidenced in the various "Old Charges." It is also partially due to the fact that England, Ireland, and Scotland were predominantly Christian nations.

2 See Katz, *Jews and Freemasons in Europe*, 16; for a prayer specified

lodges suggests a level of separation and hesitation among the brethren.[3] Claims of a Templar lineage within Freemasonry in France during the 1730s and 40s may have contributed to hostile attitudes toward Jews and Moslems.[4] Moreover, perhaps in an attempt to defend against the increasing attacks coming from the Catholic Church, Masons across Europe emphasized the Christian character of their systems. They developed Christian high-degree rites, which often resulted in the universalistic element being marginalized and fewer Jews entering Freemasonry. Still, Catholic prohibitions did not let up. The cause for ambiguity may have had to do with Masonic writings themselves. The foundational literature of the Craft speaks to religious tolerance, and Masonic principles can be traced back to certain philosophical ideals, including equality and individual human rights. Historian Jacob Katz has pointed out that it is no accident Freemasonry appeared simultaneously with the emancipation of Jews in Europe, developing alongside the latter group's integration into society.[5]

Anderson's *Constitutions* of 1723, which will be explored in depth later in the essay, states the following:

> [...I]n ancient Times Masons were charg'd in every Country to be of the Religion of that Country or Nation, whatever it was, yet 'tis now thought more expedient only to oblige them to that Religion in which all Men agree, leaving their particular Opinions to themselves; that is, to be *good Men and true*, or Men of Honour and Honesty, by whatever Denominations or Persuasions they may be distinguish'd....[6]

for Jewish Freemasons, see Dermott, *Ahiman Rezon*, 43. This prayer is addressed by Christopher Murphy in this volume; see pages 137–38 and 426.

3   See Katz, *Jews and Freemasons*, 11–25.

4   Katz, *Jews and Freemasons*, 11–25.

5   Katz, *Jews and Freemasons*, 2–5.

6   Anderson, *Constitutions* (1723), 50.

This First Charge perhaps pertained to the manifold denominations and persuasions of Christianity that had wrought such terrible conflict in Europe.[7] Christianity, it has been argued, was "that Religion in which all Men agree." However, this Charge provided the bedrock for those Masons desiring inclusion of other religious faiths. In the eighteenth century, this other faith was mainly Judaism.[8]

That this became a central issue for early Masons can be seen in the revised 1738 version of Anderson's *Constitutions*:

> A MASON is oblig'd by his Tenure to observe the Moral Law, as a true *Noachida*.... In ancient Times the *Christian Masons* were charged to comply with the *Christian* Usages of each Country where they travell'd or work'd: But *Masonry* being found in all Nations, even of divers Religions, they are now only charged to adhere to that Religion in which all Men agree (leaving each Brother to his own particular Opinions) that is, to be Good Men and True, Men of Honour and Honesty, by whatever Names, Religions, or Persuasions they may be distinguish'd: For they all agree in the 3 great *Articles* of NOAH, enough to preserve the cement of the Lodge. Thus *Masonry* is the Center of Union and the happy Means of conciliating Persons that otherwise must have remain'd at a perpetual Distance.[9]

7   See Katz, *Jews and Freemasons*, 11–25; For more information on this sprawling debate, see Bogdan *&* Snoek, *Handbook*; Jones, *Freemasons' Book of the Royal Arch*; Schuchard, *Restoring the Temple of Vision*; and Stevenson, *The Origins of Freemasonry*.

8   The first documented Muslims and Hindus started being initiated into Freemasonry during the eighteenth and nineteenth centuries, respectively, in India. See Millar, *Crescent and the Compass*; also Harland-Jacobs, *Builders of Empire*.

9   Anderson, *New Book of Constitutions* (1738), 143–44. See Katz, *Jews and Freemasons*, 14.

The important thing to notice is the inclusion of the name of Noah to the Charge, thereby forging a common bond or linkage among peoples. Genesis 10:1–3 lists the sons of Noah as Shem, Ham, and Japheth: "…and unto them were sons born after the flood. The sons of Japheth; Gomer, and Magog, and Madai, and Javan, and Tubal, and Meshech, and Tiras. And the sons of Gomer; Ashkenaz, and Riphath, and Togarmah." According to Sacred Tradition, the descendants of this genealogy populated the Arabian peninsula, Egypt, Northern Africa, Asia Minor, the Caucasus Mountains, and eventually Europe. By inserting references to a Noachide genealogy, Masons of the eighteenth century—while still advocating Christianity—incorporated Jewish Talmudic elements into the Craft and established its universalistic foundation.

The Context of Early Freemasonry

Questions over the deistic or theistic nature of Freemasonry have been debated by scholars without reaching a unanimous conclusion. Often, this charge "*Concerning* GOD *and* RELIGION" has been pointed to in defense of a deistic view. It is possible for some theorists to foreground the Enlightenment social context of eighteenth-century Freemasonry to such an extent that it becomes easy to assume early Masons were primarily deist.[10] However, most of these early Masons leading up to the formation of the Grand Lodge of England were, in addition to being largely Christian, a mixture of scientists, philosophers, mathematicians, and clergy, and they funneled their interests into the developing fraternal system of Freemasonry. Indeed, the quaint theory of secularization which describes the process of the *disenchantment*

10   See Weisberger, *Speculative Freemasonry and the Enlightenment*; also, Jacob, *The Radical Enlightenment*.

of the world, first articulated by German sociologist Max Weber (1864–1920) as the rationalization of all knowledge and the suppression of magic and superstition, has long been discredited among modern scholars.[11]

Among early brethren was John Theophilus Desaguliers (1683–1744), a man whose life still retains an arura of mystery, though he became the Craft's third Grand Master. Desaguliers, an Anglican cleric and well-known experimental scientist, is sometimes thought to have been deist, an interpretation that bolsters the deism narrative associated with the early fraternity.[12] This essay highlights the broader dimensions of Desaguliers' religious ideas and tracks the fundamental theism of Freemasonry. Desaguliers' personal conceptions surrounding religion and philosophy were entirely positive, and his views influenced the success of the Premier Grand Lodge.

A note on methodology: The focus of this essay is on intellectual history, sometimes called history of ideas. While it utilizes partial forensic evidence and archival sources—as well as textual support—the main goal is to explore context, the climate of ideas, in which Desaguliers was active and out of which the Premier Grand Lodge emerged. In academic work, this is referred to as a social history. The French sociologist Émile Durkheim argued that institutions which are formed in history are entirely

11   See "Science as a Vocation" (1917) by Max Weber; see Saler, "Modernity and Enchantment: A Historiographic Review," for discrediting disenchantment. Also, in a recent essay, Róbert Péter characterizes the secularization theory as "outmoded;" see Péter, "General Introduction."

12   For more elucidation, see *Strange Altars; a Scriptural Appraisal of the Lodge* by William Julius Acker; *Deism, Masonry, and the Enlightenment: Essays Honoring Alfred Owen Aldridge* edited by Joseph A. Lemay; *Deism in Enlightenment England: Theology, Politics, and Newtonian Public Science* by Jeffrey R. Wigelsworth; D. Knoop & G.P. Jones, "Freemasonry and the Idea of Natural Religion."

contingent upon the culture and the time period in which they emerge. For the purposes of this study, Durkheim will be taken at his word. The life of Desaguliers, the myth that he provided material for the third degree and spread it, and the appearance of the Premier Grand Lodge in 1717, are events still shrouded in mystification. No satisfactory answer has been given to forge a solid consensus. The material evidence is, sadly, lacking.

Therefore, it seems reasonable to judge the appearance of Grand Lodge era Freemasonry from the intellectual atmosphere and historical period that gave birth to it. This atmosphere and its historical players will be outlined.

The importance of Desaguliers and the events of his life remain, as mentioned, largely untreated and unrecognized by academics, except in rare occasions, usually limited to his scientific work. Masonic researchers have, of course, lent the Huguenot more attention, particularly the scholars of the Quatuor Coronati Lodge № 2076, yet much remains unknown.

The publication of a sustained academic biography on Desaguliers was released in 2011 by Audrey T. Carpenter, titled *John Theophilus Desaguliers: A Natural Philosopher, Engineer and Freemason in Newtonian England*.[13] The present essay makes use of this book as a secondary source, as Carpenter assiduously sifted through the bulk of writings on Desaguliers, including the *AQC* pieces, and collated it into a single summation. But academic histories are not Masonic histories and can therefore miss much. Thus, for the bulk of Masonic material, the work of Ric Berman will be privileged.

13   See R. William Weisberger's review of Carpenter's book in *The Social Science Journal*, in which Weisberger suggests that more of "a discussion concerning how Newtonian doctrines, deistic ideas, Whiggish beliefs, classical postulates, and Palladian tenets would have shown the connections of Masonic ritualism to the principles of the Enlightenment." (697)

Magical Religion and Masonic Science

John Theophilus Desaguliers was the son of Jean Desaguliers, a Protestant minister who had been exiled from France as a Huguenot. Protestant life in France toward the end of the seventeenth century was extremely difficult, and the Desaguliers family emigrated to England in 1692 when John Desaguliers was a child. Despite his French origins, as a man Desaguliers was assimilated into English society, remaining connected to the "emigre Huguenot community with its self-preserving support for the Hanoverian *status quo*, belief in education and promotion of latitudinarian religious tolerance."[14]

During the first half of the eighteenth century, England, particularly London, was engaged in a vigorous debate. Contemporaneous intellectuals were grappling with the emergence of a type of double-consciousness: one religious, the other scientific. Academics were engulfed in a "new science," which presented a different way of viewing the world as promoted by Francis Bacon in his *New Atlantis*, which was published posthumously in 1627.

This new world of the eighteenth century would be completely reconcilable to intellect and reason, its parts classifiable, its mysteries uncovered, its secrets revealed. This was an exciting era, with many among the elite optimistic about the progressive improvement of society. Everything, all of nature, could be comprehended, improved—just as Bacon had portrayed it. The old view of a world governed by hierarchies of spiritual beings, whose representatives held priestly offices, was breaking down, replaced by the mechanized world of gears, pulleys, and levers, unliving perhaps, but deducible.

The introduction of Mechanical Philosophy had given fresh intellectual insight into the mysteries of creation. A new, growing class of scientific initiates who aimed to control the inner

14   Berman, *Foundations of Modern Freemasonry*, 40.

components of world order, working under a banner of progress, began to appear as historical actors among the religious and philosophical elites. With the horrors of the French Revolution nowhere on the horizon—much less the Reign of Terror—the sky seemed the limit. Scientific priests gradually emerged to displace the rank of purely religious priests, increasingly seen as keeping the people in superstitious ignorance.

At least, this is the story the history textbooks often give. In reality, the intellectual events taking place during the early 1700s were more nuanced, more complex; they resist this clear picture of reification that history textbooks like to project. Science and religion, at this time, remained the bedfellows of philosophy and mystical ideas, even magic. These systems of knowledge functioned together and the balance of seemingly opposing viewpoints was embodied in the natural philosophers, precursors of the modern scientists.

In her book *Religion, Magic, and Science in Early Modern Europe and America*, historian Allison Coudert argues that:

> ...the idea that the Scientific Revolution consisted of the acceptance of the so-called "Mechanical Philosophy," in which all that existed in the material world were atoms or corpuscles in constant motion, has given way to a new view in which atomism, Aristotelianism, and vitalism, together with a panoply of religious, occult, and esoteric theories, are all recognized as contributing to both the emergence of modern science and reactions against it.[15]

Nowhere is this more evident than in the works of Newton and Desaguliers; it is no accident that the first Grand Lodge of Masons appeared on the world stage in London during the first quarter of the eighteenth century, precisely when these ideas

15   Coudert, *Religion, Magic, and Science*, xxiii.

had seized the cultural consciousness of England. Judging from Anderson's 1723 *Constitutions*, the Craft clearly proposes to balance these opposing viewpoints. The fraternity accomplishes the same feat which had been the task of its earliest and most influential members. Men like Newton—even more so his pupil Desaguliers, a prominent Freemason—assisted in the conception of "divine science," or the scientist of nature, as emphasized in Masonry.

Examples of this can be found in various Masonic writings of the time. Consider, for instance, this exchange from a 1730 exposure:

> Ex.   My Friend, if you pretend to be
> Of this Fraternity,
> You can forthwith and rightly tell
> What means the Letter G.[16]
>
> Resp.   By Sciences are brought to Light
> Bodies of various Kinds,
> Which do appear to perfect Sight;
> But none but Males shall know my Mind.[17]

The theme of Masonry as the science for understanding nature as the handiwork of the Great Architect was nearly ubiquitous in early Masonic writings. For instance, Freemason William Smith expounded on the concept of God as represented by Truth, offering:

> IN all our Pursuits of Knowledge we make Truth in the Particular the Summit of our Aim.... Was it not Truth

---

16   The Letter G is a symbol of the divine name in Freemasonry, described in this document as hanging in the midst of Solomon's Temple.

17   Pritchard, *Masonry Dissected*, 22.

that form'd the wide Expanse of Nature, and rang'd it in such Beauty and Harmony? In fine, it was Truth that gave to every Being to be what it is.[18]

Scottish Freemason Charles Leslie captured this essence in his 1739 work, *Masonry: A Poem*:

> *Sages* and *Magi*, all the ancient wise,
> Whom contemplation led beyond the skies,
> Who trac'd the order of the starry frame,
> And earth and nature's universal scheme,
> Tho' bless'd with Science's great celestial store,
> Yet still have sought to add this KNOWLEDGE more.[19]

Historian Margaret C. Jacob has cogently articulated that "men of a variety of political and religious persuasions ... found meaning in the new science and by the early eighteenth century British Freemasonry gave institutional expression to this new scientific culture. The official Masonic Lodges stand as a metaphor for their age. Ruled by grand masters drawn from the peerage, strictly hierarchical in structure yet cautiously egalitarian at their meetings and banquets, governed by 'charges' or rules constitutionally enforced, yet indifferent to religious affiliation, the Lodges mirrored a larger social and ideological consensus."[20] Connections therefore can be drawn between the Royal Society and the emergence of Freemasonry. The influence of Rosicrucian ideas on Francis Bacon, as revealed by Frances Yates, played a part in forming the Royal Society and the conception of modern science, which in turn bled over into Masonry.

---

18   Smith, *The Book M*, 1:11–12.
19   Leslie, *Poem*, 17.
20   Jacob, *Radical Enlightenment*, quoted in Peterfreund, *William Blake*, 58.

Although there is no direct evidence Newton was a Mason, he certainly studied many of the concepts that came to dominate Freemasonry. He was a member of the Royal Society and spent long hours studying alchemy and drawing diagrams of King Solomon's Temple, practices that informed his iteration of mathematical calculus. He owned a copy of the *Zohar* and reportedly studied the Jewish form of mysticism known as the Kabbalah.[21]

Coudert, meanwhile, has shown the ways in which Leibniz's application of the Kabbalah influenced his thinking when developing another iteration of calculus almost at the same time as Newton. One man studying Solomon's temple, the other Kabbalah, yet both coming up with similar mathematical systems—a clear example of the mutual exchange of religious and scientific ideas at work during this time. Kocku von Stuckrad describes the current academic assessment of Newton:

> Newton's very personification of the "new science" has led to much of his work lying outside the narrow limits of mathematics being forgotten. This impression is slowly beginning to be modified by the attention now focused on his contributions to Hermetism, alchemy and astrology.... Towards the end of the seventeenth century he wrote a commentary on the Hermetic *Tabula Smaragdina*. [...] In his work *Theologiae gentilis origines philosophicae* ("The Philosophical Origins of Pagan Theology"), on which he began to work in 1683, he disclosed that an authentic natural philosophical religion had once existed, which recognised the true structure of the cosmos. He thought this had been formulated in a symbolical form in Pythagoreanism.[22]

21   See von Stuckrad, *Western Esotericism*, 92–93; see also, Manuel, *Religion of Isaac Newton*.

22   von Stuckrad, *Western Esotericism*, 93.

Ezekiel Foxcroft (1633–1674), the scholar who made the first translation of the Rosicrucian text *The Chymical Wedding of Christian Rosenkreutz* in London in 1690, was also known to Newton.[23] Leibniz, of course, went on to attack Newton's theory of gravity as representing an occult force that had no basis in scientific legitimacy.[24] Coudert, however, convincingly reveals that Leibniz had his own occult forces at play in the development of his scientific thought. She writes: "That Locke and Leibniz were both good and loyal friends of Francis Mercury van Helmont (1614–1698), an alchemist and kabbalist, and that both owned and read his kabbalistic works shows how anachronistic our modern categories are when applied to this earlier period."[25]

Desaguliers, whom Newton had appointed as curator of the Royal Society, assisted in the spreading of Newtonian thinking throughout London during the early eighteenth century. The *Principia* was a major work that, despite significant push-back from the Church, played a key role in revealing the mathematical processes of nature. Newton strove to understand the role of divinity in the universe, which he viewed as being active in the calculable natural laws governing reality, which he observed, experimented with, and articulated in his writings. Yet all of his scientific work, alchemy, and biblical studies led him to the conclusion that an omnipotent creator god existed and could be comprehended through an empirical study of nature. His ideas produced harsh reactions from the Church, who viewed this version of the creator god as a challenge to the role of Christ in history.

However, though he kept his beliefs a secret during his life, Newton was in fact a Christian, albeit of a different kind.

23   Fleming, *Dark Enlightenment*, 123.
24   See Janiak, *Stanford Encyclopedia of Philosophy* entry: "Newton's Philosophy."
25   Coudert, *Leibniz and the Kabbalah*, 159.

Audrey Carpenter explains that "it is now known that [Newton] espoused a branch of such anti-trinitarianism known as Arianism, following the teachings of the fourth-century heretic priest, Arius."[26] Arianism, so much as it is presumed to be understood by historians, leverages the role of the Father above that of the Son; hence, by this line of thought it becomes possible to understand some negative responses to Newton's obsession with the mechanics of the Father's creation.

Whatever constituted Newton's view of Christ, it must not be confused with deism, which basically accepts the belief in intelligent design based on its scientific exemplification. Deists proposed that humans were created in the image of God, endowed with rationality, and were thus allowed to live moral lives and to be creators as God was a creator. However, deists rejected the idea of divine intervention and subscribed to the view that God had, in fact, abandoned the human race to its own devices after creating the world.

This was clearly not the view of Newton, as even a cursory examination of his more esoteric beliefs reveals; nor was it the view of Desaguliers, as will be shown; nor is it the favored view of English Freemasonry, as is sometimes supposed. This historical period represents a form of theistic science, infused with everything from philosophy, esotericism, Christianity, and the most stripped down models of mathematical theorizing.

Desaguliers and the Development of the Craft

Freemasonry is about balance, equilibrium, and syncretism, traits characteristic of the early modern era. People, mostly elites, but others too, were grappling with these issues and observing what was taking place. It is clear from the current historical van-

26   Carpenter, *John Theophilus Desaguliers*, 3.

tage point, with the benefit of hindsight, that too much religion can create dogmatism, too much science can create materialism, too much atheism can create obsession with politics. How to harmonize and balance these influences? For some, men like Desaguliers, Martin Folkes (1690–1754), and Alexander Pope (1688–1744), Freemasonry provided the perfect laboratory space in which to work out these intellectual quandaries, as well as during the meetings of the Royal Society—despite the fact that, technically, religion and politics were not allowed to be debated at the meetings of either society. Nevertheless, these spaces acted as mediums for the cultural proliferation of such ideas.

Desaguliers received his education at Christ Church in Oxford and was eventually ordained by the Church of England. Around this time he studied under John Keill (1671–1721), an early Newtonian, and was introduced to natural philosophy, Newton's *Optics*, and Newton's view of creation. Desaguliers was fascinated by what he learned, particularly the experimental approach to natural philosophy and the principles on which the work was founded. After completing his education, he built a reputation for himself lecturing on science (for which he seemed to have more of an active interest than ministering) and delivering university demonstrations on Newtonian principles and water engineering. He also gave private demonstrations to the Royal Society. He married in 1712 and stalked about London in his black clerical dress; more than once, given his variety of interests, he was compared to a conjuror.[27] He became known for performing what has come to be called *public science*; that is to say, science that was demonstrated and taught in the public sphere of coffee houses, associations, and through the print medium, to the so-called mass public. Freemasonry played a huge role in this. In London, this became Desaguliers' famous *A Course of Experimental Philosophy*, which was very popular and

27   Ibid., 37.

was even attended by nobles. The mechanical associations behind astronomy, hydraulics, and optics were illustrated through
experiments for Desaguliers' eager students. He described his
approach to natural philosophy as follows:

> Natural Philosophy is that Science which gives the Rea-
> sons and Causes of the Effects and Changes which naturally
> happens in Bodies.... We ought to call into question all
> such things as have an appearance of falsehood, that by a
> new Examen we may be led to the Truth.[28]

In this, the advancement of his course, Desaguliers was crucial in the spread of Newtonian physics to the wider public, ideas
which were not widely known or comprehended. Such ideas
were traditionally under the province of prestigious universities,
but Desaguliers advanced public education, another enterprise
for which Freemasonry was to become renowned. Desaguliers
made extra income from these public lectures, while in the Royal
Society he exemplified his experiments in accordance with Newton's wishes that there be practical demonstrations on Newtonian principles at their meetings. Desaguliers was realizing the
practical application for these Newtonian principles, not just
their intellectual importance. Thus, his mission became:

> To contemplate the Works of God, to discover Causes from
> their Effects and to make Art and Nature subservient to
> the necessities of life, by a skill in joining proper Causes to
> produce the most useful Effects, is the business of science.[29]

The First Cause for Desaguliers was, of course, God. So it is
unsurprising that he simultaneously pursued a clerical career,

28   Quoted in Berman, *Foundations*, 49.
29   Quoted in Weisberger, et al., *Profiles of Revolutionaries*, 33.

not simply for fiscal gain, and as his popularity grew from his lecture series he was also asked to give various sermons, even to the royal family. He appears to have approached his religious thinking with as much enthusiasm and sincerity as he did his scientific thinking, though he received more notoriety for the former. This is not a casual observation, but deliberately pointed out. A man who was in the position to balance both high-level scientific and religious learning without contradiction was to play a crucial role in the development, success, and spread of early Grand Lodge era Freemasonry, for clearly Desaguliers left his intellectual footprint on the Gentle Craft.

He was appointed rector of several small villages, though he appears to have struggled with his parish work due to frequent travel. However, prominent appointments came as chaplain to the Duke of Chandos, a nobleman with whom he would become closely associated. He also worked for and received patronage from the Duke. He eventually became chaplain to Fredrick, Prince of Wales, and although this was likely an unpaid position, Desaguliers promoted it proudly. He later initiated the Prince into Freemasonry.[30]

Hence, the context in which he was most actively involved the increasing popularity and development of natural philosophy and the mechanical view of nature. This worldview began with Descartes but achieved new heights with Newton. Desaguliers, for his part, worked in experimental physics, but the two contemporaneous natural philosophers maintained a close intellectual relationship.

But what about Freemasonry? The Craft was supposedly reinvented in 1717 after a long history (hard to know how long) of usage within the operative trade guilds of stone workers in England and Scotland, based on Old Charges. However, it is preferable to suggest that it was, at that time, given a public face

---

30   See Berman, *Foundations*, 53; Carpenter, *John Theophilus Desaguliers*, 20–50.

and a centralized institutional organization; this does not go against the narrative of reinvention, for indeed it was made into something new, something spectacular, and Desaguliers and the other men who formed and nurtured the Premier Grand Lodge helped to shape it.

Many of founders of the Royal Society had also been Freemasons, attracted, perhaps, to the emphasis on geometry and the mathematics of architecture. As Newtonian principles gained influence, connections between mathematical laws for constructing cathedrals and the laws for constructing the world developed close parallels. That the Royal Society founders and men like Desaguliers were attracted to this kind of work and desired to build upon it makes sense.

Sources vary as to when exactly Desaguliers became a Mason; it was prior to 1717, for that year he was very active in the fraternity and remained so until his death. He was likely a member of the Rummer and Grapes Lodge, now known as № 4. This lodge, along with three other smaller London lodges, gave birth to the Premier Grand Lodge and Anthony Sayer was elected first Grand Master. Following Sayer, George Payne, a close acquaintance of Desaguliers, was elected. After him, Desaguliers himself was installed as third Grand Maseter. Lodges proliferated around England, with a focus on restoring old traditions and adding a dash of formality to the meetings. By 1720, they spread throughout London and the surrounding countryside. Later, in 1721, the Duke of Montagu was elected Grand Master, inaugurating the custom that all subsequent British Grand Masters be of the royal family or aristocracy.

Desaguliers continued to be active in the Grand Lodge of England, often serving as Deputy Grand Master and offering the necessary element of procedural consistency to degree work and lodge organization. He assisted in the order and regulations of meetings, suggesting procedures by which brothers could communicate harmoniously and not talk over each other. Carpenter reports that one of his proposed bylaws took aim at the use of hazing tricks during the fraternity's initiation rites, which were already coming under public attack.[31] Desaguliers lectured on several occasions against anti-Masons, while at the same time furthering the cause of charity within the lodges.[32] In both endeavors, he found a good deal of success.

In 1723, Desaguliers along with Payne and Anderson produced the *Constitutions* for the sake of directing the fraternity and making the Craft less dependant upon physical manuscripts of the Old Charges. The frontispiece of the 1723 *Constitutions* depicts a wealth of symbolism. Masonic researcher Shawn Eyer, FPS, summarizes the images as follows:

> The scene depicts one Grand Master (the Duke of Montagu) passing the scroll of the Constitutions to the next (Philip, Duke of Wharton). Both Grand Masters are supported by their officers.
>
> In the deep background it is possible to see what is most likely a depiction of the splitting of the Red Sea. This motif—recalling the successful flight of the Israelites from the Egyptians to the promised land—might signify here the survival of a tradition that had been in danger, but was now entering a time of security.
>
> In the foreground of the picture is the Greek word Eureka (Archimedes' famous exclamation *heurêka*, "I have found it!") below a representation of the 47th proposition of Euclid, a symbol which is traditionally associated with Past Masters.
>
> In the sky directly overhead we see the sun approaching its meridian height, allegorized in the figure of Apollo

31   Carpenter, *John Theophilus Desaguliers*, 93.
32   Carpenter, *John Theophilus Desaguliers*, 96–98.

Helios, Greek God of the Sun.

The overall impression of the picture is one of great triumph on many levels: the philosophical and scientific (represented by the 47th problem), organizational and traditional (symbolized by the five noble orders of architecture and illustrated by the cordial transfer of power and the scroll of Constitution between the Grand Masters), and the spiritual and transcendent (the crossing of the Red Sea and the approbation of heaven signified by Apollo). These various elements may strike us today as disjointed, but at the time they were viewed as harmonious.[33]

The "as above, so below" nature of the image hints at the theistic type of science contained in Freemasonry.

Of note in the *Constitutions* is the unique history of the Craft highlighting Adam, Enoch, and Noah as progenitors of Masonry, as well as the progressive charge on God and religion. Despite the (unevidenced) claims of writers that Desaguliers and Anderson were at odds over the contents of the *Constitutions*, the dedication by Desaguliers clearly shows the two Masons' substantial mutual agreement. Desaguliers would ultimately participate in the Masonic services at Anderson's funeral, and serve as a pallbearer.[34]

The mythical history presented in the 1723 version of Anderson's *Constitutions*—most certainly penned by Anderson himself, though not without some direction, at least, from Desaguliers—refers to Masonry as the Royal Art or Noble Science and describes the origin of this alternative scientific method biblically and links it all the way back to Adam. Specifically, the history states that

33   Shawn Eyer, "An Exploration of Themes Expressed in the Frontispieces of Early Masonic Literature, 1723 to 1775." Unpublished paper.

34   See Robbins, "Dr. Anderson," 25.

ADAM, our first Parent, created after the Image of God, *the great Architect of the Universe*, must have had the Liberal Sciences, particularly *Geometry*, written on his Heart; for even since the Fall, we find the Principles of it in the Hearts of his Offspring, and which, in process of time, have been drawn forth into a convenient Method of *Propositions*, by observing the Laws of *Proportion* taken from *Mechanism*: So that as the *Mechanical Arts* gave Occasion to the Learned to reduce the Elements of *Geometry* into Method, this noble Science, thus reduc'd, is the Foundation of all those Arts, (particularly of *Masonry* and *Architecture*) and the Rule by which they are conducted and perform'd.[35]

As should be obvious upon reading this first paragraph, the Newtonian influence of Mechanical Philosophy is evident and even granted divine status. Those who believe that Desaguliers sat in silent opposition to Anderson's mythical account should consider his dedication to the Duke of Montagu, then Grand Master, in the same edition, in which he states:

I need not tell your GRACE what Pains our learned AUTHOR has taken in compiling and digesting this Book from the old *Records*, and how accurately he has compar'd and made every thing agreeable to *History* and *Chronology*, so as to render these NEW CONSTITUTIONS a just and exact Account of *Masonry* from the Beginning of the World to your *Grace's* MASTERSHIP, still preserving all that was truly ancient and authentick in the old ones....[36]

After all, Newton's own articulation of God, expressed in his *Principia*, reads more like Masonic philosophy than it does mod-

35 Anderson, *Constitutions* (1723), 1–2.
36 Anderson, *Constitutions* (1723), [iv–v].

ern science, a characteristic Desaguliers shared and incorporated into the development of the Premier Grand Lodge's Masonic culture. Newton writes:

> This most beautiful System of the Sun, Planets and Comets, could only proceed from the counsel and dominion of an intelligent and powerful being. And if the fixed Stars are the centres of other like systems, these, being form'd by the like wise counsel, must be all subject to the dominion of One; especially, since the light of the fixed Stars is of the same nature with the light of the Sun, and from every system light passes into all the other systems: and lest the systems of the fixed Stars should, by their gravity, fall on each other mutually, he hath placed those Systems at immense distances one from another.
>
> This Being governs all things, not as the soul of the world, but as Lord over all: and on account of his dominion he is wont to be called *Lord God παντοκράτωρ*, or *Universal Ruler*: for *God* is a relative word, and has a respect to servants; and *Deity* is the dominion of God, not over his own body, as those imagine who fancy God to be the soul of the world, but over servants. The Supreme God is a Being eternal, infinite, absolutely perfect.... It is the dominion of a spiritual being which constitutes a God. And from his true dominion it follows, that the true God is a Living, Intelligent, and Powerful Being. [...] He is not Eternity or Infinity, but Eternal and Infinite; he is not Duration or Space, but he endures and is present. [...] Whence also he is all similar, all eye, all ear, all brain, all arm, all power to perceive, to understand, and to act; but in a manner not at all human, in a manner not at all corporeal, in a manner utterly unknown to us.[37]

37   Newton, *Mathematical Principles of Natural Philosophy*, 2:389–91.

Deism vs. Theism and the Third Degree

Desaguliers increased both in talent and career, traveling extensively, and often combining his various interests. In 1721, he made
his famous trip to Edinburgh to assist with the water supply there
and visit one of the oldest lodges, Mary's Chapel Lodge № 1.
In the past, the general theory was that Desaguliers provided
material for the third degree and then introduced it to Scotland
at Edinburgh. This has been shown not to be the case. While,
for a time, Masonic scholars trafficked in this assumption, the
more recent research of Trevor Stewart and others has shown it
to be false.[38] Rather, Desaguliers made several important connections and likely exchanged information about the London
Grand Lodge with his Scottish brethren.

The rest of the theory, more plausible, is that around this period, when the Premier Grand Lodge was formed, nobles interested in hermetic sciences, alchemy, and other mystical doctrines
were admitted into lodges with the operative workers and began
disseminating their ideas. These nobles were also interested in
modern physical science, were deeply philosophical and religious, and they started influencing the lodges and the principles
of Freemasonry. This, after all, was the spirit of the age: a balance
of religion, science, and esotericism. Desaguliers was one such
man, a real product of his time, who tremendously impacted the
intellectual structure of Freemasonry as an institution.

The question arises, apart from this circumstantial evidence
based on a trip to Edinburgh, why had Desaguliers been thought
the progenitor of the third degree? The predominant reason is a
single piece of evidence. In a curious 1910 address on Antediluvian Freemasonry that was delivered by the librarian of the United
Grand Lodge of England, a brother named Henry Sadler, which
he based on certain newspaper cuttings that he found in the

38   See Stewart, *Desaguliers in Edinburgh*.

Grand Lodge archives. An account of Sadler's findings is given in *Early Masonic Pamphlets* (1945), edited by Douglas Knoop, G. P. Jones, and Douglas Hamer. One of the newspaper cuttings, from 1726, regarded antediluvian Masonry and may have alluded to Desaguliers indirectly. The advertisement could be the earliest reference to the third degree, namely "the Widow's Son killed by the Blow of a Beetle."

The newspaper advertisement is for an upcoming lodge meeting, at which a certain "doctor" of the "moderns" will go over some of the most recent Masonic innovations, including "Tape, Jacks, Movable Letters, Blazing Stars, etc., to the great Indignity of the Mop and Pail." It then goes on to claim that the history of the Temple of Solomon, the Middle Chamber, the wages of a Fellow Craft, and the pillars will all be explained, as they are unknown to almost everyone, including the Freemasons. Notable, of course, is that the history of "the Widow's Son kill'd by the Blow of a Beetle" would also be explained, as well as the burial site, and why it is necessary for a "Master" to understand such things. Other references to the third degree are also included.[39]

This represents all the evidence anyone has for Desaguliers as the source of the Hiramic legend. As is self-evident, this is clearly not much. Furthermore, upon reading the text, one cannot help but think of those erroneous though convincing passages found in many a Masonic expose. Such a view also disregards the Graham Manuscript of about 1725, which shares many of the same elements as the Master Mason degree. Found in Yorkshire in the 1930s, the Graham Manuscript describes a legend featuring Noah that is very similar to the culmination of the Hiramic narrative. To accept the associations of Desaguliers with the third degree, as suggested by Sadler's newspaper advertisement, one would have to ignore the existence of the Graham Manuscript. Hence, the claims about Desaguliers and the third degree of Ma-

39   See Knoop & Jones, *Early Masonic Pamphlets*, 192–94.

sonry do not have much traction.

Nevertheless, Desaguliers' Masonic travels took him into many locations for a variety of reasons. He went to Bath on several occasions, and once he even gave a lecture and observed a total eclipse of the sun that was occurring. In Holland, he had been master for the initiation of Francis, Duke of Lorraine, adding to the list of nobles with which Desaguliers was becoming connected. It is likely he Masonically visited France, his homeland, on occasion and fraternized with, among others, the famous French philosopher Montesquieu, who was also a Mason.[40]

Based on a survey of the literature, Carpenter theorizes that Desaguliers took so great an interest in Freemasonry because of his Huguenot background, that since he was an "outsider" he could find support in a society that admitted men of diverse backgrounds. While the present essay does not dispute this, it argues that another main causal factor for Desaguliers' Masonic enthusiasm was the philosophy of the fraternity, which matched his unique eighteenth-century position of clergyman and Newtonian scientist, providing a perfect medium for the transmission of such ideas. This is evidenced by Desaguliers' intellectual cross-connections between Masonry, the Church of England, and active membership in the Royal Society—three seemingly opposing institutions by today's standards. Paul Elliot and Stephen Daniels have argued that Masonry was stimulated by, as well as encouraged, the further study of natural philosophy in the eighteenth century.[41] The Mechanical Philosophy of Newton was so precise in its arrangement that belief in God seemed rational, although some came to adopt deistic attitudes as a result, which became a controversial subject for the Church. And yet, deism was not the primary basis for Freemasonry, nor was it the attitude

40 Carpenter, *John Theophilus Desaguliers*, 106–107.
41 See Elliot & Daniels, "The 'School of True, Useful and Universal Science.'"

of Desaguliers. What is expressed in Masonry is the simultaneous adherence to both the scientific and theistic positions, which was the complicated stance Desaguliers embodied. What Masonry teaches is the science of divinity, a spiritual approach to the study of the natural world. From the evidence, Carpenter draws this same conclusion—that Desaguliers never held deistic views.

Insight into this can be gained by looking at Desaguliers' publishing and literary affairs. He prepared translations from both French and Latin, often for the Royal Society, on a variety of scientific and practical subjects. He oversaw the publication of certain manuscripts for the Royal Society, looking over the work of Cotton Mather's *The Christian Philosopher* (1721), which proposed the integration of science and religion, a subject Desaguliers would have appreciated. In 1728, he penned a poem with Hanoverian implications titled "The Newtonian System of the World: The Best Model of Government," in which he praises Newton and compares mechanical astronomy to ancient philosophy and modern governance. In it, he praises the incomparable Newton as the inheritor and perfector of an ancient science, remarkably like the Noble Science of Freemasonry described in the mythical history of Anderson's *Constitutions*:

> In *Plato's* school none cou'd admitted be,
> Unless instructed in *Geometry*;
> But here it might, (nay must) aside be laid,
> And calculations that distract the Head.
> Thus got his Vogue the Physical Romance,
> Condemn'd in *England*, but believ'd in *France*;
> For the bold *Britons*, who all Tyrants hate,
> In Sciences as well as in the State,
> Examin'd with experimental Eyes,
> The *Vortices* of the *Cartesian* Skies,
> Which try'd by Facts and *mathematick* Test,

Their inconsistent Principles confess'd,
And Jarring Motions hast'ning to inactive Rest.
But *Newton* the unparallel'd, whose Name
No Time will wear out of the Book of Fame,
Cælestial Science has promoted more,
Than all the Sages that have shone before.
Nature compell'd, his piercing Mind, obeys,
And gladly shews him all her secret Ways;
'Gainst *Mathematicks* she has no Defense,
And yields t' experimental Consequence:
His tow'ring Genius, from its certain cause,
Ev'ry Appearance, *a priori* draws,
And shews th' *Almighty Architect's* unalter'd Laws.[42]

Most revealing is Desaguliers' support in 1718 for the preparation and translation of *The Religious Philosopher* by Dutch mathematician Bernard Nieuwentyt (1654–1718), a work which argued
for a religious foundation of science. A letter from Desaguliers to
the translator, John Chamberlayne (1699–1723), was included in
the edition, in which Desaguliers lays out his position concerning natural philosophy in no uncertain terms:

> When an Atheist has the Impudence to call himself a Phi-
> losopher, some well-meaning Persons that have not much
> looked into Nature, are apt to be prejudiced against the
> Study of it; as if the Philosophy and vain Deceit, against
> which the Apostle has warned us, had been the Contem-
> plation of the Works of the Creation....
>
> He that reads Nieuwentyt will easily see that a Phi-
> losopher cannot be an Atheist; and if it were true, that a
> smattering of Physicks will give a proud Man a Tincture of
> Atheism, a deep search of Nature will bring him back to a

42   Desaguliers, "The Newtonian System of the World," 20–22.

Religious Sense of God's Wisdom and Providence...

[Your translation] will perhaps do more good than the Original because in giving us [the Author's] Arguments for Natural Religion, you have omitted those which his too Eager Zeal made him also draw from the Modern Philosophy for Reveal'd Religion; the Weakness of which latter might give those Free-Thinkers occasion to triumph, who would be struck dumb at Convictions from the former.[43]

From such statements, Carpenter concludes:

Many thinking people, either openly or covertly, considered themselves deists and it was to them that this comment presumably referred. Desaguliers' true beliefs are hard to ascertain, but he certainly acknowledged a Universe designed by an all-powerful deity. As an ordained minister of the Anglican faith—in part financially dependent on this—he appeared openly to be a committed Christian. His masonic affiliation encompassed belief in an all-powerful God, but in no particular religion. He apparently kept clear of controversial physico-theological discussions and behaved as a conventional clergyman, but one who concentrated more on practical matters than on his ministry.[44]

Carpenter offers cautious assessment and conjecture regarding the several opposing intellectual activities in which Desaguliers was engaged. However, the author struggles to draw out a solid conclusion, which has been the case with others who have tackled this subject. For a Mason, the simultaneous presence of both physical science and theistic reverence is neither problematic nor discouraged. But to the outsider this double-mindedness might

43   See Nieuwentyt & Chamberlayne, *Religious Philosopher*, [xiii].
44   Carpenter, *John Theophilus Desaguliers*, 201.

be hard to accept: it is even hard to accept for some Masons. Still, careful attention to the teachings of Masonic rituals inculcates exactly this type of simultaneous doubleminded-nature, a worldview stemming from figures like Newton, Pope, and Desaguliers.

Despite indication of Desaguliers offering several Masonic orations through the years, none survive today in manuscript form. The only extant piece of explicitly Masonic writing known to be his is the 203-word dedication in the 1723 *Constitutions*, quoted above. Desaguliers' praise for Anderson's "*History* and *Chronology*," particularly when considered alongside examples of his non-Masonic writing, supports this essay's assertions regarding Desaguliers' spiritual beliefs.

The "Chronology" referred to is the lore of the Craft's mythic roots, also noted above: God creating Adam with "the Liberal Sciences… written on his Heart" through which the generations of Man could observe "the Laws of *Proportion* taken from *Mechanism*."[45] In his dedication, Desaguliers is attesting that such a myth represents the true origin of Freemasonry, thereby allowing the reader a view into Desaguliers' own religious perspectives.

Contra-Enlightenment and the Politics of Freemasonry

It is, perhaps, important to point out that not everyone in the eighteenth century enthusiastically adopted a Newtonian model of the world—for instance Herder, Goethe, Vico, and Leibniz. Also, British poet William Blake fiercely opposed Newton's Mechanical Philosophy, expounding a type of spiritual immanence instead, a soul and spirit of creation that is pre-nature and underlying the material world, and not necessarily calculable via a mechanical interpretation—a Platonic as opposed to an Ar-

45   Anderson, *Constitutions* (1723), 1–2.

istotelean view (this is a general analogy). Blake's anti-Newton worldview can be illustrated briefly in some of his poetry. In "London" (1794), a poem critiquing the effects and influence of Mechanical Philosophy in spurring the Industrial Revolution, he writes:

> I wander thro' each charter'd street,
> Near where the charter'd Thames does flow.
> And mark in every face I meet
> Marks of weakness, marks of woe.
>
> In every cry of every Man,
> In every Infants cry of fear,
> In every voice: in every ban,
> The mind-forg'd manacles I hear.[46]

The "mind-forg'd manacles" referred to the spread of Newtonian principles in London, which for Blake meant the spiritual death of the people to materialism. Blake's opposite pole can be seen in his preface to *Milton: A Poem* (c. 1804):

> Bring me my Bow of burning gold:
> Bring me my arrows of desire:
> Bring me my Spear: O clouds unfold!
> Bring me my Chariot of fire!
>
> I will not cease from Mental Fight,
> Nor shall my sword sleep in my hand:
> Till we have built Jerusalem,
> In England's green & pleasant Land.[47]

46   Blake, "London," lines 1–8.
47   Blake, *Milton: A Poem*, 2.

What was the "mental fight?" Nothing short of Blake's personal psychic battle against adopting the Newtonian worldview himself. In terms of Masonry, Blake absolutely saw the value in some of its aspects and spiritual lessons, yet he remained critical due to its association with Newtonian principles.[48] Blake's artistic rendering of Newton depicts the scientist sitting on a square stone and wielding a compass to draw out geometric lines. Meanwhile, Blake was preoccupied with his own ideas about rebuilding the Temple as the establishment of a New Jerusalem in England, a project that finds currency in Masonic literature. And yet, Blake felt Masonry was going about it in the wrong way and strove to correct it. Stuart Peterfreund argues that Blake's Masonic corrections "suggest that, for him, the cardinal sin of Freemasonry is its failure, in the midst of much activity that Blake accounted instructive and worthwhile, to identify as human the originary creative act."[49] In short, Blake saw the human body as the form divine, from which all true creation emanated, and therefore ought to be studied and apprehended in advance of the apparent natural laws of the physical world.

Blake's hostility to Newtonian philosophy, and consequently to Freemasonry, all of which is copiously described by Peterfreund in his book *William Blake in a Newtonian World* (1998) brings us to the work of Masonic scholar Ric Berman. Berman's book, *The Foundations of Modern Freemasonry: The Grand Architects* (2015), argues that the gradualist narrative of writers like John Hamill and others, stating that Freemasonry teleologically developed from the old stonemason guilds into modern English Freemasonry, is unfounded. Indeed, Stevenson has shown that if purely "operative" lodges ever did exist at all in Scotland, they were certainly more than mere trade associations and likely contained esoteric content in the form of the Mason's Word and

48 See primarily the work of Marsha Keith Schuchard here.
49 Peterfreund, *William Blake*, 63.

the Master's Part.[50] Berman lays out his intriguing argument that "Desaguliers and others within the upper circles of English Grand Lodge appropriated Freemasonry such that it became a vehicle for the expression and transmission of their ideas and ideals [which] has significant implications for not only the history of Freemasonry but also for any analysis of contemporary culture."[51]

This essay is in agreement with Berman's thesis, adding to his conclusion by demonstrating that the intense resistance of Blake to Newton's Mechanical Philosophy and modern English Freemasonry reveals that something much like Berman describes was absolutely taking place. However, Berman's assumption that science and politics are the only real causal factors at play, while spiritual interests are of no consequence, does not do justice to the data. To reiterate, this essay contends that Freemasonry as it developed in the first part of the eighteenth century appealed to men like Desaguliers and his associates because it provided the perfect system for balancing seemingly contradictory positions, that of being pro-science as well as pro-religion.

Furthermore, scholars of esotericism have shown that the modern categorization of religion, magic, and science into reified territories of knowledge simply was not how things were done in the early modern period. Equally as important as the influence of science, economics, and politics on Freemasonry, the spiritual and esoteric aspirations of religion were just as influential, evidenced by the concept of the Craft as a Royal Art or Noble Science—which is to say, a *spiritual science*. To what extent this scientific methodology was already present in Freemasonry under the Old Charges—whether conceptually or practically—is a question requiring analysis.

Delving deeper into Berman's insightful observations, the ques-

50   See Stevenson, *The Origins of Freemasonry*, 1–12.
51   Berman, *Foundations*, 6.

tion he sets out to answer is that, if the transitional theory of the development of Freemasonry is incorrect, then how to account for the broader emergence and spread of Speculative Freemasonry? His answer is that Desaguliers and his associates utilized the existing fraternity, which had fallen into relative disuse, and reinvented it to spread their political and intellectual agenda. The Mechanical Philosophy of Newton, which Desaguliers espoused, almost certainty made its way into modern Freemasonry. However, with Newtonian philosophy came the occult, alchemical, and esoteric underpinnings that, as scholars now know, Newton secretly utilized in the development of his scientific system. Desaguliers and others brought this type of philosophy into Freemasonry; indeed, they may have chosen the fraternity precisely because it lent itself to such types of knowledge, thereby allowing these early Grand Lodge era Masons to carry out their own intentions.

When Berman writes that Desaguliers "altered English Freemasonry fundamentally," it must be remembered that such an alteration included all the above-mentioned secret interests of Isaac Newton, as well as the overall spiritual situation of the early modern period more generally. In the early 1720s, Desaguliers was very active and more and more members of the nobility and aristocracy were becoming Masons. Berman identifies this as a time when the fraternity was becoming "fashionable." What was also fashionable, as has been mentioned, was to include theistic and scientific concepts together within the same intellectual paradigm without perceived contradiction, producing a variant pedagogy and a more holistic form of knowledge about the world. This point cannot be stressed enough, since the same holistic view is the driving force in Freemasonry.

For the most part, Berman paints the picture of a Desaguliers who, as a Huguenot émigré, remains relatively as an outsider within British high society, utilizing Freemasonry, the Royal Society, and his clerical position mainly to promote himself and remain gainfully employed. While he does draw some attention to Desaguliers' religious inclinations through discussions of Latitudinarianism—a sort of antinomian group of seventeenth-century theologians—in the end, following Larry Stewart, he does not lend them much weight. Further, based on correspondence between Desaguliers and the Duke of Chandos, Berman draws a conclusion that Desaguliers did not "favor" his clerical work at all and did it for financial and social maneuvering.[52]

This depiction of Desaguliers should be resisted because it fails to take into account his spiritual ideas concerning natural philosophy, which he articulated so clearly in his letter to the translator of *The Religious Philosopher*. That document reveals how Desaguliers' doubleminded-position of theism plus Newtonian science agrees with the Masonic philosophy inculcated in the trigradal system. The importance of this similarity must not be slighted or overlooked. After all, Berman himself describes the "re-engineering" of Masonry as a process that Desaguliers and his associates engaged in, transforming it, yes, into a politically viable institution, but also into to a new form of pedagogy which trafficked in the balancing of science and religion. Desaguliers could have as easily been involved in Freemasonry for these reasons, as for personal promotive reasons. In the end, it had to have been a mixture of both.

Conclusion: Esotericism and the Craft

Berman does include sections of his book exploring, predominantly, the draw of the religious pluralism of the fraternity; however, he does not explore the initiatory aspects of spiritual development offered by the degrees, esoteric Biblical symbolism, and mystery religion elements as they are presented in ritual

52   Ibid., 54.

form. If these elements are extraneous, a kind of excess goofing off among the members to pass the time, while focusing on the real work—to achieve political leverage—then how can researchers explain the complex pedagogical nature of these initiations? Why couldn't these spiritual aspects be included among the primary motives for interest in the fraternity by men like Desaguliers, Payne, Folkes, and others?

To be sure, there is not sufficient material evidence to answer this question satisfactorily. Such questions have, and still haunt Freemasonry. Thus, it is useful to conclude this examination of the intellectual history surrounding early modern Freemasonry with a look into the spiritual initiatory aspects present in the degrees, which are there because they are, in fact, a systemic part of the Craft.

What exactly is a degree? According to Masonic writer Henry W. Coil, FPS:

> By a degree in Freemasonry we mean some esoteric ceremony, no matter how brief, which advances the member or candidate to a higher rank, including the communication to him of particular distinguishing words, signs, grips, tokens or other esoteric matter, those of each degree being denied to members of lower degrees as firmly as they are denied to complete strangers.[53]

There are several major intellectual aspects of the Masonic degrees worthy of highlighting. Each, no matter how they came to be incorporated into the system—whether from the Old Charges, from the influence of Masons like Desaguliers and others, or from "time immemorial"—still impact the system of Freemasonry in the profoundest and strongest way. Without them, the fraternity would cease to be recognizable as Masonry and

---

53   Coil, *Encyclopedia*, 159.

would devolve into a mere social club, drinking/eating society, or labor association. These aspects are philosophy, initiation, mysticism, and science.

In the ancient world, Greek philosophy was often caught up with the so-called mystery religions and their peculiar doctrines and initiatory rites. Those who underwent the trials and circumstances of the mystery religions were philosophers but also initiates, who met at sacred places such as Plato's "Grove of Academia" to discuss the mysteries of nature. This sacred knowledge, which today is simply referred to as philosophy, meaning "love of wisdom," became accessible to the initiates only once they had gone through certain tests. All mystery religions had ceremonies, mystery plays, and degrees of initiation in which the candidate was blindfolded and led by a guide into the temple. There, in ritual form, the candidate was shown the *hiera*, or "sacred objects," by the Hierophant, a priestly functionary who was referred to as the "shower of sacred things." Then the candidate was presented the *deiknymena*, or "things shown," and told the *legomena* or "things said." They passed through consecutive degrees of initiation, each with their own set of working tools and bearing such degree titles as Raven, Bride, Soldier, Lion, Persian, Sun-Runner, and Father, for instance, in the Mithraic mystery religion.[54]

Why did the ancients develop such practices? The Greek philosophers held that the soul (or souls) of a human being remained trapped inside the physical body as a type of prison. Only specific rites and initiations were thought to free the soul and lead it to wider visions and a more definite sense of its destiny. According to Plato, real philosophy should be a preparation for death. The true philosopher should have no fear of death. Plato, as well as other Greek thinkers, insisted that initiation was largely concerned with the significance of death, a message that is reiterated in the Masonic lessons.

54   See Clauss, *Roman Cult of Mithras.*

The clearest example of this is found in the culmination of the Master Mason degree, as it was hinted at in the c. 1726 advertisement noted above. Within the ritual narrative, the attainment of the Third Degree could only occur following the "Blow of a Beetle." The 1730 exposure first detailing this Degree instructs that the reward for this death were the "Master-Jewels":

> Q. What are the Master-Jewels?
> A. The Porch, Dormer and Square Pavement.
> Q. Explain them.
> A. The Porch the Entring into the *Sanctum Sanctorum*, the Dormer the Windows or Lights within, the Square Pavement the Ground Flooring.[55]

The death of the Third Degree resulted in access to a holier, more enlightened state of being. But even predating the evidence of that particular point in Masonic ritual, death was still a focus. In these earlier examples, death was a sentence for those deemed unworthy. One of the earliest known ritual manuscripts of the Grand Lodge era is the Kevan MS, dated to c. 1720. It demonstrates that during the preparation, the candidate for the degree was made to feel imperiled, after being "Sufficiently frightned w^{T} a thousand Grimasses & posturs." He is then made to swear that if he violates his oath—i.e., demonstrates his unworthiness—he will offer his "throate...be Cut."[56] In either situation, death was inevitable; the remaining question was would one die in disgrace, or would one pass onto a higher state of being.

The study of philosophy and initiation—in other words, the continual contemplation of death—was intended to produce a form of mysticism or recognition of the internal divine. Mysticism as a term stems from the word Greek μύω, meaning "to

55   Pritchard, *Masonry Dissected*, 29.
56   Kevan MS. In Carr & Jones, *Early Masonic Catechisms*, 41.

close." In ancient Greece and Rome, mystical simply referred to secret rituals and religious initiation. As Christianity developed, the term came to include both an esoteric hermeneutics applied to sacred scripture, and later as a personal experience of the divine. Mystics are usually theists, with the aim of transforming their human situation, whether personally or collectively, and they include a wide range of ideas and practices.

A prime example is the German Christian mystic and theologian Jakob Böhme (1575–1624), whose spiritual system centered on gaining more light, freeing the soul from darkness and liberating it through the accumulation of mystical illumination. His complex engravings share many of the emblematic designs of Freemasonry, such as the All-Seeing Eye, the Tetragrammaton inside the golden triangle, King Solomon's Temple, the stone cube, Jacob's Ladder, and more. Even St. Augustine developed a complex system of ascension from the mundane to the divine through a continual bestowal of intellectual light from the Creator upon the aspirant. The characteristic of any mystical practice—which Freemasonry shares systemically—centers on experience vs. intellect, heart vs. mind, re-absorption into the One or union with God through a flowing light, and finally on a personal transformation.

But Freemasonry also contains a heavy dose of natural philosophy, an emphasis on science, which is to say the use of reason to comprehend matter. The essence of such an approach to the natural world can be traced back to texts like the *Magia Naturalis* written by Giambattista della Porta and first published in Naples in 1558. This work stressed the underlying order of the world that could be discerned in the Book of Nature. Natural philosophers like Newton postulated two books: the Bible and the Book of Nature. This view is what led Robert Boyle (1627–1691), Newton's influential predecessor, to famously conclude that natural philosophers were the real priests because they could read the

Book of Nature.

This new scientific method placed more importance on empirical investigations of the natural world than ever before in history. An example of this is the Flammarion engraving, which was delineated by an unknown artist and first appeared in Camille Flammarion's 1888 book *L'atmosphère: Météorologie Populaire*. This image depicts a man with a staff, dressed in something close to a monkish habit, kneeling while poking his head through the firmament to glimpse beyond the star-studded canopy into spaces beyond. What he sees there are the cogs, gears, and wheels of creation, the often invisible yet empirically calculable mechanisms that control and create the universe. A caption below reads: "A missionary of the Middle Ages recounted that he found the point where the heaven and the Earth touch...."[57] The degrees of Freemasonry, with their focus on geometry, architecture, and the application of math within the useful arts and broader natural world, leads candidates to a similar view of the cosmos, as that of the traveler in the Flammarion engraving.

By acknowledging the presence of these major aspects in the degrees of Freemasonry, and accepting them as a systemic part of the whole, Masons can appreciate the complex nature of the Craft, which the founders of the Grand Lodge of England, in particular Desaguliers, helped to establish. The special space that modern Masonic lodges facilitate is one of a harmonious relationship between theism and science. This essay has endeavored to illustrate Desaguliers crucial role in setting Masonry along this unique course. Three hundred years after its emergence, the Premier Grand Lodge and Desaguliers' legacy still inform the rich Masonic studies of the Craft.

---

57   Camille Flammarion, *L'atmosphère: Météorologie Populaire*, 163.

Bibliography

Acker, Julius William. *Strange Altars: A Scriptural Appraisal of the Lodge.* Saint Louis, Missouri: Concordia House, 1959.

Anderson, James. *The Constitutions of the Free-Masons.* London: William Hunter, 1723.

—————. *The New Book of Constitutions of the Antient and Honourable Fraternity of Free and Accepted Masons, Containing Their History, Charges, Regulations, &c.* London: Richard Chandler, 1738.

Berman, Ric. *The Foundations of Modern Freemasonry: The Grand Architects: Political Change and the Scientific Enlightenment, 1714–1740.* Rev. second edition. Brighton: Sussex Academic, 2015.

Bogdan, Henrik, & Snoek, Joannes Augustinus Maria. *Handbook of Freemasonry.* Leiden: Brill, 2014.

Carpenter, Audrey T. *John Theophilus Desaguliers: A Natural Philosopher, Engineer and Freemason in Newtonian England.* London: Continuum, 2011.

Carr, Harry & G.P. Jones, Eds. *Early Masonic Catechisms.* London: Quatuor Coronati, 1975.

Clauss, Manfred, & Gordon, Richard. *The Roman Cult of Mithras: The God and His Mysteries.* New York: Routledge, 2001.

Coil, Henry Wilson. *Coil's Masonic Encyclopedia.* New York: Macoy Pub. & Masonic Supply, 1961.

Henry W. Coil Library and Museum of Freemasonry. "Moderns Grand Lodge Constitutions." *http://www.masonicheritage.org/exhibits/moderns.html.* Accessed: April 30, 2017.

Coudert, Allison. *Leibniz and the Kabbalah.* Dordrecht: Springer, 2011.

—————. *Religion, Magic, and Science in Early Modern Europe and America.* Santa Barbara, Calif.: Praeger, 2011.

Desaguliers, John Theophilus. *The Newtonian System of the World, the Best Model of Government: An Allegorical Poem.* London: Printed by A. Campbell, for J. Roberts, 1728.

Dyer, Colin F. W. *William Preston and His Work.* Shepperton, UK: Lewis Masonic, 1987.

Elliott, P. & Daniels, S. "The 'School of True, Useful and Universal Science'? Freemasonry, Natural Philosophy and Scientific Culture in Eighteenth Century England." *British Journal for the History of Science* 39(2006): 207–30.

Eyer, Shawn. "An Exploration of Themes Expressed in the Frontispieces of Early Masonic Literature, 1723 to 1775." Unpublished paper.

Flammarion, Camille. *L'atmosphère: Météorologie Populaire*. Paris: Hachette, 1888.

Fleming, John V. *The Dark Side of the Enlightenment: Wizards, Alchemists, and Spiritual Seekers in the Age of Reason*. New York: W.W. Norton & Co., 2013.

Gould, Robert. *Gould's History of Freemasonry Throughout the World*. New York: Charles Scribner's Sons, 1936.

Hall, A. Rupert, *Philosophers at War: The Quarrel Between Newton and Leibniz*. Cambridge: Cambridge University Press, 1980.

Harland-Jacobs, Jessica L. *Builders of Empire: Freemasons and British Imperialism, 1717–1927*. Chapel Hill: University of North Carolina Press, 2013.

de Hoyos, Arturo. *Freemasonry in Context: History, Ritual, Controversy*. Lanham, Md.: Lexington, 2004.

Jacob, Margaret C. *The Radical Enlightenment: Pantheists, Freemasons and Republicans*. London: George Allen & Unwin, 1981.

Janiak, Andrew. "Newton's Philosophy." *Stanford Encyclopedia of Philosophy*. Stanford University, 13 Oct. 2006. Web. 29 Apr. 2017.

Jones, Bernard Edward, Harry Carr, & Arthur R. Hewitt. *Freemasons' Book of the Royal Arch*. London: Harrap, 1972.

Katz, Jacob, & Oschry, Leonard. *Jews and Freemasons in Europe 1723–1939*. Cambridge, Ma.: Harvard University Press, 1970.

Knoop, Douglas, & Hamer, Douglas. *Early Masonic Pamphlets*. Reprinted and Edited by D. Knoop, G.P. Jones, & Douglas Hamer. Manchester: Manchester University Press, 1945.

Knoop, Douglas, & G.P. Jones. "Freemasonry and the Idea of Natural

Religion." *Ars Quatuor Coronatorum* 56 (1946), 38–43.

Lemay, Joseph A., & Aldridge, Alfred Owen. *Deism, Masonry, and the Enlightenment: Essays Honoring Alfred Owen Aldridge.* Newark: University of Delaware, 1987.

Manuel, Frank Edward. *The Religion of Isaac Newton: The Fremantle Lectures 1973.* Oxford: Clarendon, 1974.

Millar, Angel. *The Crescent and the Compass: Islam, Freemasonry, Esotericism, and Revolution in the Modern Age.* Melbourne, Australia: Numen, 2015.

Newton, Isaac. *The Mathematical Principles of Natural Philosophy.* London: Benjmin Motte, 1729.

————. *The Principia: Mathematical Principles of Natural Philosophy.* Berkeley, Calif.: University of California Press, 1999.

Nieuwentyt, Bernard, & Chamberlayne, John. *The Religious Philosopher, Or, The Right Use of Contemplating the Works of the Creator.* London: J. Senex, 1718.

Peterfreund, Stuart. *William Blake in a Newtonian World: Essays on Literature as Art and Science.* Norman: University of Oklahoma, 1998.

Péter, Róbert. "General Introduction." In Péter, Róbert & Révauger, Cécile, Eds. *British Freemasonry, 1717–1813. Volume One: Institutions.* London: Routledge, Taylor & Francis Group, 2016.

Preston, William. *Illustrations of Masonry.* London: J. Wilkie, 1775.

Ramsay, Michael. *Oration.* In Gould, *Gould's History of Freemasonry Throughout the World.* New York: Charles Scribner's Sons, 1936: 3:10–15.

Robbins, Alfred F. "Dr. Anderson of the 'Constitutions.'" *Ars Quatuor Coronatorum* 23(1910): 6–28.

Saler, Michael. "Modernity and Enchantment: A Historiographic Review," *The American Historical Review* 111(2006): 692–716.

Schuchard, Marsha Keith. *Restoring the Temple of Vision: Cabalistic Freemasonry and Stuart Culture.* Leiden: Brill, 2002.

————. *Why Mrs Blake Cried.* London: Century, 2006.

Stevenson, David. *The Origins of Freemasonry.* Cambridge: Cambridge

University Press, 1988.

Stewart, Trevor. *Desaguliers in Edinburgh 1721*. Sunderland, UK: Septentrione Books, 2007.

von Stuckrad, Kocku. *Western Esotericism: A Brief History of Secret Knowledge*. Durham, UK: Acumen, 2013.

Weisberger, Richard William, Dennis P. Hupchick, & David L. Anderson. *Profiles of Revolutionaries in Atlantic History, 1700–1850*. Boulder: Social Science Monographs, 2007.

Weisberger, Richard William. "John Theophilus Desaguliers: A Natural Philosopher, Engineer and Freemason in Newtonian England." *The Social Science Journal* 51(2014): 696–97.

———. *Speculative Freemasonry and the Enlightenment: A Study of the Craft in London, Paris, Prague, and Vienna*. Boulder: East European Monographs, 1993.

Wigelsworth, Jeffrey R. *Deism in Enlightenment England: Theology, Politics, and Newtonian Public Science*. Manchester: Manchester University Press, 2009.

Assessing Authentic Lodge Culture

Moving Beyond the Tavern Myth

CHRISTOPHER B. MURPHY

A POPULAR THEORY holds that early Grand Lodge era Freemasonry lacked in any significant meaning or purpose. It holds that early Lodges espoused no philosophy beyond, perhaps, a basic moral code. It holds that these Masons gathered as simple drinking clubs, supper clubs, or mutual aid societies. It holds that the "mysteries" merely refer to a stonemason's vocational knowledge, and that Masonic "secrets" are just the modes of recognition, or worse, that *the only secret is there are no secrets*. The rationale behind this perception often includes an explanation pointing to the location of these early Lodges: the tavern. The theory follows that because Freemasons gathered in such establishments, their Communications must have centered on indulgence and camaraderie, rather than on spiritual, philosophical, or intellectual advancements. To be clear, this author does not dispute that early Lodges met in taverns; they certainly did. Taverns were the civic and social centers of many European and Colonial cities and villages, and it is entirely in keeping with the time that Freemasons would have met in such establishments. In fact, the literature of the era, and the records kept by the Fraternity itself, proves as much. But it is crucial to acknowledge that the setting does not determine the work; in other words, meeting in taverns does not *ipso facto* make Masonic labors frivolous.

Based on its root, this author has dubbed this misperception the "Tavern Myth."[1] But rather than challenging the location of early Lodges, the Tavern Myth should be understood as a term representing the overarching themes that minimize and trivialize the practice and self-concept of early eighteenth century Freemasons; it is a catch-all term that encompasses any assertion that Freemasonry was held by its members to be a trifling, silly, or otherwise unimportant undertaking. It should also be noted, that this very issue did not escape the attention of early members of the society. For instance, in 1768, it prompted Freemason James Galloway to comment, "Besides! our meeting at the houses of publicans, gives us the air of a *Bacchanalian* society, instead of that appearance of gravity and wisdom, which our order justly requires."[2] The fact that this letter inspired the building of the first Freemasons Hall in London supports how prevalent and destructive Freemasons of the time found the Tavern Myth.

1   Christopher B. Murphy, "The Tavern Myth: Reassessing the Culture of Early Grand Lodge Era Freemasonry." *Philalethes: The Journal of Masonic Research and Letters* 68 (2015): 50–61.

2   Letter from Freemason James Galloway to Freemason Wellins Calcott, October 01, 1768. In Calcott, *Candid Disquisition*, 118. A.C.F. Jackson makes an interesting observation, contrasting English and French Lodges of the eighteenth century, "Though inns were normal meeting places for lodges in England, they were not part of the inn and would move if they wished. In France, however, the inn-keeper could hold the warrant of the lodge, often being its master for life. Such a master was not troubled by traditions nor the quality of his initiates when his main object would be to attract custom." See Jackson, *English Masonic Exposures*, 4.

The most reliable means of examining the authentic culture of early Freemasonry is to consult the primary documents from that era. Within these surviving writing, various themes emerge which speak directly to early Masonic *praxis* and *pistis*, their actions and beliefs. These overwhelmingly speak in opposition to the assertions of the Tavern Myth. With regard to *What Masons Did*, the evidence speaks to expectations of decorum and of temperance, as well as a clear delineation between the serious work of the Lodge and the post-Communication feasts and celebrations. With regard to *What Masons Believed*, the evidence speaks to men seriously engaging with their Craft, and viewing themselves as stewards of a divinely-sourced and truly ancient Institution.

Praxis

The thrust of the Tavern Myth states that Masonic assemblies were held chiefly for drinking and feasting. Because these were times of merriment, the mood within these Lodges must have been raucous, albeit perhaps structured to a certain degree by simplistic ritual. There is very little, however, within Masonic writing of the time to support this assertion. On the contrary: the vast majority of early Masonic literature speaks to clearly defined expectations of proper decorum when in Lodge assembled. This included the essential requirement of temperance among Freemasons, and a clear delineation between the serious work of the Lodge and the celebrations that followed.

"In the LODGE while CONSTITUTED"

Various Charges outlining the proper behavior for Masons date at least as far back as the fourteenth-century, in what are known as the "Old Charges" or "Gothic Constitutions." Recognized as the oldest of these Masonic documents, the Regius Poem (c. 1425) comprises, in part, fifteen articles and fifteen points of conduct. This form of instruction extended through all of the known Old Charges, and later appeared in the governing documents of the most viable and influential of the English-speaking Grand Lodges.

In 1723, the founding philosophical document of the Grand Lodge era was published, *The Constitutions of the Free-Masons*. Compiled by James Anderson, and modeled after the Old Charges, this document was divided into two main parts: the "Traditional History" of the Craft, and various rules of conduct, presented as Charges. In these rules, Anderson wrote:

> VI. *Of* BEHAVIOUR, viz.
> 1. *In the* Lodge *while constituted.*
> You are not to hold private Committees, or separate Conversation, without Leave from the *Master*, nor to talk of any thing impertinent or unseemly, nor interrupt the *Master* or *Wardens*, or any Brother speaking to the *Master*; Nor behave yourself ludicrously or jestingly while the *Lodge* is engaged in what is serious and solemn; nor use any unbecoming Language upon any Pretence whatsoever; but to pay due Reverence to your *Master, Wardens*, and *Fellows*, and put them to worship.[3]

There are several important ideas presented in this Charge. Foremost is the recognition that the labors of the Lodge did, indeed, include those things that were "serious and solemn." Additionally, during such times, Brethren were to act with due decorum and due respect. There is the admonition inherent in this

3   Anderson, *Constitutions of the Freemasons* (1723), 53–54.

Charge that chatting, silliness, and general irreverence undercut the important work of the Lodge. Similarly, acting in such unbecoming ways was disrespectful to the Brethren there assembled. As such, Brethren were directed to avoid such behavior.

There is some evidence that expectations of solemnity met with the approbation of other influential Freemasons of the period. The 1724 bylaws of the Lodge in the Maid's Head in Norwich, for example, notes that such expectations were "recommended by our Worthy Brother Dr. Desaguliers."[4] Of course, with that said, it hardly needs to be pointed out that Anderson's *Constitutions* were approved by the Grand Lodge; we know, therefore, that the Charges set forth within met with the approbation of the rulers of the Craft.

As a mark of the importance of Anderson's work, multiple subsequent books of constitutions were based on his words. In 1730, Grand Secretary John Pennell published his *Constitutions* for the Grand Lodge of Ireland,[5] following the same pattern. In 1734, Benjamin Franklin reprinted Anderson's work "for the Use of the Brethren in NORTH-AMERICA."[6] In 1738, Anderson published his second edition of the *Constitutions*,[7] which was later adopted by the Grand Lodge of Ireland. In 1740, the Grand Lodge of Scotland put into the use William Smith's 1735 *Pocket Companion for Free-Masons*.[8] And thus, in the first twenty-three years of the Grand Lodge era, England, Ireland, Scotland, and the colonies of North America all had governing documents containing Charges identical, or nearly so, to those written by

4   Knoop & Jones, *A Short History*, 96.

5   Pennell, *Constitutions of the Free Masons*.

6   James Anderson, *Constitutions of the Freemasons* (Philadelphia: Benjamin Franklin, 1734), [i].

7   Anderson, *New Book of Constitutions*.

8   Smith, *Pocket Companion*. For its use by the Grand Lodge of Scotland, see Chetwode Crawley, "Old Charges," 48.

Anderson.[9] These officially-sanctioned documents were joined by several other books of constitutions and pocket companions, also containing charges.

Smith's *Pocket Companion*, for instance, contains a charge to be read to newly admitted Brethren. This charge specifies that the observance of proper decorum is to ensure that the "Beauty and Harmony" of the Lodge is not "disturbed or broke."[10] In other words, proper behavior was the norm, and to eschew such expectations of decorum would mean to stand out in opposition to the rest of the Brethren therein assembled.

For context, consider the 1738 letter from "Brother EUCLID." In its description of early lodge culture, the letter describes a self-reinforcing system of lofty purposes both supporting and inspiring proper decorum:

> Indeed, the *antient Lodges* were so many Schools or *Academies* for teaching and improving the *Art* of *Designing*, especially *Architecture*; and the present *Lodges* are often employ'd that Way in *Lodge-Hours*, or else in other agreeable Conversation, tho' without Politicks or Party Causes; and none of them are ill employ'd, have no Transactions unworthy of an honest Man or a Gentleman, no personal Piques, no Quarrels, no Cursing and Swearing, no cruel Mockings, no obscene Talk, nor ill Manners: For the *noble* and eminent *Brethren* are affable to the *Meanest*; and *These* are duly respected to their Betters in *Harmony* and *Proportion*; and tho' on the *Level*, yet always within *Compass*, and according to the *Square* and *Plumb*.[11]

9   Smith and Franklin use Anderson's exact phrasing; Pennell omits "and put them to worship"; see Crawley, "Old Charges," 53.
10 Smith, *Pocket Companion*, 44.
11 Anderson, *New Book of Constitutions*, 228.

These rules of conduct survived throughout the 1700s, and were reiterated throughout the decades. In addition to the appearances in various *Constitutions*, these expectations are also found in the ritual exposures of the era. For instance, in the 1760 exposure of the Antients' ritual, *Three Distinct Knocks*, the Master declares:

> This Lodge is open, in the name of God and holy St. *John*, forbidding all cursing and swearing, whispering, and all profane Discourse whatsoever ....[12]

The Masters of Moderns' lodges set the Craft to work in an identical manner, as captured in the 1762 exposure *Jachin and Boaz*.[13]

In his 1772 *Illustrations of Masonry*, William Preston published two reminders of proper lodge conduct. He reprinted the 1769 charge which affirmed that "In all regular meetings of the fraternity [Brethren are] to behave with due order and decorum."[14] He also printed the comments he offered at his grand Masonic Gala:

> No private committees are to be allowed, or separate conversations encouraged, the Master and the Wardens are not to be interrupted, or any brother speaking to the Master, but the brethren are to observe due decorum, and under no pretence to use any unbecoming language, but pay proper deference and respect to the presiding officers.[15]

The Tavern Myth holds that revelry—not solemnity—typified Masonic Lodges; yet these examples show that the expectation

---

12   W___O___V____n, *Three Distinct Knocks*, 65.
13   Anon, *Jachin and Boaz*, 6.
14   Preston, *Illustrations*, 196.
15   Ibid., 5–6.

was for far more reverent conduct. To be sure, there were certainly some Masons, or perhaps entire lodges of Masons who acted "ludicrously or jestingly" and who said things "impertinent or unseemly." It must be acknowledged, however, that by doing so, those Brethren were violating the rules established by their respective Grand Lodges.

"...the shameful Sin of Drunkenness"

A core concept of the Tavern Myth is the presumption that drunkenness amongst Masons was the norm. This conception of early Freemasonry is expressed in many forms, and it tends to be exaggerated the further it descends from the academic narrative. For instance, influenced by scholarly writings emphasizing the Tavern Myth, the Masonic layman Howard Stewart wrote that early Grand Lodge era Masonry was "a time of almost total intemperance.... To have called the average Mason of that period a speculative Mason would have necessitated extending the phrase 'a peculiar system of morality' to include lewdness and drunkenness."[16]

As stated above, the narrow view of early Freemasonry seems to look no further than the physical location of Lodge meetings. Within the perspective of the Tavern Myth, it seems inconceivable that Masons could meet in the presence of alcohol, and still exercise temperance—this despite clear evidence to the contrary.

As noted above, the Charges for Freemasons of the Grand Lodge era were derived from older, pre–1717 texts known as the Old Charges. These Old Charges shared a common format, and are generally discernable from the work of Anderson and those who followed. There is one early Grand Lodge era book of con-

---

16   Stewart, "Speculari—Speculatus—Speculativus." Quoted in Eyer, "And Hinder Not Music," 110.

stitutions that pre-dates Anderson, and essentially bridges the gap between these Old Charges and the 1723 *Constitutions*. The full title of this 1722 pamphlet is *The Old Constitutions belonging to the Antient and Honourable SOCIETY of Free and Accepted MASONS*, but is often referred to in the scholarship as Roberts' *Constitutions*, after its publisher. It offers the following charge given to Entered Apprentices:

> You shall not haunt, or frequent any Taverns or Ale-houses, or so much as go into any of them, except it be upon your Master or your Dame, their or any of their Affairs, or with their or the one of their Consents.[17]

Roberts' *Constitutions* is much closer to the Operative Charges than to the far more Speculative Charges of Anderson. However, Roberts should also be considered for its Speculative application, and be recognized as the first of such charges offered in the Grand Lodge era. Freemasons were therefore dutybound to avoid what Provincial Grand Master Isaac Head would call the "shameful Sin of Drunkenness."[18] Edward Oakley was very cognizant of this Masonic duty, and cautioned his Brethren to be mindful of prospective members:

> I therefore, according to my Duty, forewarn you to admit, or even to recommend to be initiated Masons, such as are Wine-Bibbers or Drunkards...all which Principles and Practices tend to the Destruction of Morality, a Burden to Civil Government, notoriously scandalous, and entirely repugnant to the Sacred Order and Constitutions of Free and Accepted Masons.[19]

17   Roberts, *Old Constitutions*, unnumbered.
18   Head, "Charge." In Head, *Confutation*, 75.
19   Oakley, "Speech." In Cole, *Antient Constitutions*, 28–29.

James Hoey seemed to be speaking in direct opposition to the Tavern Myth when he declared that the rumors of widespread drunkenness among Masons were "notoriously false." He continued:

> ...it is an established law in every lodge, that no Mason shall exceed a certain quantity of liquor, which is likewise fixed at a standard much within the bounds of moderation. The pleasures of the flowing bowl are the most inconsiderable gratifications indulged in the society of Masons, whose refined tastes direct them to nobler enjoyments, the social repast of the soul, the contemplation of wisdom, and the animating precepts of virtue.[20]

Even a decade earlier, when Freemasons engaged in such indulgence, it was met with disdain. For instance, in his famed 1726 speech before the Grand Lodge of York, Freemason Francis Drake lamented the "pernicious Custom of drinking too deep" which he had seen take place "in our own Most Amicable Brotherhood of *Free-Masons*."[21]

The "nobler enjoyments" Hoey speaks of were among the central themes of the Masonic oration offered in 1737 by the Chevalier Ramsay:

> Our festivals are not what the profane world and the ignorant vulgar imagine. All the vices of heart and soul are banished there, and irreligion, libertinage, incredulity, and debauch are proscribed. Our banquets resemble those virtuous symposia of Horace, where the conversation only

---

20   Hoey, *Masonry The Turnpike-Road to Happiness*, 19.

21   Francis Drake, *A Speech Deliver'd to the Worshipful and Ancient Society of Free and Accepted Masons*, 3; see also, Eyer, "Drake's Oration of 1726."

touched what could enlighten the soul discipline the heart, and inspire a taste for the true, the good, and the beautiful.[22]

Ramsay was speaking of the Craft calling its votaries to higher things. Its gatherings, therefore, were not scenes of vice or indulgence; to be so would allow the senses to be dulled, and the loftier goals in Lodge would be neglected. This admonition was echoed by Irish Freemason, Fifield D'Assigny in his answer to the "enemies of Freemasonry," when he advised "Let not excess of Liquor destroy your REASON or waste your SUBSTANCE..."[23]

In the 1770s, Freemason William Hutchinson enumerated the preferences of the Craft: "CHARITY, BENEVOLENCE, JUSTICE, TEMPERANCE, CHASTITY, and BROTHERLY LOVE...."[24] The counterpoints to these laudable pursuits included evils of every ilk—"DARKNESS, OBSCENITY... HATRED and MALICE."[25] It is noteworthy that Hutchinson listed "DRUNKENNESS" as the equal to these other ills.

This very drunkenness was dismissed by the Lord Cadwallader, the Grand Master of the Moderns Grand Lodge in 1764. Such "scenes," he stated, "... reflects an Odium and Disgrace upon the whole Body of *Free-Masons*... our Constitutions and Principles are diametrically opposed to such" conduct.[26] Because of this, at times, such intemperance met with expulsion:

> During my Stay in one LODGE I knew four of this bad
> Stamp, and heard of many more; all which were expelled

22   Ramsay, "Oration." In Gould, *History*, 3:11–12.

23   D'Assigny, *Answer to the Enemies*. In Williams & Cerza, *D'Assigny*, 84.

24   Hutchinson, *Spirit of Masonry*, 91.

25   Hutchinson, *Spirit of Masonry*, 91.

26   Cadwallader, *Charge Delivered at the Constitution of the Lodge No. cxxx*, 14.

the LODGE, but one of these four Out-casts, who was ejected for being frequently intoxicated...[27]

Within these examples, two simple and corresponding
themes emerge: Temperance as duty, and the *absence* of Temperance being anathema to Freemasonry. The Tavern Myth is
irreconcilable with this reality of Masonic expectation.

"when all grave Business is over..."

None of the above should be construed as a denial of the festivities enjoyed by our early Brethren, nor should the virtue of Temperance be confused with abstinence. One needs only to look to
the volumes of Masonic songs and toasts to find evidence that
Freemasons have always rejoiced in fellowship. But these times
were decidedly separate from the serious work of the Lodge.
The Tavern Myth conflates Lodge workings with Lodge fellowship; it mixes Labor and Refreshment. Underlying the Tavern
Myth is a "minimalistic" preconception of early Grand Lodge era
Freemasonry which holds that the lodge culture was extremely
simplistic, that there was little or no symbolism employed in the
work, that the only secrets were the grips and words, that there
were no important or significant intellectual engagements taking
place during Masonic communications, etc. As such, from this
perspective, Labor and Refreshment are conceptually insepara-
ble: within the context of the Tavern Myth, there was nothing to
separate. But ample evidence to the contrary is clear.

As with the question of decorum within the lodge, the 1723
Constitutions clearly states the Masonic expectation regarding
post-lodge decorum:

27   Disgusted Brother, *Secrets of the Free-Masons Revealed*, 9.

> 2. Behaviour *after the* LODGE *is over and the* Brethren *not gone.* You may enjoy yourself with innocent Mirth, treating one another according to Ability, but avoiding all Excess, or forcing any Brother to eat or drink beyond his Inclination, or hindering him from going when his Occasions call him, or doing or saying any thing offensive, or that may forbid an *easy* and *free* Conversation; for that would blast our Harmony, and defeat our laudable Purposes.[28]

This charge is a telling compliment to the first charge of behavior "in the Lodge while constituted" cited above. The former Charge speaks of serious and solemn engagements. This Charge, on the other hand, speaks to the "innocent Mirth" enjoyed by Brethren, but specifically when "LODGE *is over.*" Yet even within these times of celebration, there is the expectation that Masons will exercise due temperance, thereby underscoring the points made above. So eloquent is this Charge that William Preston left it essentially unchanged half a century later: "When the Lodge is closed, you may enjoy yourself with innocent mirth, but you are careful to avoid excess."[29]

The language of the 1723 charge was also adapted for use in a Masonic song by Brother L. Umfreville, published in 1736:

> If Temperance supports this Frame,
> Its Rules are its Divine Command;
> Nor does it, if exempt from Blame
> A free and jovial Mirth withstand.[30]

Considering other Masonic songs, the most well-known may

---

28   Anderson, *Constitutions of the Freemasons*, 54; see also, Dermott, *Ahiman Rezon*, 31.

29   Preston, *Illustrations*, 43.

30   Smith, *The Book M*, 2:45.

be "The Enter'd Apprentice Song." Credited to Freemason Matthew Birkhead, and dating to at least 1709, various forms of this song appeared in many different Masonic pamphlets.[31] When it appeared in Anderson's 1723 *Constitutions*, it carried this instruction: "To be sung when all *grave Business* is over, and *with the* MASTER's *Leave*."[32] Outside of the charges themselves, this may be the earliest documented reference to the division between labor and refreshment.

The division was captured in the public realm by *The Dublin Weekly Journal* in 1725. The June 26th issue from that year included an account of a St. John's Day procession by the Grand Lodge of Ireland and its constituent lodges. The article describes a fine meal, complete with "120 Dishes of Meat" and "entertainment."[33] The article specifically notes that all of the festivities of the evening came "*after* performing the Mystical Ceremonies of the Grand Lodge which are held so sacred, that they must not be discovered...."[34]

The line between "Mystical Ceremonies" and the times of mirth was so clear, that some members of the public world seemed not to know that there was any celebration at all. This was suggested in Masonic song appearing in 1731:

> The world is all in darkness,
> About us they conjecture,
> But seldom think,
> A song and drink,
> Succeeds the Mason's lecture[35]

---

31   See Knoop, et al., *Early Masonic Pamphlets*, 36–40.

32   Anderson, *Constitutions* (1723), 84.

33   *Dublin Weekly Journal*, June 26, 1725, 52.

34   *Dublin Weekly Journal*, June 26, 1725, 52. Italics added.

35   Cole, *Antient Constitutions of the Free and Accepted Masons*, 36.

This stanza implies that, in at least some circles, Masons were known for their labors, and not necessarily for the frivolity of a Lodge at rest. Minimally, it shows that the "song and drink" was a distinct practice, held separate and apart from the serious work of illuminating the Brethren against the contrast of the profane world "all in darkness."

Interestingly, a version of this song appeared in a satirical publication a year prior. In that version, the last three lines of this stanza read, "But little think, We nought but drink: For that's the Masons Lecture."[36] While the 1730 version does not as clearly speak to the separation between Labor and Refreshment, it does speak to an early acknowledgement of the possibility of the Tavern Myth: the perception that Freemasons only meet to get intoxicated.

Brother Euclid's letter also speaks to this point. The pseudonymous argument "Against unjust Cavils" places the onus of post-lodge intemperance squarely on the shoulders of misguided men:

> Others complain that the Masons *continue too long in the Lodge* [and become] *intoxicated with Liquor!* But they have no Occasion to drink much in *Lodge Hours*... and when the *Lodge* is closed (always in good Time) any Brother may go home when he pleases: So that if any stay longer and get intoxicated, it is at their own Cost, not as *Masons*, but as other imprudent Men may do; for which the *Fraternity* is not accountable....[37]

On January 21, 1738, a Masonic exposure appeared in *Read's Weekly Journal or British Gazetteer*, in London. It outlined the several parts of an Initiation, including Candidate's reception,

---

36   Farmer, *New Model*, 25.
37   Anderson, *New Book of Constitutions*, 227.

restoration to Light, and the manner in which the Candidate is taught the modes of recognition. Then:

> This Ceremony being performed and explained, the Recip-
> iendary is called Brother; after which they sit down, and,
> with the Grand Master's Leave, drink the new Brother's
> Health: Everybody has his Bottle.[38]

Similar to the report in the *Dublin Weekly Journal* cited above, this exposure explicitly states that the toasts and merriment occur after the initiation rituals. This is echoed in the 1760 exposure, *Three Distinct Knocks*: the Candidate is made a Mason, he takes his Obligation, the Lodge is mopped away, and only then the assembled brethren drink and cheer.[39] In establishing these themes, Shawn Eyer, in his 2009 work "Silence and Solemnity in Craft Masonry," offers an important observation with regard to anti-Masonic writing of the period. He writes, "Nor do the exposés of the Craft suggest a rowdy intemperance during actual rituals—an accusation that would have been prominent had such conditions been either universal or widespread."[40]

This very practice of dividing Labor from Refreshment was simply and beautifully captured by Thomas Dunckerly, Provincial Grand Master, when he addressed the Craft in 1769:

> To subdue the passions, and improve in useful scientific
> knowledge, to instruct younger brethren, and initiate the
> unenlightened, are the principal duties of the lodge: which
> when done, and the word of God is closed we indulge with
> the song and cheerful glass, still answering the same de-

38   *Read's Weekly Journal or British Gazetteer* (London), January 21, 1738.
39   W___O___V____n, *Three Distinct Knocks*, 61.
40   Eyer, "Silence and Solemnity in Craft Freemasonry," 105.

cency and regularity, with strict attention to the golden mean.... [41]

Pistis

As important as it is to maintain an accurate account of the what Freemasons did, it is vital to understand what Freemasons believed; beliefs drive actions. It is the conceit of the Tavern Myth that there was nothing of substance in early Freemasonry, nothing to inspire philosophical and spiritual reflection in early Lodges. In support of this perspective, Wallace McLeod, FPS, stated that "not until some time around the year 1770," was there "included something for the mind" in Freemasonry.[42] In another essay, he advised that the Masonry of the 1720s through 1760s did not deserve to be "called speculative," stating that what he deemed to be the "non-operative non-speculative period" lasted "until 1770."[43]

But just as misperceptions around practice are not supported by the evidence, the Tavern Myth's assertions regarding Masonic self-concept is likewise faulty. The Masonic writing of the eighteenth century reveals the expression of wide-ranging religious, philosophical, and mystical beliefs, dating from at least 1722. These are evident in the manner in which Masons discussed their Craft, and also in the disdain for those within the brotherhood who would not rise to maintain their worth. It is evident in the reverential way they discuss their secrets. Ultimately it is evident in how they conceived of their institutions as perennialist, gnostic, and above all, holy.[44]

---

41   Dunckerly, "A Charge." In Calcott, *Candid Disquisition*, 140.
42   McLeod, *Candid Disquisition*, 1.
43   McLeod, "The Causes of Ritual Divergence," 92.
44   The terms *gnosis* and *gnostic* used here not in the formal sense of

"...so far from the notion of futility..."

Even the most cursory glance at the literature of the time reveals the seriousness with which Freemasons regarded their Fraternity. One need not even begin to delve into the mystical and philosophical themes in early Freemasonry to find this evidence; the significance is clearly illustrated by the terms they used to describe it:

"a chosen Generation, a royal Priesthood"[45]
"divine Science"[46]
"*Craft* divine!"[47]
"sublime Science of Masonry"[48]
"Sacred Order"[49]
"sacred Privilege"[50]
"*Sacred Brotherhood*"[51]
"mystical Rites"[52]
"Mystery Divine"[53]
"Perfection of the Art of *Masonry*"[54]
"royal Science"[55]

ancient so-called "gnosticism," but in a more generic sense of a "special knowledge of spiritual mysteries." (OED).

45 Samber, *Long Livers*, v.
46 Ibid., xiii.
47 Anderson, *Constitutions of the Freemasons*, 83.
48 Oakley, "Speech." In Cole, *Antient Constitutions*, 26.
49 Ibid., 29.
50 Smith, *The Book M*, 1:25.
51 Ibid., 19.
52 Disgusted Brother, *Secrets of the Free-Masons Revealed*, 22.
53 Smith, *The Book M*, 2:47.
54 D'Assigny, *Answer to the Pope's Bull*. In Williams & Cerza, *D'Assigny*, 66.
55 Leslie, *Masonry: A Poem*, 6.

"HAIL GLORIOUS CRAFT! Distinguish'd Science, HAIL!"[56]
"*Art Divine*"[57]
"mighty A RT, thou gracious Gift of Heaven"[58]
"sacred Art, by Heav'n design'd"[59]
"daughter of Heaven!"[60]
"heavenly genius!"[61]
"the children of LIGHT"[62]

These beliefs of the Craft being "divine" and "sacred" are ubiquitous aspects of the self-concept of Freemasonry during its years of classical development, as will be demonstrated below. Also of interest here is the manner in which the terms "art" and "science" are used practically synonymously when describing Masonry. In the classical sense, as well as within Masonic parlance, both terms—*art* and *science*—speak to a body of specialized knowledge, beautifully applied, and were not assigned the nearly dichotomous definitions they carry today.

Other Masons spoke out directly against the accusation that theirs was an unimportant endeavor. In answer to an anti-Masonic attack, Irish Mason James Hoey composed his *Masonry The Turnpike-Road to Happiness in this Life, And Eternal Happiness Hereafter*. In his rejoinder, published in 1768, Hoey spoke to this particular element of the Tavern Myth:

… affirming the mysteries of Masonry to be so far from the

56   Ibid., 1.
57   Spratt, *The General Regulations*. In Williams & Cerza, *D'Assigny*. 115.
58   Dermott, *Ahiman Rezon*, 11.
59   Ibid., 176.
60   Gaudry, "Address". In Calcott, *Candid Disquisition*, 155.
61   Codrington, "Lecture Delivered in the Union Lodge." In Oliver, *Golden Remains*, 1:202.
62   Hutchinson, *Spirit of Masonry*, 91.

nature of futility, that, (as is well known to every brother) they are absolutely the most important that can be conceived by the human understanding.[63]

Masonic luminary William Preston also spoke to this idea when he addressed the Grand Lodge at the famed Grand Masonic Gala in 1772:

> Many have been deluded by the vague supposition that the mysteries of masonry were merely nominal, that the practices established amongst us were slight and superficial....[64]

Hoey and Preston were both speaking to Masonic audiences, and with subsequent publication, to a non-Masonic audience as well. Each spoke to the Masonic self-concept of the labors of the Fraternity being far from "slight and superficial." This was not a new perspective. At the beginning of the century, Edward Oakley derided those brethren who only viewed the Craft as some "idle loose diversion."[65] Understanding that early Freemasons seriously engaged with their Craft is the essential foundation of understanding the deeper implication of the Masonic science.

"...Perils amongst False Brethren within..."

An additional piece of evidence underscoring Masonic sincerity is the idea of *False Brethren*. In fine, False Brethren were those men who were granted the honors of the fraternity, but who either willfully and repeatedly behaved in a manner inconsis-

63   Hoey, *Masonry The Turnpike-Road to Happiness*, 8.
64   Preston, *Illustrations*, 22–3.
65   Oakley, "Speech." In Cole, *Antient Constitutions*, 31–2.

tent with the values of the Craft, or whose capabilities simply rendered a true understanding of the Craft impossible.

There is an acknowledgement that, to a certain extent, the admission of the unworthy is unavoidable. When addressing the Grand Lodge of Scotland in 1763, David Erskine Baker made this point by using an example almost above reproach:

> ...some small alloy of dross, blended among even the *noblest* Metal, must ever be absolutely inevitable...[even Jesus'] CHOSEN TWELVE...were not exempted from the having one false BROTHER among them.[66]

Other prominent Masons of Baker's time echoed his concern. At the Grand Masonic Gala, William Preston lamented that "the privileges of masonry have been too common."[67] Likewise, Wellins Calcott observed, "the craft has suffered greatly in its reputation and happiness by the admission of low and inferior persons."[68] But even before the time of Calcott and Preston, such concerns were prevalent, and the leaders of the Craft a generation earlier were offering similar cautions. For instance, when Edward Oakley, Past Provincial Senior Grand Warden, addressed a collection of Masons in 1728, he specifically spoke out against those "unworthy Brothers." Such men who sought the rank of Freemason in a "vain flight of curiosity," or for "Pride and Ambition" were clearly ignorant of the aim and purpose of the Craft. He continued:

> It is generally to be observ'd, that of these are the False Brethren, who fail in their Duty and Obedience, by their Ignorance, and being Strangers to the Intent and Consti-

---

66   Baker, *Oration in Honour of Free-Masonry Delivered*, 13–14.
67   Preston, *Illustrations*, 20.
68   Calcott, *Candid Disquisition*, 212.

tution of the Sciences....[69]

Part of the Masonic "Duty" was to subdue the passions. Men who could not or would not, were also chided as False Brethren. Writing from Ireland in 1744, Fifield D'Assigny spoke of those who joined the Craft "under pretence of searching for knowledge" but who reveal themselves as "they fall into scenes of gluttony or drunkenness."[70] But D'Assigny was clear that the such was not only reflective of the faults of the individual brethren. He also laid the responsibility upon:

> several Lodges, too many have been fond of a trifling treat, and have sold their birthrights at a mean price even for a mess of pottage; and instead of taking a due and especial care to enquire into the reputation of character of the candidate, they have often imprudently hurried him into the Craft....[71]

It is revealing that much of the warnings against False Brethren have religious tones, if not explicitly religious phrasing. While William Hutchinson does not use the phrase "False Brother," it is clear who he is addressing when he cautions Masons not "to betray the watch-word" to the unworthy. To do so, and to admit such as would become a False Brother "is like aiding the sacrilegious robber to ransack the holy places, and steal the sacred vessels devoted to the most solemn rites of religion...."[72]

Right Worshipful Provisional Grand Master Thomas Dunck-

69 Oakley, "Speech." In Cole, *Antient Constitutions*, 31

70 D'Assigny, *Serious and Impartial Enquiry*. In Williams & Cerza, *D'Assigny*, 46.

71 D'Assigny, *Serious and Impartial Enquiry*. In Williams & Cerza, *D'Assigny*, 40.

72 Hutchinson, *Spirit of Masonry*, 187.

erly similarly used religious motifs when describing what traits make a Brother "worthy":

> LIGHT and truth being the great essentials of the royal craft…and that we are not worthy of the true fellowship unless we walk in the light, and do the truth. O, sacred light! whose orient beams make manifest that truth which unites all good and faithful Masons in a heavenly fellowship.[73]

In his speech delivered before the Grand Lodge of York in 1726, Francis Drake identified the False Brother as having little grasp of the Art. He stated, "False Brethren, 'tis true, may build Castles in the Air; but a Good Mason works upon no such fickle foundation."[74] He went on to state that the Freemason's duty when in Lodge is to "declare our Principles of Brotherly Love, Relief and Truth to one another. After which, and a strict Observance from the Malice of our Enemies without the Lodge, nor *in Perils amongst False Brethren* within."[75] Of particular note in this instance is that, earlier in this oration, Drake identified these three "Grand Principles"[76] as part of the "Mystery" of Freemasonry "apparent to the whole World."[77] In other words, as essential as Brotherly Love, Relief, and Truth are, they constitute only the *exoteric* elements of the Craft. This leads one to ask, if a brother cannot grasp the *exoteric* how can he ever be expected to fully understand the *esoteric* lessons of Freemasonry?

William Smith of Gateshead, the compiler of *The Book M, or*

---

73   Dunckerly, "Lecture on Masonic Light, Truth, and Charity." In Oliver, *The Golden Remains of the Early Masonic Writers*, 1:137–8.
74   Drake, *Speech*, 14. Emphasis in original.
75   Ibid.
76   Ibid., 11.
77   Ibid.

Masonry Triumphant, was scathing in his rebuke of these False Brethren in a speech given before an assemblage of London Freemasons, circa 1734:

> ...those *wicked Masons*...shall receive Punishment instead of Reward, for spoiling the Work of the grand Architect, by introducing Confusion instead of Order, and blending the two Opposites of Light and Darkness together. These erect vain Fabricks, according to their own depraved Imaginations, supporting them by Ignorance, Debility and Deformity, which, when the Trumpets blow, come down with mighty Ruin on the Builders Heads. Let the Names of those be eras'd out of the Book *M*, and their Devices scatter'd as Dust before the Winds.[78]

This reference to "the Book *M*," may be to a lost text referenced in the Rosicrucian *Fama Fraternitatis* published in 1614; but it is a definite invocation of the 1722 work *Long Livers*, by Freemason Robert Samber. Writing under the pseudonym Eugenius Philalethes, Jun., Samber dedicated his book "to the Grand Master, Masters, Warden *and* Brethren, of the Most Antient and most Honourable Fraternity of the Free Masons of *Great Britain* and *Ireland*."[79] In this 54-page dedication—which is the earliest surviving essay interpreting the teachings of early Grand Lodge era Freemasonry—Samber speaks clearly against False Brethren, while also evoking *The Book M* in language and tone very similar to Smith's more than a decade later:

> Let these be ever excluded the Congregation of the Faithful; let their Names be rased for ever out of the Book *M*, and be buried in eternal Oblivion, whose Portion will be

78   Smith, *The Book M*, 1:23.
79   Samber, *Long Livers*, iii.

Hypocrites, Makebates, Incendiaries, and Spillers of Blood, red, black and purple.[80]

In an interesting adaptation of the mythic Traditional History of Freemasonry, Samber outlines several characters found in the Old and New Testaments as False Brethren. Of Adam's son, Cain, Samber wrote:

> [Cain] was malicious, envious, incorrigible by God's Correction, a dissembling Traytor, a Spiller of fraternal Blood, and accursed Wanderer and Vagabond, and who added Blasphemy to his Malediction; in short a FALSE BROTHER.[81]

Samber goes on to name Judas Iscariot as "the first *False Brother* under the Law of Grace,"[82] and recounts "that the next terrible Punishment of a *False Brother* was on *Ananias*...[who] was struck dead by holy Brother St. *Peter*."[83] He continues, stating that such False Brethren:

> make their Belly their God...they are unworthy Dogs, Animals which are not only to be debarred from eating the Children Bread, but to be shut out from licking up the Crumbs that fall from their Table.... And who all, unless they opportunely repent, will be overtaken by the rigorous Judgements of God for their Falshoods and Perjuries, as were their Brother Caitiffs, those perfidious Traitors and Liars, *Cain, Judas* and *Ananias*.[84]

80   Ibid., xlviii-xlix.
81   Ibid., xix.
82   Ibid., xxxvii.
83   Ibid., xxxvii. Alluding to the story in Acts 5:1–5.
84   Ibid., xlviii-xlix.

Samber also noted that the False Brethren are the source of the true ailments of the Craft:

> Our holy Brother, St. *Paul*, though he suffered infinite Perils, as he recounts himself, yet the Perils among *False Brethren* were what seemed most to touch his righteous Soul; for most dangerous are a Man's Enemies, when they are of his own House.[85]

Again, this is a sentiment echoed by D'Assigny: He specifically identified "These despicable traders or hucksters in pretended Masonry"[86] as the primary source of the "decay" which had set into the Craft. To answer this problem, D'Assigny first advises a Mason to aid in reforming a False Brother's errors; barring that, he quotes St. Paul himself, in his admonishment to "Withdraw yourself from every Brother that walketh disorderly."[87]

The simplest admonition is found in Scott's 1754 *Pocket Companion*: "guard against... false Brethren."[88] By doing so, the Craft will flourish.

Clearly, these warnings about False Brethren are sufficiently widespread and consistent to be considered a normal part of the lodge culure of early Grand Lodge era Freemasonry. As such, they pose a significant problem for the adherents of the view that there was nothing of significance or import in early Freemasonry. If that interpretation of Masonic history were generally true, it would be difficult to imagine a circumstance in which a

---

85   Samber, *Long Livers*, xlviii. In certain cases, as here, an allusion may exist to the penultimate event of the ritualistic drama of Craft Freemasonry, in which the theme of the "enemy within the ranks" is impressively communicated.

86   D'Assigny, *Serious and Impartial Enquiry*. In Williams & Cerza, *D'Assigny*, 43.

87   Ibid., 2. Alluding to 2 Thessalonians 3:6.

88   Scott, *Pocket Companion and History*, 1754, viii.

brother could be "false." If, for instance, early lodges truly were only drinking and supper clubs, no Brother would be chided for focusing on eating and drinking. If there truly was no philosophy or spirituality in early lodges, it is impossible to imagine a scenario in which Masons would be outraged by brethren *not* engaging in spiritual or religious labor. In other words, the very fact that there was such a term as "False Brother" demonstrates that there existed higher purposes for Freemasons, beyond "making their Belly their God." The Masonic writers of the early Grand Lodge era who wrote so derisively of False Brethren did so because they expected their lodge brothers to aspire to far more than simple entertainment and refreshment.

"... the Essential Secrets of masonry..."

The Tavern Myth propounds that the modes of recognition and the ritual of the Fraternity constitute the totality of Masonic secrets; there are no deeper secrets than those. Knoop and Jones asserted something like this by stating that the modes of recognition are the "essence of the Freemason's esoteric knowledge."[89] This minimalistic narrative therefore perpetuates the idea that the secrets of the Fraternity are, by definition, easily attainable, and, in fact, are already in the possession of anyone who has read any of the multiple exposures printed throughout the centuries.

Arguably the most widely read and well known exposure in the history of the Craft is Samuel Pritchard's 1730 *Masonry Dissected*. This exposure also has the distinction of being the earliest publication to reveal a catechism of the third degree in addition to those of the first and second degrees. Accordingly, Pritchard discloses the grips and passwords of the Entered Apprentice, Fellow Craft, and Master Mason. The Tavern Myth maintains

89   Knoop & Jones, *Short History*, 72.

that by doing so, Pritchard had revealed all of Masonry's secrets. And yet, we have Masonic writers explicitly stating the opposite. For instance, in the months following the publication of *Masonry Dissected*, an anonymous rejoinder was published under the title, *The Perjur'd Free Mason Detected*. This pamphlet explicitly stated that not only did the secrets of Freemasonry remain undisclosed by such exposures, but they could never be thus disclosed:

> yet the Secret remains untouch'd and the Traytors have only exposed themselves in those attempts... and let the World see in short that they have not been able to come at the Secret itself, and really know nothing of the Matter.[90]

The anonymous author of *An Apology for the Free and Accepted Masons* concurs:

> Every Thing published with Regard to the Secrets of Masonry are mere Chimeras and ridiculous Fancies. The publick seek after Words and Signs. These ingenious Gentlemen gratify that itching Curiosity by patching up some quaint Conceits... the better to impose on mistaken Credulity....[91]

These statements support the position voiced by Edward Oakley in his famous 1728 oration. Oakley states that the modes of recognition are "the most insignificant Parts of the Sacred Mystery"[92] and voices disdain for those who mistakenly "think they are sufficiently qualified, if they can make themselves known to be Masons."[93]

---

90   A Free Mason, *Perjur'd Free Mason Detected*, 6.
91   Anon., "Apology." In Scott, *Pocket Companion*, 280.
92   Oakley, "Speech." In Cole, *Antient Constitutions*, 31.
93   Oakley, "Speech." In Cole, *Antient Constitutions*, 31–2.

Of course, Freemasonry is known to inculcate a certain set of values. This is part of the public image of Freemasonry today. Perhaps it was this position that prompted a twentieth-century Mason to say that, "We should remember that the realities of Freemasonry are neither secret nor mysterious."[94] However, in the early Grand Lodge era, there was a more complex Masonic reality. To simply deny the mysterious elements in Freemasonry—then or now—ignores the stated delineations between the Fraternity's exoteric and esoteric lessons. The most clearly articulated of these statements was given in Drake's 1726 oration:

> I have already shewn you that Masonry is the oldest Science the World has produced...for this Reason the fundamental Rules of this Art have been handed down from Age to Age, and very justly thought fit to be made a Mystery on. A Mystery however that has something in it apparent to the whole World, and which alone is sufficient to answer all the Objections that Malice or Ignorance can throw, or has urged against us; of which, to mention no more, our three Grand Principals of Brotherly Love, Relief, and Truth to one another, are very shining Instances.[95]

Drake is commending Freemasonry's belief in Brotherly Love, Relief, and Truth, but makes it clear that these are merely the exoteric lessons of the Craft; in his words, that part of the Mystery "apparent to the whole World." He goes on to state that the esoteric elements of the Craft are what draw "so many Kings, Princes, and Noblemen" to seek to be "initiated into the Mysterious Part of it."[96] A pamphlet titled *A Defence of Masonry*, published in 1730 as a rejoinder to *Masonry Dissected*, made a

94   Roy, "Pillars of the Temple." In Roy, *Dare We Be Masons*, 80–81.
95   Drake, *Speech*, 11.
96   Ibid.,12.

similar point. The anonymous author of that pamphlet—almost certainly Premier Grand Lodge insider Martin Clare[97]—wrote, "*Architecture, Geometry* and *Mathematicks* [are] rather *Technical and Formal*… than essentially attached to the *Grand* DESIGN."[98] This also suggests an exoteric/esoteric divide between the Operative and Speculative elements of Masonry.

More than this, however, there is a body of Masonic writing that suggests that the secrets of Freemasonry can never be disclosed. These secrets, wrote Robert Samber, "are deeply hidden from common View, and covered with Pavilions of thickest Darkness, that what is sacred may not be given to Dogs, or your Pearls cast before Swine, and turn again and rent you."[99] Of this notion, one Masonic song (1734) offered:

> Of that happy Secret when we are possest,
> Our Tongues can't explain what is lodg'd in our Breast:
> For the Blessing's so great it can ne'er be express'd.[100]

Another song (1756) echoed the message:

> As Bees from Flowers Honey brings,
> Sweet Treasure to their Master's Store;
> So Masons do all sacred Things,
> And Wonders from the distant Shores;
> To enrich the Lodge with Wisdom's Light,
> Where babbling folly's lost in Night.[101]

The belief underlying these ideas is that the secrets of the Fra-

---

97   Wonnacott, "Martin Clare."
98   Anderson, *New Book of Constitutions*, 217.
99   Samber, *Long Livers*, lii. The Biblical allusion is to Matthew 7:6.
100 Anon., *Prologue, and an Epilogue and Songs*, 10.
101 Dermott, *Ahiman Rezon*, 169.

ternity can only be understood by "Wisdom's Light"—Masonic secrets can only be comprehended via Masonic enlightenment. Any efforts through these exposures to reveal Masonic secrets are likened to "babbling" in the darkness. This belief was explicitly stated in the oldest known private Masonic oration, the 1734 *Dissertation Upon Masonry*: "The Essential Secrets of masonry indeed are Everlastingly Safe, & never can be Revealed abroad, because they can never be understood by such as are unenlightened."[102] Here, not only is it affirmed that the secrets are safe despite these exposures, but further, any truth that is therein contained is useless to the uninitiated. Only a Mason can discern the deeper meaning of any accuracies reflected in an exposure. The pseudonymic *Brother* EUCLID's *Letter to the Author Against unjust Cavils*, printed in the second edition of Anderson's *Constitutions* in 1738, made the same point regarding exposures:

> for all of 'em put together don't discover the profound and sublime Things of old Masonry nor can any Man, not a Mason, make use of those incoherent Smatterings (interspers'd with ignorant Nonsense and gross Falsities) among bright Brothers, for any Purpose but to be laught at; our *Communications* being of a quite different sort.[103]

Isaac Head, the Provincial Grand Master of the Scilly Isles, framed this belief from the perspective of those who seek to uncover Masonic secrets unlawfully: "[E]very Method, which the Malice of Men or Devils could invent" have "endeavored to extract from *the faithful Craft* those Secrets which have in all Ages been hid from the Unworthy and Profane, and from such

---

102 Anon, *Dissertation*; see Eyer, "A Dissertation Upon Masonry," 74–75. See Shawn Eyer's article in this volume, especially pages 173–75.

103 Anderson, *New Book of Constitutions*, 226.

will ever remain an impenetrable Secret."[104]

Fifield D'Assigny said that without such illumination, even men who had been advanced through the degrees would remain in darkness:

> And I wou'd not have the World imagine, that they can ever arrive at the Perfection of the Art of *Masonry*, without first undergoing *a certain Operation*, which will entirely remove that Film that at present hangs over their visionary Orb; for altho' they may be of Opinion that they see already very well, I durst venture to say, that they are as much in darkness at this time, as an unfortunate Prisoner, who is confi'd in such a Dungeon, that the least glimmering Ray of Light cannot possibly creep into him.[105]

Robert Samber concurs:

> none but the Sons of Science, and those who are illuminated with the sublimest Mysteries and profoundest Secrets of MASONRY may understand.[106]

Wellins Calcott reflected the same Masonic belief half a century later:

> I am not at liberty to undraw the curtain, and publicly discant on this head: It is *sacred*, and ever will remain so; those who are honoured with the trust, will not *reveal* it except to the truly qualified brother, and they who are ignorant

104 Head, *Confutation of the Observation on Free Masonry*, 19.
105 D'Assigny, *Answer to the Pope's Bull*. In Williams & Cerza, *D'Assigny*, 66.
106 Samber, *Long Livers*, li.

of it cannot betray it.[107]

The evidence is overwhelming: To receive Masonic secrets requires a revelation, and could not be understood via print—if they could be printed at all. On the other hand, at their most basic, Masonic tokens, signs, and due guards are simply hand movements, and the passwords are merely vocalizations; any of these can be disclosed to virtually any person in a matter of seconds. Any assertions that Masonic secrets were easily shared is to deny the recorded beliefs of Freemasons themselves. Further, any assertions that the Craft is bereft of any secrets, of any stripe, demonstrates either a denial or ignorance of what the founders of the Craft personally believed.

"... a ffree gift of God to the children of men..."

One essential characteristic of early Masonic self-concept revolves around the antiquity of the institution. Masonry was viewed to be coeval with creation itself, emanating from the Great Architect and manifesting throughout His works; this myth is captured in what is known as the Traditional History. Of note is that much of the writing of, and pertaining to, the Traditional History reflects a Judeo-Christian worldview, with many overtly Christian references. When reading these, it is essential to recall the Premier Grand Lodge's charge "*Concerning* GOD *and* RELIGION:"

> [Masons are obliged] to that Religion in which all Men agree, leaving their particular Opinions to themselves; that is, to be *good Men and true*, or Men of Honour and Honesty, by whatever Denominations of Persuasions they may

---

107   Calcott, *Candid Disquisition*, 19.

be distinguish'd....[108]

As such, given that religious pluralism and religious tolerance are hallmarks of the early Grand Lodge era, explicitly Christian statements in Masonic writing should be seen as reflecting the fact that Freemasonry is a product of Western culture, rather than as an endorsement of Christianity. The content of early Masonic literature is ample demonstration that religious rhetoric was used without evangelical intent. Moreover, it has been found by numerous scholars that Freemasonry's religious language contains more than a simple expression or restatement of the standard concepts of the dominant religious culture.[109]

The first version of the Traditional History published in the Grand Lodge era is found in the pages of Anderson's 1723 *Constitutions of the Free-Masons*, and starts with these words:

> ADAM, our first Parent, created after the Image of God, *the great Architect of the Universe*, must have had the Liberal Sciences, particularly *Geometry*, written on his Heart....[110]

Thus begins the essential mythology of Freemasonry, with God nesting the secrets of the Craft at the very center of the first man. The legend finds the Mystic Art passed through Adam to the line of Seth, and on to Godly Enoch who inscribed the knowledge onto the primordial pillars. These were rendered so as to survive even beyond God's judgement. After the flood, the Art was promulgated by Noah and his sons, Shem, Ham, and Japheth, and passed forward to the true Masons who were puri-

---

108 Anderson, *Constitutions of the Freemasons*, 50.
109 See Hackett, *That Religion in Which All Men Agree: Freemasonry in American Culture*, 51, and Eyer, "'The Essential Secrets of Masonry'" (in this volume).
110 Anderson, *Constitutions of the Freemasons*, 1.

fied by the Divine intervention at Shinar. From there, the Craft
was passed to Hiram Abiff and King Solomon, and manifested
in the building of the Temple at Jerusalem. The knowledge was
thereafter dispersed to Pythagoras, Euclid, the Egyptian pha-
raohs, Alexander the Great, Augustus Caesar and eventually to
the kings of Europe. Other tellings include Hermes Trismegistus,
Zoroaster, and the very angels of heaven also practicing the Royal
Art. This mythology defines Freemasonry's self-concept as a per-
renial tradition: a divine set of teachings gifted to man at the time
of creation, and passed throughout the successive generations.

The Tavern Myth would minimize this great saga as a simple fairy tale, as mere fancy invented to stroke the egos of Freemasons. But such an assertion is difficult to maintain when one
sees how ubiquitous the Traditional History is in eighteenth-century Masonic writing. Be it in books of constitutions, handbooks,
speeches, orations, or rejoinders, the vast majority of these writings makes reference to the Traditional History, be it to Adam,
Seth, Enoch's pillars, Noah, Pythagoras, Euclid, or some other
component. Additionally, the fact that this history was to be delivered at every making of a Mason demonstrates the importance
with which Masons regarded their legends.

To be sure, this view to antiquity was not the invention of
Anderson. Masonic writings predating 1717, often referred to as
the "Gothic Constitutions" or "Old Charges," all speak to the
Craft being developed within an Old Testament context. The
Cooke MS, c. 1450, is recognized as the second oldest of these
Gothic Constitutions, and the first detailed telling of the Tradi-
tional History. Within Cooke, the Arts and Sciences are said to
have been developed by the children of Lamech, six generations
removed from Cain, and preserved upon the Primordial Pillars.
This story itself was adapted from such medieval works as the
Polychronicon and those of Venerable Bede.[111]

111   See Cooke MS, lines 140, 142, 201, 202, 217, 235, 321, 350, and 372.

While it is true that many medieval trade guides created legendary tales of their specific crafts, there was something peculiar about the Traditional History of the Masons. This was observed, for instance, by David Stevenson, who commented that the "mythical trade history" of the Masons in the fifteenth-century "was unusually elaborate." He added that the "lore was to make a significant contribution to freemasonry through its emphasis on morality, its identification of the mason craft with geometry, and the importance it gave to Solomon's Temple and ancient Egypt in the development of the mason craft."[112] Therefore the importance of the Masonic Traditional History cannot be diminished simply because non-Masons had similar stories in the middle of the second millennia.

While Anderson was familiar with the Old Charges of the operative Masons, he consulted a far older source for his inspiration: the works of first-century Jewish historian Flavius Josephus. It was Josephus, in his *Antiquities of the Jews*, that inspired Anderson to credit the Arts and Sciences, and their means of preservation, to the line of Seth. There is proof that this new version was approved by the rulers of the Craft. John Theosphilus Desaguliers, for instance, in his Dedication to Anderson's *Constitutions*, specifically praised the

> Pains our learned AUTHOR [Anderson] has taken in compiling and digesting this Book from the old *Records*, and how accurately he has compar'd and made every thing agreeable to *History* and *Chronology*, so as to render these NEW CONSTITUTIONS a just and exact Account of *Masonry* from the Beginning of the World to your *Grace's* MASTERSHIP.[113]

---

112   Stevenson, *Origins*, 6.
113   Anderson, *Constitutions* (1723), [ii–iii]

Additional praise for Anderson's version of the Traditional History is preserved in the 1726 speech by Francis Drake. The Grand Junior Warden states that Anderson "has taken so much true Pains to draw [the history of Freemasonry] out from the Rubbish... as justly merits the highest Gratitude from his Brethren."[114] Drake calls Anderson a "diligent Antiquary."[115] While one may be tempted to argue that Drake was only praising Anderson's description of historical works of architecture, Drake's comparison of Anderson to Joseph Addison should be consulted: while Drake quotes Addison at length, he begins with Addison's architectural description of the Tower of Babel. As such, Drake is clearly considering the architecture of both Anderson and Addison from a mythic perspective.

This concept of perennialist Freemasonry being cleared from the "Rubbish" has correspondence to another early Masonic writing, the 1730 *Defence of Masonry*:

> And for aught I know, the *System*, as taught in the regular *Lodges*, may have some Redundancies or Defects, occasion'd by the Ignorance or Indolence of the old Members. And indeed, considering through what Obscurity and Darkness the *Mystery* has been deliver'd down; the many Centuries it has survived; the many Countries and Languages, and *Sects*, and *Parties* it has run through; we are rather to wonder it ever arriv'd to the present Age, without more Imperfection. In short, I am apt to think that MASONRY (as it is now explain'd) has in some Circumstances declined from its *original Purity!* It has run long in muddy Streams, and as it were, under Ground: But notwithstanding the great Rust it may have contracted, and the forbidding Light it is placed in by the *Dissector*, there is (if I judge right) much

114   Drake, *Speech*, 4.
115   Ibid.

of the *old Fabrick* still remaining; the essential Pillars of the Building may be discover'd through the Rubbish, tho' the Superstructure be over-run with Moss and Ivy, and the Stones, by Length of Time, be disjointed.[116]

Here, the anonymous defender of the Craft—generally identified by scholars as Martin Clare—acknowledges that Masonic teachings have been sullied through the generations. But such misuse and neglect does not remove the essential purity of the institution, and certainly is not permanent. In the words of Freemason Charles Leslie, it is the duty of Craftsmen "to reform these abuses which have crept in amongst us," thereby allowing the Craft to "again shine out in its primitive lustre, and discover itself to be of a truly divine original."[117]

When Chevalier Ramsay addressed the Craft in 1737, he spoke of the *prisca theologia* of Masonry by way of comparing it to other mystery traditions of antiquity:

> ... the famous festivals of Ceres at Eleusis, of Isis in Egypt, of Minerva at Athens, of Urania amongst the Phoenicians, and of Diana in Scythia were connected with ours. In those places mysteries were celebrated which concealed many vestiges of the ancient religion of Noah and the Patriarchs.[118]

Note that Ramsay not only acknowledges correspondence between Freemasonry and other ancient mystery traditions, he states that all flow from the "religion of Noah." This is important as it predates Anderson's 1738 statement that the Masonic "reli-

---

116 [Clare], *A Defence of Masonry*. In Anderson, *New Book of Constitutions*, 219.

117 Leslie, "Vindication." In Anon., *The Free Masons Pocket-Companion*, 161.

118 Ramsay, "Oration." In Gould, *History of Freemasonry*, 3:12.

gion in which all men agree" was defined by a shared belief in
"the 3 great *Articles* of NOAH."[119] It is also significant in that in
the Holy Covenant that followed the Great Flood, God gave his
commandments to Noah. Therefore, these "great Articles" are
themselves a source of perennialist Masonry.

The self-concept of the Craft being a Divine gift is also reflected in the ritual of the early eighteenth century. For instance,
the Irish exposure, *The Whole Institutions of the Free-Masons
Opened* (1725) calls Masonry "our Holy Secret."[120] The Graham
MS, dating to 1726, expands on this belief:

> [W]hy was it called free masonry—first because a ffree gift
> of God to the children of men secondly free from the in-
> truption of infernal spirits thirdly a ffree union amonge the
> brothers of that holy secret to remain for ever.[121]

This early catechism reinforces the concept of the Craft's divine provenance. Additionally, it speaks of Masonry's ability to
keep its votaries free from evil. Again, in total, the knowledge is
deemed to be holy.

"...unfold the Mysteries of Godliness..."

Because the Craft was viewed by these early Brethren as descended from the Divine, a knowledge of Masonry was therefore framed as a means by which to understand the Divine. One
means of reaching this *gnosis* was through Geometry itself. Interestingly, in this sense, one may be able to divide Geometry

---

119   Anderson, *New Book of Constitutions*, 144.
120   Anon., "The Whole Institutions of the Free-Masons Opened." In
        Carr & Jones, *Early Masonic Catechisms*, 87.
121   Graham MS, in Carr & Jones, *Early Masonic Catechisms*, 90.

into its operative and speculative forms. For instance, in one early anonymous work, *The Rise and Progress of Freemasonry*, it is advised:

> But Freemasons consider geometry as a natural logic; for as truth is ever consistent, invariable, and uniform, all truths may and ought to be investigated in the same manner. Moral and religious definitions, axioms, and proportions, have as regular and certain dependence upon each other as any in physics or the mathematics.[122]

The writer is here comparing the abstracts of the physical realm to those of the metaphysical. Both types of abstracts can be tested by Geometry—in effect, a working tool of natural logic. Additionally, it was through understanding Creation, that the Mason could come to understand the Creator. Geometry was seen as the medium for this understanding: Geometry was the science by which to comprehend the natural world, and was therefore the language of divine revelation. Robert Samber wrote:

> But alas! my Brethren, what are we and our little Globe below, to that stupendous Celestial Masonry above! where the Almighty Architect has stretch'd out the Heavens as a Curtain, which he has richly embroidered with Stars, and with his immortal Compasses, as from a *Punctum*, circumscribed the mighty ALL; is himself the Center of all Things, yet knows no Circumference?[123]

These concepts were echoed by William Smith of Gateshead:

---

122 Anon., "On the Rise and Progress of Freemasonry." In Oliver, *The Golden Remains of the Early Masonic Writers*, 1:44.

123 Samber, *Long Livers*, viii.

THE Principles of *Geometry* were eternally in the Mind of
the great *Elohim*, e'er yet the Heavens were displayed, or
the Earth form'd, and when that happy Distinction in his
Will arose, when Nature should flow out from ideal into real
Existence; then was the whole Creation rang'd out in sweet
Geometric Order, before its great Original, and approved
and blest by him: And by this Divine Science only are we enabled to trace out the wondrous Works of the *Deity*, and give
reasonable Solutions of the various *Phænomena* of Nature.[124]

And again by the first Chaplain of the Premier Grand Lodge,
John Henley:

GOD our all-wise Master having disposed the Fabric of the
Universe in Number, Weight, and Measure; having laid
the Foundation of the Earth, stretched the Line upon it,
and hung it, in *Job's* Phrase, upon nothing, by a mysterious
Geometry....[125]

Each of these passages speaks to geometry as the means by
which to comprehend divine works. By learning this operative
science, Freemasons believed they could fully comprehend the
works of Nature; by comprehending Nature, Masons could understand the guiding hand that created these works.

But a contemplation of geometry was not the only Masonic
means of achieving spiritual insight. A theme found within the
various Masonic prayers of the early 1700s, for use in the first
degree, speaks to Freemasonry's role in connecting a Mason with
God. Consider this prayer from the 1730 *Constitutions* of the
Grand Lodge of Ireland:

124 Smith, *The Book M*, 1:1.
125 Henley, *On Scripture Masonry*, 1. This passage contains Biblical
     allusions to Wisdom of Solomon 11:20, Job 26:7 and 38:4–5.

And we beseech thee, O LORD GOD, to bless this our present Undertaking, and grant that this, our new Brother, may dedicate his Life to thy Service, and be a true and faithful Brother among us, *endue him with Divine Wisdom, that he may, with the Secrets of* Masonry, *be able to unfold the Mysteries of Godliness and Christianity.*[126]

This is more than an invocation; this is more than a statement that Freemasonry can move a man closer to God. This prayer communicates the Masonic belief that the Secrets of Freemasonry not only come from God ("Divine Wisdom") but actually can enable one to understand important spiritual insights ("the Mysteries of Godliness"). Close versions of this prayer for esoteric knowledge appeared in various *Pocket Companions* from 1754 to 1765,[127] as well as in Dermott's *Ahiman Rezon* and Calcott's *Candid Disquisition* of 1769.[128] Isaac Head modified the prayer slightly, writing:

> ...with the Attainment of the Knowledge of the Arcana of Masonry, may be also revealed the sacred and sublime Mysteries of Godliness and Christianity.[129]

Grand Master Cadwallader similarly preached:

> And may *the God of Love and Truth* enlighten you in the true Knowledge of the sacred Mysteries, and guide you continually in the due Observance of his most holy Laws....[130]

126 Pennell, *Constitutions*, 59; see also Dermott, *Ahiman Rezon*, 46.
127 E.g., Scott (1754), 309; Galbraith (1765), 101; Auld & Smellie (1765), 151–52.
128 Dermott, *Ahiman Rezon*, 46; Calcott, *Candid Disquisition*, 198–99.
129 Head, *Confutation*, 102; cf. Drake, *A Speech*, 1.
130 Cadawallader, *Charge Delivered at the Constitution of the Lodge No. CXXX*, 15.

And William Preston used similar language in his 1772 *Illustrations*:

> ...by the secrets of this art, he may be better enabled to unfold the mysteries of godliness, to the honor of thy holy name.[131]

It was not only the Christian Mason who benefitted from this Masonic *gnosis*. Beginning in 1756, the *Ahiman Rezon* of the Grand Lodge of the Antients, and lasting into several subsequent editions, Grand Secretary Laurence Dermott evoked the Hebrew Patriarchs in this prayer for use in Jewish Lodges:

> ENLIGHTEN us, we beseech thee, in the true Knowledge of Masonry: By the Sorrows of *Adam*, thy first made Man; by the Blood of *Abel*, thy holy one; by the Righteousness of *Seth*, in whom thou art well pleased; and by thy Covenant with *Noah*, in whose Architecture thou was't pleased to save the Seen of thy beloved; number us not among those that know not thy Statutes, nor the divine Mysteries of the secret Cabbala.[132]

While the terminology of Dermott's prayer may be different than that of Pennell's, the concept of the teachings of Masonry as the conduit for Divine knowledge remains. Yet another Masonic prayer, first published in 1735, pleads for spiritual wisdom amidst a host of other holy requests:

> O Great and Holy Triune Being, whose Name is TRUTH,

131   Preston, *Illustrations*, 210.
132   Dermott, *Ahiman Rezon*, 43. For further discussion of this prayer, see Murphy, "'A Just and Exact Account of Masonry,'" pages 137–38 in this volume.

> let Error be still absent from us, make Knowledge and Virtue our eager Pursuits; grant us Wisdom to know Thee, and Strength to support us in this our spiritual Warfare; and open the Eye of Truth within us, that, discerning thy ineffable Beauties, we may be drawn off from the vain and sordid Pleasures of this Life, to fix our Loves on Thee, the only Fountain of Happiness.[133]

There are complex ideas contained in this passage, relating to the religious and philosophical underpinnings of Freemasonry. It reiterates the teaching that the Craft can keep a man free from evil. Further, there is urgency in this language, describing a "spiritual Warfare." This conveys that the individual's quest for the greater good is not a guaranteed victory. Moreover, the author names the Great Architect "TRUTH," and later calls for spiritual aid to "open the Eye of Truth within us." This perhaps reflects a Masonic belief in an inner divinity. Such a teaching may be found in today's lodges in the symbolism of the Ashlars: the Perfect Ashlar is contained within the Rough Ashlar, waiting to be released and revealed. But just as the Ashlar requires labor to perfect, so must the Mason labor toward awakening his inner divinity. In 1752, Isaac Head made this symbolism explicit, sermonizing that the smoothing of the stone was bringing "the rough, unhewn Block of the mere natural Man, into the Likeness of our Maker...."[134]

The oldest known surviving private Masonic oration, the 1734 *Dissertation Upon Masonry*, speaks directly to this concept. The Dissertation speaks of St. Paul's visions as noted in his letter to the Corinthians, wherein he describes being brought into the Third Heaven. The anonymous orator[135] acknowledges that while

133 Smith, *The Book M*, 1:46. Anon., *Dissertation*; see Eyer, "A Dissertation Upon Masonry," 66.
134 Head, "Charge." In Head, *Confutation*, 79.
135 The author of the *Dissertation* may have been Rev. Thomas

St. Paul's letter had been the subject of much prior scholarship, none had yet fully grasped the message of the text. He advised, "…learned annotators & Interpreters of Scriptures" were not "of ye lodge" and therefore "Could not possibly Conceive the apostle's true meaning in this mysterious part of" the letter to the Corinthians.[136] In other words, the author of the *Dissertation* is reiterating this early Masonic belief that only through the "Secrets of Masonry" can man hope to discern the "Mysteries of Godliness." It takes the knowledge inculcated in "ye lodge" to understand that St. Paul is describing more than simply a vision of heaven. Rather, he is describing a Masonic initiation, a journey into the third Degree within a body of Masons. The importance of his *Dissertation* cannot be overstated when considering Masonic self-concept: it is one thing to assert that Masonry offers a unique form of insight; it is another thing entirely to espouse a wholly original reading of the Holy Scriptures. And yet, one exposure from 1759 reports that such a practice dates to antiquity:

> …Those Antient MASONS *associated* to explain the *Scriptures*, to preserve the Knowledge of *Architecture*, and to endeavor to make *Improvements* therein, to cultivate *Brotherly Love, Friendship*, and *Hospitality*… This *sacred Rite*, or Custom (*as they term it*) is still kept up among them….[137]

This particular passage harkens back to comments made by Francis Drake in his 1726 speech before the Grand Lodge of York, regarding the exoteric and esoteric content of Masonic labor. In this instance, Brotherly Love is joined by Friendship, Hospitality, and Architecture as those things that are, in Drake's words, "apparent to the whole world"; but explaining the Scriptures within

Harward. See Shawn Eyer's article in this volume.
136   Anon., *Dissertation*; see Eyer, "A Dissertation Upon Masonry," 66.
137   Disgusted Brother, *Secrets of the Free-Masons Revealed*, 6.

a tyled lodge remains part of the Freemasons' "sacred rite."

Another example of Masonic exegesis of the Holy Bible is displayed by James Anderson, that "learned Brother," who reconciled the "Difference betwixt the Book of *Kings* and the Book of *Chronicles* concerning the Princes of Master Masons conducting the Works of the holy Temple according to *Solomon's* Directions."[138]

Additionally, this opportunity for Masonic *gnosis* led the first Grand Chaplain, John Henley, to declare, "The Book of God, his Will, and his Works, are Patterns of sacred Masonry."[139] This assertion was extended into a soteriological point by Fifield D'Assigny in his *Answer to the Pope's Bull* against the Craft:

> That the Secret of Free Masonry was the very Basis of Religion, and so greatly conducing to the Welfare of Mankind, as to be even essential to the Salvation of their Souls.[140]

William Hutchinson noted the symbolic orientation of the Lodge room as evidence of this Masonic belief; "We place the spiritual lodge in the vale of JEHOSOPHAT, implying thereby, that the principles of masonry are derived from the knowledge of God... "[141] Further, he spoke of Masonic *gnosis* within the context of perennialism, stating that all of the "mysteries [of nature] were open to [Adam's] understanding" and "it is an uncontrovertable truth, that he has a competent knowledge of the mighty, the tremendous CREATOR OF THE UNIVERSE."[142] Hutchinson continued, avowing that Adam would "necessarily teach to his

138   Smith, *The Book M*, 1:41.
139   Henley, *On Scripture Masonry*, 3.
140   D'Assigny, *Answer to the Pope's Bull*. In Williams & Cerza, *D'Assigny*, 67.
141   Hutchinson, *Spirit of Masonry*, 94.
142   Hutchinson, *Spirit of Masonry*, 4.

family the sciences which he had comprehended in Eden, and the knowledge he had gained of NATURE and her GOD" and some would "faithfully transmit them to posterity."[143]

"Because they were holy; and so we ought."

Recalling that the perennialism of the Craft is conveyed via a thread of teaching which descends from Adam, it is not surprising to read the frequent allusions to Adam as the first Freemason. The most well known of these examples is likely the opening of Anderson's *Constitutions*, noted above. In addition to the iterations repeated in the Traditional History, there are frequent mentions of this in the several Masonic songs of the era. For instance, from a 1733 song collection:

> Old Grandfather *Adam*, deny it who can,
> A *Mason* was made as soon as a Man...[144]

And this stanza, from a song first appearing in the 1756 *Ahiman Rezon*:

> To rule the Day the Almighty made the Sun,
> To rule the Night he also made the Moon;
> And God-like *Adam*, a Master-Mason free,
> To rule and teach Posterity;
> Sanctity of Reason, and Majesty of Thought,
> Amongst Free-Masons should be sought[145]

These songs, and those like them, cast Adam in a Speculative

143 Hutchinson, *Spirit of Masonry*, 6.
144 Anon., *Prologue, and an Epilogue and Songs*, 5.
145 Dermott, *Ahiman Rezon*, 172.

light. Interestingly, other songs portray Adam as an Operative builder as well; for instance:

> When *Adam* was King of all Nations,
> HE form'd a Plan with all Speed;
> And soon made a sweet Habitation,
> For him and his Companion *Eve*.[146]

In 1724, a counter to Anderson's *Constitutions* was published by a Sam Briscoe which spoke, in part, to this portrayal. *The Secret History of the Free-Masons*, commonly referred to as the "Briscoe Pamphlet," was a recapitulation of the charges and Traditional History printed by J. Roberts two years earlier. Moreover, it spoke of Adam not only as a Freemason, but did so in a manner that underscored these perennialist ideas:

> It is universally agreed on all Hands, from sacred Writ, the *Jewish Talmudists*, the *Magi* among the *Egyptians*, and the *Arabick Catena*, that *Adam* was the First Architect, copying after his *grand Original* the Maker of all Things.[147]

In this excerpt from Briscoe, we are not told of Freemasonry as a manifestation of Perennialism, but rather we are shown that the concept of Adam as an architect appears in a variety of esoteric traditions. Recall also that the Traditional History casts Adam as created with the "Liberal Sciences, particularly *Geom-*

---

146 Dermott, *Ahiman Rezon*, 133

147 Briscoe, *Secret History of the Free-Masons*, 29–30; Interestingly, Briscoe cites the Arabick Catena MS, which states that Adam inscribed the secrets of the Craft upon his own sarcophagus, to be transported after the Great Flood. This story of transmitted knowledge was more usually seen in Masonic writing as being done upon two pillars by the children of Lamech, or by either Seth or Enoch, as noted above.

etry, written on his Heart."[148] Another theme related to Adam's heart is woven into the writing and self-concept of the time. Both the Graham MS (1726) and the Essex MS (1750) contain the following catechetical exchange:

> How were you made a free mason—by a true and a perfect Lodge—what is a perfect Lodge—the senter of a true heart.[149]

Similarly, the famous exposures from the 1760s, *Three Distinct Knocks* and *Jachin and Boaz*, contain the following:

> *Mas.* Where were you first prepar'd to be made a Mason?
> *Ans.* In my Heart.[150]

Through these examples, evidence of a narrative embedded within the Adam mythos emerges, whereby Adam is created with Masonry in his heart—in which are held "all the VIRTUES unpolluted."[151] All Masons are thereafter modeled after this first Brother, and first prepared in the same manner in which Adam was created, while the Lodge room becomes likened to the heart itself.

This theme supports the self-concept of the Lodge room as a sacred space. In some versions of Craft lore, Adam's fall from grace is presented as a failure to subdue the passions. For example, one early writer lamented, "Had it not been for that fatal Apple, Adam would have remained the first Free Mason."[152] Wil-

---

148 Anderson, *Constitutions* (1723), 1.

149 Graham MS, see also the Essex MS; both in Carr *&* Jones, *Early Masonic Catechisms*, 90 *&* 183.

150 W___O___V____n, *Three Distinct Knocks* , 66; Anon, *Jachin and Boaz*, 14.

151 Hutchinson, *Spirit of Masonry*, 4.

152 Anon., *Free Masons Apology*, in Pritchard, *Masonry Farther Dissected*, 24.

liam Smith puts a finer point on the accusation:

> Our first Father Adam was left without excuse, when he
> transgress'd the Divine Command...but after his Default
> the Passions usurp'd the Throne of Reason....[153]

This, then, creates a highly religious context for the Freemason's chief duty: "Q. What do you come here to do? A. Not to
do my own proper Will, But to subdue my Passion still...."[154]
In fine, it frames the Freemason's responsibility as a correction
of original sin; a purification of self. Indeed, the Masonic duty
to subdue your passions may well be seen as a symbolic representation of the internal battle between the "infernal spirits"
noted in the Graham MS, and the Divine "TRUTH" referenced
above. The labors of Freemasonry are thereby the means of this
purification. For example:

> Pleasures always on thee wait,
> Thou reformest *Adam's* Race,
> Strength and Beauty in thee meet,
> Wisdom's radiant in thy Face.[155]

It therefore follows that the Lodge room, as the site of Masonic labor, then becomes a locus of holy purity and perfection.
Symbolically, this belief was represented by frequent allusions
to the Lodge room being Eden. William Smith described the
Masonic initiation as a purification, and after being "invested
with innocence" the newly made Brother can begin to receive
the Glory:

153 Smith, *Pocket Companion*, 1.
154 Pritchard, *Masonry Dissected*, 9.
155 Smith, *The Book M*, 2:36.

> The World now from West to East, from South to North,
> affords nothing but Objects of Delight and Surprize; now
> the mystick Gate of Paradise is open'd, and the Tree of Life
> presents itself, and such as do not transgress the Lodge's Pre-
> cept, will be admitted to eat the immortal Fruit thereof.[156]

The Tree of Life is explained in the Book of Genesis as the key
to immortality. It was the *primi parentes'* transgression—their
eating of the Tree of Knowledge—that prevented their access to
immortality. Genesis 3:24 describes the gates of Eden thereafter
being guarded by cherubim with a "flaming sword."[157] At least
one Masonic song uses this imagery when describing the mysteries of the tyled Lodge:

> Where Cherubs guard the Door
> With flaming Swords before....[158]

A similar stanza is sung:

> WHILST Masons guarded stand,
> With flaming Sword in hand....[159]

Grand Lodge Chaplain Henley used this same imagery when
he advised that Masons ought to "preserve a pure and unblemish'd life and Conversation." Grand Chaplain Henley followed
with an important caution behind his admonishment: "Remember the fate of that primitive Mason, who being found unworthy
of the happy State he was placed in, was justly driven thence by

156 Smith, *The Book M*, 1:25.
157 Authorized Version.
158 Anon., *Curious Collection of the Most Celebrated Songs*, 3.
159 Farmer, *New Model*, 21. This stanza is from a song entitled "The
     FAIRIES" composed by Mr. Leveridge.

order of the great mason, and an Angel was sent to Guard the entrance against him with a Sword of fire."[160]

Another Masonic song directly links the bliss of paradise with the establishment of reason over passions:

> Where scepter'd Reason from her Throne,
> Surveys the *Lodge*, and makes us one;
> And Harmony's delightful Sway
> For ever sheds ambrosial Day;
> Where we bless'd *Eden's* Pleasure taste,
> Whilst balmy Joys are our Repast.[161]

The Edenic association extended to the physical orientation of the Lodge room, as well. The Graham MS (1726) describes the Lodge's easterly orientation as originating, in part, because "our first parance was placed Eastward in edin...."[162]

The Lodge was similarly compared to other perfect realms. More than 80-years before the phrase "celestial lodge above"[163] entered the Masonic lexicon, an early Masonic writer was referencing "holy Brother St. *Peter*."[164] This notion developed into a song, published in 1751, by an Irish Mason. The author highlighted the Saint's role as the Tyler of the Celestial Lodge:

160 Anon., *Dissertation*; see Eyer, "A Dissertation Upon Masonry," 73.

161 Anon., *Curious Collection of the Most Celebrated Songs*, 40.

162 Anon., "Graham MS." In Carr & Jones, *Early Masonic Catechisms*, 91.

163 The prominent American cleric and Masonic leader William Smith (1727–1803) used this phrase in 1795, in a St. John the Baptist Day sermon in Philadelphia. Please note that this William Smith is different than the compiler of *A Pocket Companion* and *The Book M.* For a transcript of the sermon with critical notes, see Shawn Eyer, "A Dissertation Upon Masonry, 1734, with Commentary and Notes." For an extended analysis of the document, see Eyer's article, "'The Essential Secrets of Masonry'" (p. 151ff).

164 Samber, *Long Livers*, xxxvii.

Let's lead a good Life whilst Power we have,
And when that our Bodies are laid in the Grave,
We hope with good Conscience to Heav'n to climb,
And give *Peter* the Pass-word, the Token, and Sign.

Saint *Peter* he opens and so we pass in,
To a Place that's prepar'd for all those free from Sin;
To that heav'nly Lodge which is tyl'd most secure,
A Place that's prepar'd for all Masons that's pure.[165]

Wellins Calcott continued in this comparison. He advised that through a faithful discharge of the tenets and virtues of the Craft "then we may reasonably hope to attain the cœlestial *pass-word*, and gain admittance into the lodge of our *supreme grand master, where pleasures flow for everyone.*"[166] Grand Master Cadawaller named this reward as "Eternal Residence in the LODGE above...."[167]

Recall also the 1734 *Dissertation.* In this oration, the author interprets St. Paul's letter to the Corinthians as a Masonic initiation. But the initiation is not into the temporal Lodge. Instead, this was an initiation into the Celestial Lodge, when St. Paul glimpsed behind the veil. The author continues in outlining the many ways that the temporal Lodge room exemplified Heaven.

Henley also reinterpreted a section of the Volume of Sacred Law, in another demonstration of this Masonic belief. While speaking of the Traditional History, he invokes the story of Jacob. Genesis 28:9–16 relates when Jacob, weary on his journey toward Haran, laid his head upon a stone to rest. Upon dreaming, Jacob had a vision of angels ascending and descending a ladder extend-

---

165 Spratt, *New Book of Constitutions*, 23.
166 Calcott, *Candid Disquisition*,175.
167 Cadawallader, *Charge Delivered at the Constitution of the Lodge No. cxxx*, 15.

ing from the heavens. Henley described this as God's revelation to Jacob of "the Holy Lodge."[168] Similar imagery was used in a London lecture circa 1735:

> ...and so ancient is the Lodge, that no Records can fix its Origin. For, how can it be otherwise than permanent, which has its Foundation fix'd on the stable Centre of the Earth, and its Heaven-aspiring Superstructure supported by Columns of Divine Attributes.[169]

The *Ahiman Rezon* also spoke of heaven in such terms, with the wit often read in the writing of the Antients' Secretary Laurence Dermott. In his introduction, Dermott promised a "full Account of the Transactions of the first Grand Lodge, particularly the excluding of the unruly Members, as related by Mr. *Milton*."[170]

Just as common as references to the Lodge room as Eden or Heaven are the more general descriptions of the Lodge room as sacred space. Ritual exposures and discovered MSS from the 1720s through the 1760s speak of the Lodge room being situated in its specific manner to as to emulate places of worship. For instance, from the 1724 exposure, GRAND *Mystery of Free-Masons Discover'd*:

> Q. What Lodge are you of?
> The Lodge of St. *John*.
> Q. How does it stand?
> A. Perfect East and West, as all Temples do?[171]

And from *A Mason's Confession* (1727):

---

168   Henley, *On Scripture Masonry*, 13.
169   Smith, *The Book M*, 1:25.
170   Dermott, *Ahiman Rezon*, vii.
171   Payne, *Grand Mystery of Free-Masons Discover'd*, 8.

Q. How stands your lodge?

A. East and west, as kirks and chapels did of old.

Q. Why so?

A. Because they were holy; and so we ought.[172]

Additional examples are found in catechisms dating to 1725, 1726, 1730, 1750, 1760, and 1762. There are also abundant examples of this belief revealed in Masonic songs.

From 1731:

Come sing for Joy, thro' us 'tis found
That all this Lodge is sacred Ground.[173]

From John Bancks, 1737:

A STATELY DOME o'erlooks Our East,
Like Orient PHOEBUS in the Morn:
And TWO TALL PILLARS in the West
At once support US, and adorn,
Upholden thus, the Structure stands,
Untouch'd by sacrilegious Hands.[174]

From Alexander Kennedy, 1756, describing the Initiation ceremony:

All Stumbling Blocks he took away,
That I might walk secure;

---

172 Anon. "A Mason's Confession." In Carr *&* Jones, *Early Masonic Catechisms*, 104.

173 Creake *&* Cole, *Curious Collection of the Most Celebrated Songs,* 1.

174 Bancks, *Miscellaneous Works, in Verse and Prose*, 36.

And brought me long e'er Break of Day,
To Wisdom's Temple-Door;
Where there we both Admittance found,
To mystic Paths on hallow'd Ground.[175]

From Alexander Dixon, 1756:

How bless'd are we from Ignorance free'd
And the base Notions of Mankind,
Here every virtuous moral Deed
Instructs and fortifies the Mind;
Hail! Ancient hallow'd solemn Ground,
Where Light and Masonry I found.[176]

From the same hand:

When we assemble on a Hill,
Or in due Form upon the Plain;
Our Master doth with learned Skill
The sacred Plan and Work explain:
No busy Eye, nor Cowan's Ear,
Can our grand Myst'ry see or hear.[177]

All of this—the allusions to Eden, Heaven, temples, and churches—underscores that the work of Masonry was understood by early Masons to be a sacred and holy endeavor. It should be noted that early anti-Masons often alleged that Lodges were contrived simply to take advantage of the curious.[178] It might

175 Dermott, *Ahiman Rezon*, 158.
176 Ibid., 167.
177 Ibid.
178 See Anon., *Free-Masons Accusation and Defense*, and Pritchard, *Masonry Dissected*, for examples of such an indictment.

therefore be suggested that public writings comparing the Lodge to a paradise, or stating that the Craft was delivered by God, were done to lure in Petitioners—and their membership fees. But there is no reason why private ritual would reflect such a belief, unless that belief was, in fact, part of the fabric of the Fraternity.

Conclusion

There is a widely held belief that early Freemasonry lacked in any deeper meaning or purpose than as a social outlet, with perhaps some added benefit of mutual aid. This view portrays early Masons as a collection of men as unconcerned with philosophy or spirituality as they were preoccupied with the hogshead and stein. The rationale behind why such a perception is held is often rooted in the fact that Masons convened in Taverns; the idea therefore follows that Masonic assemblies were a time of raucous intemperance. What the above has begun to outline, however, is the overwhelming evidence that runs contrary to the Tavern Myth, and speaks in direct opposition to such a minimalist narrative.

The passages and examples noted herein do not constitute a comprehensive listing of these practices. Numerous additional examples which further defy the Tavern Myth can be found in the various *aides des mémoires*, exposures, constitutions, pocket companions, speeches, sermons, and Masonic exegeses written throughout the first century of the Grand Lodge era. They tell the same story: early Grand Lodge era Freemasons held themselves to clear behavioral expectations, viewed their labors as a serious means by which to engage with Deity, and which afterward celebrated their mutual Brotherly Love with a bumper and song. While there were certainly Brethren and Lodges that eschewed this model, such does not change the essential design of the Craft.

To some, these sentiments may seem irreconcilable with the view of contemporary Freemasonry. It is vital to remember, however, that the Brethren who wrote and practiced these things were the ones who actually crafted the Freemasonry that we have ultimately inherited. Further, many of the examples presented here were drawn from officially-sanctioned Grand Lodge documents, and/or were penned by recognized Masonic leaders of the era. As such, these pervasive religious and philosophical concepts in the beginning decades of the 1700s represent normative Craft teachings of the time, and the expectation of decorum and temperance represent the actual behavioral standards endorsed by early Grand Lodge era Freemasonry.

By turning to the writings of the early Freemasons themselves, contemporary students of the Fraternity can discern key features of foundational Masonic culture. These writings often emphasize the seriousness with which the Masons of the early 1700s conducted themselves, and the deeply spiritual way in which they perceived the work of the lodge.

Bibliography

Anderson, James. *The Constitutions of the Freemasons, Containing the History, Charges, Regulations, &c. of that most Ancient and Right Worshipful Fraternity*. London: William Hunter, 1723.

———. *The Constitutions of the Freemasons. Containing the History, Charges, Regulations, &c. of that most Ancient and Right Worshipful Fraternity*. Philadelphia: Benjamin Franklin, 1734.

———. *The New Book of Constitutions of the Antient and Honourable Fraternity of Free and Accepted Masons, Containing Their History, Charges, Regulations, &c*. London: Richard Chandler, 1738.

Anonymous. *An Apology for the Free and Accepted Masons*. In Scott, *The Pocket Companion and History of Free-Masons*. London: J. Scott, 1754: 237–81.

———. *A Curious Collection of the Most Celebrated Songs in Honour of Masonry*. London: B. Creake, 1731.

———. *A Dissertation Upon Masonry, Deliver'd To a Lodge In America June the 24th 1734, Christ's Regm*. Unpublished speech contained in the C.W. Moore MS. Samel Crocker Lawrence Library, Boston, Ma.

———. "Essex MS." In Carr & Jones, Eds. *Early Masonic Catechisms*. London: Quatuor Coronati, 1975: 182–83.

———. "Graham MS." In Carr & Jones, Eds. *Early Masonic Catechisms*. London: Quatuor Coronati, 1975: 89–96.

———. *The Free-Masons Accusation and Defense, in Six Genuine Letters*. London: J. Peele, 1726.

———. *The Free Masons Apology as it Was Published at Paris, In March, 1737*. In Pritchard, *Masonry Farther Dissected*. London: J. Wilford, 1738: 23–24.

———. *Jachin and Boaz: Or, An Authentic Key to the Door of Free-Masonry*. London: W. Nichols, 1762.

———. *A Mason's Confession*. In Carr & Jones, Eds. *Early Masonic Catechisms*. London: Quatuor Coronati, 1975: 99–107.

———. *The Old Constitutions Belonging to the Ancient and Honour-*

able Society of Free and Accepted MASONS. London. J. Roberts, 1722.

————. *On the Rise and Progress of Freemasonry*. In Oliver, *The Golden Remains of the Early Masonic Writers*. London: Richard Spencer, 1847: 1:32–46.

————. *A Prologue, and an Epilogue, and Songs, Spoken and Sung to the Antient and Rt. Worshipful Society of Free-Masons, at the Theatre-Royal, on Thursday November the 29th, 1733, being Mr. GRIFFITH'S Benefit*. Dublin: Geo. Faulkner, 1734.

————. *The Whole Institutions of the Free-Masons Opened*. In Carr & Jones, Eds. *Early Masonic Catechisms*. London: Quatuor Coronati, 1975: 81–82.

Auld, William, & William Smellie. *The Free Masons Pocket-Companion*. Edinburgh: Auld & Smellie, 1765.

Baker, David Erskine. *An Oration in Honour of Free-Masonry Delivered Before the Honourable and Worshipful the Grand Lodge of Scotland, 30th November 1763, Being St. Andrew's Day*. Edinburgh, 1763.

Bancks, John. *Miscellaneous Works, in Verse and Prose*. London: Mr. Ares, 1737.

Bancks, Jonathan. *Proposals for Printing by Subscription, Miscellaneous Works, in Verse and Prose, of Mr. John Bancks*. London: Mr. Ares's Printing House, 1737.

Bogdan, Henrik. "Freemasonry and Western Esotericism." In Henrik Bogdan & Jan A.M. Snoek, Eds., *Handbook of Freemasonry*. Leiden: Brill, 2014: 277–305.

Briscoe, Samuel. *The Secret History of the Free-Masons, Being an Accidental Discovery, of the Ceremonies Made Use of in the several Lodges*. London: Sam Briscoe, 1724.

[Cadwallader, Blayney]. *A Charge Delivered at the Constitution of the Lodge No. CXXX, at the Swan in Wolverhampton on Tuesday the 30th of October 1764*. Birmingham: James Sketchey, 1765.

Calcott, Wellins. *A Candid Disquisition of the Principles and Practices of the Most Ancient and Honourable Society of Free and Accepted*

Masons. London: Brother James Dixwell, 1769.

Carr, Harry & Jones, G.P., Eds. *Early Masonic Catechisms*. London: Quatuor Coronati, 1975.

[Clare, Martin]. *A Defence of Masonry*. In Anderson, *The New Book of Constitutions of the Antient and Honourable Fraternity of Free and Accepted Masons, Containing Their History, Charges, Regulations, &c*. London: Richard Chandler, 1738: 216–26.

Codrington, John. *On the Design of Masonry, Delivered In the Union Lodge, Exeter, No. 370, DPGM, 1770*. In Oliver, *The Golden Remains of the Early Masonic Writers*. London: Richard Spencer, 1847: 1:196–216.

Cole, Benjamin. *The Antient Constitutions of the Free and Accepted Masons, Neatly Engrav'd On Copper Plates*. London: B. Creake, 1731.

Crawley, W. J. Chetwode. "Contemporary Comments on the Freemasonry of the Eighteenth Century." *Ars Quatuor Coronatorum* 18 (1905): 201–216.

———. "The Masonic MSS in the Bodleian Library." *Ars Quatuor Coronatorum* 11 (1898): 4–44.

———. "The Old Charges and the Papal Bulls." *Ars Quatuor Coronatorum* 14 (1911): 47–64.

D'Assigny, Fifield. *An Impartial Answer to the Enemies of Free-Masonry*. Dublin: Edward Waters, 1741. In Williams, Louis & Alphonse Cerza, Eds. *D'Assigny*. Bloomington: The Masonic Book Club, 1974: 70–87.

———. *A Serious and Impartial Enquiry Into the Cause of the Present Decay of Free-Masonry in the Kingdom of Ireland*. Dublin: Edward Bate, 1744. In Williams, Louis & Alphonse Cerza, Eds. *D'Assigny*. Bloomington, Ill.: The Masonic Book Club, 1974: 19–48.

[D'Assigny, Fifield]. *An Answer to the Pope's Bull; With the Character of a Free Mason*. Dublin: Edward Waters, 1738. In Williams, Louis & Alphonse Cerza, Eds. *D'Assigny*. Bloomington: The Masonic Book Club, 1974: 63–69.

Dermott, Laurence. *Ahiman Rezon: Or, A Help to a Brother*. London:

James Bedford, 1756.

Disgusted Brother. *The Secrets of the Free-Masons Revealed.* London: J. Scott, 1759.

[Drake, Francis]. *A Speech Deliver'd to the Worshipful and Ancient Society of Free and Accepted Masons. At a Grand Lodge, Held at Merchant's Hall, in the City of York, on St. John's Day, December the 27ᵗʰ, 1726.* York: Thomas Gent, 1727.

———. *A Speech Deliver'd to the Worshipful and Ancient Society of Free and Accepted Masons. At a Grand Lodge, Held at Merchant's Hall, in the City of York, on St. John's Day, December the 27ᵗʰ, 1726.* London: B. Creake & B. Cole, 1734.

Dublin Weekly Journal, June 26, 1725, 52.

Dunckerly, Thomas. *A Charge, Delivered to the Members Of the Lodge of Free and Accepted Masons, Held At the Castle-Inn, Marlborough. In Calcott, A Candid Disquisition of the Principles and Practices of the Most Ancient and Honourable Society of Free and Accepted Masons.* London: Brother James Dixwell, 1769: 137–44.

———. *Lecture on Masonic Light, Truth, and Charity Before the Lodges at Plymouth, 1757.* In Oliver, *The Golden Remains of the Early Masonic Writers.* London: Richard Spencer, 1847: 1:137–56.

Eyer, Shawn. "A Discourse on Good Behaviour for the Guidance of the Members of the Craft." *Philalethes: The Journal of Masonic Research and Letters* 69(2016): 64–67.

———. "A Dissertation upon Masonry, 1734, with Commentary and Notes." *Philalethes Journal of Masonic Research and Letters* 68(2015): 62–75.

———. "'And Hinder Not Music': The Role of Music and Song in Traditional Freemasonry." *Philalethes: The Journal of Masonic Research and Letters* 67(2014): 110–24.

———. "Defining Esotericism from a Masonic Perspective." *The Journal of the Masonic Society* No. 2 (Autumn 2008): 16–21.

———. "Drake's Oration of 1726, with Commentary and Notes." *Philalethes: The Journal of Masonic Research and Letters* 67(2014):

14–25.

————. "Exploration of Themes Expressed in the Frontispieces of Early Masonic Literature, 1723 to 1775." Unpublished paper.

————. "Silence and Solemnity in Craft Freemasonry." *Ahiman: A Review of Masonic Culture and Tradition* 1(2009): 102–119.

————. "The Inward Civility of the Mind: The 1735 Grand Oration of Martin Clare, F.R.S." *Philalethes: The Journal of Masonic Research and Letters* 69(2016): 58–63.

Farmer, Peter. *A New Model for the Rebuilding of Masonry on a Stronger Basis Than the Former.* London: J. Wilford, 1730.

A Free Mason. *The Perjur'd Free Mason Detected.* London: T. Warner, 1730.

Galbraith, Joseph. *The Free Masons Pocket Companion: Containing The Origin, Progress and Present State of that Antient Fraternity.* Glasgow: Joseph Galbraith, 1765.

Galloway, James. "Letter to Wellins Calcott, October 01, 1768." In Calcott, *A Candid Disquisition of the Principles and Practices of the Most Ancient and Honourable Society of Free and Accepted Masons.* London: Brother James Dixwell, 1769: 116–22.

Gaudry, J.S. *An Address to the Lodge Of Perfect Friendship, Held At the Shakespeare and Greyhound Inn and Tavern At Bath, On the Festival Of St. John the Evangelist, A.L. 1768, A.D. 1768.* In Calcott, *A Candid Disquisition of the Principles and Practices of the Most Ancient and Honourable Society of Free and Accepted Masons.* London: Brother James Dixwell, 1769: 152–56.

Gould, Robert. *Gould's History of Freemasonry Throughout the World.* New York: Charles Scribner's Sons, 1936.

————. *The History of Freemasonry.* New York: John C. Yorston and Company, 1885.

Hackett, David G. *That Religion in Which All Men Agree: Freemasonry in American Culture.* Berkeley, Cal.: University of California Press, 2014.

Head, Isaac. "A Charge, Delivered to a Constituted Lodge of Free and

Accepted Masons, at the King's-Arms, in Helstone, Cornwall, on Tuesday April 21, A.D. 1752. A.L. 5752." In Head, *A Confutation of the Observations on Free Masonry By an Anonymous Author of a Pamphlet, Entitled Masonry the Way to Hell.* Exeter: A Brice & B. Thorn, 1769: 71–81.

————. *A Confutation of the Observations on Free Masonry By an Anonymous Author of a Pamphlet, Entitled Masonry the Way to Hell.* Exeter: A. Brice & B. Thorn, 1769.

[Henley, John]. *Select Orations on Various Subjects.* London: John Tillotson, 1737.

Hoey, James. *Masonry the Turnpike-Road To Happiness In This Life, And Eternal Happiness Hereafter.* Dublin: James Hoey, 1768.

Hughan, William James. *The Old Charges of British Freemasons.* London: Simpkin, Marshall & Co., 1872.

Hutchinson, William. *The Spirit of Masonry.* London: J. Wilkie, 1775.

Jackson, A.C.F. *English Masonic Exposures, 1760–1769.* London: Lewis Masonic, 1986.

Knoop, Douglas, & G.P. Jones. *A Short History of Freemasonry to 1730.* Manchester: The University Press, 1941.

Knoop, Douglas, G.P. Jones & G. Hamer, Eds. *Early Masonic Pamphlets.* London: Quatuor Coronati, 1978.

————. *The Two Earliest Masonic* MSS. Manchester: Manchester University Press, 1938.

Leslie, Charles. *A Vindication Of Masonry and Its Excellency Demonstrated In a Discourse At the Consecration Of the Lodge Of Vernon Kilwinning, On May 15, 1741.* In Anon., *The Free Masons Pocket-Companion.* Edinburgh: Auld & Smellie, 1765: 153–64.

————. *Masonry: A Poem.* Edinburgh: W. Sands, A. Brymer, A. Murray and J. Cochran, 1739.

Mackey, Albert G. *An Encyclopædia of Freemasonry and its Kindred Sciences.* Philadelphia: Moss & Co., 1879.

Mazet, Edmund. "Freemasonry and Esotericism." In Antoine Faivre & Jacob Needleman, Eds., *Modern Esoteric Spirituality.* New York:

Crossroad, 1992: 248–76.

McLeod, Wallace (Ed.). *A Candid Disquisition of the Principles and Practices of the Most Antient and Honourable Society of Free and Accepted Masons*. Bloomington, Ill.: The Masonic Book Club, 1989.

———. "The Causes of Ritual Divergence." In McLeod, Wallace. *The Grand Design: Selected Masonic Addresses and Papers of Wallace McLeod*. Highland Springs, Va.: Anchor Communications, 1991: 87–98.

Murphy, Christopher B. "The Tavern Myth: Reassessing the Culture of Early Grand Lodge Era Freemasonry." *Philalethes: The Journal of Masonic Research and Letters* 68 (2015): 50–61.

Oakley, Edward. *A Speech Deliver'd To the Worshipful Society Of Free and Accepted Masons*. In [Drake], *A Speech Deliver'd to the Worshipful and Ancient Society of Free and Accepted Masons. At a Grand Lodge, Held at Merchant's Hall, in the City of York, on St. John's Day, December the 27th, 1726*. London: B. Creake & B. Cole, 1734: 25–34.

Oliver, George. *The Golden Remains of the Early Masonic Writers*. London: Richard Spencer, 1847.

———. *The History of Masonic Persecution in Different Quarters of the Globe*. London: Richard Spencer, 1867.

Payne, T. *The Grand Mystery of Free-Masons Discover'd*. London, T. Payne, 1724.

Pennell, John. *The Constitutions of the Free Masons. Containing the History, Charges, Regulations, &c. of that most Ancient and Right Worshipful Fraternity*. Dublin: J. Watts, 1730.

Preston, William. *Illustrations of Masonry*. London: J. Williams, 1772.

[Pritchard, Samuel]. *Masonry Dissected*. London: J. Wilford, 1730.

———. *Masonry Farther Dissected*. London: J. Wilford, 1738

Ramsay, Michael. *Oration*. In Gould, *Gould's History of Freemasonry Throughout the World*. New York: Charles Scribner's Sons, 1936: 3:10–15.

Read's Weekly Journal or British Gazetteer (London), January 21, 1738.

Roy, Thomas. "The Pillars of the Temple." In Thomas Roy, *Dare We*

Be Masons, and Other Addresses. Boston: Anthoensen Press, 1966: 80–85.

[Samber, Robert, writing as Eugenius Philalethes, Jr.]. *Long Livers: A Curious History of Such Persons of Both Sexes Who Have Liv'd Several Ages, and Grown Young Again*. London: J. Holland, 1722.

Schuchard, Marsha Keith. *Restoring the Temple of Vision: Cabalistic Freemasonry and Stuart Culture*. Leiden: Brill, 2002.

Scott, J. *The Pocket Companion and History of Free-Masons*. London: J. Scott, 1754.

Shaftesley, John. "Jews in English Freemasonry in the Eighteenth and Nineteeth-centuries." *Ars Quatuor Coronatorum* 92 (1979): 25–63.

Smith, William. *A Pocket Companion for Free-Masons*. London: E. Rider, 1735.

———. *The Book M: Or, Masonry Triumphant*. Newcastle upon Tyne: Leonard Umfreville & Co., 1736.

Spratt, Edward. *The New Book of Constitutions of the Most Ancient and Honourable Fraternity of Free and Accepted Masons*. Dublin: Edward Bate, 1751.

———. "A Collection of Songs." In Spratt, *The New Book of Constitutions of the Most Ancient and Honourable Fraternity of Free and Accepted Masons*. Dublin: Edward Bate, 1751.

Stevenson, David. The Origins of Freemasonry. Cambridge: Cambridge University Press, 1988.

Stewart, Howard. "Speculari—Speculatus—Speculativus." *Philalethes Journal of Masonic Research and Letters* 48(1995): 113.

W——O—— V——n. *The Three Distinct Knocks On the Door of the Most Antient Free-Masonry*. London: H. Srjeant, 1760.

Williams, Louis & Alphonse Cerza, Eds. *D'Assigny*. Bloomington: The Masonic Book Club, 1974.

Wonnacott, William. "Martin Clare and the Defence of Masonry (1730)." *Ars Quatuor Coranatorum* 28 (1915): 80–110.

About the Contributors

Ric Berman is the author of numerous Masonic books, including *The Foundations of Modern Freemasonry: The Grand Architects—Political Change and the Scientific Enlightenment, 1714-1740* (2012), *Schism: The Battle That Forged Freemasonry* (2013), and *Loyalists and Malcontents: Freemasonry and Revolution in the Deep South* (2015). In 2016, he was selected as the United Grand Lodge of England's Prestonian Lecturer. He is a Past Master of the Marquis of Dalhousie Lodge № 1159 (English Constitution); Treasurer of Quatuor Coronati Lodge № 2076 (EC), England's oldest research lodge; PM of the Temple of Athene Lodge № 9541 (EC), the research lodge of the Province of Middlesex; and PZ of Marquis of Dalhousie Chapter № 1159 (EC). Ric has a Masters in Economics from Cambridge University and a Ph.D. in History from Exeter; he is a Visiting Research Fellow at Oxford Brookes University and a Fellow of the Royal Historical Society.

Shawn Eyer, FPS, is a Masonic scholar with research interests strongly focused upon the development of Freemasonry in the seventeenth and eighteenth centuries, explored through the careful reading of early Masonic literature, with special attention to intertextuality, thematic progression, and ritualistic praxis. He has authored dozens of articles on Masonry, and is the editor of *Ahiman: A Review of Masonic Culture and Tradition*, and of *Philalethes: The Journal of Masonic Research and Letters*, North

America's oldest independent Masonic education journal. Professionally, he is engaged as the Director of Communications and Development of the George Washington Masonic National Memorial Association.

Jedediah French, MPS, is a member of Templum Rosae Lodge in Oakland, California. He is also a member of the Sacramento York Rite Bodies and a 32nd degree in the Sacramento AASR. His articles have been published in *Philalethes: The Journal of Masonic Research and Letters, The Plumbline,* and *The Square.* He regularly gives presentations on Masonic education and is currently working toward his Ph.D. in the Study of Religion at the University of California, Davis.

David Harrison, FPS, is a Masonic historian in the United Kingdom, and a member of the Lodge of Lights № 148 in Warrington, England. He researched the development of English Freemasonry for his Ph.D. at the University of Liverpool, which was published by Lewis Masonic as *The Genesis of Freemasonry* (2009). Other works by Harrison include *The Transformation of Freemasonry* (2010), *The Liverpool Masonic Rebellion and the Wigan Grand Lodge* (2012) and the *York Grand Lodge* (2014). His most recent publication is *A City of York: A Masonic Guide.*

Christopher B. Murphy, MPS, is a frequent contributing writer to *Philalethes: The Journal of Masonic Research and Letters,* with a focus on early Grand Lodge era literature and culture. He has lectured in Lodges and at Masonic events throughout the United States. He is the current Worshipful Master, and Charter Junior Warden, of Fibonacci Lodge № 112, as well as the Secretary for the Vermont Lodge of Research № 110, of the Most Worshipful Grand Lodge of Vermont, Free and Accepted Masons. Murphy resides in southern Vermont with his wife and two sons.

Dana Scofield, MPS, is a Past Master of Franklin Lodge № 4 and is currently the Senior Warden of Fibonacci Lodge № 112 under the auspices of the Most Ancient and Honorable Society of Free and Accepted Masons of the State of Vermont. He is a member and contributing writer for *Philalethes: The Journal of Masonic Research and Letters*, current board member of the Masonic Restoration Foundation, and a Masonic scholar focusing on eighteenth-century Masonic culture and philosophy. He lives in northern Vermont with his wife and two daughters.

Nathan St. Pierre, MPS, holds a Ph.D. in Music Education from George Mason University, a Master of Education degree in Kodàly Music Education from Loyola University Maryland, and a Bachelor of Music Degree from The Hartt School, University of Hartford. Initiated into Freemasonry in 2009, he is a member of The Lodge of the Nine Muses № 1776 in Washington, D.C. He served as Master of the Lodge from 2013 to 2017. He is a recurring contributor to *Philalethes: The Journal of Masonic Research and Letters*.

The Philalethes Society

Established in 1928, the Philalethes Society is devoted to the promotion of the highest quality Masonic education and research. It was created on October 1, 1928, when a small group of Masonic writers gathered at the Masonic Library at Cedar Rapids, Iowa, for a very serious purpose. They were some of the most renowned Freemasons of their day: Robert I. Clegg (editor of new editions of Mackey's classics), George H. Imbrie (editor of Kansas City's *Masonic Light*), Cyrus Field Willard (formerly of the *Boston Globe*), Alfred H. Moorhouse (editor of *The New England Masonic Craftsman*), Henry F. Evans (editor of Denver's *Square and Compass*), and William C. Rapp (editor of Chicago's *Masonic Chronicler*).

They combined their efforts to create the Philalethes Society because they valued the importance of Masonic education. It was the intention of the founders that the Philalethes Society would effectively serve the needs of those in search of deeper insight into the history, rituals and symbolism of Freemasonry. Reflecting their intentions that day, founding president Cyrus Field Willard said:

> Those who have been members of the Fraternity for a number of years have known men who were little more than "good fellows," but because they were appointed to some minor position by a friend who was Master, they contin-

ued to go "up the line" until eventually they landed in the Master's chair. And after serving in the office for a year, they had signally failed "to set the Craft to work and give them instructions whereby they might pursue their labors." It was the realizing sense of this that prompted the formation of an association to bring together in one body the writers who felt that the great mass of Freemasons in the United States should have more information on the fundamentals of Freemasonry.

The Greek word φιλαλήθης (pronounced "fill-a-*lay*-thayss") was used by ancient writers such as Aristotle and Plutarch, and means "a lover of truth." The word came into Masonic circles through alchemical mystic Robert Samber (1682–1745), who used the pseudonym Eugenius Philalethes; Samber's use, in turn, was an homage to Thomas Vaughan, an earlier alchemist who had used the same name. Finally, a Rite of Philaléthes was founded in Paris in 1772, devoted to the study of esotericism. Founding President Cyrus Field Willard wrote in 1937 that the Philalethes Society took its name from the Parisian Philaléthes.

In the earliest days, the Society described itself as "An International Body of Masonic Writers." Official membership was limited to forty Fellows, who were drawn from writers and editors of the many Masonic newspapers and magazines that existed before the Second World War. As the founders explained:

> Its Fellowship is limited to 40, like the French Academy, but the Correspondence Circle is unlimited in number. [...] Its purpose is to bring together the Masonic writers of the world who seek the Truth in Masonry.

This structure consciously imitated both the Académie Française (in the limitation of forty Fellows) and the world's premier lodge of Masonic research, Quatuor Coronati № 2076 in London, England (in allowing non-members to participate through an unlimited "Correspondence Circle"). Members of the Correspondence Circle were also called "corresponding members."

Today, members of the Correspondence Circle are merely referred to as "Members." The number of members who are designed Fellows is still restricted to forty.

Among the original forty Fellows were Cyrus Field Willard, Harold V. B. Voorhis, Rudyard Kipling, Oswald Wirth, Robert I. Clegg, Louis Black, J. Hugo Tatsch, Charles S. Plumb, Harry L. Haywood, J. S. M. Ward, and Charles C. Hunt.

Fellows elected since that time have included Masonic notables such as Carl H. Claudy (1936), Arthur Edward Waite (1937), Allen E. Roberts (1963), S. Brent Morris (1980), John Mauk Hilliard (1981), Wallace McLeod (1986), Thomas W. Jackson (1991), Norman Vincent Peale (1991), Robert G. Davis (1993), Leon Zeldis (1994), Rex R. Hutchens (2011), and Arturo de Hoyos (2013).

In the Society's early days, all of its publications appeared in other, established Masonic periodicals, many of which were edited by Fellows of the Society. For example, the Denver *Square and Compass* ran hundreds of Philalethes items during that period. Many of the Society's earliest publications were issued under the slogan, "With Rough Ashlar and Tracing Board," and under the motto, "There is No Religion Higher than Truth." Both of these maxims reflected the viewpoint that Freemasonry is a serious and deeply personal quest for Truth and Light.

Unfortunately, the Great Depression took a toll on many of the independent Masonic periodicals, and, soon after that, the hardships of World War Two caused nearly all of them to cease publication. It was only after the war ended that the Philalethes Society was able to release the first issue of *Philalethes*. The first issue, dated March, 1946, was edited by Walter A. Quincke, FPS.

Philalethes: The Review of Masonic Research and Letters has long served as the *de facto* journal for North American Freemasonry. Today, the journal is published quarterly, and every edition aims to present thought-provoking, substantial articles on Masonic symbolism, ritual, history, art and philosophy, as well as careful book reviews and insightful editorial content.

For information about membership
in the Philalethes Society,
please visit the Society's website,
www.freemasonry.org

Index

Aaron (Biblical character) 138

Abel (Biblical character) 138, 139, 432

Abibalus, King of Tyre 19, 20n21

Abram / Abraham (Biblical patriarch) 16, 17, 63

Acaster, E. John T. ✶ 72n60

acceptation 38 (*see also* Freemasonry—acceptance of gentlemen)

Achab (see Ahab)

Acker, William Julius 352n12

Adam (Biblical patriarch) 8, 9–11, 54, 61, 70, 82, 93, 100, 101, 108, 138, 139, 218, 225, 242, 287, 300, 306, 366–67, 375, 414, 423, 424, 432, 435–41

  liberal sciences / geometry implanted within, 8, 9, 61, 108, 225, 375

  created after the Image of God, 61, 225, 367–68, 423, 433

  formed his sons into a lodge, 108

  paradisiacal or sylvan lodge of, 9–10, 204, 242

  sarcaphagus of, 139

  state of bliss, 9–10, 204

Addison, Joseph (1672–1719) 426

Adept 118

Adoniram (Biblical character) 20

Africa 15, 18, 25, 29, 66, 351

Ahab, King of Israel (Biblical character) 26

Ahabath Olam (*'ahavat 'olam*) 140, 144

Ahiman (Biblical character) 133n253, 135 (*see also* Dermott, Lawrence—*Ahiman Rezon*)

Ahiman: A Review of Masonic Culture and Tradition 457

Aholiab (Biblical character) 17, 21, 63, 72

Alberti, Leon Battista (1404–1472) 126

Alcamenes (fifth century BCE) 29–30n28

alchemy 358, 359, 369, 379

Aldrich, Henry (1647–1710) 45

Alexander the Great (356–323 BCE) 29–30n28, 30, 424

Alexandria 31

  Lighthouse of, 31

allegory 90, 171, 185, 209n125, 238,
    364–65
All Hallows Church, Lombard
    Street, London 45
All-Seeing Eye (Masonic symbol)
    125, 384
allusions 205
altar 11, 125
Ambrosebury, Wiltshire 41n37
America (Masonic legend of) 15
American colonies 87, 95–96,
    154–56, 159–63, 169, 189, 192,
    209, 247, 274–75, 394
    as battlefield between Antients
    and Moderns, 274–75
    Masonic culture of, 152–209
    Masonic education within,
    183–84
    Masonic publishing in, 247
Amhurst, Nicholas (1697–1742)
    118
ample form 47n38, 48, 50, 51 (see
    also due form)
Ananias (Biblical character) 414
Anaxagoras (c. 510–c. 428 BCE)
    29–30n28
Anaxarchus (c. 380–c. 320 BCE)
    137
Anderson, Rev. James ✴ (c.
    1680–1739) 4–5, 50, 51, 52, 71,
    75, 83–84, 85, 91, 97, 100–101,
    104–120, 121, 134, 143, 145,
    216–39, 365, 393–95, 425–26,
    435
    assigned to author the Constitu-
    tions, 50, 51
    committee of fourteen "learned
    Brothers," 50, 51
    News from Elysium (1739), 4,
    228–39

Grand Warden pro tem., 52
Royal Genealogies (1732), 228
songs by, 80–81, 91, 110
The Constitutions of the Free-
    masons, Containing the Histo-
    ry, Charges, Regulations, &c.
    of that most Ancient and Right
    Worshipful Fraternity (Lon-
    don, 1723) xi, 4, 50–52, 54, 55,
    56–82, 83, 84, 90, 92, 95, 101,
    102, 105, 117, 122, 145, 163, 169,
    174n56, 177, 179, 217–24, 233,
    236, 255, 281, 287, 289, 295,
    297, 305, 349–50, 356, 365–67,
    372, 375, 393–95, 401–402,
    403, 407n47, 422–23, 425–26;
    endorsed by Desaguliers, 57,
    221, 367, 425; examination of
    Hebrew Bible in, 177; frontis-
    piece of, 57–58, 72–73, 365–66;
    religious tolerance in, 255,
    305; vetted by numerous Ma-
    sonic leaders, 57
The Constitutions of the Free-
    masons. Containing the Histo-
    ry, Charges, Regulations, &c.
    of that most Ancient and Right
    Worshipful Fraternity (Phila-
    delphia: Benjamin Franklin,
    1734) 55, 95–96, 160, 394
The New Book of Constitutions
    of the Antient and Honourable
    Fraternity of Free and Accept-
    ed Masons, Containing Their
    History, Charges, Regulations,
    &c., second edition (1738)
    4, 55, 59, 71, 104–120, 121–22,
    134, 137–38, 143n305, 174n56,
    179, 218, 221–24, 227, 235, 237,
    323, 350, 394, 404, 420, 427–

28; as partial basis for Dermott's *Ahiman Rezon*, 247;
esotericism claimed for, 227
*The History and Constitutions
of the Most Ancient and Honourable Fraternity of Free and
Accepted Masons*, third edi-
tion (London, 1746) 120
Androcides of Cyzicum (fourth
century BCE) 29–30n28
angels 192, 424, 441, 442
Angerona (Roman goddess) 137
Annapolis, Maryland 194
Anne, Queen of Great Britain
(1665–1714) 43, 44–45, 323n25
Anno Lucis (see Year of Light)
Antediluvian Masonry 9–13,
369–70
Antients (see Grand Lodge of England, Antients)
antimasonry 67–68, 90, 93, 96,
118–20, 127–29, 140, 365, 408
Antipatris 31
Apelles of Kos (fl. fourth century
BCE) 29–30n28, 231
Apollo 28, 58, 72, 73, 365–66
*Apology for the Free and Accepted
Masons, An* (1754) 417
Apollodorus (fouth century BCE)
29–30n28
appropriation theory 378 (*see also*
transition theory)
apron 89, 115–16, 131, 260, 270, 320
operative apron, 320
Arabian peninsula 15n13, 17, 25,
351
Arabick Catena 139, 142, 437
arcana of Masonry 431
arch 89, 99
Archimedes (c. 287–c. 212 BCE)

66, 365
Archiphron 236
architects / architecture 2, 7–8, 9,
10–45, 54, 63–66, 67, 69–70,
82, 107, 110, 119, 138, 225, 232–
37, 287, 289, 315, 366, 367, 385,
395, 419, 432, 434
as synonymous with Masonry,
54
cultivated by Cain and Seth, 12,
287
five noble orders of, 22, 366
proportions taken from the
human body, 29
revival of, 69
sacred architecture, 18
understood by clergymen of
"former ages," 67
(*see also* Corinthian order, Doric order, Ionic order)
Areopagus 28
Arianism 360
Aristotle (384–322 BCE) 29–30n28
Aristotelian philosophy 355, 375
arithmetic 30n29, 281 (*see also*
arts and sciences)
Arius 360
Armitage, Edward ✶ (1859–1929)
163–64n32
Ars Quatuor Coronatorum
122n215, 158, 163–64n32
ark of Noah 12, 70, 109, 138, 139,
432
as a Masonic Lodge, 12, 109
as a "Piece of Architecture," 12
(*see also* Antediluvian Masonry, Deluge, Noah)
ark of the covenant 23
Artaxerxes 115
Artemon (fl. 230 CE) 29–30n28

arts and sciences 53, 62, 88, 109,
     145, 233, 281, (see also gram-
     mar, rhetoric, logic, arith-
     matic, geometry, music &
     astronomy)
   incribed onto primordial pil-
     lars, 62, 222
   survival of antediluvian knowl-
     edge of, 53, 109
Arundel marbles 36
Arundell, William ✕ (fl. 1754) 330
Ahasuerus (Biblical character) 115
Ashkenaz (Biblical character) 351
Ashlar (Masonic symbol) 433
Ashmole, Elias ✕ (1617–1692) 37,
     41–42, 127–28, 289, 325
Ashtaroth 25
Asia 15–16, 25
Asia Minor 18, 25, 26–27, 29, 351
Ashkelon 19
Assyria 14, 19, 25, 27
Astarte 19
astrology 231, 358
astronomy 30n29, 44, 63, 231,
     281, 362, 372 (see also arts and
     sciences)
   development of in the ruins of
     Babel, 63
atheism 112, 143, 300, 361, 373–74
Athelstan (c. 894–939) 66, 101,
     128, 288, 314
Athelstane-Edwin legend 128
Athens 28, 29, 114, 200, 427
atomism 355
Augustan style 33–34, 37–38, 41,
     43, 45, 66, 69, 84, 99, 234
Augustus Caesar (63 BCE–14 CE)
     30, 31–32, 35, 66, 424
Auld, William (fl. 1760–1771)
     431n127

Baal 14, 26
Baasha, King of Israel (Biblical
     character) 26
Babel, Tower of 13, 53, 62–63, 72,
     100, 108n172, 110, 113, 178–79,
     201, 230, 236–38, 426
   Andersonian account of, 13–15,
     62–63
   and astronomy, 63
   and the Grand Design, 109,
   built by Noachidæ, 62, 109,
Babylon 27, 28, 29, 292
   hanging gardens of, 27
Bacchus 92 (see also Nimrod)
Bacon, Francis (1561–1626) 354,
     357
Bactria 25, 111
Baigent, Michael ✕ (1948–2013)
     325
Bailey, Francis ✕ (fl. 1721) 49
Baker, David Erskine ✕ (1730–
     1767) 410
Baldwin, Richard (d. 1777) 124
Baltimore Convention of 1843 206
Bancks, John ✕ (1709–1751) 118,
     217, 291–92, 444
Barnewall, Henry Benedict,
     4th Viscount Barnewall ✕
     (1708–1774) 98
Baron, John 326
Baron, William 326
Baronet, Sir George Tempest ✕
     (1675–1745) 328
Bate, Edward 121
Bath, England 371
Bathurst, Charles ✕ (b. 1702, fl.
     1726) 94
Bathurst, Ralph (1620–1704) 45
     (see also New Chapel, Trinity
     College)

Beal, John ☩ (d. 1724) 50, 52
Beauty (in the Masonic sense) 17, 18, 24, 29, 63, 92, 101–102, 142, 188, 190, 201, 206, 239, 303, 357, 395, 433, 439 (*see also* Strength, Wisdom)
Beckwith, Josiah (b. 1734) ☩ 329
Beckwith, Thomas (1731–1786) 315, 329
Bede (c. 672–735) 59, 84–85, 128, 224, 314, 424
Bedern Hall 320
Bedford, James ☩ (fl. 1754) 132
Bedlam Hospital, London 40
Belshazzar (Biblical character) 27
benediction 208
Bennet, Henry, 1st Earl of Arlington (1618–1685) 41, 42
Benson, Robert, 1st Baron Bingley ☩ (c. 1676–1731) 328
Berkeley House, Piccadilly, London 37
Berman, Ric ☩ 5, 353, 354n14, 362n28, 363n30, 377–80, 457
Bethel 26
Bezaleel (Biblical character) 17, 20–21n21, 63, 72
Bible 64, 70, 83–84, 85, 97–98, 100, 113, 115, 121, 124, 130, 133n253, 136, 137, 139, 152, 163–64n32, 165–66, 169, 174n56, 176–77, 178, 185, 194–206, 208–209, 222–223, 230, 305, 340n125, 351, 359, 384, 405, 414, 415, 419, 433–35 (see INDEX OF TRADITIONAL SOURCES for individual verses)
  as "Divine Furniture" of the lodge, 130
  as a "Pattern of sacred Masonry," 435
  "dark" passages of, 176, 208
Birkhead, Matthew ☩ (d. 1722) 80, 82, 91, 294, 403
Black-Swan (tavern) 124
Blackerby, Nathaniel (d. 1742) 264
Blake, William (1757–1827) 375–78
Blanchard, Bartholomew ☩ (fl. 1783) 333
Blanchard, William ☩ (1749–1836) 316, 317, 333
Blayney, Lord Cadwallader, 9th Baron Blayney ☩ (1720–1775) 400, 431
Blazing Star (Masonic symbol) 125, 370
bliss 130, 187–88, 191, 201, 204, 292, 441
Blunt, Bro. ☩ 269
blue (Masonic symbolism of) 115–16
Boaz (see pillars, Hiramic)
Bodleian Library 163–64n32
Body (as technical term in Freemasonry) 12, 166n36, 197, 198, 274, 322, 400, 434
Bogdan, Henrik ☩ 166n36, 175–76, 350n7
Böhme, Jakob (1575–1624) 384
Boitard, Louis-Philippe (fl. 1733–1767) 125
Bonai 20, 64, 223
Book *M*, the (Rosicrucian tradition) 413–14 (*see also* Smith, William, of Gateshead)
Book M, or Masonry Triumphant, The (1736) (see Smith, William, of Gateshead)
Book of the Antient Constitutions

of the Free & Accepted Masons, A (1728) 55
Book of Nature 384–85
Booth, John ✶ 337, 338
Boreham, James ✶ 327
Borthwick, Capt. Richard ✶ (d. 1702) 42
Boston, Massachusetts 129, 154–56, 159n21, 160–63, 192
Boyle, Richard, 3rd Earl of Burlington (1694–1753) ✶ 37, 82
Boyle, Robert (1627–1691) 384
Bradford 334
Bradley, B. ✶ 340
bright masons/bright men (see Freemasons—as "bright")
Bramwell, F. H. ✶ 340
Brewers 321
Bricklayers 322–23
Brierley, Samuel ✶ 336–37, 338
Britain/Britons 15, 33–52, 66, 69, 82, 88, 241–75, 313–41, 372, 413
British Museum 325n32
Broad, John ✶ (fl. 1787) 335
Brockwell, Charles Rev. ✶ (d. 1755) 129, 161–62
brotherly love 75, 100, 133, 167, 168, 190, 197, 199, 200, 204, 400, 412, 418, 434
    as a heavenly trait, 167, 168
Browne, John ✶ (fl. 1798–1802) 333n55, 334
Bruce, Sir William, 1st Baronet of Kinross (c. 1630–1710) 41
Brydges, James (1673–1744), 1st Duke of Chandos 363
Buckingham House, St. James's Park, London 44
Bullock, Steven C. 158–59, 209, 275

Bultflow, John 320
Bunyan, John (1628–1688) 177n62
Burton, John (1710–1771) 315, 330
Bussey, Jacob ✶ (fl. 1779–1788) 335, 340
bylaws 76
Byron, William, 5th Baron Byron (1722–1798) 259
cabala/cabbala (see kabbalah)
cabalists/cabbalists (see kabbalah)
Caesarea 31
Cain (Biblical character) 11, 54, 287, 414, 424
    as a "false brother," 414
    line of 61, 288
Calcott, Wellins ✶ (1726–c. 1780) 87, 139, 391n2, 406n140, 408n60, 410, 421–22, 442
    A Candid Disquisition (1769) 87n, 408n60, 410, , 421–22, 431, 442
Calcutta 110, 114
Cambridge 34
Cambridge University 161
Campbell, Katherine 282, 293, 296–97
Canaan/Canaanites 16–18, 20
Candia 28
Canning, George ✶ (1770–1827) 316
Canterbury, England 322–23
Canton of Bern 124, 128
Carlile, Richard (1790–1843) 317
Carmarthen, Wales 88, 90, 410
Carnarvon, Henry Brydges, Marquis of ✶ (c. 1708–1771) 105, 270
Carnegy, S.W.B. ✶ (fl. 1843) 206n120
Carpenter, Audrey T. 353, 359–60,

363n30, 365, 374

Carpenter, George, 2nd Baron Carpenter ✻ (c. 1694–1749) 264

Carpenters 322–23

Carr, Harry ✻ (1900–1983) 234n31–32, 383n56, 428n120, 428n121

Carthage 18

Cartwright, John ✻ (fl. 1756) 141

Carvers 231, 322–23

Carysfort, John Proby, 1st Lord Carysfort ✻ (1720–1772) 126, 259

Castle Abby, Northamptonshire 37

Castle Howard, North Yorkshire 45

Castorius 72

catechism 1, 86, 100, 134, 170, 175, 184, 255, 265, 416, 428, 438, 444

Catholicism 84, 124, 244, 245, 349

Caucasus Mountains 351

Cavendish, William, 2nd Duke of Devonshire (1672–1729) 44

cedars of Lebanon 20, 24

Celestial Hierarchy 188

celestial lodge 185, 187–91, 135, 198, 199, 200–201, 205–206

as lodge triumphant, 189

cement (in a figurative sense, see lodge—cement of)

Centre of Union/Unity 179, 350

Ceres 114, 427

Cerza, Alphonse ✻ (1905–1987) 97n139, 98n145, 99n146, 99n148, 407n54, 408n57, 435n140

Chaldea / Chaldees 14–16, 25, 27, 29, 62, 66, 225, 231

Chamberlayne, John (1666–1723) 373, 380

Chancellor Robert R. Livingston Masonic Library, the (New York City) 153n2, 162

Chandler, Richard (c. 1713—1744) 104

Charges, Masonic 63, 67, 71–76, 85, 88, 102, 112–15, 126, 129–30, 132, 137–38, 143–44, 145, 226–27, 255, 305, 392–93, 402

concerning religion, 71–73, 126, 143–44, 349–51, 422–23

charity 77, 100, 117, 126, 140, 168, 247, 252–53, 208, 262, 269, 412, 418

in the sense of brotherly love, 168

(see Grand Lodge of All England at York—charity practices of, Grand Lodge of England—charity practices of, Grand Lodge of England, Antients— charity practices of)

Charlemagne (742–814) 126

Charles I (1600–1649) 35, 40, 323n25

statue at Temple Bar, 40

Charles II (1630–1685) 37–42, 44, 323n25

statue at Temple Bar, 40

Charles V and I (1500–1558) 229–34, 235

Chatsworth, Derbyshire 44

Cheapside, London 42

checkered pavement (see Mosaic Pavement)

Chelsea {London} 41, 43

Chemosh 25

cherub / cherubim 23, 204, 206,

441
  as celestial Tyler, 204
Cheshire, England 321n20, 332
Chester, England 321–22, 323, 328
Chesterton, Maryland 194
Chevening, Kent 41n37
Chicester, England 44
China 16, 25, 108n172
Chirurgeons Hall (Barber-Sur-
  geon's Hall), London 37
Christ Church, Oxford, 361
Christ Church, Philadelphia 205,
  206
Christian Masons 130, 132, 144,
  139, 432
Christianity 2, 18, 32, 72, 114, 130,
  132, 143–44, 159, 177, 185, 191,
  208, 209n125, 244, 305, 318,
  330, 348–51, 359–60, 423, 432
  Mysteries of, 177
Church, Catholic (see Catholi-
  cism)
Church of England 244, 361, 371,
  374
Church of Ireland 244n12
Churchill, John, 1st Duke of Marl-
  borough (1650–1722) 44
Chymical Wedding of Christian
  Rosenkreutz, The (1616) 359
Cibber, Caius Gabriel (1630–1700)
  40, 42
Civil War (see English Civil War)
civility 77, 116
clandestine Masonry 116, 252
Clare, Martin (1688–1751) �֎ 153,
  419, 426–27 (see also A De-
  fence of Masonry)
  December 11, 1735 Grand Ora-
  tion of, 129, 153, 189–91
Clare-market (area of London) 97

Clark, J. 99
Claret, George (1783–1850) �֎
  102n157
classism 253, 275
Claudius 72
Clauss, Manfred 382n54
Clayton, Sir Robert (1629–1707)
  43
Clegg, Isaac ✖ (fl. 1790) 336–37
clergy 40, 47, 52, 67–68, 69, 70,
  80, 162, 232, 233, 330, 351, 352,
  354, 361, 371, 374
Clorfene, Chaim 113n185
Codrington, John ✖ (fl. 1770)
  408n61
Coil, Henry Wilson ✖ (1885–1974)
  157–58, 381
Cole, Benjamin ✖ (1695–1766) 55,
  88–94, 96, 102–103, 117, 145,
  280–81, 301n81
Cole's Constitutions, or A Book of
  the Antient Constitutions of
  the Free & Accepted Masons
  (1728) 55, 89, 91, 280–81
Cole's Constitutions, second edition (1731) 55, 88–94, 96,
  117–18, 145, 398n19, 403n35,
  407n48, 411n69, 417n92,
  417n93
College of Philadelphia 194
Colling, John 327
Coke, Edward 75–76
communication (Masonic meeting) 35, 46, 47, 48, 51, 66, 70,
  76–79, 116, 194–95, 253, 390,
  392, 401, 420
communio sanctorum, Masonic
  concept of:
  in A Dissertation upon Masonry, 189

in Martin Clare's oration, 189–91
in *The Book M*, 188–89
Company of Masons (London) 38, 42, 289
Hall of, 41–42
Compass (Biblical symbol) 305
Compass / Compasses (Masonic symbol) 89, 99, 119, 195, 395
Mason's Confession, A (1727) 234
Conflagration, General 26, 222
conflict resolution 168
confusion of tongues (Biblical legend) 13–14, 62–63, 108n172, 178–79, 201, 230, 237 (*see also* Mason's Faculty)
Constitutions (in abstract) 67, 199, 200, 366
contrafactum 292–94
Constantine the Great 313
conversation 52, 75, 119, 168, 393, 395, 396, 402
Cooke MS (see Masonic manuscripts—Cooke MS)
Cooke, Ross Frank (1915–1997) 158
Cooper, John L., III ✡ xvi
copper plate (see engraving)
Cordwell, John ✡ (d. March 26, 1755) 47
Corinth 29
Corinthian order 29, 41, 89
corner-stone 199
Cornwall 163–64n32
Coudert, Allison 355, 358–59
counter-mythology 8, 62 (*see also* Traditional History)
Couper, Robert 320
cowans (see profane)
Cowper, William (d. 1740) ✡ 263, 264
Cranstoun, James, 8th Lord Cranstoun ✡ (1755–1796) 259
Crawley, W. J. Chetwode ✡ (1844–1916) 92n120, 97n140, 111n182, 135, 228n27, 395n9
Creake, Benjamin (fl. 1726) 88
Crete 28
Cross, Jeremy Ladd ✡ (1783–1861) 102n157
Crown (tavern) 132
Cryer, Neville Barker ✡ (1924–2013) 314n3, 319n14, 319n16, 320n17, 322, 324–25, 326n35, 327n37, 330n49, 334, 335
Culdees 317, 332
Curious Collection of the Most Celebrated Songs in Honour of Masonry, A (1731) 89–93, 102–103 (*see also* Cole's *Constitutions*)
Curl, James Stevens ✡ 184
Cush (Biblical character) 13, 237
Cypron 31
Cyrus II, King of Persia 27–28

Daedalus 28
Dagon 18
Damascus 24, 26
Dan 26
Dan, tribe of 64–65
Danby Gateway, Oxford 36
Daniel, Thomas ✡ (fl. 1787) 335
Daniels, Stephen 371
Danish Invasion, the 66
Danvers, Henry, 1st Earl of Danby, (1573–1643) 36
darkness (as ignorance) 129, 400, 403, 413, 421, 426

Darnley, Edward Henry, 2nd Earl of ✠ (1715–1747) 117

D'Anvers, Caleb (see Amhurst, Nicholas)

D'Assigny, Fifield ✠ (1707–1744) 76n77, 134, 137, 143–44, 284, 400, 411, 415, 421, 435
  An Answer to the Pope's Bull; With the Character of a Free Mason (1738), 134, 407n54, 421, 435
  An Impartial Answer to the Enemies of Free-Masonry (1741), 134, 137n270, 400
  A Serious and Impartial Enquiry in to the Cause of the present Decay of Free-Masonry in the Kingdom of Ireland (1744), 134, 411

David, King of Israel 19, 21, 230
  Cedar palace of, 19

Davies, Malcolm ✠ (1952–2010) 287, 289, 295, 299, 301, 302, 308–309

de Hoton, William, Jr. ✠ 318

de Hoton, William, Sr. ✠ 318

de Hoyos, Arturo ✠ 153n2

de Pakenham, Thomas (d. 1361) 319

de Veil, Thomas ✠ (1684–1746) 264–65
  invested a knight, 265
  satirized in Hogarth's Night (1736), 264

Deacon, Masonic office of 85, 255
  mentioned in Pennell's Constitutions (1730), 85

decorum 74, 79, 116, 395

Defence of Masonry, A (1730), 118–19, 170n49, 418–19, 426–27

(see also Clare, Martin)

degree, first (see Entered Apprentice degree); second (see Fellow Craft degree); third (see Master Mason degree)

deiknymena (Gr. "things shown") 382

Deism 72, 143, 208, 351–52, 360, 371–75
  prohibited, 143
  vs. theism, 351

Delafaye, Charles ✠ (1677–1762) 80, 81–82, 91, 264

della Porta, Giambattista (c. 1535–1615) 384

Deluge 12–13, 53, 62, 63, 72, 84, 98, 109, 222, 423, 428

demit 77

Denham, John (c. 1614–1669) 38

Deputy Grand Master 21, 35, 38, 48, 50, 52, 57, 74, 77, 78, 117, 221, 241n1, 257, 263, 264, 364

Deputy Master 109

Dermott, Anthony (1760–1784) 244

Dermott, Lawrence ✠ (1720–1791) 6, 132–43, 45, 241–50, 259–61, 265–67, 272–73, 288, 432
  a Protestant, 244
  biographical details of, 243–47
  appointed Grand Secretary of the Antients Grand Lodge (1752), 243
  initiated at Lodge Nº 26 (1741), 244
  Masonic songs by, 141
  Master of Lodge Nº 26 (1746), 244
  occupation as painter, 244
  owner of the Five Bells Tavern,

246

occupation as vintner, 246

Dermott's *Ahiman Rezon* (1756) 55, 132–43, 145, 241–43, 242–43, 249, 255, 259–60, 288, 349–50n1, 402n28, 408n58, 408n59, 432

  editions of, *247*

  meaning of Hebrew title, 133n253

  second edition (1764), 260, 265–66

  third edition (1778), 270

  success of, 245, 247

Dermott, Thomas (b. 1699) 243

Desaguliers, John Theophilus ✶ (1683–1744) 4, 47–48, 57q, 58q, 134, 221, 252, 348–85, 394, 425

  A Course of Experimental Philosophy, 361

  author of dedication of Anderson's *Constitutions* of 1723, 57–58, 221, 367, 375

  depicted by John Pine, 57

  did not profess Deism, 372

  grand oration of June 24, 1721 (lost), 50

  part of possible "inner circle" of Freemasons, 254–55

  poetry of, 372–73

  religious views of, 352–53, 362, 371–75

  view regarding charity funds, 252

Descartes, René (1596–1650) 363

diabolism 119

Diana (Roman goddess) 114, 236, 427

Diocletian (244–312) 72

Diodorus Siculus (first century

BCE) 14n12, 223

Dipoenus (fl. 580 BCE) 29–30n28

discipline 77

Dissertation upon Masonry, A (1734) 5–6, 152–209, 420, 433–34

  as earliest surviving private Masonic oration, 156–57, 207, 433

  as third oldest surviving Masonic oration, 153

  authorship of, 161–63

  circulation of, 193–206

  discovery of, 154

  esotericism in, 169–78

  importance of, 207–209

  later influence of, 204–206

Divine Providence (see Providence)

Divine Wisdom (see God—as Wisdom, Wisdom)

Dixon, Alexander (fl. 1756) ✶ 142

Doniger O'Flaherty, Wendy (b. 1940) xiii

Doric order 29, 40, 89

Dormer window 383 (*see also* Master-Jewels)

Dowsett, Thomas ✶ 269

Drake, Francis ✶ (1695–1770) 94, 100, 156, 314–15, 316, 325–26, 329–32, 340, 399, 412, 418, 425, 434–35

  Eboracum (1736), 314–15, 331, 340

  1726 Grand Oration of, 94, 100, 102–103, 153, 207, 314, 315, 327, 330, 399, 412, 425, 431n129, 434–35

Drake, John 326

Drawswerd, Thomas 320

Dresiphon 236

dress, modes of 289

druids 119

Drumlanrig, Nidsdale 41n37

Duncombe Park, Helmsley 45

drunkenness 75, 119, 397–401, 411
    (*see also* gluttony)
    disapproved of, 397–401, 411

Drury Lane 88

Dublin, Ireland 83, 121, 128n240,
    244

Dublin Weekly Journal, The 403,
    405

Dudley House 258

due form 17, 32, 34, 40, 46, 47n38,
    49, 51, 445 (*see also* ample
    form)

due guards 422

Duke of Chandos, the (Brydges,
    James, 1st Duke of Chandos)
    363, 380

Duke of Sussex, the (see Freder-
    ick, Augustus, the Duke of
    Sussex)

Dunckerley, Thomas ✸ (1724–
    1795) 405–406, 411–12

Durkheim, Émile (1858–1917)
    352–53

Dwindle, Mary (seond wife of
    Laurence Dermott, d. 1766)
    245

Dyer, Colin F. W. ✸ (1910–1987)
    171n51

East 92

Eboracum (see York)

Ecbatana 27

Edelstein, Dan xii

Eden 9–11, 93, 101, 185, 186, 192,
    204

as "the first Temple," 9–10
    Masonic lodge as, 93, 185, 186

Edinburgh 41, 369

education (see Masonic instruc-
    tion)

Edward IV (1442–1483) 130

Edwards, Lewis ✸ (1888–1969)
    217n1

Edwin of Northumbria (c. 586–
    633) 66–67, 101, 313, 314, 318,
    330
    as "Grand-Master," 66–67, 314,
    330

egalitarianism 119, 145, 202

Egypt / Egyptians 14–15, 16–17, 19,
    25, 28, 32, 114, 230, 231, 232,
    237, 287, 292, 351, 365, 424,
    425, 427

Eleazar (Biblical character) 18, 138

Eleusinian mysteries 114, 382, 427

Eliade, Mircea (1907–1986) xiii

Eliot, John ✸ (1754–1813) 192

Elizabeth Stuart, Queen of Bohe-
    mia (1596–1662) 35, 45
    incorrectly stated as represent-
    ed on Wren's Temple Bar Gate
    (actually Anne of Denmark),
    40

Elizabeth I (1533–1603) 68, 90

Elliot, Capt. Joseph ✸ (fl. 1717) 46

Elliot, Paul 371

elves 90–91

emphatic expressions 165, 194
    (see esotericism)

empiricism 359

England 33–52, 95, 114, 264, 270,
    287, 348n1, 354, 356, 363, 372,
    376, 394
    class distinctions within 253
    as New Jerusalem, 377

English Civil War 318, 322, 323, 325

engraving 11, 55, 57, 72, 73, 89, 95, 99, 107, 108n172, 125, 222, 270, 294, 365, 384–85

Enlightenment 138, 185, 284, 351–55, 420, 421, 431, 432

Enoch (Biblical patriarch) 61–62, 100, 222, 366, 423, 424 (*see also* pillars, primordial)

Enosh (Biblical character) 11

Entered Apprentice degree 77, 226, 416, 431
  in the Traditional History, 22, tokens and passwords transposed with Fellow Craft degree by Moderns, 250

"Enter'd 'Prentices Song" 82

Ephesus 27

epilogues 102–103 (*see also* prologues)

equality 75

equity 194–95, 199

Essenes 119

esoteric / esotericism xiv, 100, 105, 165–66, 169–78, 194–206, 207–209, 225–28, 355, 360, 369, 377–78, 380–85, 412, 418–19, 431, 433–34
  academic scholarship on, 172n54
  as "emphatical meaning," 165, 194
  as "Philosophical and Masonic sense," 194
  classification of, 170–78
  esoteric readings of the Bible, 165, 176–77, 194–206, 208
  "latent doctrines" of Freemasonry, 171

only an "expert Brother" understands, 105, 227
  taxon 1: social-exclusionary, 80, 107, 170–71, 173–74, 177, 181, 195, 225–26, 381
  taxon 2: textual-interpretive, 80, 171–78, 182, 207–208, 412, 420, 434
  taxon 3: systematic, 171–72, 172n54
  (*see also* secrets, Masonic)

ethnomusicology 283

Euclid (fl. 300 BCE) 54, 65, 66, 100, 424
  47th Problem of (Masonic symbol) 58, 65–66, 120, 365–66

"Euclid, Brother" (allonym for early eighteenth century Mason, possibly James Anderson) 118, 119–20, 395, 404, 420

Eudoxus of Cnidus (c. 390– c. 337 BCE) 29–30n28

Euphranor of Corinth (fourth century BCE) 29–30n28

Euphrates 225

Eupompus (fourth century BCE) 29–30n28

eureka (Gr. "I found it") 29, 58, 365

Europe 267, 349, 350, 351

exclusionary membership 168, 398, 409–14
  a heavenly emulation, 168

exegesis 209, 434–35

Exodus, the 63

exoteric 100, 412, 418–19, 434 (*see also* esotericism)

experimental physics 361–63, 369, 373–74

exposés 64, 81, 92, 101–102, 170, 175, 179–80, 234–35, 250–51, 284, 303, 317, 351, 356, 370, 383, 396, 404–405, 416–18, 420, 428, 434, 438–39, 443–445, 446
measures taken against, 250
exposures (see exposés)
Eye of Providence (see All-Seeing Eye)
Eyer, Shawn ✡ 5–6, 94n133, 113n186, 125n228, 128n238, 129n244, 189n87, 365–66, 399n20, 405, 420n102, 433n133, 434n136, 457–58

Facultye of Abrac 181
Fairfax, Charles ✡ (fl. 1688–1714) 329
Fairfax, Robert ✡ (1666–1725) 328, 329
Faivre, Antoine 172n54
false brethren 119, 252, 409–16
compared to Judas, 410
only pretend to search for knowledge, 411

Fama Fraternitatis (1614) 413
Farmer, Peter 89, 91–93, 96, 294, 404n36
A New Model for the Rebuilding of Masonry on a Stronger Basis Than the Former (1730) 89, 91–93
feast (see festive board)
Fellow Craft degree 74, 226, 370, 416
in the Traditional History, 20, 22, 29, 30, 37, 41, 64
"Key" of, 80, 226
songs for, 90, 295
tokens and passwords transposed with Entered Apprentice degree by Moderns, 250
wages of, 370
festive board 35, 38, 42, 44, 46, 47, 48, 49, 50, 51, 78–79, 81, 281, 299
singing during, 280–309
Five Bells Tavern (in the Strand, London) 245–46
flamberge 204n112
Flammarion, Nicolas Camille (1842–1925) 385
Flanders 128
Flavel, John (c. 1627–1691) 200
Fleming, John V. 359n23
Fletcher, Charlotte 194n96
Fletcher, William ✡ 337
Flying Post 92 (*see also* exposés)
Folkes, Martin ✡ (1690–1754) 361, 381
foundational narrative xii (*see also* mythistory)
Fountain tavern, the Strand, London 51
four crowned martyrs 72–73
Foxcroft, Ezekiel (1633–1674) 359
France 128, 349, 354, 355, 371, 372
Francis I (1494–1547) 229–34
Francis, the Duke of Lorraine ✡ (1708–1765) 371
Frankfort 128, 134
Franklin, Benjamin ✡ (1705/6–1790) 95–96, 97, 160, 195, 209, 292, 394, 395n9
his American edition of Anderson's *Constitutions* (1734), 55, 95–96, 160, 394
Franklin, Peter (1692–1766) 292

Frederick, Augustus, the Duke of
    Sussex ✡ (1773–1843) 316
Frederick Lewis, Prince of Wales
    ✡ (1707–1751) 105, 107, 117,
    363
Free Mason's Vade Mecum (1736)
    106–107
Freemasonry:
    acceptance of gentlemen, 35, 38,
        51, 52
    as a "Distinguish'd Science," 408
    as a "divine Science," 407
    as a "famous Art, Science, or
        Mystery," 118
    as a "ffree gift of God to the
        children of men," 428
    as a "Holy Secret," 428
    as a "Mystery Divine," 407
    as a "Sacred Brotherhood," 407
    as a "Sacred Institution," 164
    as a "Sacred Order," 407
    as a "sacred Privilege," 407
    as a "regular system of moral-
        ity conceived in a strain of
        interesting allegory, which
        readily unfolds its beauties to
        the candid and industrious
        enquirer," 171
    as an "Art Divine," 92
    as "El Shaddai," 18
    as God-given, 81, 92, 129, 408,
        422–24, 428
    as "gracious Gift of Heaven,"
        408
    as "heavenly genius," 408
    as "mystical Rites," 407
    as the "Art Divine," 408
    as "the Center of Union," 46, 71,
        350
    as the "Craft Divine," 81, 407

    as the "Daughter of Heaven,"
        129, 408
    as the "Kingdom of Masons,"
        200
    as the "Noble Art," 300
    as the "Noble Science," 366
    as the "Perfection of the Art of
        Masonry," 407
    as the "Royal Art," 12, 15, 23, 26,
        27, 28, 33, 34, 65, 80, 81, 137,
        179, 201, 225–26, 236, 366
    as the "royal craft," 412
    as the "royal Science," 407
    as the "sacred Art, by Heav'n
        design'd," 408
    as the "sublime Science of Ma-
        sonry," 407
    as "this most Ancient and Hon-
        ourable Society," 190
    epicurean narrative of, xiv–xv
    etymology / early use of name,
        26, 30, 288, 322n22, 428
    heterodoxy within, 159
    meritocracy within, 74
    not Deistic, 360
    perfected at the building of Sol-
        omon's Temple, 24, 65
    phenomenological study of x
    pre-dates the Grand Lodge era,
        2
    propagated after Solomon's
        Temple completed, 25–26, 65
    prosopography of, x
    reductionist narrative of, 5
    the "Arcana" of, 431
    tradition that some clergy op-
        posed, 67–68
Freemasons:
    as "a chosen Generation," 407
    as "a royal Priesthood," 407

as "bright," 11, 20, 28, 43, 420

as "Professors of the Royal Art," 179

as "the children of Light," 408

as "Travellers" or "Solomon's Travellers," 13, 25, 26, 28, 112, 235–36, 238, 350

dispersed after Solomon's Temple completed, 65

"elite religious status" of, 191

excel other men, 81

heavenly Masons 190, as "Divine Philosophers," 188–89, as "Spirits," 190

must not involve civic courts in their disputes, 74

"old Masons," 11n3, 19n20, 22n22, 41, 42, 46, 47, 51, 108, 174n56, 222

penalties for misbehavior of, 74

qualifications of, 38–39, 73–74, 76–77

voting sign of, 116, 145

Freemasons Hall (London) 391

Freemasons' Monthly Magazine 154–55, 158; mistakenly referred to as *Moore's Masonic Magazine*, 158

French language 128, 372

French, Jedediah 4, 348–89, 458

French Revolution 348

Frodsham, Bridge (d. 1768) 315

frontispieces 89, 95, 99, 107, 125, 365–66

funeral service, Masonic 366

Galbraith, Joseph ✶ (fl. 1765) 431n127

Galbraith, Samuel ✶ 269

Galen 231

Galloway, James ✶ (fl. 1768–1796) 391

Gascoigne, Sir Thomas, 8th Baronet ✶ (1745–1810) 333

Gateshead, England 179

Gath 19

Gaudry, J.S. (fl. 1768) ✶ 408n60

Gauge (Masonic symbol) 326

Gavel (Masonic symbol)
the "magna kevell" at York, 319

Gaul 15, 26

Gaza 18, 19, 174

Gelbart, Matthew 291

General Regulations (see Regulations)

Geneva Bible 84

Genius of Masonry 92, 291, 292

geometry 2, 9–12, 16, 17, 20–21n21, 29–30, 54, 62, 65–66, 67–68, 69, 102, 108, 110, 145, 225, 281, 287, 367, 372, 385, 419, 423, 428–30 (*see also* arts and sciences)

as synonymous with Masonry, 54,

as the "Basis" of Masonry, 102

as the "Foundation" of Masonry, 61

condemned as "Conjuration," 67–68

implanted in Adam, 10, 68, 225, 287, 367, 423

in the Traditional History, 9, 10, 54, 61, 67–68, 108, 423

God created the universe using, 9, 108, 305, 430

"recover'd its Ground," 69

Zoroastrians and, 110

George I (1660–1727) 35, 45, 46,

49, 266
George IV ✫ (1762–1830) 316
George, Prince of Denmark and Norway, Duke of Cumberland (1653–1708) 44
Georgian architecture 315
Germany 15, 26, 128, 348
Ghiblim 20, 64, 223
Gibbons, Grinling (1648–1721) 39
Gifford, Richard ✫ (1725–1807) 264
Gildas the Wise (c. 500–570) 128
Gilding, Brother ✫ (fl. 1754) 131
Glovers 321
gluttony 411, 414 (*see also* drunkenness)
Glycon (sculptor of the Farnese Hercules, third century CE) 29–30n28
gnosis 406, 406n44, 428, 432, 435
God 9–10, 16, 17, 19, 62, 71–73, 85–86, 110, 113, 130, 137, 138, 143, 145, 177, 186, 188, 191, 195, 196, 199, 204, 235, 300–301, 304–307, 359, 362, 367–68, 373–74, 375, 396, 422–28, 423, 429–35
as Jehovah, 18, 23, 24, 235
as "our all-wise Master," 430
as "sovereign Grand Master," 306
as "the all Mighty architecte, son of the virgin," 169
as "the Almighty Architect," 9, 188, 373, 429
as "the Almighty Artist," 306
as "the Center of all Things," 429
as "the Eternal," 19, 143
as "the first great Master of Masonry," 301
as the "Fountain of Happiness," 433
as "the God of Glory," 16
as "the God of Truth," 188
as "the Grand Architect of the World," 190
as the "Grand-Master of the Universe," 9
as "the Great Architect of Heaven and Earth," 85
as "the great Architect of Nature," 102
as "the Great Architect of the Universe," 24n24, 61, 225, 305, 367, 423
as "the Great Architect of the world," 195
as "the great *Elohim*," 430
as "the great Geometrician," 169
as "the omnipotent Grand-Master," 204
as "the one true God," 18, 24, 235
as "the tremendous Creator of the Universe," 435
as Providence, 111
as Truth, 188, 356–57, 432–33
as Wisdom, 17, 302, 420
created the universe using geometry, 9, 108, 305, 430
implored to "enlighten our Minds with Wisdom and Understanding," 85
inspiration by, 12, 17, 20, 24, 26, 61, 63, 65, 129, 235
intervention by, 18, 62, 72, 360, 424
Newtonian concept of, 368
presence of, 18, 23, 63, 65

(*see also* Shechinah)
Trinitarian concept of, 130, 432
Goethe, Johann Wolfgang von ✡ (1749–1832) 375
gold (Masonic symbolism of) 115–16
golden calves 26
Gomer (Biblical character) 351
Goodrick-Clarke, Nicholas (1953–2012) 172n54
Goodricke, Sir John, 5th Baronet (1708–1789) 315
Goodricke, Sir Henry, 4th Baronet ✡ (1677–1738) 329
Goose and Gridiron tavern (St. Paul's Churchyard, London) ix, 1, 46, 348
Gore, Christopher ✡ (1758–1827) 192n92
Gordon, Patrick (c. 1644–1736) {Governor of Pennsylvania} 160
Goston, Brother ✡ 117
Gothic architecture 33, 66, 84, 233–34, 318
as "Gothick Ignorance," 69
Gothic Constitutions (see Old Charges)
Gould, Robert Freke ✡ (1836–1915) 114n188, 248–49, 249q, 318, 327, 328, 331n52, 334n59
grammar 30n29 (*see also* arts and sciences)
Grand / Great Architect of the Universe (see God)
Grand Chaplain 333
Grand Design, the 13, 15n13, 18, 22, 27, 110, 237, 419
nature of in the Traditional History, 110
Grand Lodge of All England at York (1725–c. 1792) 5, 88, 94, 100, 153, 313–41, 399, 412, 434
charity practices of, 140
ended in or after 1792, 333
relics of, 340
Grand Lodge of England (1717–1813; also known as the Moderns and the Premier Grand Lodge) 1–2, 69–82, 98, 142, 161, 177, 189, 243, 250–75, 221, 227, 239, 289–90, 295, 305, 313, 327–28, 330, 331, 333, 348, 351, 352–53, 364, 368, 369, 378, 385, 394, 400, 419, 422, 430
anti-Catholicism within, 253,
anti-Irish sentiment within, 253,
attempted to destroy the Antients by an act of Parliament, 274
chaplain of, 163–64n32
charity practices of, 76–77, 116–17, 127, 140, 247, 252–53, 262, 268, 270–71, 365
class distinctions within, 253, 275
communications of, 70,
constitution process for lodges of, 98
criticized as gluttonous, 259–60,
defined, 77
discrimination against Irish Freemasons by, 253–54, 261–62
elections, 79, 116
exclusion of the Holy Royal Arch, 133, 255–56

exodus of members and lodges
    from, 258–59
"inner circle" within, 254–55
interest in other cultures, 110–
    111
lack of Deacons, 255,
minutes of, 251–59, 270–71
quarterly communications of,
    35, 46–48, 51, 66, 70, 76–79,
    253
not recognized in Ireland or
    Scotland, 254
omission of catechetical lec-
    tures, 255
regalia of, 115–16
suffered from arrogance and
    poor leadership, 256
tercentenary of, 1, 6,
transposition of first and sec-
    ond degree words by, 250
transposition reversed, 254
union with the Antients, 256,
    290 (see United Grand Lodge
    of England)
Grand Lodge of England, Antients
    (1751–1813; also known as the
    Most Ancient and Honour-
    able Society of Free and Ac-
    cepted Masons according to
    the Old Constitutions)
    6, 132–43, 241–75, 290, 333,
    432 (see also United Grand
    Lodge of England)
acceptance regardless of social
    class, 275
anti-establishment flavor of,
    248
broad religious tolerance of,
    245
charity practices of, 140, 247,

262, 269
demographics of, 267
disapproved of belonging to
    numerous lodges simultane-
    ously, 138
Grand Master's throne, 247
membership certificates issued
    by, 269
parity with Moderns' religious
    policy, 143–44
perceived as potentially sedi-
    tious, 269–70
popularity in England, 276
popularity in America, 248, 276
proposed to have the more tra-
    ditional approach, 250
recognized by the Grand Lodge
    of Ireland, 254
recognized by the Grand Lodge
    of Scotland, 254
union with the Moderns, 256,
    290 (see United Grand Lodge
    of England)
Grand Lodge of England South of
    the River Trent (1779–1789)
    316–17n8
aligned with the Grand Lodge
    of All England at York, 316–
    17n8
Grand Lodge of Georgia
    (Antients, Est. 1786) 247
Grand Lodge of Ireland 83–87, 97,
    100, 122, 248, 253, 254, 394,
    403
charity practices of, 140
parity with English practice, 83,
    122
Grand Lodge of Maryland (An-
    tients, Est. 1787) 194, 247
Grand Lodge of Massachusetts

(United in 1792) 153n2, 154–55, 162

Grand Lodge of New York (United in 1827) 162

Grand Lodge of Nova Scotia (Antients) 247

Grand Lodge of Pennsylvania (Antients, Est. 1786) 194, 198, 205–206, 247

Grand Lodge of Pennsylvania (Moderns, Est. 1734–1750) 194

Grand Lodge of Scotland 97, 100, 248, 254, 331, 394, 410

Grand Lodge of South Carolina (Antients, Est. 1787) 247

Grand Lodge of Virginia (Antients) 247

Grand Master (Masonic officer) 46, 47, 48, 49, 50, 51, 52, 74, 94, 98, 105, 108n172, 132, 236, 238, 252, 257, 328, 329, 333, 352, 364, 365, 366, 367, 400, 405, 413, 431
of the Christian Church, 32
in Masonic legend, 13, 16, 17, 19, 24, 25, 26, 27, 30, 31, 34, 35, 36, 37, 38, 39, 40, 41, 42, 44, 45
restricted to nobility within Moderns, 74

Grand Secretary (Masonic officer) 83, 116, 122, 333, 335, 340
regalia of, 115–16

Grand Stewards (Masonic office) 78, 127

Grand Warden (Masonic officer) 46, 47, 48, 49, 50, 51, 52, 74, 88, 100, 108n172
legendary, 17, 18, 20, 21, 22, 31, 34, 35n35, 38, 39, 40, 41, 42, 44

prerequisite for office of Master, 77

Great Architect of the Universe (see God)

Great Fire of London (see London—Great Fire)

Gregory, John (1607–1646) 139n274

Greece / Greeks 15, 18, 25, 28–30, 32–33, 65, 114, 137, 200, 232, 223, 232, 287, 365–66, 382–84

Greek philosophy 382 (see also Aristotelian philosophy, Platonic philosophy)

Greenleaf, Lawrence N. ✣ (1838–1922) 157–58

Greenwich 41, 44

Griffith, Thomas ✣ (1680–1744) 122

grip (see modes of recogition)

Guildhall at York 320

Gunn, Michael ✣ 337, 338

Gunnerysbury House, Brentford 37

Hackett, David G. 159, 161, 208, 209,

Hagarty, James ✣ 244

Half-Moon Tavern, Cheapside, London 42

Halliwell MS (see Masonic Manuscripts—Halliwell MS)

Ham (Biblical character) 12, 13, 62, 113, 237, 351, 423

Hamer, Douglas (1897–1981) 152n, 370

Hamill, John M. (b. 1947) ✣ 60, 112, 377

Hampton Court Palace, London 43
"where a bright Lodge was

held," 43

Hanegraaff, Wouter J. 171n53, 172n54

hanging gardens of Babylon (see Babylon—hanging gardens of)

Hanoverians 330, 354, 372

Hargrove, William ✹ (1788–1862) 317–18, 320n19, 325n33, 326n35

Harland-Jacobs, Jessica 350n8

Harmony 52, 119, 188, 357, 395, 402

Harodim 20, 25, 64, 223

Harpocrates (Greek god) 137

Harris, Moses ✹ 92

Harrison, David ✹ 5, 313–41, 458

Harward, Thomas Rev. ✹ (d. 1736) 162–63, 433n135

Hassall, John ✹ 335–36, 338, 339

Hawkins, William ✹ (fl. 1722) 51, 52

Hawksworth, Sir Walter ✹ (d. 1735) 329

Haydn, Joseph ✹ (1732–1809) 293

Haywood, Harry L. ✹ (1886–1956) 146–47

hazing 365

Head, Isaac ✹ (fl. 1752–1769) 87, 129–30, 163–64n32, 398, 420–21, 431

heaven 11, 24, 62, 63, 65, 85, 130, 135, 166–69, 186, 195–206, 222, 235, 300, 306, 366, 385, 424, 429, 433–34, 443, 445
  Freemasonry descended from, 122, 129, 135, 142, 300–301, 302, 408
  "heaven or paradice," 166, 168, 182, 195–206
  lodge resembles it, 157, 166–69, 186, 197–206, 442

Throne of, 188

Heber (Biblical character) 13

Hebrew language 63, 64, 95, 125, 133n253, 135, 139, 177, 201, 222

Hebron 19

Helmsley House (see Duncombe Park)

Henley, John "Orator" ✹ (1692–1756) 163–64n32, 177, 430, 435
  On Scripture Masonry (1737), 163–64n32

Henry VI (1421–1471) 67, 75, 128, 134

heraldry 107

Herbert, William, 6th Earl of Pembroke (c. 1641–1674) 34, 35, 36

Hercules 19 (*see also* pillars of Hercules)

Herder, Johann Gottfried von (1744–1803) 375

hermeneutics 290, 384

Hermes Trismegistos 54, 424

Hermeticism 2, 171, 358, 369

Herod the Great (c. 74 BCE–1 CE) 30–32

Hershfeld, Georgia 153n2

Het Loo Palace, Netherlands 44

heterodoxy 208

Hextall, William Brown ✹ (1847–1923) 92n120

hiera (Gr. "sacred objects") 382

Hierophant 382

Higden (c. 1299–c. 1363) 59 (*see also Polychronicon*)

Higgins, Godfrey ✹ (1772–1833) 316–17, 332
  Anacalypsis (1836), 316–17

High Priest 26, 135–36, 236, 288
  breastplate of, 135

higher degrees 250, 335, 339, 349

Hillel (110 BCE–10 CE) 31
Himley 258
Hindus 350n8
Hippocrates 231
Hiram Abiff (Biblical character)
  20–25, 50, 64–65, 95, 107, 187,
  232, 370, 424
  divinely inspired, 24
Hiram Abiff's chair (for the Depu-
  ty Grand Master) 50
Hiram, King of Tyre (Biblical
  character) 19, 20, 20–21n21,
  24, 64–65, 125, 167n41, 223,
  232
Hiram: or the Grand Master-Key
  (1764) 256
Hobsbawm, Eric 282, 285–86, 288
Hobby, Thomas ⚒ (fl. 1720) 48
Hoey, James ⚒ (fl. 1768) 399,
  408–409
Hogarth, William ⚒ (1697–1764)
  264
  Night (1736), 264
Holborn (area of London) 88
Holland 128, 348, 371
Hollinwood 332, 336n65, 337, 338,
  339
Holy Spirit 85 (see God)
Holy of Holies 65, 106, 383
  esoteric nature of, 106
Holy Royal Arch 133, 138, 140,
  255–56, 317n10, 338, 339, 341
  as "the Root, Heart and Mar-
  row of Free-Masonry," 140,
  255
  lodge of, at Jerusalem, 140
Holy Saint(s) John 167n41
Holyrood Palace, Edinburgh 41
Hooke, John ⚒ 56
Horace 90, 399

Horne, Alex ⚒ (1897–1988) 2
Horton, Mrs. 103
Hotham-House, Yorkshire 41n37
House of the Temple, Library of
  153n2
Howard, Charles, 3rd Earl of Carl-
  isle (c. 1669–1738) 45
Howard, Thomas, 21st Earl of
  Arundel (1586–1646) 36
Howard, Thomas, 8th Duke of
  Norfolk (1683–1732) 36
Hughan, William James ⚒
  (1841–1911) 130n249, 135, 249,
  316, 325n32, 325n33, 326n34,
  326n36, 327n37, 334
Huguenots 354, 371, 379
Hunt, Walter H. ⚒ 153n2
Hunter, William 56
Hutchins, Zachary 192
Hutchinson, William ⚒ (1732–
  1814) 400, 408n62, 411, 435
hydraulics 362
Hyndeley, William (fl. 1480–1510)
  319, 320

Ideal Lodge 184–85, 301
illud tempus xiii
imposters 251–252
India 25, 110–111, 115, 317, 350
Interregnum period 37
initiation 9, 178, 185, 191, 381 (*see
  also* making)
  prayer at, 85, 430–32
installation ceremonies 132
intertextuality 189n87, 193–206
Ionia 29
Ionic order 29, 89
Iowa Masonic Library and Museum 153n2
Ireland 83–87, 95, 97–101, 121, 140,

244, 247, 255, 267–68, 270,
    348n1, 394, 411, 413
emigration from, 267–68
Irish prosecuted and convicted
    disproportionately in En-
    gland, 263
Irish Freemasons in London
    discriminated against, 133,
    253–54, 261–62
Irish delegation, the (1735) 253–54
irregular lodges 251
irregular Masons 254
Isaac (Biblical patriarch) 16, 63
Ish Chotzeb 20, 64, 223
Ish Sabbal 10, 64, 223
Ishmael (Biblical character) 63
Isis 114, 427
Islam 349, 350n8
Israel / Israelites 13n8, 18–26, 138,
    365
    legendary lodges of, 18, 27–28
Italian revivers of classicism 33–34
Italy 9, 15, 25, 29, 34, 35, 128
Ithamar (Biblical character) 138

Jabal (Biblical character) 11, 82
    first taught geometry, 82
Jachin (see pillars, Hiramic)
Jachin and Boaz (1762) 396
    decorum stressed in, 396
Jackson, A.C.F. ✠ (1903–2000)
    391n2
Jackson, H. ✠ (fl. 1754) 131
Jackson, John ✠ (fl. 1756) 141
Jackson, Thomas W. ✠ 2–3
Jacob (Biblical patriarch) 16, 384
Jacob's Ladder 384
Jacob, Margaret C. 351n10, 357
Jacobitism 257, 329, 330
Jamaica 269

James II and VII (1633–1701) 42–
    43, 44, 323n25
James VI and I, James Charles Stu-
    art (1566–1625) 34–35, 69
    a "Mason King," 69
    statue at Temple Bar, 40
Janiak, Andrew 359n24
Japan 16
Japheth (Biblical character) 12, 15,
    62, 84, 113, 351, 423
Japhetites 15, 236
Jared (Biblical character) 11–12
Javan (Biblical character) 351
Jebusi 19
Jedidiah (see Solomon)
Jehosophat (see Vale of Jeho-
    sophat)
Jehu, King of Israel (Biblical char-
    acter) 26
Jenkyns, Tobias ✠ (fl. 1700–1720)
    329–30
Jermyn, Henry, 1st Earl of Saint
    Albans (1605–1684) 38
Jeroboam I, King of Israel (Bibli-
    cal character) 26
Jerusalem 19–25, 28, 31–32, 65,
    140, 186, 230, 250, 270, 288,
    376, 424
    Phasael Tower, 31
Jesus 169, 360, 410
    as "the all Mighty architecte,
        son of the virgin," 169
    as "the Lord Jesus Christ Im-
        manuel," 32
    as "the Word made Flesh," 32
    as the "Great Architect of Heav-
        en and Earth," 85–86
    as "the "Great Architect or
        Grand Master of the Chris-
        tian Church," 32

jewels (Masonic medals) 115–16,
    145, 340
Jewish lodges 132, 138–39, 144,
    348–49, 432
  in the Traditional History, 18,
    27–28
Jews 27–28, 30, 31, 63, 113, 114n187,
    132, 138–40, 144, 185, 235, 245,
    305, 348–50, 351, 358, 425, 432,
    437
Johnson, Gilbert Yorke ✠ (1885–
    1968) 322n22, 335n63, 340
Joiners 322–23
Jones, Bernard E. ✠ (1879–1965)
    350n7
Jones, Gwilym Peredur (1892–
    1975) 234n31–32, 370, 383n56,
    428n120, 428n121 (see also
    Knoop, Douglas)
Jones, Inigo, Sr. 34
Jones, Inigo (1573–1652) 8, 34–37,
    41, 43–44, 48, 69, 108, 224
  as Vitruvius Britannicus, 34
  on Stonehenge, 108, 224
Jones, Stephen ✠ (1763–1827)
    102n157
Jones, T. 98
Jórvik (see York)
Joseph (Biblical character) 16, 21
Josephus, Flavius (37–c. 100 CE)
    11n3, 32, 59, 108, 108n172, 109,
    145, 222, 425
Joshua (Biblical character) 17–18
Jubal (Biblical character) 11
Judah 26–28, 230, 235
Judaism 113, 132, 305, 350–51, 358
Judas Iscariot (Biblical character)
    410, 414 (see also false broth-
    er)
Junior Grand Warden (Masonic

office) (see Grand Warden)
Jupiter 19
Jupiter Hammon 18
Justice 199

kabbalah 2, 119, 138, 171, 185, 209,
    250, 358, 359, 432
  as a source of Masonic ideas,
    250;
  the "divine Mysteries of the se-
    cret Cabbala," 138
Kain (see Cain)
Kainan (Biblical character) 11
Katz, Jacob 348n2, 349–50
Kay, William 324
Keill, John (1671–1721) 361
Kennedy, Alexander ✠ (fl. 1756)
    141
Kensington, England 43, 44, 45
kevell (see Gavel)
Key of a Fellow Craft 226
Kilde, Jeanne Halgren 307
King James Bible 84
King's Arms tavern (St. Paul's
    Churchyard, London) 49,
    51, 52
Kingsland 98
Kingston, James (1693–1761), 4th
    Lord of 253
Kinross, Scotland 41
Kirk, Robert (1644–1692) 176–77
knife and fork Masons 259–60
Knights Templar, Masonic 317n10,
    335, 338, 349
Knoop, Douglas ✠ (1883–1948)
  and G.P. Jones, 153n3, 153n4,
    177n62, 294n58, 319n16, 323,
    324n28, 352n12, 370, 394n4,
    403n31, 416
Knowledge 10, 138, 194–95, 199,

357, 405, 431, 433

Kreuger, Bill �֎ 153n2

Kuhlke, Olaf ✖ 186, 186n84

Kypling, Mark ✖ 326–27

labor (Masonic) 391, 393, 401,
    403–405, 409, 433, 434, 439,
    446

labyrinths 28

Lamball, Jacob ✖ (c. 1695–1759)
    46

Lamech (Biblical character) 12,
    54, 82

  children of, 58–59, 61–62, 82,
    145, 424

Lancashire, England 37, 321n20,
    332, 335, 339

Lancaster, William (1650–1717) 45
    (see Queen's College)

Landmarks 62, 79, 133, 242, 250,
    254, 266

  Grand Lodge may not alter, 79

Lane, John ✖ (1843–1899) 337n66

Latitudinarianism 380

Latin 36, 40, 83–84, 97–98,
    319n14, 372

Laurie, William Alexander ✖
    (fl. 1845–1860) 248q

Laycock, Joseph ✖ (fl. 1734–1740)
    179

lectures, Masonic 9, 51, 186, 206,
    297, 403–404

Lee, Samuel (1625–1691) 177n62

legomena (Gr. "things said") 382

Leibniz, Gottfried Wilhelm (1646–
    1716) 358–59, 375

Leland-Locke Pseudepigraphon
    (aka the Leland MS) 128, 134,
    154, 180–82, 193

  first published in 1753, 193n94

transcribed in the C.W. Moore
    MS, 180n75, 193

Lemay, Joseph A. 352n12

Lemnos 28

Lemon, Robert ✖ (fl. 1830) 316

Lennox, Charles, 1st Duke of Rich-
    mond, 1st Duke of Lennox
    (1672–1723) 44

Leon, Rabbi Jacob Jehudah (1602–
    1675) 135

Leopold I (1640–1705) 228

Leslie, Charles ✖ (c. 1720–1782)
    3, 217, 234, 357, 407n55,
    408n56, 427

Letter G (Masonic symbol) 356

Level (Masonic symbol) 119, 202,
    294, 395

Levites 20–21n21, 22, 31

  as "skilful Architects," 31

lewis (son of a Mason) 117

lewis (stonemasonry implement)
    117

liberal arts and sciences (see arts
    and sciences)

liberty of conscience 110

Libya 18

Light (in the Masonic sense) 105,
    167, 227, 412, 413, 420, 421

  "the "glimmering Ray," 421

  "the peculiar light" of Masonry,
    167, 199

  "the true Light," 105, 227

Lincoln's Inn Fields, London 37

Lindsay, John, 20th Earl of Craw-
    ford ✖ (1702–1749) 98

Lindsey House, London 37

Locke, John (1632–1704) 155,
    189n87, 359

  pseudo-Locke, 180–181

lodge / lodges:

activities of, 119

as a civil government, 199–200

as "a microcosm of an ideal world," 301

as a microcosm of creation, 102

as a "Monarchy," 166–67, 199–200

as a "resemblance of the Paradisaical lodge, and even of Heaven itself," 204

as "a safe and pleasant Relaxation from Intense Study or the Hurry of Business, without Politicks or Party," 52

as an "Oblong Square," 234, 235

as "grounded in scripture," 198

as having "fallen from primitive order and perfection," 204

as "hallowed Ground," 302

as "sacred Ground," 301

as "Seminaries," 137

as timeless, sacred space, 186–87

cement of, 12, 51, 113, 144, 199–200, 350

Christian, 130, 132, 139

compared with heaven or paradise, 166–67, 184–93, 198–206

constitution of, 52, 98, 138

defined, 73

early growth in number of, 289

form of, 234–35

"formed" lodges, 24, 235

instruction within, 35, 50, 51, 156, 168, 182, 183–84, 207–209, 255

lists of, 103

Jewish, 132, 138–39, 144, 348–49, 432

meetings called "communica-

tions," 420

militant and triumphant, 189

music of, 280–309

opened in the name of God, 396

opening prayer of, 206

operative, 319, 377

prayer during, 85

"principles and doctines of," 204

reflects the harmony of the heavenly Temple, 206

refreshment, 401–406

regalia of, 115–16

ritual variations among, 250; (see also celestial lodge, Ideal Lodge; INDEX OF MASONIC LODGES AND ORGANIZATIONS)

solemnity of, 392–97

supports of, 101–102

logic 30n29 (see also arts and sciences)

Lomax, Alan 282, 284

London, England 34–52, 55, 69, 88, 95, 97, 102, 104, 117, 124, 153, 156n9, 229, 238, 258, 261–63, 267, 289, 313, 314, 323, 330, 340, 348, 354, 359, 361, 376, 391, 413

Freemasons Hall, 391

Great Fire, 39–41

the "drooping Lodges" of, 69

London Journal, The 295

Lord Carteret's Head (tavern) 83

lost word 187

Louis XIV (1638–1715) 228

Lowther, Luke 327

Lymm, England 323

Lyon, Thomas, 8th Earl of Strath-

more and Kinghorne ✶
(1704–1753) 259
Lysippus (fourth century BCE)
29–30n28

MacAlpine, J.M.K. ✶ 122n215
Macclesfield 332
Mackey, Albert Gallatin ✶ (1807–
1881) 72n60, 157–59, 248
*An Encyclopædia of Freemason-
ry and Its Kindred Sciences*
(1879), 157
MacNulty, W. Kirk ✶ (b. 1932)
290
Madai (Biblical character) 351
Magi 62, 66, 80, 225, 357, 437
Magians 14, 29, 110–111, 126
Magog (Biblical character) 351
Mahalaleel (Biblical character) 11
making (ritual of initiation into
Freemasonry) 76, 85
charge at, 102
no more than five at a time, 76
prayer at, 85, 102
Mali, Joseph xii–xiv
Man / Male (as Masonic technical
term) 165, 194–97, 356
Manchester, England 335, 339, 341
Manley, Richard ✶ (fl. 1730–1740)
264
Manningham, Thomas ✶ (d. 1794)
271
manuscript records (see Masonic
manuscripts)
Manwaring, Col. Henry 37
Mark Master Mason degree 334–
35, 338, 339, 369–70
Marleborough House, St. James's
Park, London 44
Marmora Arundeliana (1612) 36

Marsham, John (1602–1685) 224
Martell, Charles (c. 686–741) 66
Mary II (1662–1694) 43
Maryland 194
Mason Word, the (or Mason's
Word) 1–2, 62, 176, 377–78
compared to a Rabbinical tradition by Robert Kirk, 176–77
Mason's Faculty 14, 62, 69, 135,
167, 178–82
as a means of esoteric transmission, 180–82
as a secret, information-bearing
language, 181
as "ancient universal Practice of
conversing without speaking,"
62, 179
as "the original language," 201
as "the Pantomime Fashion,"
135
as "Universelle Longage of Maconnes," 181
as "universal understanding,"
176
can only be learned by Masons,
178, 201–202
supposed to be "greatly lost,"
180
Masonic instruction 35, 50, 51,
156, 168, 182, 183–84, 207–
209, 255
Masonic manuscripts
destruction of, 35n35, 42, 48,
106
Cooke MS (c. 1450) 53–54,
54n2, 55, 58, 59, 82n90, 85,
128, 219n5, 223, 280, 308, 424;
quoted in Anderson's *Constitutions* of 1723, 58
Dowlands MS (c. 1600) 130

Embleton MS (c. 1680) 139

Essex MS 438n149

Graham MS (c. 1725) 370, 428, 438–39, 441

Halliwell MS (c. 1425) 53, 54, 58–59, 59, 219n5, 288–89, 393

Hope MS (c. 1680) 334

Kevan MS (c. 1720) 383

Charles W. Moore MS (c. 1755–1770) 154, 161–62, 163–69, 173–80, 193–206 (see also A Dissertation upon Masonry)

Leland MS (wrongly denoted a manuscript—see Leland-Locke Pseudepigraphon)

Levander York MS (c. 1740), 323–24

Old York Manuscript Constitution (see Hope MS)

Manuscript Roll № 7 (1712–1730) 340

Manuscript Roll № 10 (1761–1792) 340–41

Plot MS, 127

Rawlinson MSS, 163–64n32

Sloane MS № 3848, 325

Wilklinson MS (c. 1730), 234

York MS № 1, 316, 317n9, 324, 325–26

York MS № 4 (c. 1693), 326, 327n37, 334

York MS № 7, 327

Masonic research x–xv

methodology of, xi

neglect of primary sources within, xiii–xv, 152, 157–58, 217n1, 299, 397, 401, 406

rejection of mythographic narrative within, xi, xiii–xv, 59–60, 217n1, 219, 220, 299

Masons Company 323 (see also operative masonry)

Master (Masonic office) 9, 22, 26, 31, 38, 42, 44, 45, 46, 47, 49, 51, 60, 74, 76, 78, 79, 82, 85, 96, 115, 136, 140, 160, 199, 226, 244, 251, 253, 256, 271, 289, 295, 299, 336, 337, 338, 341, 365, 371, 391n2, 393, 396, 403, 413, 419

must have been a lodge Warden first, 77

Master-Jewels, Masonic 383

Master Mason degree 156, 166, 187, 207, 369–70, 415n85, 416, 434

as "third & Chief degree of Masonry," 166, 197

compared with the "third heaven," 166, 182, 185, 187, 195–98, 433–34

in the Traditional History, 64

"Master" as a rank equivalent to Fellow Craft, 77

Master's Part, the 378

materialism 239, 361, 376

mathematics / mathematicians 14, 16, 48, 62, 225, 231, 351, 358, 359, 360, 364, 368, 372–73, 385, 419, 429

Mather, Cotton (1663–1728) 372

Mayfair, London 258

McLeod, Wallace E. ✳ (b. 1931) 139, 406

McLucas, Anne Dhu 290–91

mechanical philosophy 10, 225, 354–55, 367, 375–76, 378–79

Medes / Media 25, 27

Medieval period 293, 304–305,

328, 332
membership certificates 269
Menatzchim 20, 25, 64, 223
Mesopotamia 16, 25
Methuselah (Biblical character) 12
Mercury 229
mercy seat 23, 65
Mereworth House, Kent 45
Merlin 107
Merryman, Elizabeth (third wife
      of Laurence Dermott) 246
Merryman, John ✠ 246
Meshech (Biblical character) 351
metaphors 205
Meton of Athens (fifth century
      BCE) 29–30n28
Metrodorus the Architect (fourth
      century CE) 29–30n28
Micklegate Bar 330
Middle Chamber 370 (*see also*
      Temple at Jerusalem)
Middlesex 246, 262, 263, 264–65
Mile End, Middlesex 246
Miles, Mr. (fl. 1728) 88
military architecture 63
Millar, Angel ✠ 350n8
Mills, Henry ✠ 337
Milner, William, 1ˢᵗ Baronet Mil-
      ner ✠ (1696–1745) 329
Milton, John (1608–1674) 135
      Blake's *Milton, A Poem*, 376
Mishnah 140
Mitzraim / Mizraim (Biblical char-
      acter) 14–15, 237
Minerva 28, 114, 427
minutes 76
Mithraism 382
Moderns (see Grand Lodge of
      England)
modes of recognition 14, 105, 197,

203, 208, 250, 381, 401, 416–17,
      422
legendary origins of, 14
transposition of first and sec-
      ond degree by the Moderns,
      133, 250
Molech 25
Monod, Paul Kléber xii
Montagu, John, 2ⁿᵈ Duke of Mon-
      tagu ✠ (1690–1749) 48–52, 57,
      70, 76, 126, 221, 364, 365, 367
depicted by John Pine, 57, 365
Montesquieu / Charles-Louis the
      2ⁿᵈ, Baron of Montesquieu ✠
      (1689–1755) 371
Monument to the Great Fire of
      London 40 (*see also* Lon-
      don—Great Fire)
Moon (Masonic symbol) 89, 99,
      125, 436
Moore, Charles Whitlock ✠
      (1801–1873) 154–57, 158,
      159n21, 193, 206n120 (*see also*
      Masonic Manuscripts—C.W.
      Moore MS)
Moorfields, London 245
Moorgate, London 40
morality 73, 77, 133
Moray, Sir Robert ✠ (c. 1608–
      1673) 289
Morgan, John ✠ (fl. 1750–17512)
      244n11
mortar 199
Morris, Rob ✠ (1818–1888) 157–59
Morris, S. Brent ✠ 153n2
Morrice, Thomas ✠ (fl. 1718) 47,
      49, 50
Mosaic Pavement of Solomon's
      Temple (Masonic symbol)
      58, 125

Mosaic style of architecture 18

Moses (Biblical character) 17–19, 23, 63, 71, 138, 230, 287

as a Grand Master in the Traditional History, 17, 63

as "our holy Brother Moses," 138

Most Ancient and Honourable Society of Free and Accepted Masons according to the Old Constitutions (see Grand Lodge of England, Antients)

Mount Ararat 12

Mount Moriah 24

Mount Zion 24

Mozart, Wolfgang Amadeus ✷ (1756–1791) 293

Mulvey-Roberts, Marie 264n90

Murphy, Christopher B. ✷ xvi, 1–6, 53–151, 99n148, 113n186, 153n2, 177n64, 191n90, 349–50n1, 432n132, 458

Murray, John, 4th Duke of Atholl ✷ (1755–1830) 273–74

Muse / Muses 91, 298

music / Musick 5, 11, 23, 30n29, 81, 95, 136, 145, 280–309 (see also arts and sciences; songs, Masonic)

Mycon (fifth century BCE) 29–30n28

mysteries 86, 119, 132, 136, 177, 191, 205, 238, 339, 380, 382–84, 390, 409, 418, 426, 427, 431, 432

as imperfectly transmitted, 426–27

of "Godliness and Christianity," 86–87, 431

of pagans as the "vestiges of the ancient religion of Noah and the Patriarchs," 114

mystery plays 328

mysticism xiv, 90, 207–209, 284, 355, 358, 369, 381, 383–84, 406

mythistory xii–xiv, 7

as "historical mythologisation," xii

as "parahistory," xii

(see also foundational narrative, mythography, Traditional History)

mythography xi–xii

mythopœic history (see Traditional History)

Naphthali, tribe of 64–65

natural philosophy 361–63, 371

Neale, Susanna (first wife of Laurence Dermott) 245

Nebuchadnezzar II, King of Babylon (Biblical character) 27, 232

neoplatonism 172

Nettl, Bruno (b. 1930) 282, 283, 285–86, 287

New Chapel, Trinity College, Oxford 45

New Printing House, Cambridge 45

Newcastle-under-Lyme 257

Newgate Prison, London 247

Newton, Isaac (1642–1727) 355–56, 358–61, 363, 367–68, 371, 372–79, 384

Newtonian thought xiv, 353n13, 364, 367, 371, 375, 379

Nichostatus 72

Nieuwentyt, Bernard (1654–1718) 373–74

Nimrod (Biblical character)

13–14, 58, 62, 92, 100, 180, 230, 236–38
  as Grand Master in the Traditional History, 92, 180, 237
  known as Bacchus, 92
  known as Belus, 13n8, 180
Nineveh 14, 27
Ninus (Biblical character) 14
Ninus (Masonic legendary character who brings knowledge of Masonry to Germany and Gaul) 25–26
Noachida / æ 12–13, 109–115, 119, 139, 350–51
  all of humanity descended from, 12
  "all of one Language," 109,
  as "first Name of Masons, according to some old Traditions," 13n7, 109
  builders of Tower of Babel, 109
  preserving and transmitting antediluvian wisdom, 109, 111
  Zoroastrians an example of, 111
Noachide covenant, 428 (see also Noah—three great articles of)
Noachide Laws (see Noah—three great articles of)
Noah (Biblical Patriarch) 12–13, 62, 66, 98, 100, 108n172, 109, 125–26, 138, 139, 236, 287, 351, 366, 370, 423, 424, 427, 432
  three "great Articles of," 113, 125–26, 350, 428
  sons of, 12–13, 62, 63, 109, 113, 139, 236, 238, 351, 423
  preservation of antediluvian knowledge, 12, 62–63, 109
  raising of, 370
  (see also Deluge, Noachida / æ)

Norris, Henry ✻ (fl. 1730–1740) 264
North Riding 326
Northumbria 313–14
Norway 15

Oakley, Edward (fl. 1728) ✻ 88, 94, 156, 163–64n32, 398, 409, 410–11
  oration of, 94, 153, 163–64n32, 191n89, 207, 398, 407n48, 407n49, 410–11, 416, 417
oaths (see obligations)
Oats, Brother ✻ 91, 117, 118, 130
obligations (Masonic) 119
oblong square (Masonic symbol) 36, 234, 235 (see also lodge)
observance (Masonic) 132, 412, 431
Old Charges 2, 16n14, 25, 38, 47, 50, 53–55, 62, 74, 81, 88, 127, 134, 139, 145, 176, 219n5, 221, 280, 304, 316, 323, 324, 325–27, 331, 334, 348n1, 363, 365, 367, 378, 381, 393, 397, 424
  faulted by Grand Lodge, 50
Oldham, England 332, 336, 338, 339, 341
Oliver, George (1782–1867) ✻ 128n240, 408n61, 429n122
Olympiads 28
officers 73–74
Omri, King of Israel (Biblical character) 26
Önnerfors, Andreas ✻ 297, 298, 299, 307
Opera House, Haymarket, London 44
operative masonry 55, 288–89, 308, 318–25, 348n1, 369, 377,

398, 419

optics 361, 362

oral tradition 17, 19, 249, 250, 290–91, 296

Oswald of Northumbria (c. 604–642) 314

Ovid (43 BCE–18 CE) 88, 89

Oxford 36, 40, 45, 361

Paine, Thomas (1737–1809) 331

painting / painters 14n10, 29–30, 34, 35, 70, 232

Palace of Hamilton, Clydesdale 41n37

Palladian architecture 258, 353n13

Palladio, Andrea (1508–1580) 34, 69, 232

Palmes, George ✶ (d. 1774) 329

Palmes, John ✶ (1732–1783) 329

Palmyra 25

Pamphilus of Amphipolis (fourth century BCE) 29–30n28

Papirius Prætextatus (fl. 272 CE) 136–37

Paracelsus (1493–1541) 231

paradise 9–11, 166, 192

"Paradisaical Lodge," 204, cf. 9–10

(see also Eden, heaven)

Parrhasius of Ephesus (fifth to fourth century BCE) 29–30n28

Parian marble 22

Parker, John ✶ 333

Parliament, English 67–68, 257, 274, 328

Parthenon (see Temple—of Minerva at Athens)

passions 101, 140, 190, 405, 411, 438–39, 441

password (see modes of recogition)

Past Master / Past Masters (Masonic title) 74, 365

Paul of Tarsus (see St. Paul the Apostle)

Payne, George ✶ (d. 1757) 47–50, 76, 255, 364, 381

part of possible "inner circle" of Freemasons, 254–55

Peleg (Biblical character) 13

Paneas 31

Peckwater Quadrangle (Peek-Water-Square), Christ Church College, Oxford 45 (see also Henry Aldridge)

Peneus 29–30n28

Penket, Richard 37

Pennell, John (fl. 1730–1739) ✶ 83, 97, 98, 102, 122, 145, 394

Pennell's Constitutions (1730) 55, 83–87, 101, 102, 128, 130, 134, 145, 177, 191n90, 394, 395n9, 430–31, 432

Pennsylvania Gazette, The 160

Persepolis 27

Persius (first century CE) 29–30n28

perennialism 61, 115, 126, 136, 145, 406, 426–47

Perfect Ashlar (see Ashlar)

Perjur'd Free Mason Detected, The (1730) 417

Persia 25, 27, 28–29, 200

Péter, Róbert 172n54, 352n11

Peterfreund, Stuart 377

Petergate 327

Petrus Gyllius (1490–1555) 223

Pharos (see Alexandria—Lighthouse of)

Phasaelis 31

Phenicians / Phoenicians 114, 230

Phidias (c. 480–430 BCE) 29–
    30n28

Philadelphia, Pennsylvania 95,
    159n21, 160, 193–94, 205, 206,
    267, 275, 441n163
    switched allegiance to Antients
    Grand Lodge (1759), 267

Philalethes, Eugenius, Jr. (see
    Samber, Robert)

Philalethes Society, the xvi, 153,
    460–63

*Philalethes: The Journal of Masonic
    Research and Letters* xv–xvi,
    153, 158, 189n87, 457, 458, 459,
    462–63

Philips, Clifford William ✹
    (fl. 1730) 264

Philistines 19, 174n56

philosophy / philosophers 351,
    354–55 (*see also* mechanical
    philosophy)

Philostratus, Lucius Flavius
    (c. 170–c. 250) 29–30n28

Phoenicia / Phoenicians 18–19, 28,
    174n56, 230, 427

Piatigorsky, Alexander (1929–
    2009) x, 191

Pick, Fred Lomax ✹ (1898–1966)
    336n65, 337n67, 337n69–71,
    338n73

pillar, broken (Masonic symbol)
    99

pillars, Hiramic 177

pillars, primordial 11, 11n3, 54, 58,
    68, 100, 108–109, 172, 222, 423,
    424, 437n147
    made of brick and stone, 11n3
    of Enoch, 11, 11n3, 62, 108, 222,

    423, 424,
    of Lamech's children, 54, 58,
    424, 437n147
    of Seth, 108, 222

pillars, three 89

pillars of Hercules 25

Pine, John ✹ (1690–1756) 57, 73,
    107

Pink, Andrew 295, 296

Pisistratus (d. 528 BCE) 28

pistis 392, 406–35

plasterers / plastering 14n10, 35

Plato (428–348 BCE) 29–30n28,
    66, 372, 382
    as "the divine Plato," 29–30n28,
    66

Platonic philosophy 66, 372,
    375–76, 382

Pliny the Elder (23–79 CE) 223

Plot, Robert (1640–1696) 124,
    127–28

Plumb (Masonic symbol) 98, 119,
    123, 395

Plumbline, The 458

pocket companions (in general)
    97

politics 93
    disputes forbidden, 51, 75, 93,
    119, 395

Polychronicon (c. 1350) 424

Polycletus (fifth century BCE)
    29–30n28

polymorphic concept of Freema-
    sonry 126, 136

Pompey the Great (106–48 BCE)
    32

Pontefract Castle 316, 325, 331

Porch (of Solomon's Temple) 383
    (*see also* Master-Jewels)

Pope, Alexander ✹ (1688–1744)

245, 361, 375
The Dunciad, 245q
Porters 78
Post-Boy 92 (*see also* exposés)
Powis House, Ormond Street, London 44
praxis 55–56, 145, 392–406
Praxitiles (fourth century BCE) 29–30n28
prayer 85–86, 102, 122, 129, 130, 138–40, 144, 177, 191, 206, 430–33
preferment 74,
prelapsarian world 192 (*see also* Eden)
Premier Grand Lodge (see Grand Lodge of England)
Prescott, Andrew 228n26, 317
Preston, Robert 324–25
Preston, William ✹ (1742–1818) 87, 171, 284, 316, 316–17n8, 330, 340, 396, 402, 409, 410, 432
his definition of Masonry as "a regular system of morality conceived in a strain of interesting allegory," 171
Illustrations of Masonry, 87n103, 102n157, 171, 340, 396, 432
Price, Henry ✹ (c. 1697–1780) 161, 209
primordial pillars (see pillars, primordial)
prisca theologia (see perennialism)
Prichard, Samuel (fl. 1730–1735) 118–19, 170n49, 250–51, 416–17
Masonry Dissected (1730), 101–102, 118–19, 170n49, 235, 250–51, 356, 383, 416–17, 418, 445n178

priests (Jewish) 22, 31 (*see also* High Priest)
as "skilful Architects," 31
processions, Masonic 49, 50
profane 63, 105, 190, 201, 303
as "the Bulk of the people," 201
as "the Gross of Mankind," 190
prologues 102–103 (*see also* epilogues)
Protestantism 244–45, 264 (*see also* Catholicism, Church of England, Christianity)
Nonconformist 245
Providence 111, 125, 302, 374
Provincial Grand Master (Masonic officer) 164, 398, 405, 420
Prudence 75, 232–33, 238
Ptolemeus Philadelphus (309–246 BCE) 66
Public Advertiser 134 (*see also* Leland-Locke Pseudepigraphon)
public science 361–62
Puritanism 192
pyramids 15, 230, 237
Pythagoras 28–29, 54, 65–66, 100, 126, 424
holding a "Lodge of good Geometricians," 29, 126
Pythagoreanism 28–29, 66, 119, 137, 358

Quakers 245
Quatuor Coronati Lodge of Research № 2076 457 (see INDEX OF MASONIC LODGES AND ORGANIZATIONS)
Queen's College, The, Oxford 45

Ramsay, Chevalier Andrew Mi-

chael ✴ (1686–1743) 114, 153,
   399–400, 427
oration of, 153, 399–400, 427
Raulins, Mr. 103
Raynor, Jonathan ✴ (fl. 1790)
   336–38
*Read's Weekly Journal, or British
   Gazetteer* 404–405
Reason 199
recognition, modes of 178
   "the most insignificant Parts of
   the Sacred Mystery," 417
recognition, of Masonic Grand
   Lodges 248,
red (Masonic symbolism of)
   115–16
Red Bible tavern 88
Red Sea 17, 365–66
Reformation, the 318, 320
refreshment (see festive board)
regalia 115–16
Regius Poem (see Masonic Manuscripts, Halliwell MS)
regularity 73, 77, 251–55
Regulations 76–80, 115–17, 140,
   145
religion 93, 110, 231
   disputes forbidden, 75, 93
"Religion in which all Men Agree"
   71, 85, 112, 115, 305, 349, 350,
   422, 428
religious tolerance 72–73, 85, 110,
   167, 142–43, 203, 208, 245, 255,
   348–51, 380, 423
   "good people of all Religions,
   Sects, perswasions & Denominations, of all nations &
   countrys... of all Generations
   of men in all ages since the
   Beginning of Mankind," 167,

167–68n41
   in the Charges of a Free-Mason, 255, 351
Renaissance xiv, 284, 293
Revis, John ✴ (fl. 1734–1756)
   110–111, 114
rhetoric 30n29 (*see also* arts and
   sciences)
Rider, E. 97
Riphath (Biblical character) 351
*Rise and Progress of Freemasonry,
   The* (c. 1730) 429
ritual 82, 101, 111, 146, 170, 175–76,
   184, 186, 206, 208, 234–35,
   248–50, 254–56, 269, 272, 273,
   275, 287, 289–97, 299, 303, 308,
   317, 333, 375, 380, 382–83, 392,
   405, 416, 428, 439, 443–44,
   446
   variations in, 250
rivalry of Antients and Moderns
   248–52, 290
Roberts' *Constitutions, or The Old
   Constitutions Belonging to
   the Ancient and Honourable
   Society of Free and Accepted
   Masons* (1722) 55, 398
Robbins, Sir Alfred Farthing ✴
   (1856–1931) 366n34
Robinson, Sir William, 1st Baronet
   ✴ (1655–1736) 329–30
Rochdale, England 332n54, 341
rods, ceremonial 115–16
Rogalsky, Yakov 113n185
Roman architecture (see Augustan
   style)
Romain Britain 313, 315, 318
Romans 18, 66, 72, 136–37, 181,
   200
Rome 66, 200, 232, 287, 384

Rose (tavern) 124
Rosicrucianism 357, 359, 413
Rotherham 317, 332, 335
Rough Ashlar (see Ashlar)
Royal Arch (see Holy Royal Arch)
Royal Art, the (see Freemasonry)
Royal Exchange, London 39
Royal Hospital, Chelsea, London
    41, 43
Royal Society, the 289, 357–59,
    361, 362, 364, 371, 372, 379
Royster, Paul 96n137, 160–61n24
Rubens, Peter Paul (1577–1640) 35
Russell, Francis, 2nd Earl of Bed-
    ford (c. 1527–1585) 36
Rylands, W.H. ✠ (1847–1922) 321,
    323n24

sacred history 152, 185, 351
Sadler, Henry ✠ (1840–1911) 249,
    369–70
Salem, Massachusetts 161
Saler, Michael 352n11
Samaria 26, 31
Samber, Robert ✠ (1682–1745)
    163–64n32, 178, 191n89,
    407n45, 407n46, 413–15, 429,
    461
Samuel Crocker Lawrence Library
    153n2, 162
Samson (Biblical character) 19,
    173, 174
  name expunged from Masonic
    tradition, 174n56
Sanconiathon 19n20, 174n56
sanctum sanctorum (see Holy of
    Holies)
Sanhedrin 22
Sankey, Edward ✠ 325
Sankey, Richard ✠ 325

Sardis 26
Savage, Thomas, 3rd Earl Rivers
    (c. 1628–1694) 38, 41
Sayer, Anthony ✠ (c. 1672–1742,
    first Grand Master of the Pre-
    mier Grand Lodge) 1, 46–47,
    364
Scarborough Spa, Yorkshire 104
Scholfield, John ✠ 337
Schuchard, Marsha Keith 350n7,
    377n48
scientific revolutions 355
Scilly Isles 163–64n32, 420
Scituate, Massachusetts 161
Scofield, Dana ✠ 4–5, 216–40
Scotland 41, 43, 44, 68, 87, 249,
    255, 270, 283, 287, 348n1, 363,
    369, 377–78, 394
Scott, John ✠ (fl. 1754) 124, 145
  Pocket Companion (1754) 55,
    124–31, 134, 145, 163–64n32,
    190n88, 415, 431n127
sculpture / sculptors 14, 15, 20, 26,
    28, 29, 34, 35, 39, 40, 42, 67,
    70, 223, 231
Scyllis (sixth century BCE) 29–
    30n28
Scythia 15, 25, 114, 427
Sebaste 31
Secretary (Masonic office) 76, 145,
    294
  song of, 294
secrets / secrecy 48, 67–68, 75,
    79–80, 80–81, 86, 100, 105–
    106, 132, 136–37, 168–78, 191,
    225–28, 302–304, 390, 416–22,
    431
  a heavenly trait, 168–69
  "the Essential Secrets" of Free-
    masonry, 169, 173, 175, 420

the secret of Masonry as "the
    very Basis of Religion," 435
    (*see also* esotericism)
secularization theory xiv, 351–52
Senex, John (d. 1740) ✶ 56
Senior Grand Warden (Masonic
    office) (see Grand Warden)
Senior Warden (Masonic office)
    76, 269, 337
seraph / seraphim 206
sermons, Masonic 161, 163–64n32,
    186, 194–206 (see lectures,
    Masonic)
Seth (Biblical patriarch) 11, 61,
    63, 100, 108, 138, 139, 222, 287,
    423, 424, 425, 432, 437n147
    and astronomy, 63
    line of, 61–62, 288
    (*see also* pillars, primordial)
seven wonders of art (seven won-
    ders of the ancient world) 15,
    23, 27, 230
Shammai (50 BCE–30 CE) 31
Shaftesbury House, Aldersgate
    Street, London 37
Shaftesley, John M. ✶ 114n187
Sharp, Cecil (1859–1924) 282,
    283–84
Shechinah (*see also* God—pres-
    ence of) 17
Sheldon, Gilbert (1598–1677)
    39–40
Sheldonian Theatre, Oxford 40
Shem (Biblical patriarch) 12, 62,
    113, 351, 423
Shekinah (divine presence) 63, 65
Sherman, John M. ✶ (1899–1993)
    162–63
Shiloh 18
Shinar, plain of 12–15, 23, 62–63,

84, 109, 141, 237, 424
Sibelius, Jean ✶ (1865–1957) 293
Sicily 28, 232
Sicyon 28, 29
Siddall, William ✶ (fl. 1776–1784)
    333
side orders 2, 250
Sidon 18, 19
signs, Masonic 178, 197, 203, 417
    of distress, 178
silver (Masonic symbolism of)
    115–16
Slade, Alexander ✶ (fl. 1754)
    174n56, 179–80
Smellie, William (1740–1795)
    431n127
Smith, Horace Wemyss (1825–
    1891) 206n118
Smith, Leonard ✶ (fl. 1726) 329
Smith, William ✶ (fl. 1734–1764)
    97, 99, 100–102, 108, 145, 292,
    394
    Smith's *Pocket Companion*
    (London, 1735) 55, 97–103,
    107, 108, 130, 134, 138, 144, 145,
    394–95
    Smith's *Pocket Companion*
    (Dublin, 1735) 97, 98–99
Smith, William (of Gateshead,
    County Durham) ✶ (fl. 1736)
    217, 356–57, 412–13, 429–30
    *The Book M, or Masonry Tri-
    umphant* (1736) 179, 187–89,
    191, 217, 356–57, 402n30,
    407n50, 407n51, 407n53,
    412–13, 429–30, 432–33
Smith, Rev. Dr. William ✶ (1727–
    1803) 192–93, 193–206
    academic career of, 194
    Ahiman Rezon edited by (1783),

206n119

and George Washington, 205–
206

author of common American
lodge opening prayer, 206

Masonic career of, 194

possessed a copy of the 1734
Dissertation, 204–205

Smiths 321

Snoek, Jan 187n85, 350n7

Socrates (c. 470–399 BCE) 29–
30n28

solemnity 392–97

Solomon, King of Israel (Biblical
character) 19–27, 63–65, 72,
91, 107, 125, 137, 167n41, 194,
196, 223, 230, 232, 235, 424 (*see
also* Temple at Jersusalem—of
Solomon)

as legendary "Grand Master
Mason," 19

as "Prince of Peace and Architecture," 19

palaces of, 24

Solomon's chair (for the Grand
Master) 36, 50

Solomonian style of architecture
27

Somerset House, London 36

Songhurst, William J. ✪ (1860–
1939) 251n44, 253–54

songs, Masonic 80–82, 88–94,
95–96, 117–18, 122–23, 131, 132,
140–42, 145, 186, 280–309,
401, 402–403, 419

1709 earliest publication of, 294

as a form of Masonic education, 299

closely associated with toasts,
122, 299

generally intended to be performed by all, 281

printed collections of, 88, 89–
94, 96, 102, 106–107, 117–18,
121, 122, 124, 131, 132, 140–42,
284, 294, 295, 307

recurring themes within, 300–
307

taxonomy of, 296–97, 298

"A Mason is Great and Respected," 298

"A Mason's Daughter," 92–93

"A New Song," 96

"A System More Pure Ne'er Was
Modell'd by Man," 298

"An Ode on Masonry," 131

"Arise, Gentle Muse, and Thy
Wisdom Impart," 298

"As Masons once on Shinar's
Plain," 141

"Attend, attend the Strains," 141

"Attend loving Brethren and to
me give Ear," 141

"Bless'd be the Day that gave to
me," 141

"Blest Masonry! Thy Arts Divine," 298

"Come as you prepar'd," 122–23

"Come, boys, let us more liquor
get," 123

"Come, come my Brothers
dear," 123

"Come fill up a Bumper, and let
it go round," 142

"Come Lend Me Your Ears,
Loving Brethren, A While,"
306

"Come follow, follow me," 123

"From the Depths let us raise,"
141

"Guardian Genius of our Art Divine," 92, 292

"Hail! Masonry divine," 142

"Hail, sacred Art! by Heaven design'd," 122

"Hail Secret Art," 302–303

"Hail to the Masons Sacred Art," 402

"Hark! The Hiram Sounds to Close," 298

"How bless'd are we from Ignorance free'd," 142, 419

"How happy a Mason whose Bosom still flows," 142

"If Unity be good in every Degree," 142

"King Solomon, that wise projecter," 123

"Let Masons be merry each Night when they meet," 142

"Let worthy Brethren all combine," 142

"Masons Song," 91

"Of All Institutions to Form Well the Mind," 298

"Of Masonry: An Ode," 118, 291–92

"On You Who Masonry Despise," 298, 304

"Once I Was Blind and Cou'd Not See," 141, 302

"Progress of Masonry," 141

"See in the East the Master plac'd," 141

"Some Folks have with curious Impertinence strove," 303–304, 419

"Song in the *Generous Free Mason*," 91, 118

"The Candidate's Song," 90

"The Curious vulgar could never devise," 123

"The Deputy Grand Master's Song" (1731), 117

"The Enter'd 'Prentices Song" or "Free-Mason's Health," 82, 122, 123, 131, 294, 297–99, 403 (parody of) 295

"The Fairies, with the Mason's Chorus," 91

"The Fairy Elves Song," 91

"The Fellow-Crafts Song," 81, 295, 297, 298

"The Grand Warden's Song," 117

"The Master's Song: Or, the History of Masonry," 51, 80–81, 96, 177, 236–37, 295, 297, 298, 300

"The New Fairies: Or, The Fellow-Craft's Song," 90, 91, 301, 304

"The Secretary's Song," 118, 294

"The Swordbearer's Song," 118

"The Treasurer's Song," 117

"The Warden's Song, or Another History of Masonry," 81, 110, 295, 297, 298

"The Warden's Song, at Closing the Lodge," 298

"The World is all in Darkness," 403

"Tis Masonry unites Mankind," 131, 141

"To Masonry your voices raise," 141

"To the science that virtue, and art do maintain," 123

"Urania sing the Art divine, Beauty, Strength, and Wisdom grace each line," 142

"We brethren, Free-Masons, let's mark the great name," 123

"What tho' they call us Masons fools," 141

"When a Lodge of Free-Masons, are cloath'd in their Aprons," 131

"When Earth's Foundation First Was Laid," 123, 306

"When Masonry by Heaven's Design," 142

"Whoever wants Wisdom, must with some Delight," 142

"With cordial Hearts lets drink a Health," 142

"With Harmony and Flowing Wine," 141, 298

"With plumb, level, and square, to work let's prepare," 123

"Ye ancient sons of Tyre," 141

"You People Who Laugh at Masons Draw Near," 300, 305

Sophie Amalie of Brunswick-Lüneburg, Queen of Denmark and Norway (1628–1685) 35, 45

South, Robert (1634–1716) 40

Southampton House, Bloomsbury, London 37

Sparta 200

Spencer, Samuel ✵ (Grand Secretary, Premier Grand Lodge, 1757–1768, d. 1768) 241–42q, 261–62

    A Defence of Free-Masonry (1765), 241–42q, 249–50q, 260–62

Spitalfields {area of London} 271

Spratt, Edward ✵ (fl. 1743–1756) 121, 122, 145

Spratt's *Constitutions* (1751) 55, 121–23, 134, 145, 408n57

    as partial basis for Dermott's *Ahiman Rezon*, 134, 247

Square (Masonic symbol) 89, 99, 107, 119, 195, 202, 395

Square, The 458

Square Pavement 383 (*see also* Master-Jewels, Mosaic Pavement)

St. Alban legend 128

St. Augustine (354–430 CE) 384

St. Bennet's Church, London 37

St. Isadore (c. 560–636) 59

St. John (unspecified) 396

St. John the Baptist (Biblical character):

    Feast Day of, ix, 35, 38, 46, 47, 49, 51, 78, 100, 153, 154, 155, 159, 160–61, 192, 194, 255, 289, 327, 403, 441n163

St. John the Evangelist (Biblical character):

    Feast Day of, 38, 48, 51, 88, 129, 161n26, 205, 255, 327

St. John's College (Annapolis, Maryland) 194

St. Mary Woolnoth Church (mistakenly referred to as St. Mary Wool-Church) 41

St. Mary-le-Bow Church, London 41

St. Paul the Apostle (Biblical character) 21, 129–30, 163–66, 163–64n32, 182, 185, 195–98, 202, 208, 415, 433–34

    as an "Enemy to the Lodge" before admission, 164

    as Freemasonry's "Glory & Support" after admission, 165

as "skilfull architect," 163
as a mythical Freemason, 163, 163–64n32, 182
as "holy Brother," 129–30, 163–64n32, 414
as esoteric teacher, 177
his "Trance and Vision," 196
vision of the third heaven, 182, 185, 195–98, 433–34
St. Paul's Cathedral (Old Saint Paul's), London (1300) 34, 40
St. Paul's Cathedral, London (Wren, 1697) 40, 42, 43, 45, 88, 132, 323
St. Paul's Church, Covent Garden, London 36
St. Peter the Apostle (Biblical character) 414
as "holy brother St. Peter," 414
St. Peter's Church, Philadelphia 193–94
St. Pierre, Nathan ✡ 5, 280–309,
Staffordshire 127, 256, 257, 258
Stainsborough, Yorkshire 41n37
Stanhope, Philip Dormer, 4th Earl of Chesterfield ✡ (1694–1773) 49
Stars, Seven (Masonic symbol) 89
Stationers' Hall, London 49, 51
Statute of Artificers of 1563 69, 90–91, 320
Sterling-House near the Castle 41n37
Stevenson, David 219, 350n7, 377–78, 425
Steward (Masonic office) 115
regalia of, 115–16
Stewart, Howard ✡ 397
Stewart, Larry 380
Stewart, Trevor ✡ 184n78, 369
Stewart, William, 1st Earl of Blessington (1709–1769) 247
1756 edition of *Ahiman Rezon* dedicated to, 247
Stewart, House of 34–45
Stoke Park, Stoke Bruerne 37
Stone, Nicholas (1587–1647) 34–35, 48
lost manuscript of, 35n35, 48
Stonegate 327
Stonehenge 107–108, 224
Stourton, Wiltshire 44–45
Strand, the {section of London} 246
Strength (in the Masonic sense) 18, 24, 92, 101–102, 142, 190, 239, 433, 439 (*see also* Beauty, Wisdom)
Strong, Edward, Jr. (Master of the London Company of Masons in 1718) 40, 44
Strong, Edward, Sr. (Master of the London Company of Masons in 1696) 40, 42, 44
Stukeley, William ✡ (1687–1765) 224n19
Sun (Masonic symbol) 58, 72, 89, 97–98, 99, 125, 365–66, 436
Susiana 27
Switzerland 124
sword of fire (Masonic symbol) 204
Swordbearer (Masonic officer) 118
symbolism 90, 157, 166n36, 177–78, 184, 293, 326, 358, 401
Symphorianus 72
Syria 11n3, 25, 26, 109, 200, 222, 232, 292

Tabernacle 17, 18, 23, 63, 72, 138

as a work of architecture / ma-
    sonry, 63
as a Lodge, 138
as model for the Temple of Sol-
    omon, 63
moved into Solomon's Temple,
    23
Tacitus 32
Tadmor (see Palmyra)
Taillor, John 320
Talmud 113n185, 351, 437
tapers, three 125
taverns 398 (see also INDEX OF
    MASONIC LODGES AND OR-
    GANIZATIONS)
    as Masonic settings, 391
    Masonic desire to vacate for
    public image concerns, 391
Taylor, David ✷ 325n33
Taylor, James ✷ 336, 338
Taylor, Thomas ✷ 339
Tees Valley 326
temperance 397–404
temple:
    first (see Eden)
    at Bethel, 26
    at Dan, 26
    at Jerusalem (see Temple at Je-
    rusalem)
    at Paneas, 31
    at Sebaste, 31
    of Apollo, 28
    of Asclepius, 28
    of Ashtaroth, 25
    of Astarte at Tyre, 19
    of Baal at Nineveh, 14
    of Baal at Samaria, 26
    of Chemosh, 25
    of Dagon in Gaza, 18–19
    of Diana, 236

of Hercules at Tyre, 19
of Janus, 32
of Jupiter at Tyre, 19
of Jupiter Olympius, 28
of Jupiter Hammon, 18
of Minerva at Athens, 28
of Molech, 25
of Solomon (see Temple at Je-
    rusalem)
of Theseus, 28
of Zerubbabel (see Temple at
    Jerusalem)
Temple at Jerusalem 109, 186, 230
    of Herod, 31–32; dedication of,
    32; erected by priestly ma-
    sons, 31; Holy of Holies with-
    in, 31; Holy Place within, 31;
    inferior to Solomon's Temple,
    32; Portico of, 31
    of Solomon, 17, 19–24, 27, 32,
    63–65, 72, 93, 100, 125, 135,
    167n41, 177, 185, 190, 222–23,
    230, 235–36, 356n16, 358, 370,
    384, 424, 425; as "the 2d and
    Chief of the 7 Wonders of
    Art," 23; as "the finest piece
    of Masonry upon Earth," 23;
    portico of, 22; sanctum sanc-
    torum of, 22
    of Zerubbabel, 28, 31, 32, 110;
    violated by Pompey the Great,
    32
    porters of, 135
    Tabernacle a type or foreshad-
    owing of, 17, 63
Temple Bar Gate, London 40
Tendler, Carl Hermann ✷ (1829–
    1889) 163–64n32
tenets, Masonic 412, 418
tetragrammaton 384

Thales of Miletus
   (c. 624–c. 546 BCE) 28
*The Old Constitutions Belonging
   to the Ancient and Honorable
   Society of Free and Accepted
   Masons* (1722) 55
theater 102, 122, 293
Theatrum Sheldonianum (see
   Sheldonian Theatre)
Theodore of Cyrene (fifth century
   BCE) 29–30n28
Theological Virtues 100
Theseus 28
third degree (see Master Mason
   degree)
Thompson, Edward (fl. 1729) ✵
   329
Thornhill, James (1675–1734) ✵
   107
Three Blue Bonnets (tavern) 83
Three Distinct Knocks (1760) 396,
   405
   decorum stressed in, 396
Thurmond, Mrs. 103
Tigris 13, 225, 237
Tiler (see Tyler)
Timanthes (fourth century BCE)
   29–30n28
Timson, Joshua ✵ (fl. 1722) 51
Tiras (Biblical character) 351
Tirzah 26
toasts 35, 47, 82, 92, 122, 296, 299,
   401, 405
Togarmah (Biblical character) 351
token (see modes of recogition)
Tola (Biblical character) 18
Tories 257
Tower Hill {area of London} 246
Tower of Babel (see Babel, Tower
   of)

tracing board 99, 107, 462
   the "tracyngbordes" at York,
      320
tradition, Masonic 9, 11n3, 13n7,
      14n11, 19n20, 22n22, 24n24,
      25–26, 70, 109
Traditional History xii, 7–8, 9–52,
      54, 58–72, 84–85, 88, 91, 92,
      100–101, 107–112, 125–27,
      133–36, 145, 152, 163, 179, 184,
      186, 218–26, 235–38, 287–89,
      297, 366–67, 414, 422–28
   as counter-mythology 7
   critically edited by the Premier
      Grand Lodge, 50, 51
   Dermott's version of, 133–36,
   drawn from ancient sources,
      109
   incompatible with Deism, 72
   involvement of Desaguliers, 366
   key portions of Anderson's 1738
      version of, 9–52
   (*see also* mythistory, mythogra-
      phy)
transgressive themes 62–63,
      178–79
transition theory 377, 379 (*see also*
      appropriation theory)
transmission 285
trestleboard (see tracing board)
triangle 384 (*see also* Tetragram-
      maton)
trigradal system 157–58, 182–83,
      207, 380
Trinity 130 (*see also* God)
Trojan War 28
Troy 18, 28
Truth 100, 129, 138, 188, 356–57,
      412, 418
Tubal (Biblical character) 351

Tubal Kain (Biblical character) 11
Tudors / Tudor period 34, 320
Tygris (see Tigris)
Tyler (Masonic officer) 47,
    204n112, 270–71
    celestial Tyler, 204, 441–42 (*see
    also* celestial lodge)
type / typological interpretation
    157, 177, 185–86, 209n125
Tyre 18–21, 20–21n21, 24, 64–65,
    141, 167n41, 223, 250

Umfreville, L. (fl. 1736) ✷ 402
Union of 1813 (see United Grand
    Lodge of England)
United Grand Lodge of England
    256, 290, 333, 369
    acceptance of the Holy Royal
    Arch, 256
United States of America 194
universalism 71–73, 87, 91, 112,
    113, 142, 143–44, 145, 167n41,
    200–201, 203, 265, 266, 305,
    348, 351
Universe 188
University of Pennsylvania 194
Ur 15, 16
Urania 114, 131, 427
Uzziah, King of Judah (Biblical
    character) 28

Vale of Jehosophat 435
    location of the "spiritual lodge,"
    435
van Helmont, Francis Mercury
    (1614–1698) 359
Versluis, Arthur xii, 172n54
Vespasian 222
Vibert, Lionel ✷ (1872–1938)
    134–35

Vico, Giambattista (1668–1744)
    375
Vikings 313
Villalpando, Juan Bautista (1552–
    1608) 23
Villeneau, Josiah ✷ (fl. 1721) 49,
    50
Villiers, George, 2nd Duke of Buck-
    ingham, 20th Baron de Ros,
    (1628–1687) 41
virtue / virtues 92, 100, 238, 433
    (*see also* Theological Virtues)
vitalism 355
Vitruvius (fl. 40 BCE) 66, 231
Volume of Sacred Law (see Bible)
von Stuckrad, Kocku 172n54, 358
Vulgate 20n21, 83–84

Waite, Arthur Edward ✷ (1857–
    1942) 314, 317, 318, 334n59,
    335n62
Wales 88, 90
Waller, Edmund (1606–1687)
    173n55
Ward, Caesar (c. 1710—1759) 104
Ward, John, 1st Viscount Dudley
    and Ward ✷ (1704–1774)
    256–59
Warden (Masonic office) 8, 37, 38,
    74, 77, 79, 109, 226, 289, 295
    in Masonic legend, 12, 22, 26,
    31, 35,
    regalia of, 115–16
    (*see also* Junior Warden, Senior
    Warden)
Ware, James (1594–1666) 224
Ware, Richard ✷ (fl. 1720–1740)
    48
Warren, John ✷ (1753–1815) 192
Warrington, England 37, 323, 325

Washington College (Chesterton, Maryland) 194

Washington, George ✳ (1732–1799) 205–206

Watkins, Larissa 153n2

Watts, J. 83

wealth, disregard for 202

Webb, John ✳ (1611–1672) 38, 39, 40, 41, 108
  on Stonehenge, 108, 224

Webb, Thomas Smith ✳ (1771–1819) 339

Weber, Max (1864–1920) 352

Weeks, James Eyre ✳ (c. 1719–c. 1754) 132
  Solomon's Temple: An Oratorio (1753), 132

Weisberger, R. William ✳ 351n10, 353n13, 362n29

Werneth, England 338

Westminster {area of London} 117, 262, 263, 264, 265,

Weymouth, Thomas, 2nd Viscount ✳ (1710–1751) 110–111, 257n61

Wharton, Philip, Duke of ✳ (1698–1731) 51–52, 57, 82, 365
  depicted by John Pine, 57, 365

Wheildon, William W. 154n5

Whigs 255

Wing-House, Bedfordshire 41n37

white (Masonic symbolism of) 115–16, 136

White, William Henry ✳ (1777–1866) 316

Whitehall 34–35, 36, 41, 42

Whitehead, James ✳ 337

Whitehead, John ✳ 329

Whole Institutions of the Free-Masons Opened, The (1725) 428

Whytehead, T.B. ✳ (1840–1907) 329, 331n52, 341

Widow's Son 64–65, 169 (see also Hiram Abiff)

Wigelsworth, Jeffrey R. 352n12

Wilbury House, Wiltshire 45

Wilkinson, Tate (1739–1803) 315

William III, Prince of Orange (1650–1702) 42, 43

William the Conqueror (c. 1028–1087) 315, 318

Williams, Bro. ✳ 90

Williams, Louis Lenway ✳ (1899–1990) 97n139, 98n145, 99n146, 99n148, 407n54, 408n57, 435n140

Wilson, Sir William ✳ (1641–1710) 42

Wilton House, Wiltshire 37

Winchester, England 314

Wisdom 17, 18, 20–21n21, 24, 68, 85–86, 101–102, 138, 142, 169, 177, 190, 191, 194–95, 199, 232–33, 238, 239, 298, 302, 374, 382, 391, 399, 419–20, 431, 432–33, 439, 445 (see also Beauty, Strength)

Wise, Thomas ✳ (Master Mason to the Crown, 1678–1685) 42

Wolley, Edward ✳ (fl. 1792) 333

Wolverhampton 256, 257

women 21, 25, 64–65, 73, 93–94, 231

Wonnacott, William ✳ (1868–1926) 419n97

Wood, Robert Leslie ✳ (fl. 1977) 334n58

words (see modes of recogition)

Working Tools (aggregate Masonic symbol) 99, 107

Worlidge, Thomas (1700–1766)
99
Worshipful Master (see Master)
Wren, Sir Christopher ✳ (1632–
1723) 8, 38–46, 108n172, 323
neglect of, 45, 46
Xenocrates (c. 396–313 BCE)
29–30n28
Xerxes I (518–465 BCE) 29

Yates, Dame Frances (1899–1981)
357
Year of Masonry (Lat. *Anno Lucis,*
"Year of Light") 10n1, 32, 56,
83, 95, 104
York 67, 104, 140, 249, 313–40, 370
(*see also* Grand Lodge of All
England at York)
Freemasons Hall, 334n59, 340
known as Eboracum in Roman
times, 313
known as Jórvik to the Vikings,
313
Merchant Adventurers' Hall,
314, 315, 327, 328, 330

Micklegate Bar 330
York Cathedral 314, 317n10, 326,
330
York Chronicle, The 316, 333, 335
York Minster Fabric Rolls 319
York MSS (see Masonic manu-
scripts)
York Stairs (Buckingham Wa-
ter-gate), London 37
Yorkshire Gazette, The 341

Zerubbabel (Biblical character)
Zerubbabel (biblical character) 28,
29, 100, 110 (*see also* Temple
at Jerusalem—of Zerubba-
bel)
Zeuxis (fifth century BCE) 29–
30n28
Zohar (c. 1275) 358
Zoroaster / Zoroastres (10th century BCE) 110–11, 114–15, 126,
424
as "Grand Master of Magians,"
110–111, 126
Zoroastrians 110–11, 114–15

Traditional Sources

BIBLE, APOCRYPHA & PSEUDEPIGRAPHA

Genesis 1:31 9

Genesis 6:10 113

Genesis 10:1–3 351

Genesis 11:1–2 12

Genesis 11:1–9 178

Exodus 32:6 17

Judges 15:19 174n56

1 Kings 5:16 222–23

1 Kings 5:18 222–23

1 Kings 7:13–15 20–21n21

1 Kings 7:14 64

1 Kings 9:20–23 64

1 Kings 11:23 133n253

Isaiah 56:7 22

Psalms 82:11 97–98

Proverbs 31:4–5 137

Job 26:7 340n125

Job 38:4–5 305, 430n125

Ecclesiastes 1:2 25

Ecclesiastes 2:21 194–95, 199

Ecclesiastes 9:8 136

Ecclesiastes 12:13 25

Esther 1:8 115

1 Chronicles 9:17 133n253

2 Chronicles 2:2 64

2 Chronicles 2:13 20

2 Chronicles 2:13–14 20–21n21

2 Chronicles 2:14 64

2 Chronicles 2:18 222–23

2 Chronicles 4:6 21

Wisdom of Sirach 32:1–3 136

Wisdom of Sirach 32:3 144

Wisdom of Solomon 11:20 169,
    340n125

Matthew 7:6 419

Matthew 18:20 85

John 1:5 121

John 11:20 31

Acts 5:1–5 414

1 Corinthians 13:11 165, 195

2 Corinthians 6:8 124

2 Corinthians 12:2–5 165–66,
    195–98

2 Corinthians 12:4 205

2 Corinthians 13:11 163–64n32

2 Thessalonians 3:6 415

1 Peter 2:17 83–84

Jude 14–15 222

CLASSICAL MATERIALS

Diodorus Siculus,
    Historical Library 1 14

Euclid, *Elements of Geometry*
    1, prop. 47 29

Horace, *Blandusia* 3.13 90

Josephus, *Antiquities of the Jews*
    1.2.3 11n3, 108–109, 222
    15.11.1–7 32

Tacitus, *The History*
    5.9 32

Ovid, *Epistulæ ex Ponto*
    2.9.47 88, 89

Masonic Lodges & Organizations

LODGES

〜 *England — Immemorial*   〜 *England — Moderns*

Lodge at Warrington [E. Ashmole,   Lodge № 2 (Moderns, 1740)
  1646] 37, 325   At the Horn Tavern
                                           Westminster, London
At the Goose and Gridiron   = Rummer & Gapes,
  St. Paul's Churchyard   Immemorial
  London, 1691   264, 271–72
  (Moderns № 1, 1729)
    ix, 43, 46, 316, 340   Lodge № 5 ("№ V")
                                           Const. July 11, 1721
At the Crown Ale-House   Three Cranes tavern,
  Parker's Lane near Drury Lane   Poultry, London
  Lincoln's Inn Fields, London   82
  (Moderns № 2, 1729)
    46   Lodge № 9 (Moderns, 1729)
                                           Const. May, 1722
At the Rummer and Grapes   One Tun tavern
  Channel Row   Noble-Street, Falcon Square
  Westminster   London
  (Moderns № 3, 1729)   92
    43, 46, 364
                                         Lodge № 11 (Moderns, 1729)
At the Apple Tree   Const. February 27, 1723
  Charles Street, Covent Garden   At the Fish and Bell (1750–
  London   1769), Charles Street
  (Moderns № 11, 1729)   Soho Square, London
    ix, 43, 46, 264, 271-72   = Apple Tree, Immemorial
                                           271–72
The Old York Lodge
  At the Merchant Adventurers'   Lodge № 30 (Moderns, 1729)
    Hall   Const. 1724
  At the Star Inn (Stonegate)   At the Maid's Head
  At the White Swan (Petergate)   Cook Row
  York   Norwich, Norfolk
    94, 100, 153, 313–31   394

The Lodge at the Carpenters'
Arms ("Three Compasses")
    7ᵗʰ in Pine's list of 1725
    Silver-Street, Golden-Square
    London
    153

University Lodge № 11
    Const. December 14, 1730
    At the Bear and Harrow
    Butcher Row, Temple Bar
    London
    256

Lodge № 88
    Const. March 28, 1732
    At the Bell and Raven
    Rotten Row, Wolverhampton
    Staffordshire
    256

Lodge № 94
    Const. November 15, 1732
    At the Ben Johnson's Head
    London
    271–74

Lodge № 117
    Const. June 25, 1735
    Later the Grand Stewards'
        Lodge (with no number)
    Shakespeare's Head
    Covent Garden, London
    189n87

Lodge № 259
    Const. January 12, 1761
    At the Punch Bowl
    Stonegate, York
    331–32

Lodge of Integrity № 252
    Const. May 8, 1766
    Bull's Head Inn, Union Street
    Manchester, Lancashire
    336

Union Lodge № 370
    Const. August 6, 1766
    At the Globe
    St. Mary's Churchyard
    Exeter, Devonshire
    408n61

York "Union" Lodge № 326
    Const. July 7, 1777
    Lockwood's Coffee House
    Micklegate, York
    333, 340

Prince of Wales Lodge № 412
    Const. August 20, 1787
    At the Thatched House Tavern
    St. James's Street (1787–1789)
    At the Star and Garter,
    Pall Mall (1789–1802)
    London
    316

Lodge of Union № 534
    Const. September 27, 1788
    Manchester
    336

Lodge of Friendship № 277
    Const. August 22, 1789
    At the Ring of Bells
    Goulborne
    Oldham, Lancashire
    332, 336–38, 341

The Lodge of Hope № 539
  Const. March 23, 1794
  Talbot Inn, Kirkgate
  Bradford, Yorkshire
    334

⚭ *England — Antients*

Lodge № 4
  Const. July 17, 1751
  a) At the Cannon
  Water Lane, Fleet Street
  London
  b) At the Temple and Sun
  Shire Lane, London
    244

Lodge № 26
  Const. November 8, 1753
  At the Rosemary Branch
  Rosemary Lane, London
    244

Lodge № 28
  Const. November 15, 1753
  At the Hampshire Hog
  London
    269

⚭ *England — York*

The Druidical Lodge № 109
  Const. December 22, 1778
  Rotherham, Yorkshire
    317, 332, 335

At the Duke of Devonshire
  Const. September 24, 1770
  Macclesfield, Cheshire
    332

The Lodge of Fortitude
  At the Sun
  Const. November 27, 1790
  Hollinwood, Lancashire
    332, 334, 335–39, 340

⚭ *England — The United Grand
  Lodge, 1813*

The Lodge of Reconciliation
  Const. December 27, 1813
  London
    333

Quatuor Coronati
Lodge of Research № 2076
    60, 341, 353, 457

⚭ *Ireland*
Lodge № 218
  Const. December 27, 1750
  Military lodge attached to the
  48th Regiment of Foot, under
  the Northamptonshire Reg't
    269

Lodge № 354
  Const. December 4, 1760
  Military lodge attached to the
  Royal Berkshire Regiment,
  attached to the 49th Regiment
    336

⚭ *Scotland*

Lodge of Edinburgh
(Mary's Chapel) № 1
  Edinburgh
    369

❧ *American Colonies*
Lodge № 126
    Const. July 30, 1733
    At the Bunch of Grapes
    Boston (Moderns)
      155–56, 160–61, 163

St. John's Lodge [№ 1]
    At the Tun Tavern
    Philadelphia (Moderns)
      160; acting as
        a Grand Lodge, 160

HOLY ROYAL ARCH

The Chapter of Philanthropy
    Werneth
      338

KNIGHTS TEMPLAR

St. Bernard's Conclave
    Hollinwood
      338

Jerusalem Preceptory № 5
    Manchester
      341

Royal Encampment of Jerusalem
    Manchester
      339

Also from Plumbstone

The Way of the Craftsman: Deluxe Edition
W. Kirk MacNulty

Contemplating Craft Freemasonry:
Working the Way of the Craftsman
W. Kirk MacNulty

Ahiman: A Review of Masonic Culture & Tradition
Edited by Shawn Eyer

The Meaning of Masonry
Walter Leslie Wilmshurst

The Masonic Initiation
Walter Leslie Wilmshurst

Sing the Art Divine:
A Traditional Masonic Songster
Nathan St. Pierre & Shawn Eyer

Masonic Perspectives:
The Thoughts of a Grand Secretary
Thomas W. Jackson

The Higher Spiritualization of Freemasonry
Karl Christian Friedrich Krause

CPSIA information can be obtained
at www.ICGtesting.com
Printed in the USA
BVOW09*2002270418
514526BV00002B/35/P